Praise for *Breakthrough*

Breakthrough is a powerful, disturbing, enlightening must-read for anyone who cares about the Israeli-Palestinian conflict and knows the present trajectory is a tragic cul-de-sac. Forer eloquently tells the story of the difficult but ultimately life-affirming process of awakening to the suffering of the Other. Read this book if you have the courage to acquire the wisdom to make the leap of empathy required to realize a new politics of peace and reconciliation.

– *Rabbi Irwin Kula,* Author of *Yearnings: Embracing the Sacred Messiness of Life.*

The journey Rich Forer took from the world indoctrination and fabrication to the land of truth and justice is a very recent one. This is why this tale is so fresh, lively and moving. Written in the most accessible style, and yet covering an impressive factual and historiographical ground, this can be an eye opener to many Americans who are still utterly misled and totally misinformed about Israel and Palestine.

– *Ilan Pappe,* Professor of History, Director of the European Centre for Palestine Studies and Co-Director for the Exeter Centre for Ethno-Political Studies.

As the author explains, where a man cannot look he cannot feel and where a man cannot feel he has not really looked. Without both, he will never understand; and if he does not understand he will never awaken his inborn ability to repair the world. Rich Forer, in his meticulously researched book, proves that if we open our eyes to "the other" we begin to feel compassion. Only then can we shake off the bondage of an emotionally conditioned and limited perspective and create *true Tikkun Olam.*

– *Cathy Sultan,* author of *Israeli and Palestinian Voices: Dialogue with Both Sides, Tragedy in South Lebanon: The Israeli-Hezbollah War of 2006* and *A Beirut Heart: One Woman's War.*

Rich Forer's *Breakthrough* is a compassionate, introspective, and thoughtful transformative moment. The book is a personal and emotional journey from bias to truth, from passionately held views to justice and peace, and from a close-minded Zionist ideology to a "world minded" commitment to righteousness and wisdom. In this well documented work, Forer tells us that being a Zionist Jew does not ipso facto mean that one should deny the rights and humanity of the Palestinians and that the search for justice and self-fulfillment on the personal and collective levels must include the reality of the Palestinian "other." The author should be commended on his "awakening," courage, and thorough research. The book is a must read for anyone seriously interested in understanding the essence of the Israeli-Palestinian conflict and in finding ways to resolve it.

– *Emile Nakhleh,* Former Senior Intelligence Service Officer and former director of the CIA's Political Islam Strategic Analysis Program; Author of *A Necessary Engagement: Reinventing America's Relations with the Muslim World.*

RICHARD FORER

BREAKTHROUGH

TRANSFORMING FEAR INTO COMPASSION

A NEW PERSPECTIVE ON THE ISRAEL-PALESTINE
CONFLICT

INSIGHT PRESS ● ALBUQUERQUE, NM

Published by Insight Press, Albuquerque, NM.
www.richardforer.com

BREAKTHROUGH: TRANSFORMING FEAR INTO COMPASSION

Edited by Christopher Boys
Cover Design by Robyn Almaleh – SaiWorks

To order this title please visit www.Breakthrough-book.com or www.richardforer.com.

Library of Congress Cataloging in Publication Data

Richard Forer, 1948-

Breakthrough: Transforming Fear Into Compassion – A New Perspective on the Israel-Palestine Conflict / by Richard Forer – First American Edition
p. cm

Includes bibliographical references and index.
1. World History   2. Spirituality

ISBN 978-0-615-40458-5
ISBN 978-0-615-41568-0 (ebook)

Library of Congress Control Number: 2010916063

Printed in the United States of America

An unquestioned mind is the world of suffering.
Byron Katie

Foreword

It is difficult to overestimate the emotional attachment of American Jews to the State of Israel. Zionism, in the words of Baby Boomers like Jewish psychologist and author Mark Braverman, has been "mother's milk" to Jews in the United States and around the world. Unconditional support for Israel is not so much an intellectual choice as a deeply rooted component of Jewish identity. Indeed, in many Jewish circles today it has become more important to believe in Israel than to believe in God. Criticism of Israel feels like a personal attack, a challenge not of a state but of who we are.

I grew up in a secular, unaffiliated Jewish household, and I knew where my allegiance lay. I saw Israel as a victimized country that simply wanted to live in peace but couldn't because of its aggressive, Jew-hating, Arab neighbors. When I was young, my grandmother, who had fled from Europe and lost most of her family in the Nazi Holocaust, talked about Israel as the one protection our family and Jews everywhere had against persecution in the future.

I first confronted an alternative narrative while traveling through the Middle East. I was taken in by families of Palestinian refugees, who told me their stories. They recounted tales of displacement, destroyed villages, land confiscation, imprisonment without trial and torture.

When I first heard these accusations, I didn't want to believe them. In fact, at first I didn't. Although my friends seemed nice enough, it seemed to me that they had been brainwashed. I set out to do some research, to prove them wrong, and quickly realized how little I actually knew about the situation. Still, I rationalized to myself that if Israel was doing anything violent, it must be because it had no other choice, that this was the only way to ensure the safety of the Jewish people. Over time, I found it harder and harder to justify my findings in the context of security. Not knowing who or what to believe anymore, I set out to see the situation for myself.

What I found shocked me beyond anything I had read or heard. I witnessed a system of complete segregation. There was one kind of road for Jews living in the West Bank and another for Palestinians. I saw Jewish Israelis paid to leave Israel and move to the West Bank, pushing off my Muslim and Christian neighbors simply because of their ethnicity and religion. I visited a Palestinian village that had been intentionally covered in raw sewage, forcing inhabitants to leave and clearing the surrounding area for subsequent Jewish-only settlement. I comforted my friend Dawud, whose six-month-old son Khaled died in his arms of an asthma attack as they were held by Israeli soldiers, unable to reach a nearby Palestinian hospital inside the West Bank. I found that non-Jews within Israel were treated as second-class citizens, and that many other Christians and Muslims in the area were being prevented from getting to work, going to school, or praying at their holy sites.

A personal transformation began that would continue for many years. My wall of certainty of Israel's innocence began to crack and eventually came crashing down. It is a scary process to question the one thing that you never doubted. Most people would do anything to avoid such an experience, so it is not surprising that criticism of Israel and Zionism is fiercely challenged. Those unable to disprove the realities of Israeli human rights violations frequently fall back on name-calling and character attacks, often labeling the messengers as anti-Semitic (or self-hating, if the messenger is Jewish).

As a Jew, I am deeply troubled by these characterizations. The human rights violations I witnessed in Israel/Palestine are profoundly contrary to the basic tenets of Judaism. There is nothing Jewish about Occupation and discrimination, and there's nothing anti-Jewish or anti-Semitic about recognizing and examining these practices; in fact, it's in line with a Jewish tradition of social justice. To equate criticism of human rights violations with criticism of Judaism is to me an offensive and dangerous mistake.

One of the things I feared most about acknowledging Israel's transgressions was that it would separate me from my Jewish community and identity. In fact, the opposite has happened. For every Jewish friend I've lost I've gained five hundred more, and I've never felt more confident of what being Jewish means to me. I've rediscovered Judaism. But it goes further than that. I've rediscovered myself.

For years I was imprisoning myself. I was my own enemy. My vulnerability came not from Hamas, Hezbollah, or Iran, but from my own prejudices and the unjust policies I supported. My journey, my "breakthrough" itself, was devastating, but what was waiting for me at the other end was well worth it. The fears that enshrouded me my whole life have melted away, and I've never felt freer and more hopeful. No longer am I afraid of the "other." I know now that there never really was an "other." It was never us versus them; nobody's freedom or security can come at the expense of another's. We are all in this together.

Of course, the injustices perpetrated against the Palestinian people are not wrong simply because they are bad for Jews. The Jewish identity crisis ensuing from realistic analysis of Israeli policies is nothing compared to the suffering experienced by Palestinians under those policies. The Palestinian movement for equal rights is just, worthy of solidarity from all people. Palestinians have borne the brunt of our fear and trauma, and our redemption cannot be seen as independent of their struggle for liberation. On the contrary, our redemption will come from the Palestinians themselves, and we must look to their guidance.

People frequently ask me how I came to support Palestinian rights given my history of unquestioning support for Israeli policies. While I've learned to articulate where I once was and where I am today, to describe what brought me from Point A to Point B seems like an impossible task. To my knowledge, there has never been a book that takes on the daunting challenge of describing and deconstructing the unbelievably complex emotional and intellectual journey from prejudice to compassion on this issue... until now!

In Richard Forer's powerful journey can be found the seeds of compassion and respect required for a just peace in the Middle East. Forer's fearless openness and commitment to peace are inspiring and contagious. Mirrored in his story are the stories of countless others, including my own and many whose journeys have yet to begin. This book may open the door to your own journey, if you are ready to enter it. For some, the endeavor may pave the way to a sense of inner peacefulness coupled with a renewed energy to work for justice. Those courageous enough to open themselves to this deeper understanding and compassion will not be disappointed.

Anna Baltzer

Anna Baltzer is an award winning lecturer and human rights worker. She is the author of *Witness in Palestine: A Jewish American Woman in the Occupied Territories* and producer of the acclaimed film, *Life in Occupied Palestine: Eyewitness Stories & Photos.*

Breakthrough

Table of Contents

Breakthrough

Introduction

On three things does the world endure: justice, truth and peace. . . .
Mishnah: Pirkei Avot (Chapters of the Fathers) 1:18a

On Wednesday, July 12, 2006, Hezbollah (party of God), the nationalistic Lebanese political and military organization, abducted two Israeli soldiers and murdered three in a cross-border raid into northern Israel. Within two hours, Israeli tanks and armored personnel carriers entered Lebanon. In the fighting that followed five more Israeli soldiers died, four when their tank drove over a powerful bomb. An unknown number of Hezbollah soldiers also died in the fighting. Israel's cabinet immediately authorized "severe and harsh" retaliation. The Second Lebanon War had begun.

Upon hearing this news, I was overcome with fear and despair. Once again Israel was the object of undeserved scorn and hatred and, in its endless struggle for permanence, was forced to strike back against blatant acts of aggression, which I took to be personal and execrable attacks against myself and all Jews. Like my fellow Jews I only wanted to live in peace. Although I had no history of discord with anyone of Arab heritage, this latest incitement proved that the adversary I had read about in Sunday school, the enemy of the Old Testament, was determined to wipe Israel and its Jewish inhabitants off the face of the Earth.

As the war raged on, I anxiously watched television and read the newspapers, anticipating a quick and successful end to the conflict. My hopes, however, were dashed by Hezbollah's unexpected strong resistance to the powerful Israeli military. I bristled at the damage to Israel and the loss of Israeli lives, victims of rocket attacks dispatched by Hezbollah.

When I read about the devastation to Lebanon, I had no difficulty rationalizing the deaths of hundreds of innocent civilians and the displacement of nearly one million. The deceased were victims of the wanton disregard their countrymen had for the sanctity of human life. There was no mistaking the fact that Islamic terrorists had intentionally embedded themselves within local populations. Hezbollah's premeditated and cynical strategy was to attract enemy bombs in order to provoke the international denunciation of Israel that would follow. These extremists had cavalierly sacrificed the lives of their own people just to smear the integrity and reputation of the Jewish nation. In the light of that depravity, the proposition that Hezbollah was fighting for the rights of its populace was nothing more than a pathetic excuse to hide its genocidal intentions. Clearly, the Arabs would do anything to achieve their heinous objective. In contrast, Israel's plan of self-defense, which some called excessive, seemed reasonable to me. "We" were fighting a war, while making every effort to avoid harming civilians, even at the cost of increased risk to our own troops.

A few years later, as I look back at that difficult period, I can see the unreserved one-sidedness of my disposition. Back then, however, no one could have convinced me that my views were biased. Facts alone dictated my position. And the fact that I was fortunate enough to have been born a Jew and American, rather than a Muslim and Arab, did not implicate me in any kind of prejudice.

A different identity, however, was silently waiting to be born and with a more sweeping perspective than I ever could have imagined. By the time Israel ended its naval blockade of Lebanon on September 8, 2006, my perception of the world had been radically transformed, my lifelong conditioning released, my tendentious beliefs overturned and my inborn compassion manifested. From this new place of freedom the roots of conflict were gracefully revealed to my conscious mind.

At the time the war began, I had, for over thirty years, seriously considered various religious and spiritual teachings. I was familiar with concepts such as Christ consciousness, enlightenment, liberation, non-separation and the death of the ego; and I was aware that these concepts could spring to life, anywhere at any time, through spontaneous spiritual awakening. Nevertheless, I was soon greatly surprised to find that I had experienced just such an awakening while studying one of the most protracted and misunderstood problems of the past century: the Israel-Palestine conflict. In this book I discuss my path to self-awareness as well as my research into the history of that conflict. My hope is that by sharing what I discovered others will break through their own invisible walls of confusion and begin to transmute their negative emotions into clarity and compassion.

Introduction

For those readers who want to set out on this journey to self-awareness, it is critical that together we examine the roles each of us plays in cultivating conditions that lead to suffering among our fellow man. We will especially need to question the certainty of our positions and understand how polarized and uninformed our views can be. Once we take that step, we will see how easily we can deceive ourselves into supporting policies that favor some at the expense of others, and how our views often induce us to deny the humanity of those whose actions arouse our fear and anger. To reach our destination we must begin to understand the seemingly senseless behavior of those we denounce. We will need to continually ask: Why? – What is the history behind their outlook? Not our particular version of their history, not the selected evidence that supports our beliefs, not the facile language we use to condemn them – but the reality of their history.

The responsibility for uncovering and verifying the facts is ours alone. If we abdicate this duty, there will be no one to blame but ourselves for the turmoil that results – not terrorists, politicians, religious groups, governments, or radical cults. Until we come to a hard-earned understanding of the causes of a particular conflict and the lessons its history contains, peace will remain a distant fantasy.

The heart of this book lies in the understanding that conflict arises not because of inherent defects in a particular culture, but because of the behavior that radiates from our unexamined beliefs. Difficult emotions, especially fear, stimulate confusion. Our natural intelligence then succumbs to cultural prejudices and unconscious thought processes that doom us to conflict. The paradigm of this archaic process is the belief in "us" versus "them," good against evil. This belief – and the dualistic thinking that produces it – has held us in its grip for most of our lives. If we honestly commit ourselves to a real peace, a new understanding will reveal itself. We shall see that in truth we have much in common with our so-called enemy. We are both the product of our history and we are both often distracted by pain and confusion. We both want to avoid suffering. Most important, we both share a common desire for peace within ourselves and within the world. This understanding of our common reality produces compassion.

My experience is that compassion is a profound relief. It is inborn. When it was reawakened I was instantly freed from irrational fear and my natural intelligence was restored. Then I knew that a real peace can never come about through aggression or as a result of one group's superiority over another. Real peace can only come about through insight and compassion.

– 1 –

In the Beginning

*Anyone who has the power to make you believe absurdities has
the power to make you commit injustices.* Voltaire

Growing up in New Jersey during the Cold War era of the 1950s and
1960s, I attended Sunday school at my reform synagogue from the time I
was six years old until a year after my bar mitzvah. Like most people I
naturally identified with my religion and culture. Knowing who I was
gave me a sense of pride and participation in something deep and
mysterious.

The overwhelming majority of Jews I knew were honest and fair in
their dealings with others and, taken as a whole, appeared to be more
socially and politically aware than other groups of people. Their respect
for different cultures impressed me as kind and considerate, especially
when contrasted with the racial slurs and ethnic stereotypes I often heard
from Gentiles.

I appreciated the humor, the food, the warmth, the intelligence and
the contributions to humanity spawned by my ancestry; but more than
anything else, I willingly embraced my Jewish heritage because of my
people's history of wandering and persecution. To question my identity
would have felt like a betrayal of an ancient tradition and indifference
toward the suffering of my people.

Public elementary school further reinforced my identity with a sense
of fairness and with the understanding that no group of people ought to
be more entitled than another. The school day regularly began with the
Lord's Prayer, the most well known prayer in Christianity. The classroom
also celebrated Christmas and Easter, yet the corresponding Jewish
holidays of Chanukah and Pesach (Passover) were completely ignored.
For me this neglect proved that my teachers were insensitive to the
feelings of their Jewish students. Sometimes I wondered if they even saw
us in their classrooms. How could they not acknowledge our existence
and our traditions?

These experiences taught me that school prayer and other religious
events are inappropriate in a public school setting because of their effect

on the self-esteem of children whose backgrounds do not conform to the prevailing religion.

After graduating from elementary school, I regularly attended Friday night and Saturday morning religious services. Occasionally, during Oneg Shabbat,* I would overhear some of the men discussing the possibility of a global nuclear catastrophe. They all agreed that the most likely place for war to be triggered was the Middle East. That region was a powder keg just waiting for a spark, and the spark was Arab hatred of Israel.

Faced with that prospect, I would often ask myself what we had done to cause the Arabs to hate us so much. The answer was simple. We had done nothing. We were Jews. That was enough. That was the rule since time immemorial. But, as I would finally figure out many years later, the most honest and accurate answers to my question were not so one-dimensional. The anger that the Arab nations felt over Israel's existence had more to do with territory than with inborn hatred for the Jewish people and their religion.

As I grew older I rarely dwelled on the enmity between Israel and the Arabs, but I never lost sight of Israel's vulnerability, situated among hostile neighbors, each resenting its very existence and insensitive to the six million unspeakable acts of cruelty that had exterminated a third of world Jewry a generation earlier.

Miraculously though, my people had turned a barren desert into a land of milk and honey. Opening its arms, Israel was an oasis of hope and freedom, a sanctuary where any Jew could make aliyah,+ a refuge where Jews who were subject to routine persecution elsewhere could find compassion and brotherhood. Sadly though, the world did not appreciate the legacy of wisdom, ethics and culture that the Jewish people had produced and that Israel represented. For me it was an undeniable truth that this proud nation was a place of benevolence and justice.

In the mid 1990s I began to pay more attention to the Middle East, its leaders and its political affairs. There were two principal reasons for

---

* A Hebrew term meaning "joy of Sabbath," which refers to a reception held following Friday night religious services.

+ Aliyah is a Hebrew word meaning ascent. It refers to Jewish immigration to Israel.

my renewed interest. Beginning in 1994 and lasting until 2000, I spent substantial intervals of time in San Francisco, studying a unique system of healing taught by an Israeli, Meir Schneider. This incomparable opportunity to learn from a true pioneer in the art of therapeutic movement and bodywork also afforded me access into the world of a proud Israeli citizen who was attracted to politics and keenly aware of the far-reaching possibilities for change taking place in his country.

Born in Russia, Meir was five years old when his family immigrated to Israel. Both of his parents were deaf and, as he explains in his autobiography:

> I was born cross-eyed, with glaucoma (excess pressure in the eyes), astigmatism (irregular curvature of the cornea), nystagmus (involuntary eye movement) and cataracts (opacity of the lens). In short, I was blind.[1]

While still a young child Meir underwent a series of unsuccessful, experimental surgeries that left both eyes permanently covered with scar tissue, severely limiting the amount of light that could penetrate to his retinal tissue. After the fifth attempt Meir's surgeon pronounced his condition irreversible.

Meir, however, refused the bleak counsel of his parents and doctors to accept his fate and learn to live with his disability. Instead, he held onto his dream, resolute that somehow, someday, he would gain the functional vision necessary to live as a sighted person.

Most blind people are not completely enshrouded in darkness. In Meir's case, he could differentiate between light and shadow and distinguish large objects in a room, such as a sofa. Someone sitting on the sofa, though, would blend in and appear to be a part of its fabric.

During his teenage years Meir met a fellow high-school student who had dramatically improved his own severe near-sightedness through the regular practice of a combination of eye exercises. The method the boy used had been devised by an ophthalmologist, Dr. William Bates, in the early part of the twentieth century. Meir's new friend shared his expertise with Meir, who was confident he had found the secret to vision he had been searching for. Fervently devoted to his new regimen, Meir sometimes practiced the exercises as much as eleven hours a day. Within eighteen months, his scar tissue notwithstanding, he was able to read his high school textbooks without the use of the Braille technique or telescopic lenses.

As his visual acuity progressed, Meir developed a talent for empowering people to gain relief from a wide range of conditions. As a result of a number of unusual cases that the medical establishment found hard to believe – involving muscular dystrophy, rheumatoid arthritis, multiple sclerosis, vision ailments and more – Meir began to establish a reputation throughout Israel as an exceptional healer. In his early twenties, however, he decided to move to California where his message that almost anything is possible if you believe in yourself could gain a larger audience. There he founded the Center for Self-Healing.

Continuing to work on his eyesight, Meir also qualified for an unrestricted California driver's license, making him probably the only person in the United States with a certificate of legal blindness who also has lawful permission to drive without corrective lenses. As Meir liked to recount, his friends courteously asked him not to drive in their neighborhoods.

My training included a long apprenticeship in which I regularly spent seven to ten hours each day, six days a week, assisting Meir in his work with his clients. Movement, touch and mental imagery were the primary tools we used to facilitate a greater kinesthetic awareness in our clients and, therefore, a greater possibility for change.

Meir sees his healing work within the context of the "world mind," a shared, finite consciousness that is "the source of everything in the world."

> The thoughts, feelings, actions, or conditions of any individual or society, or of humanity itself, spring from the world mind, and by their existence perpetuate the world mind . . . . Any individual act reverberates through the world mind for all of humanity. No individual can remain unaffected by any human act, although the effects may not be experienced consciously or immediately. Every thought and act contributes to the total picture of humanity and becomes part of humanity.[2]

The world mind, however, like humanity, is resistant to change. "But there are moments of grace or liberation, when we step outside the world mind and are momentarily free of our patterns. It is during these times that both the individual and the world mind can change."[3]

With his sense of humor, warm congeniality and avid interest in current events, Meir drew me into conversations on American and Israeli politics. Frequently, during sessions with clients, we would listen to the *MacNeil/Lehrer News Hour* on the radio. Sometimes our Jewish clients would engage us in discussions about Israel and the Middle East, about Yasser Arafat and the Palestinians, and about the prospects for peace between the two peoples.

One of Meir's favorite politicians was Israeli Prime Minister Yitzhak Rabin. Rabin had been Chief of Staff of the IDF during his country's triumphant Six-Day War of 1967, and had served as its Prime Minister from 1974 to 1977. He began his second term as leader of the Jewish State in 1992 when he replaced Yitzhak Shamir.

In 1993 Rabin entered into negotiations with Yasser Arafat, Chairman of the PLO, for the eventual establishment of a Palestinian State. On September thirteenth of that year, the two leaders met in Washington D.C., where they signed the *Declaration of Principles on Interim Self-Government Arrangements*, commonly referred to as the Oslo Accords. Later, in Cairo, Egypt on May 4, 1994, they signed the *Agreement on the Gaza Strip and the Jericho Area*, which sketched out the implementation of the first stage of the *Declaration of Principles*. On October 26, 1994, Rabin and King Hussein signed the *Treaty of Peace between the State of Israel and the Hashemite Kingdom of Jordan*. For their accomplishment in creating an outline for peace between the Palestinians and the State of Israel, Rabin, Arafat, and Israeli Foreign Minister Shimon Peres shared the 1994 Nobel Peace Prize.

On November 4, 1995, after attending a rally in Tel Aviv, Rabin was assassinated by Yigal Amir, an Israeli law student who opposed the Oslo Accords and the return of any land to the Palestinians. Later that day, at the Center for Self-Healing, I took it upon myself to inform Meir that the leader of his nation was dead. This was a very sad moment for those of us who wanted to believe that an end to this seemingly eternal conflict was on the horizon.

Breakthrough

Amir was linked to the extreme right wing group *Eyal* (Jewish Fighting Organization), whose activities consisted of passing out leaflets claiming responsibility for crimes it had not committed and efforts to disrupt the peace process.[4*] Amir also had ties to the militant, right-wing, ultra-nationalist political party, *Kach* (Thus) and to *Kahane Chai* (Kahane Lives). Kach was founded by Rabbi Meir Kahane, a Brooklyn born lawyer and rabbi who preached "terror against terror." Kahane was assassinated in 1990. Kahane Chai, led by Kahane's son, Binyamin Ze'ev Kahane, split off from Kach in the wake of that assassination. The stated goal of both groups is the restoration of the biblical land of Israel, which requires the expulsion of all Arabs.[+] Both groups are designated as terror organizations by Israel, the European Union and the United States.

The second stimulus for my renewed interest in the Middle East was a conversation I had in February 1996. My girlfriend and I were visiting my mother and her boyfriend in Florida. Our annual vacation coincided with visits from my identical twin brother and his wife, as well as my younger brother and his wife and son. Both brothers are far more observant of their Jewish tradition than I have ever been. My twin and his immediate family belong to an Ultra-Orthodox sect of Judaism. They live in a town with a large concentration of fellow Hasidim.[⊥] My younger brother is a former president of one of the largest Jewish congregations on the East coast.

One evening we all planned to meet for dinner. Due to the dietary restrictions of the Ultra-Orthodox side of my family, we could not eat at just any restaurant. My brother chose a kosher Chinese eatery for our gathering. The fact that the Chinese restaurant was kosher should not be

---

* Eyal has been inactive since 1995.

+ There are differences of opinion over what constitutes these lands. Zionists generally consider the 20th century land of Palestine as the biblical land of Israel.

⊥ Hasidism is a "Jewish mystical movement founded in the 18th century in Eastern Europe by the Baal Shem Tov that reacted against Talmudic learning and maintained that God's presence was in all of one's surroundings and that one should serve God in one's every deed and word." thefreedictionary.com/Chassidim.

surprising to those who are aware of the wise business practices of the Chinese and the affection Jews have for their cuisine.

Although we arrived at our destination before five o'clock, there was a line of customers waiting to get in. There are many Ultra-Orthodox and Orthodox Jews in the Fort Lauderdale area, the site of our rendezvous, and very few kosher Chinese dining places. That ensured a waiting list. The weather was mild and balmy, so the half-hour wait was bearable.

Standing outside, I was discussing the situation in the Middle East with my Ultra-Orthodox sister-in-law when she began to tell me about a book she and my brother had recently read that revealed pertinent and little-known details about Israel's quarrel with the Palestinians. Written by Joan Peters and published in 1984, the book's title was *From Time Immemorial: the Origins of the Arab-Jewish Conflict over Palestine.* Because of their immersion in Jewish history and culture, and the fierce sense of pride they had in their identity and in the integrity of their religion, I was confident my brother and sister-in-law had discovered the most reliable and authoritative reading material on the history of the Israel-Palestine conflict. Equally compelling was the notion that grew out of our conversation that Arabs were propagandists and liars. With that inspiration, and never doubting that the book was anything other than a truthful history of the genesis of the State of Israel, I resolved to obtain *From Time Immemorial* in the near future.

A few months later, having purchased the book, I returned to San Francisco to continue my work with Meir. Each night, back at the motel room after a long day at the Center for Self-Healing, I would spend a few hours engrossed in Peters' historical narrative. My brother and sister-in-law were right. Her book was fascinating.

For more than ten years the learning I gleaned from Joan Peters' scholarship served as an indispensable companion and the primary source I used to defend Israel from the never-ending stream of calumny its critics seemed so intent on directing at its reality. The book fortified my emotionally based conviction that anything not in harmony with a benign account of the actions of Israel and the Jewish people was anti-Semitic disinformation. After finishing the book, I recommended it to several

Jewish friends as a mandatory guide to the source of the Israel-Palestine problem. They too were comforted by Peters' findings, not knowing that many were without merit.

There was another reason the book had such an impact on me: Joan Peters was not Jewish. To my way of thinking that meant there was no temptation to omit or bend the facts in order to show Israel in a false light. Peters' past reporting on segregation and the civil rights movement in the Deep South added additional credibility to her work.

But what really guaranteed my enthusiasm was that her original purpose had been to bear witness to the plight of the Palestinian people. She pointed out that, according to her academic research, the Palestinian refugee camps that had been established in the aftermath of the 1948 Arab-Israeli War were among the most squalid places on Earth. By visiting the Occupied Territories, she expected to publicize the unsanitary living conditions and debilitating poverty she was sure to encounter. To her astonishment, however, she discovered that the camps had adequate sanitation and were noticeably superior to the dismal conditions most Arabs tolerated elsewhere in the Middle East.

Here was a non-Jewish reporter, dedicated to civil rights for all people and so compassionate that, after reporting on African Americans in the segregated South, she was willing to focus awareness on another allegedly beleaguered people, the Palestinians. And what did she bring to light? That the Palestinians had never even existed! They were Iraqis, Lebanese, Libyans, Syrians, Turks, Trans-Jordanians, Yemenis and other Arabs who were desperate for decent jobs to support their families.[*] Luckily, Jewish landholders were hiring laborers to work their fields, so they migrated to Palestine during the first half of the twentieth century to take advantage of this economic opportunity. In conjunction with that disclosure, she enunciated that the land of Palestine had been virtually empty – primarily consisting of nomadic Bedouin tribes – before European Jews began arriving in large numbers in the latter part of the nineteenth century and into the mid-twentieth century.

---

[*] In 1946, the Emirate of Trans-Jordan changed its name to the Hashemite Kingdom of Jordan.

Peters' integrity was so profound that she was able to let go of her presumptions and report the unadorned truth. Not only did her story prove to me that Israel was beyond reproach, it reinforced my conviction that most of the western world, Christian and Muslim, was biased against the Jewish people and actively involved in sabotaging their reputation, with the ultimate aim the dismantling of the Jewish State.

Through her willingness to see things in their true light and her conversion to a more judicious position on this core issue, Peters disproved the claim against Israel that the Palestinian refugee camps were places of squalor. She had performed an important service to every Jew, and to the whole world, by exonerating Israel of the accusation that it failed to treat the Palestinians with decency and humanity. *From Time Immemorial* articulated the justification for a Jewish State and provided detailed evidence that enabled me to infer that any and all accusations by Israel's enemies were not only false but anti-Semitic. The book affirmed everything that I had always believed or wanted to believe, but had never delineated in my mind.

Breakthrough

– 2 –

Resistance

If you want to understand a given perspective, and especially if you wish to understand a comprehensive worldview, an all-encompassing outlook on life, it is first necessary to rid yourself of any preconceived notions. Menachem M. Schneerson, the Lubavitcher Rebbe, *Mind Over Matter*, p. 18

One night, soon after Israel's army and air force began their invasion of Lebanon, my close friend Bill stopped by my house. From our first meeting in college four decades earlier, he had inspired me with his commitment to honesty, his remarkable ability to interpret dreams, and his willingness to help me integrate their meaning into my life. If anyone would understand how I felt, Bill would.

After we greeted each other I began to express my anger about the lack of understanding all over the Arab world for the past suffering of the Jews. I specifically emphasized the Jewish people's need for a land they could call their own, a place where they would be safe from prejudice. For me this issue was urgent and was exemplified by Hezbollah's malevolence toward Israel.

"The Arabs have always hated the Jews," I said. "During World War II Hitler was the greatest hero of the Arab world. The Arabs learned their propaganda from the Nazis and have used it to discredit the honest and generous motives of Israel. Lying has always been a part of Arab culture."

Before Bill could reply, I agitatedly moved on to the crux of the troubles in the Middle East: Israel's conflict with the Palestinians. "Bill, these so-called Palestinians are not even from that region of the Middle East. Israel is not their ancestral home. They left their villages in northern Africa and other Arab countries because the landholders they worked for paid them so little they could barely survive. By moving to the land that became Israel, they were able to acquire better jobs from kind-hearted Jewish employers."

"First of all," Bill responded, "most of the Arabs in Israel and the Occupied Territories are Palestinians who have always lived there. Israel/Palestine has been their home and the Palestinians have lived in the

Breakthrough

area for thousands of years. Many are descended from the Canaanites. European Jews took the land away from them. That's the reason for this confrontation, and the claim that a Palestinian people never existed until Arabs came from other countries is Israeli propaganda."

Shocked that Bill would defame defenseless European Jews who had emerged from the darkness of the Holocaust with nowhere to go but the land of their ancestors, I altered my approach: "The Palestinian refugee camps are a huge improvement on the filthy living conditions these people put up with in their home countries. Israel bends over backwards to treat these people with respect. It is unbelievable that anyone could ignore that fact and blame Israel for all the chaos in the Middle East."

Bill looked incredulous. "If the Israelis respected the Palestinians, they wouldn't keep building settlements on their land and destroying their villages."

I was becoming more incensed. With revulsion I declared that any person with an ounce of intelligence could see that the PLO, Al Aqsa Martyrs Brigade, Hamas,* Islamic Jihad, Hezbollah, Iran, Syria, and anyone critical of Israel, hated the Jewish people. "How can you dismiss Israel's continual desire for serious negotiations with the Palestinians? All Israel has ever wanted is to live in peace."

Certain of the moral necessity for a Jewish nation, I introduced the Diaspora into our discussion. It was important that Bill understand the Jewish experience as it occurred throughout much of Europe and the Middle East. Knowledge of the Holocaust was not enough. "Bill, Jews never possessed the same rights as the indigenous people of their host countries. They were no more than second-class citizens wherever they lived. Even now that they have their own country, they are still chastised no matter what they do. The criticism never stops."

Since I hoped that Bill would agree or at least empathize with my position if he had a broader knowledge of the facts, I explained how the Jewish people had diligently sought assimilation into Russian society but

---

* Hamas means "zeal" and is an acronym for Harakat al-Muqawama al-Islamiyya (Movement of the Islamic Resistance). Hamas is a socio-political movement that combines Palestinian nationalism with Islamic fundamentalism.

were thwarted whenever they tried to gain parity with non-Jewish residents.* "Bill, Russian Jews were seldom allowed to be legislators, professors, or other professionals. The male children were conscripted into the Russian army as young as ten years of age and, just like everyone else, the Russians turned aside while Nazi Germany instigated the systematic murder of millions of men, women and children, all in an attempt to accomplish the Final Solution."

Next I told him about the generations of pogroms in Russia and Eastern Europe that had destroyed large numbers of European Jewry.+ In the early twentieth century, after World War I and the Russian Revolution and during the years of the Russian civil war, the slaughter of Jews, mostly by anti-Bolshevik, White Army soldiers and their supporters, was a common occurrence. From late 1917 to early 1920 75,000 Jews were savagely murdered in the Ukraine. Going further back in time, to 1648, I informed Bill that in a single pogrom more than one hundred thousand Polish Jews were slaughtered under the direction of Bohdan Khmelnytsky, a Ukrainian Cossack. I gave a brief description of some of the atrocities perpetrated against innocent men, women and children that left this black mark on the face of humanity. From the *Yeven Mezulah* by Natan Nata Hannover:

> Some of them [the Jews] had their skins flayed off them and
> their flesh was flung to the dogs. The hands and feet of others
> were cut off and they [their bodies] were flung onto the roadway
> where carts ran over them and they were trodden underfoot by
> horse ... And many were buried alive. Children were slaughtered
> at their mother's bosoms and many children were torn apart like
> fish. They ripped up the bellies of pregnant women, took out the
> unborn children, and flung them in their faces. They tore open
> the bellies of some of them and placed a living cat within the
> belly and they left them alive thus, first cutting off their hands so

* At the beginning of the twentieth century, about 5.2 million Jews lived in the Russian Empire, which included Poland. The total global Jewish population at the time was about 11.2 million.

+ A pogrom is an organized, often officially encouraged massacre or persecution of a minority group, especially one conducted against Jews,
dictionary.reference.com/browse/pogrom.

that they should not be able to take the living cat out of the belly ... and there was never an unnatural death in the world that they did not inflict upon them.[1]

"This," I implored, "is why Jews must have their own country."

Then I described a story of callousness that I had frequently recited to others, one I remembered from Joan Peters' book: the Nazis had offered to deport tens of thousands of Hungarian Jewish children, but the only government willing to absorb significant numbers into their general population was the Caribbean island nation of the Dominican Republic.* + Ultimately, most of the children perished in the death camps.

Possessed by the horrors of this subject, I insisted that after the Second World War, when the terrible destruction of European Jewry was finally out in the open, the United States, England and the rest of Western Europe still refused to accept more than a nominal number of desperate Jews from the European killing fields. With disgust I bemoaned the fact that because of widespread indifference to Jewish life, over one thousand Polish Jewish survivors of the death camps, after returning to their villages, were murdered by vicious anti-Semitic mobs – a year after the fall of the Third Reich. Neither the Catholic Church nor the Polish communist rulers did anything to stop these barbaric acts.

Relentless, I repeated my contention that the only way my people would ever be free from persecution was to have a homeland of their own: "Wouldn't any human being want to live in a place free of hatred and discrimination?" I pleaded. "Do you really expect Jews to live in countries where they know they will be persecuted, tortured and murdered? Are the Jews at fault because so many Christians and Muslims are taught from childhood that we should be objects of their contempt? They're jealous that Jews have been so successful. Rather than take

---

* I could not recall the exact figure Peters quotes in her book, nor could I confirm or deny her claim. The total number of Hungarian Jews killed in the Holocaust is estimated at 450,000 or 70% of Hungarian Jews.

+ The Dominican Republic took in 100,000 refugees. Dominican dictator Trujillo was not motivated by compassion. His primary goal was to improve his image in the eyes of the American public.

responsibility for themselves, they scapegoat Jews and blame them for their own failures in life."

Bill had listened patiently, but now he reacted forcefully: "The Palestinians live under a cruel occupation. Even though some of their methods are dreadful, Hezbollah and Hamas are resisting a ruthless oppressor. This war in Lebanon wouldn't be happening if European Jews hadn't violated the rights of the Palestinians and pushed them off their land. That's the bottom line."

Self-righteously I disagreed. "Jews have lived in the land now called Israel for thousands of years. As for the European Jews, they legally purchased much of that land from the so-called Palestinians. Besides, in 1948, when Israel declared its statehood and was attacked by the Arabs, almost as many Jews as 'Palestinians' – 500,000 to 600,000 – were expelled from their homes. Jews, who had lived in Arab countries for centuries, had to leave for fear of retribution and were prohibited from returning. The 'Palestinians' left Israel only because radio broadcasts by Arab governments encouraged them to do so; and while leaving, they rarely came upon Israeli soldiers. Unlike Israel most of the Arab nations closed their borders to their own kinsmen, thereby creating the Palestinian refugee problem of today."

"That's ridiculous," Bill said, as he repeated his claim of a few minutes before: "Zionists drove the Palestinians from their aboriginal homes. They took as much of the land as they could. That's why there is a problem today."

My impassioned plea was having no effect on my friend, so I tried to reform him by calling attention to Palestinian degeneracy: "Bill, you can't compare Israelis and Palestinians. The Palestinians have no respect for human life. They deliberately target all Jews, even infants, and celebrate every single death. They're so perverted they even martyr their own children. The Israelis are the opposite. They only kill in self-defense and mourn the regrettable deaths of the innocent."

Annoyed that my analysis was falling on deaf ears, I reminded Bill that my people had continually offered land for peace but the Palestinians always sabotaged their proposals with suicide bombings or other acts of malice. And diplomatically, the Palestinians presented an attitude marked by simple intransigence and an obvious lack of concern for their own people. The prime example I referred to – my ace in the hole – was Israeli Prime Minister Ehud Barak's peace proposal in 2000 at Camp David, near the end of the Clinton presidency. Israel had offered to return somewhere between ninety-four and ninety-six percent of the Occupied Territories to the Palestinians, by far the most generous offer ever put on the table by an Israeli Prime Minister, and Yasser Arafat turned Barak down cold. I could not conceive of a more convincing argument to prove who was serious and who wasn't when it came to peace.

Shockingly, unreasonably, Bill overlooked all of my arguments. Instead, he brought up an alleged human-rights violation by Israel: "Ariel Sharon is disgusting," he charged. "He has no respect for human life. When he was Israeli Defense Minister, he was responsible for the murders of hundreds of innocent Palestinians in Lebanon." I knew that Bill was referring to the 1982 massacre at the Sabra and Shatila Palestinian refugee camps, but I quickly excused Sharon's misconduct as an unfortunate attribute of war.[*]

Exasperated with my refusal to give any weight to his arguments, Bill reverted to the Old Testament and its accounts of the conquest and slaying of tribes whose lands the children of Israel coveted. That seemed really far-fetched to me. It was hard to believe that he would castigate Israel and the Jewish people for blood that was shed so long ago. I asked him if he thought the United States should return the land that white European immigrants had taken from the Indians. He didn't quite answer affirmatively, but he seemed to agree with my sarcastic comparison of the "Palestinian Diaspora" with the displacement of the American Indians.

Since I had no sympathy with Bill's regard for the Palestinians or Hezbollah, I could see no reason to acknowledge that Israel had acted inappropriately in its dealings with either of those groups or the Lebanese population. All that Bill had accomplished throughout our entire dialogue was to leave me feeling even more defensive and anxious to preserve my version of the historic record. Each of his assertions seemed insignificant

---

[*] Israeli military intelligence estimates put the number killed during the sixty-two-hour rampage at 700 to 800. Witnesses from the Red Crescent as well as investigative journalists from *Le Monde Diplomatique*, *The Independent*, and other sources claim the dead numbered up to several thousand.

in light of the long history of enmity aimed at Israel by its Arab neighbors. Why couldn't Bill see that Israel was only defending itself against an unremitting enemy, as it had so many times before? Both of us knew that Hezbollah's military capabilities were facilitated by the coordinated efforts of Syria and Iran. Additionally, I was sure that the Palestinian group Hamas and other Islamist terror groups were also affiliated with Hezbollah. If Hezbollah and the Palestinians were willing to end their terrorist acts, they would be able to live in peace and the Palestinians could have their own country.

Anyway, I'd had enough, so I asked Bill a question that I had wrestled with for some time. "Bill, are you anti-Semitic?" He answered that he wasn't, but in my emotionally charged state I was not sure I believed him. I certainly didn't listen very carefully to his line of reasoning, because it was a foregone conclusion that anyone who could not understand the reality of this conflict was either anti-Semitic or poorly informed. With resignation, I had come to realize that only Jews could truly understand the suffering of our people. Thousands of years of anti-Semitism, so ingrained in the world's psyche, was a major cause of the disturbed thinking of well-meaning people, even my wise friend Bill.

After Bill left I felt a need to mollify my uneasiness and confusion over why so many countries constantly disparaged Israel, so I came up with the idea of drafting an Israel-Palestine peace proposal. Besides the somewhat calming effect this exercise had on my emotions, it was a way to privately express my solicitude for the innocent people of the Middle East, mostly the Israelis, as well as the multitudes around the world who would inevitably be drawn into this unrelenting feud.

There didn't seem to be any foreseeable resolution to the Israel-Palestine quarrel. After sixty years of Israeli statehood the competing factions were unwavering. Making matters worse, more and more weapons were being stockpiled by Islamist fanatics, intent on carnage. This was an issue that really worried me. By attempting to find a solution to this interminable dispute and by seeking a way to protect and save lives, I was able to find a measure of peace within myself.

* * * *

A few days later I was invited to a pro-Israel rally at the local Jewish Community Center. Although I had not attended synagogue or any other organized Jewish function for decades, I was eager to be present at this gathering to lend encouragement to my brothers and sisters in our fight for survival.

The auditorium was filled. As my congressional representative and state attorney general spoke in defense of Israel, my anxiety abated and was replaced by gratitude for their friendship. Next to assume the podium were Israel's consul general to the southwestern United States, prominent members of the Jewish community and rabbis representing each of the congregations within my city. All held unequivocally that Israel's incursion into Lebanon was necessary to protect its borders from an enemy that had no justification for its shameful acts.

A gathering of Christians, holding placards affirming allegiance to Israel, stood with us in solidarity. I felt relieved that we were not alone as we often seemed to be. Afterwards I donated money to the Jewish Federation to help Israeli children who lived in the path of Hezbollah's rockets to attend summer camp in safer, more southerly regions of Israel. I also made a donation to the American Israel Public Affairs Committee (AIPAC), a powerful lobbying group in Washington, D.C., which works to shape United States foreign policy to favor Israel.

Meanwhile, the war between Israel and Hezbollah continued. Later that week I spoke with another friend whom I thought I could count on for support and reassurance during this troubling period. Westley's ability to see and sometimes predict behavior that others were unaware of always intrigued me. He too had usually taken a stance critical of Israel but I was sure he would agree with my point of view – the intelligent and rational point of view. Disappointingly, he did not. Instead, he presented an exposition similar to Bill's, though in a different manner. Whereas there was an edge of anger to Bill's demeanor, Westley conveyed a matter-of-fact attitude, one that brooked no disagreement. Our discussion ended with my convictions still intact. Acutely frustrated that my friends had rejected my views, I could not help but reject theirs.

A few days later I received an unexpected phone call from an old friend, a call that would set the stage for a remarkable change in my relationship to the State of Israel. Sam and I had known each other since early childhood. He was calling from his home on the East coast to tell me he would be attending a bar mitzvah out West and planned to come visit me afterwards. Sam was more informed on most contemporary topics than the vast majority of people I knew. He had studied many of the consequential political problems of our time, including the Israel-Palestine conflict. During our long conversation I began to speak of the war in Lebanon. As I went through my list of reasons why Israel was blameless, he would occasionally disagree and interject his more educated assessment. He was relaxed and dispassionate, not interested in choosing sides. Instead, he just indicated where he felt I was incorrect.

Sam suggested I explore the website www.commondreams.org for some informative articles about the war and Israel's administration of Palestinian Occupied Territory. He also recommended a couple of authors whose writings, he promised, would clarify the turbulent history of the Israel-Palestine conflict. Because Sam was Jewish, and because he did not exhibit any sort of judgmental reaction to my viewpoint, I was able to accept his guidance. Fortuitously, he had given me the space to question myself without a threat to my sense of identity. Thus, I embarked upon my own investigation into the history of the animus that had been aimed at Israel throughout its existence.

Breakthrough

– 3 –
Awakening

And you shall know the truth, and the truth shall make you free.
John 8:32

When I began my study of the Israel-Palestine conflict I was determined to read the works of Jewish authors only. I knew that if I chose non-Jewish authors I would suspect bias. First, I went on the Internet and scanned reviews of books by Israeli professors Baruch Kimmerling and Tanya Reinhart, the authors Sam had referred me to.* I also glanced at a number of other works on the Israel-Palestine conflict, quickly segregating as best I could Jewish authors from the rest. Then I noticed a book by an American professor, Norman Finkelstein. The writer's surname met my chief requirement and the title drew my attention: *Beyond Chutzpah: On the Misuse of Anti-Semitism and the Abuse of History.* That was enough to encourage me to add the book to my reading list. After compiling a few other possibilities, I drove to my local library.

Browsing through the bookshelves, the first book I found was *The Palestinian People* by Kimmerling and Joel Migdal. Since I trusted Sam's advice, I didn't bother to inspect the book. I had already decided that I would borrow at least one book written by Baruch Kimmerling. Then I discovered *Beyond Chutzpah*. I perused the inside jacket. To my simultaneous surprise and horror, I read that Joan Peters' book *From Time Immemorial* had been "exposed as an academic hoax." Given my enthusiasm for Peters' work, the statement was provocative and threatening. As I was beginning to recover my balance, the jacket held another surprise: it said that Finkelstein was highly critical of the Israel-Palestine analysis that Harvard Law professor Alan Dershowitz communicated in his book *The Case for Israel*. Although I had not read that book, I had always regarded Dershowitz as an independent and fair-

* Baruch Kimmerling (1939-2007) was professor of sociology at the Hebrew University of Jerusalem and author of various books on the Israel-Palestine conflict. Tanya Reinhart (1943-2007) was Professor Emeritus of Linguistics and Comparative Literature at Tel-Aviv University and guest lecturer at the University of Utrecht in the Netherlands. She authored *Israel/Palestine: How to End the War of '48* among other books, and wrote for various publications including *Yediot Aharanot*.

minded thinker. I had admired him, along with Peters, for a long time. I had barely begun my investigation, had not even read the first page of either Kimmerling or Finkelstein's book, yet I was already faced with the prospect that long-held, nearly sacred beliefs were about to be deflated.

One thing was now clear: my inner turmoil had pushed me into a corner. Seeing something I almost wished I hadn't, the forbidden fruit as it were, I was repelled and attracted at the same time. In the face of this unforeseen impasse, I was left with no choice but to borrow Finkelstein's book from the library as the only possible relief from my dilemma. Then I remembered a fragment of a brief conversation I had put out of my mind: eight or nine years earlier, Sam had warned me that the book I had invested such faith in, *From Time Immemorial*, had been debunked by a Jewish scholar years before I first learned about it from my sister-in-law.

After I returned home the awareness that I was about to venture into terrain that did not appear to be as clearly demarcated as I had always supposed became more pronounced. Feeling somewhat anxious, I realized that I was shocked enough for one day, so I decided to sleep on my decision and see how I felt after a night's rest.

****

The following morning I sat alone in my living room. It was very quiet outside. There was nothing to distract me, nothing I really wanted or needed. At ease, I was finally ready to uncover any evidence that might clarify the issues that had caused such consternation. Resigned to the fact that I was about to discover new and unsavory details about Peters and Dershowitz, I picked up *Beyond Chutzpah*. What I never expected, as I began my journey, was just how forcefully the book would rebuke Israel's policies in the Palestinian Occupied Territories.

Over the ensuing days, I read Finkelstein's words with as much tolerance as I could muster. There was no doubt in my mind that I was studying the work of a brilliant scholar who possessed a great deal of confidence in his arguments. Furthermore, Finkelstein was meticulous about documenting the evidence he was presenting. Because of these qualities I restrained myself from abandoning his book, sensing that my endurance would lead to some kind of resolution, though I had no idea what form it might take. Most of the time my reading was marked by an inner struggle: on the one hand, a desire to get to the truth and alleviate my torment; on the other, a curiosity to ascertain whether Finkelstein was in fact a disturbed academic and anti-Semite – an ironic possibility, given that the book was purportedly about the misuse of anti-Semitism. For me the question became: Who was actually misusing anti-Semitism, he or I?

In his introduction Finkelstein compared the policies that grew out of Zionism to South African apartheid and the conquest of the American Indian.* He pointed out that the history of the Israel-Palestine conflict up until the formal establishment of the Jewish State was no longer a point of contention among serious scholars: Zionists had denied Palestinians the same rights they themselves had fought for, and were responsible for the expulsion of the indigenous people from their native land. This may have prepared me for further explosive arguments yet to come, but it did not resolve my primary question: What were the Jewish people supposed to do in a hostile world that wouldn't let them live in peace?

Part one of *Beyond Chutzpah* was entitled *The Not-So-New 'New Anti-Semitism.'* Here Finkelstein tackled the modern Jewish penchant for ascribing "any challenge inimical to Jewish interests" to anti-Semitic tendencies.[1] He criticized a wide variety of Jewish sources for their blind and uninformed support of Israel and their attempts to silence voices that spoke out against its policies, even when those voices were respected human rights organizations like Amnesty International or Human Rights Watch. He especially ridiculed the hypocritical stance of some prominent Jews in defending Christian fundamentalist leaders, like Jerry Falwell of the Moral Majority and Pat Robertson of the Christian Broadcasting Network, because they backed a "militarized Israel," while ignoring the fact that their theology "reeked of anti-Semitism."[2] For Finkelstein there were no sacred cows. He criticized leading Jewish institutions like the Anti-Defamation League (ADL) and its leader, Abraham Foxman; the Simon Wiesenthal Center and its leader, Marvin Hier; and Jewish Holocaust survivor, author, and Nobel Prize laureate, Elie Wiesel, one of the most revered men in Jewish society.

---

* Zionism is a worldwide Jewish movement that began in the late nineteenth century. Its goal is to establish and preserve a Jewish homeland. There are religious Zionists and secular Zionists. Some Zionists believe in a two-state solution with a Palestinian state in the West Bank. Others believe that in addition to Israel proper all of the West Bank belongs to the Jewish people.

I could not help but be impressed with the clarity of Finkelstein's reasoning but I was not fully persuaded. Although I was beginning to recognize that I was one of the uninformed whose views he was deconstructing, I remained very sensitive to the undercurrent of anti-Semitism in my society and the threat it posed to the Jewish people. And even though I disagreed with Christian fundamentalist leaders on almost every political and social issue imaginable, I was relieved that the one issue they did get right was Israel. I kept coming back to this question: Why was Finkelstein so one-sided, his message so critical of Israel and the prevailing Jewish ethos, with almost nothing negative to say about the Palestinian ethos? Some speculative answers I contemplated were: 1) He was simply stating the facts in order to restore reality to the discussion of anti-Semitism and its relationship to the Israel-Palestine issue; 2) He felt great empathy for the Palestinian cause and wanted the same quality of life for their society as that enjoyed by Israel, so he avoided discussing their acts of terror; or 3) He was really an anti-Semite who had a talent for distorting any issue and using it for his own reprehensible purposes. My confusion had not subsided. I saw no alternative but to continue reading.

By the third day, I began to experience a succession of distinct emotions, but was so engrossed in the book that it took awhile before I could articulate them. When I eventually shifted my attention onto my mental-emotional state, I remembered the feelings of shock and disbelief that had come over me upon reading that Israel had bulldozed hundreds of homes in the Palestinian areas, sometimes with the inhabitants still inside; that Israel was siphoning off flagrantly disproportionate amounts of water from those areas for its own use; that collective punishment was a common practice; and that Israel was the only country in the world that legalized torture.* As a Jew, I was acutely bothered that human beings

---

* Israel's High Court of Justice ruled in September 1999 that the Internal Security Agency (ISA) could not use "physical means" against detainees. In their ruling, the HCJ shielded interrogators from prosecution in "ticking bomb" situations. According to a joint report by Israeli human rights groups, B'Tselem and HaMoked: Center for the Defence of the Individual, "Absolute Prohibition: The Torture and Ill-Treatment of Palestinian Detainees," May 2007: "This ruling implicitly legitimized these severe acts, contrary to international law, which does not acknowledge any exceptions to the

were being mistreated in my name and in the name of my people. Considering that I had never treated anyone with such brutality, it seemed unfair that I should have to carry such a burden of culpability.

Pausing briefly, I put the book down and tried to find some respite from this onslaught of disturbing information. After taking a few deep breaths, I forged ahead, only to discover that Israel frequently appropriated Palestinian-owned land in the Occupied Territories for Jewish-only settlements, thereby "'drastically restrict[ing] the possibilities for economic development in general, and for agriculture in particular.'"[3] Then, from a study by Amnesty International: "'Palestinian vehicles and passengers [in Gaza] have been stuck between . . . checkpoints for hours, unable even to get out of their cars for fear of being shot . . . . Members of the Israeli security forces have frequently resorted to lethal force to enforce restrictions, killing or injuring scores of Palestinians who were unarmed and presented no threat.'"[4]

Forcing myself to continue, I learned that in 1994 Human Rights Watch reported that "'the number of Palestinians tortured or severely ill-treated' – often without even a pretense that these detainees were guilty of wrongdoing – 'is in the tens of thousands.'"[5] On the same page, B'Tselem (the Israeli Information Center for Human Rights in the Occupied Territories) was quoted as accusing Israel of being the only democratic country in the world that regarded "political liquidations as a 'legitimate course of action....'"[6]

After reading the allegations of these respected, mainstream human-rights organizations, my disbelief and shock turned into anger at my Israeli brethren for their unjustified and inhumane deeds. My anger then turned inward as I reflected on my past failure to pay attention to this struggle. My face flushed with heat and a righteous fury seethed within me for the suffering of an entire ethnic group that I had continually ignored. The cries of millions had never even touched me. Waves of

---

prohibition on torture and ill-treatment." Torture of Palestinians is still commonplace.

B'Tselem is Hebrew for "'in the image of,' and is also used as a synonym for human dignity. The word is taken from Genesis 1:27 'And God created humans in his image. In the image of God did He create him.'"

btselem.org/About_BTselem/Index.asp.

remorse passed through my body and I shuddered at the thought that I had rejected their claims of persecution as propaganda and lies. I was ashamed that I had demonized an entire culture and judged its people as irredeemable. In acknowledging my heartlessness, I was obliged to silently confess to my history of delusion and denial. Many of the positions I had taken on behalf of Israel and against the Palestinian people were factually incorrect.

These positions, so prevalent within my culture, had appeared reasonable, even unassailable. They had taken shape during the impressionable years of childhood and were suffused with the common accounts of my parents, rabbis, Sunday-school teachers, relatives and friends. Most significantly, they were founded upon two interconnected, governing beliefs, which were the substratum out of which all other judgments arose.

The first was that Israel unfailingly acted with integrity in its dealings with others. There was never any doubt in my mind that when mistakes were made, Israel's overriding rectitude ensured that the mistakes were redressed. The second and more prominent belief was one that had wielded its authority from the deeper recesses of my mind, indifferent to the fact that I had never been a religious Jew: God had promised the land of Israel to the Jewish people and, at last, after thousands of years of persecution, that promise had been fulfilled. And, just as the patriarchs Abraham, Isaac and Jacob had acted under God's guidance and protection, so too had Israel. Thus, the judgments I had regarding the Israel-Palestine issue – empowered by holy writ – were so unshakable there was never any thought of deserting them.

Under the influence of these beliefs, I had further rationalized Israel's actions with other, subordinate beliefs that I presumed were equally incontestable. Among these were that Israel, when forced to retaliate against its enemies, did so with great reluctance; that Israeli soldiers did not violate civil rights or kill indiscriminately, principles which I later learned are embodied in the IDF concept of *purity of arms*; that Israel's Supreme Court was a bastion of justice for all citizens, including the Palestinians; and that the reason the Palestinians always subverted Israel's sincere attempts to establish a fair peace was because their true goal was to push the Israelis into the sea.

Since I had always believed the United Nations was the primary arena for resolving conflict around the world, I was chronically upset with its myopia to the truth of what was happening in the Middle East and its insensitivity to the suffering of the Jewish people. Only anti-Semitism could explain such ignorance. I also couldn't comprehend why some Jews were convinced the Palestinian cause was just. That reasoning was nonsensical to me, so I had attributed their confused logic to misguidance and misinformation.

But now my mind was in the crosshairs, its conception of reality threatened by powerful reasoning and compelling research.

My shame and embarrassment receded, and a heavy sadness enveloped me for the oppressive treatment that so many Palestinians had suffered.

Although I had always considered myself capable of clarifying most matters on the basis of my own scrutiny, I saw that when it came to Israel I had brushed aside challenging questions in favor of an irrational but emotionally satisfying appraisal. I had believed what I wanted to believe. As I got more in touch with this insight, a startling awareness emerged: not one trace of the emotions I had been experiencing only minutes before was anywhere to be found. The entire constellation had apparently fallen apart; yet, I could not distinguish a point in time when these emotions, either singularly or collectively, had faded from awareness. Nor did I have a clue as to the manner in which they had left. Was their dissolution gradual or instantaneous? There was no way of telling.

Uncertain if my pain might return, I noticed that a distinct sense of freedom had taken its place. Somehow I had drifted into a restful space of emptiness where there was no inner conflict and no reactive thinking. My curiosity took over and I tried to decipher how this transformation had come to pass. Plumbing my memory, the only thing I could recall was putting the book down and pondering the incriminating charges I had just learned about.

When I concluded that an answer to my inquiry was not forthcoming – and since I wasn't in a state of mind to care one way or the other – I dismissed the exercise and sat quietly, waiting. There didn't seem to be anything else to do. Although I had no idea what I was waiting for, I was utterly patient. There was no struggle, no doubt and no dilemma, only sitting and basking in this blissful state. There was no past and no future, only the *Now*. Perhaps a sign would appear to confirm that this incomprehensible reversal of my usual consciousness was real. There was no need for any answers because I had no questions. There was no resistance to my state of being. Not looking for one experience or avoiding another, I was perfectly neutral.

A minute or two passed. I was the same person I had always been, yet I felt so different, as if I was connected to a source beyond my body. My body, or the pressure inside my body, felt like it was dispersed over a wider area, which produced more spaciousness throughout my being and filled me with a profound feeling of satisfaction. My sense of self had transcended the ordinary limits of a physical form.

This fresh sensation brought to mind the image of a balloon. A balloon is distinguished from the space in which it resides by the elastic boundaries that give it its shape and definition, or existence. The boundaries, however, are impermanent. If the balloon is punctured, the air that was inside the balloon equalizes with the air outside the balloon and there is no longer any separation, only oneness; and the balloon is quickly forgotten.

In one seamless and timeless "moment," I had moved from a state of constriction and suffering to one of newness, as if the world around me was pure and untouched, its atmosphere rarefied and, like my mind, empty of all qualities. This transition felt so natural that for a few seconds I wondered why I hadn't always lived this way. Compared to my new sense of self, it was as if I had been asleep or in a trance for most of my life and upon waking was not burdened by the emotional pain I had been carrying. I felt lighter and more unguarded, and the pain I had borne appeared to be nothing more than the content of a long, drawn-out dream. Within the dream, the pain had persisted for a lifetime, but in this newly awakened state it was only a dim and distant memory.

Where had the pain gone? Still unsure of what had just happened, I scanned the room in search of my emotions, wondering if they might have a solid life of their own and were hiding in some physical location, not particularly bothered whether I found them or not. Nothing I had done could have induced them to leave. In fact, even if I had formulated the thought that I didn't want these emotions impinging on my consciousness, I would have had no idea how to extinguish them, short of mind-numbing drugs. My experience could not be denied. The painful emotions were gone.

My attention was then drawn to my face. Running horizontally along a line just below my eyebrows and, parallel to that, along a line crossing the upper border of my cheekbones, and spanning the distance between the lateral orbital bones of my eyes, a rectangular-shaped area felt as if it was covered by a soft, gossamer-like material. Lightly pressing against my face, the "material" slowly began to unravel, moving delicately from left to right in a spiral pattern, freeing one eye and then the other from a gentle pressure that I had never felt before. In the short time it took for this strangely soothing sensation to appear and disappear, a new world had arisen, so that whatever my vision rested on was literally displayed in a brighter light, enabling me to see with a sharper clarity; and I grasped that the world was an unqualified reflection of my ever changing states of consciousness.

The Hindu religion uses the concept of Maya, the veil of illusion or ignorance, to refer to the activity whereby we superimpose our mental content onto the world and presume that what we see before us is Reality. That, at least, is how I would have defined those terms prior to this event. Now I could see and feel how the veil of illusion was much more than a figure of speech that points to a mysterious error in cognition. The veil is an actual psychophysical manifestation: a commanding – though unconscious – refusal to see the world as it really is without the addition of an entire belief system.

This realization quickly passed when, unexpectedly, I observed that I could not detect an exclusive identity, or "me," differentiated from anyone or anything else. There was no evidence of an attachment to, attraction toward, or merging with a Jewish self. Given my customary outrage at the world's non-acceptance of my people, it was hard to believe at first that I was evaluating my experience accurately. Briefly I speculated that such an evocative ending to a core identity should be accompanied by dramatic emotional, mental and physical overtones. But that was not the case. And too, as hard as I tried to reanimate my Jewish identity – not out of fretfulness, but to confirm the validity of my unanticipated observation – it would not return. So, I surrendered to the inevitability of the moment and calmly accepted that I was not separate from members of other religious or ethnic groups. I had lost my individual identity as a Jew and discovered my common humanity with all people. I was as much Palestinian as Israeli, as much Muslim as Jew. My Jewishness had never felt like a burden to me. It was "who I am" or so I'd thought. But now that I was no longer bound to one identity and separate from another, I felt a great relief. This new consciousness of non-separation gave me the freedom to reflect upon the lifelong dominion my former identity had held over me.

Initially, my reflection took the form of a simple exercise. I relaxed and settled into my body. Then, from that calm space I began to compare the new self-sense with the old. At a certain point I noticed an almost imperceptible sensation in my upper abdomen, around my solar plexus. As the sensation captured my attention a memory arose from early childhood. The memory took the form of subtle bodily recoil at the communication that who I was could be defined by others, that I was Jewish and an American. This recoil, which I experienced as doubt, was a natural response to the delimiting of my being – to being informed who I was and, therefore, who I wasn't. It was a warning from my deepest internal perception that by capitulating to a limited identity my most basic understanding of myself would be undermined. But the warning disappeared as fast as it had appeared and the communication became a part of how I would come to identify myself. I had made a choice, but the choice was not borne of thought; it was borne of innocence, vulnerability and trust. It was a decision from the heart.

As I matured into adulthood my identity became more entrenched within cultural and social boundaries, beyond which I had no awareness or understanding. These boundaries were analogous to having bridle reins connected to the sides of my head, prescribing how far I could turn in any direction. I could see only that part of the world the restraints permitted and was so habituated to the restraints that I didn't even know they existed. As a result I took for granted that the world I saw was all there was to see. With such a worldview it was not possible to comprehend the motivation for the behavior of those I perceived as threats to me and my people. What was possible was to label them "terrorists." My irrational fear had reduced them to objects intent on my demise. Only after I was free of irrational fear did I become aware that I had objectified anyone. Now I could see just how primitive my thinking had been. A reasonable need for safety had been transformed into an irrational fear that could be satisfied only by incapacitating or destroying the objects of my fear. Only then would no harm befall me. Fear persuaded me to deny the humanity of others and more easily condone their destruction. By interpreting the world through the prism of fear, my mind had created enemy images and then superimposed those images onto other people, unconsciously presuming that they actually existed as reality. I had played God by determining the substance of a man or a woman without even knowing that man or woman. Those whom I defined as enemies, as threats to my being or way of life, were transmuted by my fear into monsters, whose potential for violence could never be discounted.

I recalled a statement made by President George W. Bush during his address to Congress after the tragedy of September 11, 2001: "Either you are with us, or you are with the terrorists." Like most Americans I had agreed with the President, convinced that the uncompromising position he was taking was the path to safety. Bush also said that the terrorists wanted to kill Americans because they hated our freedoms and values. At first I wasn't sure I agreed with that statement, but after further consideration, and taking into account that Bush had access to intelligence I wasn't privy to, I decided it was an accurate assessment of the mental processes of fanatical individuals and the culture of hatred they had grown up in.

With insight into my own mental processes regarding the Israel-Palestine conflict, I now understood that Bush's declarations were not grounded in reflective analysis. They were about revenge. His reaction to the attacks of 9/11 by Islamist extremists was similar to my reaction to the attacks by Hezbollah that had precipitated the Second Lebanon War. Bush was pandering to the fear and confusion that had inundated the consciousness of America, just as I had pandered to the fear and confusion that had inundated my consciousness.

In the midst of the horror of 9/11, my emotions seduced me into tolerating policies that were not only contrary to my own self-interest and to the values Bush spoke about, but catastrophic to incalculable numbers of people who wanted to live their lives in peace. By dividing the world into opposing camps, Bush was propagating the illusion of a united Muslim-Arab conspiracy. He made it clear that America was about to embark upon a "crusade" against a strain of religious extremism that was dedicated to eradicating the principles America's founders had fought and died for. Bush's divisive mentality was fated to breed fear, confusion and hatred and, inevitably, more violence. What I had failed to consider for myself was that by demonizing others, others would learn to demonize me; and that by judging entire societies on the basis of the attitudes of a few depraved individuals, entire societies would judge my society on the basis of my attitudes.

Deceived by a belief system consisting of antagonists and protagonists and aligning myself with the presumption that one part of the world represented sanity and the other insanity, I was supporting indiscriminate and massive destruction; in a word, insanity. This careless choice emanated from a single error in consciousness: my unquestioned devotion to a limited identity. Until I acknowledged the profound influence of this primal error, my participation in the generational reenactment of hatred and retribution, of chronic hostility and mistrust, was destined to continue.

* * * *

I noticed that I didn't seem to suffer a fear of terrorists. Where once there had been fear, now there was emptiness, and this emptiness manifested as the absence of any impulse or desire to judge or define the other. My curiosity was stirred, so I designed an experiment to check the accuracy of my observation. Like someone who pinches himself to see if he is really awake, I visualized a series of horrifying scenarios that were similar to news reports that once stimulated great agitation within me. My objective was to see if I could rekindle my former feelings. I imagined bloody atrocities against innocent children and meditated on nightmare visions of my brutal death at the hands of Islamist extremists. Surprisingly, the physical and mental stress that normally sprang from such images did not appear. What materialized instead was a feeling of equanimity. There was an immeasurable relief in knowing that the rage extremists felt was not based solely upon irrational hatred. With this understanding they became human, and the irrational fear and anger I once felt for them were translated into compassion, equal to the compassion I felt for Jews. To me, this was strong evidence that without labels we would see all people as cut from the same cloth. How many of us would feel sadness at the sight of a man in obvious pain, dying? How many of us would not feel a thing if we were told beforehand that the man was a Muslim fundamentalist? Compassion became the doorway to understanding the suffering of my former enemy.

* * * *

In classical psychology projection is defined as "the attribution of one's own ideas, feelings, or attitudes to other people or to objects; *especially*: the externalization of blame, guilt, or responsibility as a defense against anxiety."[7] Although I was familiar with this defense mechanism, I had really only understood it with my intellect. Now I understood it with the natural intelligence of my heart, and I found myself able to inquire directly into the grievances that catalyze the anger of others.

I realized that my past appraisal of the motivations of the extremists had more to do with me than it had to do with them. Believing that my fear and hatred were justified, I had been certain that my intentions arose out of fairness, while theirs arose out of hatred. That was pure projection. Their anger simmered and then exploded because my culture withheld the fairness they longed for. Now I had to consider the possibility that they didn't become our enemies because of who we were; they became our enemies because of what we did.

Before, I had scoffed at their torment and ridiculed as pure fiction the reasons they gave for their anger. Now I could feel how callous that attitude had been and I understood why the level of violence in parts of the Muslim world had grown over the years and why my fellow man could act with such murderous intent and disdain for life. After years of frustration, of being shunned, of not having his hopes and needs considered, he was enraged. Demoralized by the deaths and mutilations of family and friends and anguished over the persistent inequality between his people and their occupier, he was intent on ridding his homeland of an unwelcome and foreign presence. Once I understood how these feelings ignited his passions, I knew that what the Palestinian people truly wanted was not the gratuitous deaths of Israelis but the implementation of the same God-given rights on which the State of Israel was built – self-determination and equality.

Notwithstanding my continued abhorrence for premeditated acts of violence, I had to admit that no matter how coldhearted I judged their behavior, the extremists had adopted the only means they knew to pursue the quest for justice that was hidden within the heart of their struggle. They had as much right to self-determination and equality as anyone else.

Also, I understood why so many Jews and Americans were emotional, even hysterical, in their condemnation of Islamist extremists and how – as I had once done – they generalized that reaction to include all of Islamic society.

* * * *

Our beliefs beguile us. They tell us how the world should appear. When we look out at the world, if it does not conform to our beliefs – and especially when we see conflict and violence – we suffer fear, anger and despair. We struggle with these emotions. Usually, we deny them in one of two ways: either we suppress them and disavow our humanity; or we find suitable individuals or groups to project them onto and disavow their humanity. Neither choice satisfies. But there is another choice that gets to the root of the problem: we can examine our beliefs, lay bare their emptiness and let true compassion awaken. It is my experience that this choice leads to peace.*

---

* *Epilogue: Reflections on Awakening* provides a brief analysis of possible catalysts for the awakening.

– 4 –

Alan Dershowitz and Norman Finkelstein

Do you solemnly swear to tell the truth, the whole truth, and nothing but the truth? So help you God. Witness oath taken before all criminal and civil trials in the United States

By neutralizing enemy images of Palestinians and Arabs, and by producing a deeper understanding of compassion and non-separateness, the breakthrough in consciousness imbued me with a more penetrating insight into the dynamics of conflict and relieved me of irrational fear and dualistic thinking. I already knew that for a peace to last it had to be just, but now it became obvious that in order to really find peace in the world we first had to find it within ourselves. This insight freed me to continue my research into the Israel-Palestine conflict from different points-of-view, without emotionally charged beliefs maneuvering me in the direction of one conclusion or another. If need be, I was willing to begin my research all over again, even to discover evidence that contradicted what I now intuited to be the basic history of the subject.

Although the evidence I had come upon did not make me an authority on the conflict, I knew that the Palestinian people would have a more difficult time gaining the rights they are entitled to without the help of America's powerful Jewish community. Moreover, I was aware that my past views on Israel-Palestine were commonplace within this community and that the same internal barriers and prejudices I once faced also existed among my fellow Jews. Similarly, my fellow Jews were as capable of learning about the history of the Israel-Palestine conflict as I had been. A more accurate knowledge would relieve them of much of their own irrational fear and dualistic thinking. They would see that the Palestinian struggle was not founded upon a hatred of Jews but upon a need for self-determination that was as genuine as the struggle for a Jewish state had been. Most importantly, anyone willing to seriously consider the history would likely catch a glimpse into how their unexamined beliefs contributed to the protracted character of the dispute. Convinced that my message of peace through internal transformation was of critical importance, I resolved to communicate it to others as best I could.

To that end, I decided to review Norman Finkelstein's discussion of the Israel-Palestine conflict and his withering criticism of Alan Dershowitz's *The Case for Israel*. Although I had no reason to doubt Finkelstein's scholarship, I was not willing to passively rely on it. There was a potential irony in the outside chance that Finkelstein had embellished the facts in order to disseminate a biased point of view; that my transformation had been facilitated by fiction or deceit. If that had turned out to be the case, I would be disappointed in Finkelstein, and would have to adjust my knowledge of Israel and Palestine accordingly, but I knew that any disappointment could not erase the clarity and compassion I now enjoyed.

Respect for Alan Dershowitz was another factor that persuaded me to carry out this investigation. Even though *Beyond Chutzpah* had rebutted *The Case for Israel* quite convincingly, I felt that Dershowitz deserved a degree of latitude. He had often impressed me with his readiness to speak frankly on controversial matters while others, probably for fear of repercussions, had toned down their rhetoric. And his support of liberal causes suggested that he cared about people less fortunate than himself. Furthermore, if someone had told me – as Finkelstein states in *Beyond Chutzpah* – that Dershowitz had written a book about Israel in which "The genuine challenge [was] to unearth *any* meaningful historical fact . . . ."[1] I would have thought the person had ulterior motives or was hopelessly confused. Finally, because *The Case for Israel* was a bestseller, I expected to meet a significant number of Jews who had read it. Realizing how affronted they would be if I tried to tell them that Dershowitz's book had been thoroughly discredited (assuming my investigation supported Finkelstein's conclusions), I wanted to possess the resources to respond cogently to their reactions.

With accuracy my goal, I went back through *Beyond Chutzpah* and randomly selected a number of citations for examination. On page 101 Finkelstein quotes Human Rights Watch, Amnesty International, and B'Tselem. Each of these human-rights organizations reprimands Israel for killing people in situations where there was no threat of deadly force from the other side. Some of their findings are:

> The organization found a pattern of repeated Israeli use of excessive lethal force during clashes between its security forces

and Palestinian demonstrators in situations where demonstrators were unarmed and posed no threat of death or serious injury to the security forces or to others. [Human Rights Watch] [2]

[T]he majority of people killed were taking part in demonstrations where stones were the only weapon used. . . . A large proportion of those injured and killed included children usually present and often among those throwing stones during demonstrations. Bystanders, people within their homes and ambulance personnel were also killed. [Amnesty International] [3]

[Open-fire] regulations apparently enable firing in situations where there is no clear and present danger to life, or even in situations where there is no life-threatening danger at all. [B'Tselem] [4]

Finkelstein then brings up the issue of human shields, which "refers to the conscription of civilians for military operations." On page 109 he quotes *The Case for Israel*: "[The Palestinians] use women (including pregnant women) and children as human shields." Finkelstein points out that Dershowitz fails to cite a source to back his claim up. Going further, he explains that human rights organizations have *not* "accused armed Palestinians of forcibly recruiting civilians for life-endangering operations." Rather, they "extensively document *Israel's* use of Palestinian human shields." Furthermore, Dershowitz omits any mention of this violation of international law.[5*]

On page 110 Finkelstein states:

A 2002 Human Rights Watch report found that "the IDF is systematically coercing Palestinian civilians" – including minors – "to assist military operations." For example, "friends, neighbors, and relatives of 'wanted' Palestinians were taken at gunpoint to knock on doors, open strange packages, and search houses in which the IDF suspected armed Palestinians were present. Some families found their houses taken over and used

---

* Finkelstein acknowledges that "Human rights organizations have documented instances in which armed Palestinians endangered civilians by firing on IDF soldiers from locations that exposed civilians to IDF return fire (Human Rights Watch).'"

as military positions by the IDF during an operation while they themselves were ordered to remain inside."[6]

Additional reports referenced by Finkelstein describe the deliberate targeting and killing of children in the Occupied Territories; Israel's lack of judicial investigations into these killings; "the IDF's reckless shooting, shelling and aerial bombardments of residential areas;" and the torture of minors through the use of "severe beatings, splashing cold water on detainees (the events occurred during the winter), putting the detainee's head in the toilet bowl, threats, and curses."[7]

After carefully reviewing each of the reports cited above, I determined that Finkelstein presents their findings accurately. Continuing with my investigation, I looked into additional criticisms Finkelstein makes of assertions that appear in *The Case for Israel*. For each and every citation or criticism of an assertion that I reviewed, Finkelstein is conscientious and precise. The same cannot be said of Dershowitz. Finkelstein quotes from page 42 of *The Case for Israel*:

> The developing clash between the Jews of Palestine, led by David Ben Gurion, and the Muslims, led by the uncompromising Jew-hater, Haj Amin Al-Husseini, was not over whether the Jews or Muslims would control all of Palestine . . . . Instead, it was – realistically viewed – whether the remainder of Palestine was to be given exclusively to the Muslims of Palestine or whether it would be fairly divided between the Jews and the Muslims of Palestine, each of whom effectively controlled certain areas.[8]*

In his criticism of this passage, Finkelstein points out that Dershowitz does not cite source material to substantiate the deliberations he attributes to Ben-Gurion. Finkelstein demonstrates that, in fact, Dershowitz's main source documents a contrary intention on the part of Ben-Gurion:

---

* Author's note: David Ben-Gurion, the "father of Israel," was its first Prime Minister and a key figure in achieving the Zionist goal of establishing a Jewish state in historic Palestine. Haj Amin Al-Husseini, appointed Grand Mufti of Jerusalem by the British in 1921, held that position until 1936.

Although Dershowitz ignores it, his main historical source – like all other studies of the period – concludes that both Weizmann and Ben-Gurion "saw partition as a stepping stone to further expansion and the eventual takeover of the whole of Palestine . . . . [Ben-Gurion] wrote to his son, Amos: '[A] Jewish state in part [of Palestine] is not an end, but a beginning. . . . Our possession is important not only for itself . . . through this we increase our power, and every increase in power facilitates getting hold of the country in its entirety. Establishing a [small] state . . . will serve as a very potent lever in our efforts to redeem the whole country.'"[9]*

The author Finkelstein refers to as Dershowitz's main historical source is Israeli historian Benny Morris.[+] After examining the relevant paragraph on page 138 of Morris's *Righteous Victims*, I confirmed that Finkelstein quotes Morris precisely. Then I looked at *The Case for Israel* and confirmed that Finkelstein quotes the passage from Dershowitz precisely and that Dershowitz neglects to cite source material. I then reviewed the *Notes* section of Dershowitz's book. There are fifty-nine footnotes that cite Morris's *Righteous Victims* in the first eighty-three pages of *The Case for Israel* and eighty-seven total references to Morris within the 244 pages of the book. The second most cited source is referenced twenty-one times by Dershowitz. On that basis, it is safe to say that Morris is in fact the "main historical source" for *The Case for Israel*. The conclusion I drew is that Dershowitz knowingly ignores his main historical source's account of the intentions of David Ben-Gurion and the Zionist movement regarding the division of Palestine so that he can promote his own version of history.

Another misrepresentation by Dershowitz is contained in his assertion that the Israeli Supreme Court acts with integrity in its defense of Palestinian rights. Finkelstein:

---

* Author's note: Chaim Weizmann (another key figure in achieving the Zionist goal of establishing a Jewish state in historic Palestine) was Israel's first President and President of the World Zionist Organization.

+ Benny Morris, currently professor of history in the Middle Eastern Studies Department at Ben-Gurion University, is an Israeli historian who has written extensively about the Israel/Palestinian conflict.

To demonstrate the Israel Supreme Court's defense of Palestinian rights, Alan Dershowitz quotes a Palestinian human rights activist on page 184 of *The Case for Israel*:

Even Raji Sourani, the director of the Palestinian Center for Human Rights in Gaza and a strident critic of Israel, says that he remains "constantly amazed by the high standards of the legal system [sic]."

Cited from the *New York Times*, the passage reads in full: "Despite his many frustrations with the Israeli courts, Mr. Sourani says he remains 'constantly amazed by the high standards of the legal system.' 'On many issues,' he said, 'when the courts are dealing with *purely Israeli questions*, like gay rights, I admire their rulings. *But when it comes to the Palestinians, these same people seem to be totally schizophrenic*'" (emphases added).[10]

Again, I checked *The Case for Israel* to make sure that Finkelstein quotes Dershowitz accurately and once more he has. Also, on page 184 of Dershowitz's book, I confirmed that the footnote for the quote cites the same newspaper article that Finkelstein cites. Lastly, I looked at the article itself in the *New York Times* and saw that the passage Finkelstein quotes perfectly matches the words of its author. The passage by Dershowitz is an egregious error; it effectively edits Raji Sourani's words so as to give them an explicitly different meaning than Sourani had intended.

Dershowitz's misrepresentation of the reporting of an eminent news source is patently unfair to the Palestinians and to the cause of peace. He has considerable influence within Jewish society and in liberal America in general. By misleading his readers, whose trust is based on his past dedication to equality and civil rights, Dershowitz has placed barriers in the way of the Palestinian struggle for those very same rights. What will his audience think the next time they hear a Palestinian complaint that the Israeli legal system treats them unfairly? It is regrettable that Dershowitz has chosen this path, especially if it adds one more day of suffering for anyone affected by this problem.

* * * *

Finkelstein was professor of political science at DePaul University until June 2007. A few months before he left his position, I learned that his application for tenure was under consideration and that DePaul political science professor and former department chair, Patrick Callahan, had asked Alan Dershowitz to provide the "clearest and most egregious instances of dishonesty on Finkelstein's part."[11] Dershowitz complied with Callahan's request and submitted a dossier of evidence that he alleged contained "ugly and false assertions that . . . are not incidental to Finkelstein's purported scholarship; they are his purported scholarship."[12] Dershowitz's action drew the attention of mainstream newspapers, including the *New York Times*, which reported:

> In a full-court press against Mr. Finkelstein, Mr. Dershowitz lobbied professors, alumni and the administration of DePaul, a Roman Catholic university in Chicago, to deny him tenure. Many faculty members at DePaul and elsewhere decried what they called Mr. Dershowitz's heavy-handed tactics.[13]

Petitions circulated the Internet, some urging DePaul to reject Finkelstein's bid for tenure and others asking DePaul not to succumb to pressure from groups attempting to suppress positions critical of Israel on college campuses. In the midst of the controversy, DePaul's political science department voted nine to three to grant tenure to Finkelstein, and a five-member personnel committee unanimously seconded that decision. Both, however, were overruled by the University Board on Promotion and Tenure and Finkelstein's request for tenure was formally denied. Civil rights attorney Bitta Mostofi, a graduate of DePaul's undergraduate and law schools, wrote:

> It is worth noting the oddity of even considering Dershowitz's evaluation of Finkelstein in that Dershowitz himself is not considered a scholar on the Israel-Palestine conflict. Additionally, DePaul's political science committee evaluated the accusations waged against Finkelstein and concluded that the accusations were not founded in any legitimate criticism of his scholarship. The Department invited two independent scholars from the University of Chicago and the University of Pennsylvania, chosen for their expertise on the Israeli-Palestine conflict, to evaluate the academic merit of Finkelstein's work.

They concluded that his work was an important contribution to the field.[14*]

Despite the well deserved academic reputations of the two independent scholars, I could not in good conscience completely rely on their findings. I had to see for myself if Dershowitz's dossier contains information that might discredit the evidence Finkelstein presents about Israel's treatment of the Palestinians. Again, Dershowitz's reputation prompted me to take another look. I could not dismiss out of hand what such a prominent attorney and law professor believes is evidence sufficient to warrant a particular decision. Moreover, the ad hominem nature of both men's attacks on each other was a red flag that I had better treat Dershowitz's allegations against Finkelstein as scrupulously as possible. And most importantly, Dershowitz's statement – ad hominem or not – that Finkelstein's scholarship was made of "ugly and false assertions" brought back to me the question I had wrestled with when I first began reading *Beyond Chutzpah*: Was Finkelstein an anti-Semite who had a talent for distorting any issue and using it for his own reprehensible purposes? Subsequently, I came upon an article by Frank Menetrez (Juris Doctor and PhD in Philosophy, both from UCLA).[15+] As I read the article I became satisfied that Menetrez had approached his subject with a genuine interest in discerning the truth.

Menetrez evaluated Dershowitz's list of alleged instances of dishonesty on the part of Finkelstein. Among the points of contention he reviews in the first part of his analysis are the death of Abd al-Samad Harizat while in Israeli custody, violent interrogations of Palestinian prisoners and the number of deaths that have resulted, and the use or nonuse of human rights organizations by Finkelstein and Dershowitz.

---

* Author's Note: the independent scholars are John Mearsheimer (University of Chicago) and Ian Lustick (University of Pennsylvania). I am indebted to Professor Azza Layton of DePaul University for providing me with this information.

+ Author's note: I discovered the Menetrez article at *Counterpunch.com* more than a year after I had read *Beyond Chutzpah*. It was not until two years after that, when I was once again looking through *Beyond Chutzpah*, that I discovered that Finkelstein had included the Menetrez article as the epilogue to his book. I have no recollection of having read it prior to encountering it at *Counterpunch*.

In the case of Harizat, Dershowitz writes that his death, which occurred after he had been shaken, was the result of a pre-existing medical condition and not the shaking itself. Conversely, Finkelstein cites "multiple independent investigations that did attribute the death to shaking . . . ."[16] In *Beyond Chutzpah* Finkelstein cites a report by Amnesty International and, among other references, lists Doctors Kugel and Levi from the Institute for Forensic Medicine in Tel Aviv, who performed the autopsy, and Dr. Pounder, a Scottish forensic pathology professor who observed the autopsy on behalf of the Harizat family. All acknowledged that Harizat's death resulted from shaking. Two comments are that Harizat died from "a brain hemorrhage caused by 'sudden jarring movements of the head' – that is, 'violent shaking'" and "the autopsy report of the Israeli forensic pathologists concluded that Harizat died from 'brain damage due to rotational acceleration of the head.'"[17]

On the subject of deaths caused by violent interrogations, Menetrez recounts that in *The Case for Israel*, Dershowitz states that the methods Israel uses to interrogate Palestinian prisoners are "'universally characterized as torture' even though 'they were nonlethal and did not involve the infliction of sustained pain.'"[18] Finkelstein, however, states the following:

> [H]uman rights organizations report multiple deaths of Palestinian detainees during Israeli interrogation. For example, the entry for "Israel and the Occupied Territories" in *Amnesty International Report 1993* states: "Palestinians under interrogation were systematically tortured or ill-treated. Four died in circumstances related to their treatment under interrogation." The Public Committee Against Torture in Israel reports that "approximately 20 Palestinian detainees died under suspicious circumstances while in interrogation and detention during the first Intifada."[19]

After a careful examination of Dershowitz's charges against Finkelstein, Menetrez comes to the following conclusions:

> Dershowitz never responds to, let alone refutes, any of Finkelstein's substantive claims in *Beyond Chutzpah* concerning the number of interrogation deaths, the actual independent

investigations of Harizat's death, or the fact that Dershowitz's cited source does not mention an independent investigation that attributed the death to a preexisting medical condition. . . . Dershowitz's *The Case for Israel* appears to contain multiple serious falsehoods concerning Israel's violent interrogation of Palestinian prisoners. . . . Not only does Dershowitz systematically ignore their [human rights organizations] findings, but in order to justify having done so, he seeks to malign the human rights organizations themselves.[20]

Menetrez ends that section of his examination with this paragraph:

From these facts it appears reasonable to conclude that, with the possible exception of the plagiarism issue, Dershowitz has been unable to find a single false statement in *Beyond Chutzpah*. And it follows that, as far as Dershowitz himself can now determine, his own book *The Case for Israel* is full of falsehoods concerning Israel's human rights record and the history of the Israel/Palestine conflict, while Finkelstein's book contains none.[21]

The plagiarism issue Menetrez cites is in reference to Joan Peters' book *From Time Immemorial*. Finkelstein charges that Dershowitz is guilty of "apparently unacknowledged lifting of Peters' research. . . ."[22] There are a number of passages in *The Case for Israel* that are identical or nearly identical to passages in Peters' book, yet Dershowitz often fails to cite Peters as their source. Instead, he cites the primary sources that Peters cites. Finkelstein: "Fully twenty-two of the fifty-two quotations and endnotes in chapters 1 and 2 of *The Case for Israel* match almost exactly – *including, in long quotes, the placement of ellipses* – those in *From Time Immemorial*."[23] Dershowitz countered that his use of the sources Peters had used did not constitute plagiarism.

Although I found Dershowitz's claim of innocence disingenuous, his guilt or innocence really depends on how one chooses to define plagiarism. Doubtlessly, Dershowitz was heavily influenced by Peters' book and was as anxious to buttress his pro-Israel beliefs with her conclusions as I once had been. Consequently, he made use of a number of her passages in writing his book and went directly to the sources she cited except when they were unavailable, in which case he cited her.

What carried greater weight for me was that a serious author ought to have been mindful of the fact that a significant number of scholars had renounced Peters' book for its shoddy scholarship years before Dershowitz wrote *The Case for Israel*. Menetrez writes: "Given the well-known scholarly repudiation of Peters' book, no scholar would rely on it, any more than a scholar would rely on *The Protocols of the Elders of Zion*."[24]*+

Having seen Dershowitz speak his mind over the years and having a sense that he is not the type to avoid a fight, his reaction to Finkelstein was not unexpected. Even before the tenure battle he had unsuccessfully

---

* Virulently anti-Semitic, *The Protocols of the Learned Elders of Zion* alleges that a secret Jewish and Freemason conspiracy is plotting to overthrow Christianity and capitalism. Its goal is domination of the world. Plagiarized by Czarist Russia's Secret Police in the early 1900s, the writing was first introduced in the 1860s as a French satire directed against Napoleon III.

+ Finkelstein, *Beyond Chutzpah*, p. 2: "*From Time Immemorial* was a colossal hoax. Cited sources were mangled, key numbers in the demographic study falsified, and large swaths plagiarized from Zionist tracts."

Professor of International Relations at Oxford University, Avi Shlaim, from the film *American Radical: the Trials of Norman Finkelstein*: "[*From Time Immemorial*] was completely preposterous and worthless. . . .The book was of no value whatsoever. It simply recycled very old and stale Israeli propaganda. But it was the book that American Jews wanted to have because it completely whitewashed Israel."

Colin Campbell, "Dispute Flares Over Book On Claims to Palestine," *New York Times*, Nov. 28, 1985, citing Rabbi Arthur Hertzberg (deceased), past vice-president of the Jewish World Congress and former professor of religion at Dartmouth College: "'I think that she's cooked the statistics. I think the right-wingers in Israel have an interest in cooking the statistics. The scholarship is phony and tendentious. I do not believe that she has read the Arab sources that she quotes." Also citing Yehoshua Porath, Professor Emeritus of Middle East history at Hebrew University of Jerusalem: "'I think it's a sheer forgery. . . . In Israel, at least, the book was almost universally dismissed as sheer rubbish except maybe as a propaganda weapon . . . .'"

Yehoshua Porath, "Mrs. Peters's Palestine," *New York Times Review of Books*, January 16, 1986, Volume 32, Number 21 & 22, www.nybooks.com/articles/5249: "Everyone familiar with the writing of the extreme nationalists of Zeev Jabotinsky's Revisionist party (the forerunner of the Herut party) would immediately recognize the tired and discredited arguments in Mrs. Peters's book." And: "What is surprising is that Joan Peters . . . writes as if the Zionist myths were wholly true and relevant, notwithstanding all the historical work that modifies or discredits them."

tried to block the publication of *Beyond Chutzpah* by the University of California Press. That was followed by a failed appeal to California Governor Arnold Schwarzenegger to halt the book's release. When Finkelstein's bid for tenure came up at DePaul, Dershowitz was presented with an irresistible opportunity to retaliate against his nemesis, a man he has called a "notorious Jewish anti-Semite and Holocaust-justice denier"[25] and whose deceased mother he suggested might have been a kapo in a Nazi concentration camp.*

Instead of petitioning for a just solution to the Israel-Palestine conflict, Dershowitz seems to be more interested in silencing voices of dissent. Ironically, his derogatory style has caused him to lose the respect of scholars and the trust of many readers, while also making more people aware of the writings of Norman Finkelstein.

Dershowitz may feel compelled to defend Israel from its many critics. He probably fears for the safety of its Jewish citizens and its continued existence. That is how I once felt, but having let go of that fear,

---

* Kapos (blockheads) were Jewish collaborators who assisted the Nazis in controlling and murdering Jews in concentration camps. From "Statement of Alan M. Dershowitz," www.law.harvard.edu/faculty/dershowitz/statement.html: "He suspects his own mother of being a kapo and cooperating with the Nazis during the Holocaust."

In "Who Was Maryla Husyt Finkelstein," January 13, 2006, normanfinkelstein.com/who-was-maryla-husyt-finkelstein, Finkelstein responds: "Here is the actual excerpt from my memoir that Dershowitz is allegedly quoting: Except for allusions to relentless pangs of hunger, my mother never spoke about her personal torments during the war, which was just as well, since I couldn't have borne them. Like Primo Levi, she often said that, being 'too delicate and refined, the best didn't survive.' Was this an indirect admission of guilt? Much later in life I finally summoned the nerve to ask whether she had done anything of which she was ashamed. Calmly replying no, she recalled having refused the privileged position of 'block head' in the camp. She especially resented the 'dirty' question 'How did you survive?' with the insinuation that, to emerge alive from the camps, survivors must have morally compromised themselves. Given how ferociously she cursed the Jewish councils, ghetto police and kapos, I assume my mother answered me truthfully. Although acknowledging that Jews initially joined the councils from mixed motives, she said that 'only scum,' reaping the rewards of doing the devil's work, still cooperated after it became clear that they were merely cogs in the Nazi killing machine."

I now see that the greatest threat to Israel and the Jewish people is that very fear itself and the unexamined beliefs and images that issue from it. From my perspective fear is what motivates Dershowitz's reporting. The motivation is unfortunate because it slants his conclusions to favor one side, stimulating mistrust and the likelihood of violence.

Hopefully – and soon – Dershowitz will find a way to convert his fear into clarity about the conflict and compassion for the plight of the Palestinians. Then his advocacy for peace will help to defuse the conflict and actually add to the long-term security of Israel's citizens.

As someone who was fortunate enough to shake off the bondage of an emotionally conditioned and limited perspective, I offer the unsolicited advice to Alan Dershowitz that if he admits to his misrepresentations, he will gain some peace within himself. Then, both he and his readers will benefit from a transformed understanding.

Breakthrough

– 5 –

The Righteous

Your fellow is your mirror. If your own face is clean, so will be the image you perceive. But should you look upon your fellow and see a blemish, it is your own imperfection that you are encountering – you are being shown what it is that you must correct within yourself. Rabbi Israel Baal Shem Tov ["Master of the Good Name"], 1698–1760, Founder of the Hasidic Movement

My identical twin brother lived in Israel for a few years after he graduated from college. Initially he worked on a kibbutz, before joining the Ultra-Orthodox sect of Judaism that has been the focus of his life for nearly forty years. After he returned to North America we would occasionally talk on the telephone and discuss the Israel-Palestine conflict. Invariably he expressed his opinions about the Palestinians and other Arabs in a harsh and contemptuous tone, introducing into our conversations stark judgments that he deemed incontrovertible. My immediate response to the intensity of his feelings was usually discomfort, but not enough to consider the likelihood that his anger was affecting his views. The mild skepticism that surfaced would regularly dissolve in the face of the conviction with which he spoke. He would declare that "the only thing the Palestinians respect is force," and "the only way to solve the Palestinian problem is to humiliate them."

Knowing my brother's familiarity with the Holy Land, I assumed he had a more direct understanding of the dispute than someone who had never lived there. Also, one of his children had served in the Israeli army and two others were married and living in Jerusalem. My deference to my brother was reinforced by the fact that I hadn't studied the issues for myself and by my anxiety for Israel's survival.

After my transformation my brother and I engaged in an e-mail correspondence in which he once again presented his anti-Arab opinions as fact. Now, however, I presented documented material from a variety of sources to challenge those "facts." I told him about the home demolitions, the misappropriation of Palestinian land for Jewish-only settlements, and the building of homes without permits by Jewish settlers in occupied territory while Israeli soldiers looked the other way. I told him about the violence that had accompanied the Zionist movement; about David Ben-Gurion's ambition to expand Israel's territory at the expense of the indigenous population; about the killing of Palestinian children; the use of unprovoked lethal force by the Israeli army and the atrocities committed by Jewish soldiers during the 1948 war with the Palestinians, including the destruction of entire villages. My brother spurned all of my evidence and rationalized any Israeli behavior, past, present or future, on the premise that:

> The so-called Palestinians are people who inhabit a pathological society that supports indiscriminate murder and teaches as a matter of public policy hatred of Jews and others. The barbaric acts of terrorism directed against any Jew that breathes should show you what kind of people they are. Even if their cause had legitimacy, their actions degrade it and destroy any justification for pursuing it. The Arabs today are the Nazis of our generation and their single-minded goal is to murder every Jew they can get their hands on.

He accused "Zionists like Benny Morris" of being liars and Norman Finkelstein and Noam Chomsky of being "despicable, self-hating, cowardly Jews;" they were "true traitors to the Jewish nation."[*] He called the Israeli government:

> [A] terrible, corrupt and criminal government, not because of its treatment of the Arabs but because of its treatment of its own citizens. If Israel were to do what it is capable of doing, namely, to utterly destroy the terror infrastructure and undeniably defeat the Arabs, there would be a serious de-escalation of terrorism throughout the world. For example, the Israeli army wished to surround Damascus in the Yom Kippur War and to destroy the Egyptian army that it had surrounded in the Sinai but the government didn't allow them to do so.

Many of these allegations were ones my brother had repeated for years. His ill will toward Arabs, without any admission that there could

---

[*] Noam Chomsky is a Jewish linguist and educator, currently a professor at M.I.T.

be some truth to my arguments, left me feeling rather hopeless. I decided to respond by appealing to his common sense with historical fact. During the Yom Kippur War, I explained, the Soviet Union warned the United States that if Israel did not withdraw from Syria and Egypt, they would enter the fighting on the side of the Arab countries. The United States, fearing a nuclear confrontation with the Soviets, pressured Israel to comply with this demand. I also told him how the security wall Israel was building to separate their population and the Palestinian's did not track the Green Line (the 1949 armistice line). Instead, its design called for it to encroach into Palestinian territory, so that once completed its total distance would be more than twice the length of the Green Line. As a result, the wall would divide Palestinian territory into separate cantons, similar to the South African Bantustans of the Apartheid era.

My intention was to stimulate my brother's curiosity so he might recognize that the argument over the Occupied Territories was not as simplistic as he believed. I recommended he investigate the writings of Tanya Reinhart and the reports of B'Tselem, the United Nations, Human Rights Watch and Amnesty International. Going out on a limb, I asked him to look into the tremendous body of research and eyewitness reports that validated the conclusions of Chomsky, Finkelstein and Morris. Even *The History of the Haganah* (Sefer Toldot Hahaganah), which was published by the Israeli Military Press, admits that the Zionist strategy before and during the 1948 war called for the destruction of Arab villages and the transfer of their inhabitants from the land now called Israel.[*]

My brother insisted that I must be wrong, that it wasn't "logical" for Israel to act in the ways I had described. Then, in his disdain for my logic, he stated:

> Apartheid in South Africa had a purpose that reflected religious beliefs about the inferiority of the blacks. There is no philosophical justification that I have ever heard or seen regarding the treatment of the Arabs. This is mainly due to the fact that claims of mistreatment are bogus.

---

* The Haganah were the Jewish defense force during the British mandate of Palestine, 1920-48. They were merged into the IDF, or Israeli Defense Forces.

Breakthrough

He also said, "The *Torah* clearly states that G-d gave the Land of Israel to the Jewish people." When I read that comment, I understood that I was not going to break through his inflexible certainty. My brother and I were not engaged in a real discussion. He had resorted to his *sine qua non*, the *Torah*. In so doing, he could justify without qualification his hatred of the Palestinians, his rejection of any proof that they had been mistreated, and his call for brutal force to suppress them and their Arab brethren.

Obviously my brother is not going to conduct his own research if there is a risk of uncovering evidence that contradicts his version of the Arab-Israeli conflict. Asking him to examine the issues from the standpoint of ethics or morality is futile. The *Torah* – the Pentateuch or Five Books of Moses – is the apodictic pillar he relies upon to uphold whatever beliefs he chooses to identify with. Just as fundamentalist Christians and Muslims represent the *New Testament* or *Koran*, Judaism asserts that the *Torah* is infallible; and, as my brother demonstrated in his terse commentary on apartheid, religious beliefs take precedence over compassion or equality.

My brother is correct, however, that South African apartheid was based on a religious interpretation that regarded the native population as inherently inferior to the white population. The same can be said for white American attitudes about the indigenous peoples of their land until at least the early twentieth century. And the same is true of the Ultra-Orthodox religious movements that justify the settlement of Palestinian territory with the belief that the Holy Land belongs to the Jewish people. All used or use religious interpretation as the basis with which to violate one people's civil rights for the apparent benefit of another's. In contrast, Zionism was a secular movement that publicly committed itself to the security and survival of the Jewish people.

Theodore Herzl, the father of modern Zionism, was deeply affected by the 1894 Dreyfus Affair. Alfred Dreyfus, an officer in the French army, was falsely convicted of treason, primarily because he was a Jew. Herzl, an Austro-Hungarian journalist in Paris at the time, witnessed crowds chanting "Death to the Jews." This incident convinced him to abandon his belief that Jewish emancipation and assimilation into European society was possible. Instead, he concluded that if his people were to live in freedom, they must leave the Diaspora and establish a Jewish homeland. For Herzl, a secular Jew, the Jewish question was "neither a social nor a religious one"[1] – it was a national question and the justification for a Jewish state was anti-Semitism, which Herzl saw as an "absolute condition in all nation-states wherein Jews constituted a minority."[2] Thus, non-Jews who inhabited land on which the future State of Israel was envisioned were considered obstacles to that goal. The only way a nation could become a Jewish democracy was if a preponderance of its citizens were Jewish. The solution was massive Jewish settlement combined with population transfer/ethnic cleansing of the non-Jewish inhabitants from the future Jewish homeland. Shlomo Ben-Ami, a past Israeli Minister of Foreign Affairs and Internal Security and chief negotiator at the 2000 Camp David summit, has succinctly described Zionism as "the territorial answer to the Jewish fear and this fear has never subsided since."[3]

Like South African apartheid and American manifest destiny and slavery, Zionism is inherently selfish in that it put, and still puts, the needs of its people above anyone else's. Herzl foresaw the continued persecution of the Jewish people in Europe and this, rather than Biblical and Talmudic claims, was the primary motivation for Jewish immigration to Palestine. And the colonization of Judea and Samaria since the June 1967 Six-Day War has been a direct outgrowth of Zionism's success in creating a Jewish or, more accurately, a Zionist homeland.[*] Yitzhak Shamir said: "The settlement of the Land of Israel is the essence of Zionism. Without settlement we will not fulfill Zionism. It's that simple"[4]

Reform Judaism, a relatively recent phenomenon that considers its movement a spiritual one, originally rejected Zionism because of its nationalistic ideology and its belief in the necessity of a separate state.[+]

---

* Judea and Samaria constitute the West Bank and are considered a part of the holy land by many religious Jews. Judea is the area of the West Bank that is south of Jerusalem and Samaria is the area north of Jerusalem.

+ In 1885 the Reform movement adopted a set of principles which became known as the Pittsburgh Platform. Regarding Zionism the platform stated: "We consider ourselves no longer a nation, but a religious community, and therefore expect neither a return to Palestine, nor a sacrificial worship under the sons of Aaron, nor the restoration of any of the laws concerning the Jewish state."
www.jewishvirtuallibrary.org/jsource/judaica/ejud_0002_0016_0_15835.html.

Many Orthodox Jews also oppose Zionism because it puts nationalism before the *Torah*, which is heresy. They believe that only the Moshiach (Messiah from the House of David) can establish a Jewish nation and that Zionism violates "the promise made to God not to acquire the Holy Land by human effort."[5]

> From their point of view the settlement of Jews, whether in Israel or anywhere else, must be judged by the traditional criteria: does it bring the Jews closer to the Torah and its commandments or does it drive them away from Judaism?[6]

A minority of Jewish sects, such as *Neturei Karta* (Aramaic for "Guardians of the City"), believe the Moshiach will come only when Israel ends its oppression of the Palestinian people; and they acknowledge that Jews and Arabs lived in peace for centuries until the emergence of Jewish nationalism.*

Notwithstanding the reasons why Zionism is unacceptable to many Jews, if its critics had been as prescient as Herzl, many doomed Jews might have escaped the Nazi death machine.

In 1975 U.N. General Assembly Resolution 3379 determined that "Zionism is a form of racism and racial discrimination." That determination was revoked in 1991 by General Assembly Resolution 46/86. Simply classifying Zionism as a form of racism overlooks its original intent and associates it with violent images that inevitably produce polarization and conflict. For those not familiar with the history of the Israel-Palestine conflict, such a label gives the impression that Zionist attitudes are ideologically comparable to white supremacist attitudes concerning people of color or to the Ku Klux Klan's attitude toward Catholics, Jews and African Americans. These movements are purveyors of racism. Zionism, as most Jews conceive of it, was a reaction to racism. Zionism did not single out a particular people because of who they were; it singled them out because of where they were. Zionism was an inevitable response to a uniquely virulent kind of racism. It was a movement whose primary purpose was to protect the Jewish people from

---

* The city is Jerusalem.

hatred, discrimination and death. For most Jews, Zionism is not *inherently* racist.

However, Zionism in its current manifestation is out of control. It has become an instrument of greed, plain and simple. It is the ideological force that enables the stealing of another people's land and enslaving them in a virtual prison. If those who support Israel's Zionist policies take offense when they are called racist, they should also understand that for the last forty years there has been virtually no functional difference between their movement and some of the worst racist regimes in history.

And Jewish Americans should understand that Israeli policy – as distinguished from whatever benign proclamations the government of Israel makes – is essentially Zionism. No Israeli prime minister *ever* has separated himself from Zionism. All have unreservedly embraced the movement. All have worked tirelessly to accomplish its goal: territorial acquisition. And no Israeli government since the 1967 war has put a halt to the growth of settlements in the West Bank. During Yitzhak Rabin's second term as prime minister the settler population in the West Bank grew at a faster rate than ever before. Few if any Israeli politicians have had the courage to stand up against the momentum of Zionism. Journalist Gideon Levy, writing for *Haaretz*, recently said: "Not a single Jewish MK in today's Knesset ran on a ticket calling for an end to the occupation."[7]

A common refrain of the last ten years is that Islam promotes intolerance and violence. Whatever the truth in this saying – and I believe it is more fallacy than truth – as a Jew I feel obligated to say that by its very nature Zionism promotes intolerance and violence. And Israel does *not* represent Judaism or traditional Jewish values. Its Zionist foundation distorts the very essence of Judaism. Israel is not so much a Jewish state as a Zionist state. It's foreign policy, its policy in the Occupied Territories, and its military and political resources are a machine of Zionism. And any Jew who supports Israel must understand that he is supporting Zionism and is complicit in its consequences. To imagine otherwise is an exercise in self-delusion. When I began to understand the reality of the conflict I could not immunize myself from what was being perpetrated in my name. It was impossible. I could only feel the horror of the whole thing, and how I had been complicit in it.

I say all this because I was raised a Jewish American and, for the sake of understanding and peace, I believe it is important to tell a hard truth to friends. When I reflect on my former prison, my self-imposed incarceration in a world of myths, I marvel that I had the good fortune to be released. And I remember the shock it took to wake me up. I may have been in my house reading a book, but that reading was one of the most difficult things I had done in my life. The only thing that kept me going was that I valued the necessary truths the book was communicating.

I am also aware that many Jews characterize their accusers as I once did: as insensitive to Jewish history and to the reasons that made Zionism necessary in the first place. I know they find it inconceivable that they could be called racist because they support a movement that they believe saved their people from extinction. Most Jews did not grow up indoctrinated into a culture of discrimination, and their intentions are not like that of the White Aryan Brotherhood or Ku Klux Klan. But they need to understand that for the most part criticism of Israel is not intended to ignore or minimize the history of Jewish persecution but is an emotional reaction to some of the policies Israel has adopted on behalf of the Jewish people. I also know that some Zionists find my brother's statements as extreme as I do. But all of the subjective justification and the need to be understood are irrelevant in the face of the *act* being perpetrated by Israel in the Occupied Territories. That act is affecting the lives of millions of people every day and its dehumanization and brutality are a direct result of Zionism.

* * * *

The tendency among some fundamentalists that is particularly troubling to me is the use of scriptures to vindicate pre-existing beliefs. There are passages in both the *Torah* and the *Koran* that advocate extreme punishment for minor offenses, and there are passages that encourage compassion. Both Scriptures have been used to justify discrimination and persecution, and both have been used as inspiration to promote charity and generosity. The Talmud says: "Whoever destroys a single life is as guilty as though he had destroyed the entire world; and whoever rescues a single life earns as much merit as though he had rescued the entire world."[8] And the Jewish concept of *tikkun olam*, or repairing the world, implies that Jews have a responsibility to all of society.* In Islam, the concept of *jihad* has been used by a small minority of Muslims to justify a holy war, but to many of that faith *jihad* means accepting personal responsibility through struggle with oneself. It does not mean struggling with the world and demanding that it change. The *jihad* is to discover the impact our beliefs have on the world and society at large. Then, if necessary, we can transform our understanding. The world, as it always does, will reflect our transformation.

My brother lives in a community of limited cultural diversity. Challenging points of view about the Arab-Israeli conflict are rare, as members tend to reinforce each others' views. A similar process of collective reinforcement is at work, with more or less dogmatism, in a wide variety of groups – clubs, sports teams, religious sects, and so on – and is at the root of patriotic and nationalistic tendencies.

Nonetheless, the benefits of religious community can be profound. Serious religious practitioners have always sought the company of others of similar persuasion. There is a critical understanding that informs life in a religious community: that by tendency one's attention does not remain easily concentrated in self-transcending practice; it wanders in the mind of desire and the inevitable incarnation of desire. And the modern world, with its countless promises of fulfillment, reinforces this tendency. Religious communities create environments in which people can resist succumbing to the vagaries of the mind while magnifying the potential for true fulfillment through self-understanding. Seen from this perspective, they are a particularly sane choice.

My brother's community has these benefits. What it lacks is a well-articulated mandate for vigilance against disparaging others not in the community. My brother enjoys the advantage of community but suffers from its insulation. He is especially crippled in his ability to consider the history and values that inform differing perspectives. This is in part a result of the fact that Judaism has no explicit recognition of non-

---

* *Tikkun Olam* (literally, "world repair") – sometimes translated as "perfecting the world" – is often used to refer to social activism and social justice. The phrase is used in the Mishnah (Rabbinic Teachings) and Jewish mystical teachings, such as the Kabala. Originally, tikkun olam was a mystical practice intended to restore the world to its holy state prior to human sin. See "Overview: Tikkun Olam" and "Tikkun Olam in Contemporary Jewish Thought," by Dr. Lawrence Fine, MyJewishlearning.com.

Breakthrough

separation as the foundation of religious practice. Indeed, it is virtually impossible to find a real exploration of this understanding in any of the Abrahamic religions, though it has been demonstrated, at least to some degree, in the lives of the founders and saints of these traditions. Judaism, Christianity, and Islam suffer terribly from religious provincialism and all of the cultic insanity of the "true believer" versus the "infidel," or "non-believer." Shaped by dualistic thinking, the separative ego-identity pursues its fulfillment in the very field of life that should call for humility and self-nullification.[*] I have always considered religious dogma that dehumanizes the other to be a perversion of the intent of the founders. And I do not believe that "non-believers" pose a threat to the coming of the Messiah. For me, the coming of the Messiah symbolizes a possibility that is *Here* and *Now*, merely waiting for the limited self to be transcended. The Messiah is a living consciousness, an awakening to the reality that the world is already infused with God. The obstacle to this awakening is not the other but the ego-identity's beliefs and images, especially those that involve the exploitation of religion to justify fear and hatred. The challenge – and it is really no different in a community than in an individual – is to honor the deeper principles that lie at the heart of all truly human or religious endeavors. These are tolerance, compassion and love. Explicit understanding of non-separation is not necessary for sane relationships with others; all that is necessary is devotion to the fundamental values present in any religious tradition.

Since I was certain that my brother's beliefs do not adequately represent the *Torah*, I searched for passages that illustrate the abiding humanism I know exists within Judaism. From Deuteronomy, 10:19: "You shall love the stranger; for you were strangers in the land of Egypt."[9] And, from Genesis, 18:1-5, I rediscovered the story of Abraham's hospitality to the three strangers, how he withdrew his attention from God and bowed down to the strangers, thereby honoring them with the same respect he accorded God:

---

* The concept of selflessness is found in all the world's major religions. Therevada Buddhism, for example, uses the Sanskrit word *anatta*, which is translated as No-Self, No-Soul, or egolessness. In Judaism this concept is often referred to as self-nullification or *bitul*.

1. Now the Lord appeared to him in the plains of Mamre and he was sitting at the entrance of the tent when the day was hot.
2. And he lifted his eyes and saw, and behold, three men were standing beside him, and he saw and he ran toward them from the entrance of the tent, and he prostrated himself to the ground.
3. And he said, "My lords, if only I have found favor in your eyes, please do not pass on from beside your servant.
4. Please let a little water be taken and bathe your feet and recline under the tree.
5. And I will take a morsel of bread, and sustain your hearts; after[wards] you shall pass on, because you have passed by your servant." And they said, "So shall you do, as you have spoken."[10]

After reading this story, I learned that hospitality (hachnasat orchim) is one of the *Torah*'s 613 divine commandments, or mitzvoth.

By now, knowing that facts and logic were ineffective, I made one more attempt to get through to my brother:

> We will never be able to end conflict until we are free from unexamined fear and hatred. Unless we investigate why we have such feelings we will project fear and hatred onto others. And they will respond by doing the same to us. But what we see in others will not be very different from what they see in us. What is any true religion or spiritual path about if not self-awareness and compassion? In all honesty, do you really believe the *Torah* advocates disregarding the dignity of non-Jews so that Jews prevail and another people are destroyed? Or is that your fear and hatred speaking? I prefer to see the enemy in the *Torah* as the dark side of human nature. We are all Jews and we are all Palestinians.

Characteristically, my brother was impervious to my advice. He retorted that my "thoughts bordered on the irrational," because "all" Palestinian and Arab groups had made it clear that any negotiation would be used by them as "a tool to give them time to organize for the realization of their goal, which is the eradication of Israel."

There was nothing left for me to do. Since my brother will not admit to his fears and prejudices, he presumes that actions directed at Israelis by

Palestinians are based exclusively on pathological hatred of Jews. With the same reasoning he believes that far more lethal Israeli operations in the Occupied Territories are justified by the need for self-defense. His disgust for all Arabs hinders him from grasping why some Palestinians feel disgust for their occupiers.

* * * *

When a people who have long been persecuted are at last freed from oppression, they are likely to do whatever is necessary to ensure they are never again oppressed. The unimaginable suffering Jews experienced during World War II and the centuries of discrimination and violence they were subjected to in Eastern and Central Europe, made Israel's resolve to acquire irresistible power virtually inevitable. But with great power comes great responsibility, for if history teaches us anything it is that the powerful have always succumbed to the abuses of power. To guard against these abuses is especially important for the Jewish nation. Every Jew knows the history of the Holocaust and the pogroms, and almost every Jew has direct experience of those nightmares, either personally or through the lineage of family or friends. The collective pain of Israel's Jews is in some ways unique among all the countries in the world.

When the Second Lebanon war started I too was in pain. I felt persecuted, resigned that my people would never have the opportunity to live in peace without the threat of an evil enemy waiting for the moment to murder ever more of us. The awakening I described was catalyzed by the apprehension I felt for the safety of Israel. Israel was very much my country, the Jews were my people and their history was my history. But what I was almost completely unaware of was how I had never examined my pain and the beliefs and images that created it. When all of that was brought to light and inspected, it became something else entirely. The pain was not about an event in history, or an event in the present. It had never been about something objective. It was the pain of feeling oppressed by these beliefs and images and the doubts they imposed: Who, for example, should be judged – myself included – and who had the right to act with impunity? Something real in me was struggling to break through; and continually denying it, blocking it with the rationale of my righteous mind, was filling me with pain. When innate compassion was reborn, I was at last freed from the oppressiveness of that pain.

The Righteous

The dynamic of the victim mutating into the victimizer has been a frequent feature of conflict throughout history. After the trauma of their European experience, it is a tragic irony that the Jewish people did not guard against this paradigm. Who would have thought that the Jewish people would safeguard their future through a movement – Zionism – that required the subjugation of another people?

My brother is extremely sensitive to the suffering his people have historically endured, as are most Jews, religious or not. But it is important to understand that such exclusive sensitivity toward one group can lead to insensitivity toward other groups and create a climate for fear-based judging. The danger in this kind of judging is that it occludes one's natural intelligence, the intelligence that can save a person from danger and bring some security to his situation. Pronouncements like my brother's that equate all Arabs with Nazis inflame an already highly volatile situation, but more than that, they make impossible steps that can lead to peace and security. Peace and security for Israel are not going to happen magically. Achieving these goals will require a lot of communication with the Palestinians and a lot of hard work. Both sides are going to have to take many incremental practical measures. Even to begin such a process requires a certain practical intelligence. At the very least that intelligence must acknowledge that there are justifiable grievances on both sides, and that the ability to listen and learn is essential. The righteous mind admits of no such possibility.

The tragedy in the Middle East is not the horrific violence itself. The tragedy is that so little wisdom has come from so much suffering. The wise have always understood the primary principle of life: non-separation.* This understanding enables them to build communities of tolerance and cooperation and to successfully confront difficult ethnic and racial divisions. Devotion to the primary principle of life awakens the truly powerful resources within us. During the civil rights era of the 1960s, Martin Luther King Jr. spoke tellingly of these resources. He said that for the movement of nonviolent civil disobedience to succeed it was not enough to *like* one's enemy; only *love* of one's enemy would succeed.

---

* In this paragraph I am indebted to the American Spiritual Master Adi Da for his understanding of the primary and secondary principles of life and what comprises tragedy.

He said that the history of suffering, and the inevitable suffering yet to come, was so terrible that only the deepest resource of man could prevail, and that is love. But in the Middle East suffering seems only to have reinforced devotion to the secondary principle of life: separation and apparent differences. This devotion has become so embedded in the collective mind that statements like my brother's are accepted as an accurate appraisal of the situation, even though they would have appalled the wise men of the very religious tradition to which he has devoted his life.

If we look more carefully, then, who is the enemy and who are the righteous? The enemy *is* the righteous. The enemy is the righteous mind that sees everything in terms of us against them, that calls forth evil and death upon the other. Through parallel enemy images each side portrays the other as less than human and inherently violent. But where is the inhumanity and violence? It is in our minds. Our minds are so filled with righteous fire that they have become realms of constant violence and constant suffering. We have essentially become the imagined other, whom we dread. None of us, therefore, is a victim of the other; rather, we are victims of our own self-inflicted terrorism.

The righteous mind is absolutely a personal responsibility. To understand that it is part of the collective mind is only a beginning. The work of transformation is what it has always been: an individual affair. If we can let go of our judgments, our irrational fears and our prejudices, we will begin to see with clarity and compassion. Our natural intelligence will be restored. But letting go requires preparation. That was my experience, at least. Letting go was the product of my becoming available to a force superior to my judgments. First I had to do some hard work. That work involved an uncompromising determination to discover the facts. In the process of that discovery I had to face difficult things in myself – long held beliefs and powerful emotions. And I had to face old threats; at times I knew fear as things that seemed essential to my identity were threatened.

But there was nothing threatening at all. When I look back, I see that I was simply sitting in my house reading a book. It was my great good fortune that the book was an accurate and compelling account of the subject I was most blind about, but I was never threatened. The common thread of the words I was reading was that they conflicted with my reality. That was the apparent threat. But my reality was not *Reality*. It was an illusion. That illusion could not withstand the process of separating fact from fiction, the false from the real. At a certain point the process reached a critical mass and there was no longer any work on my part. Something else did the work. Mysteriously and gracefully everything was completed in an instant, and I awakened to what I had always been.

The most satisfying fruit of finding myself was finding compassion. Just as irrational fear is always accompanied by confusion, compassion is always accompanied by clarity. I cannot overstate how directly compassion understands conflict. Compassion sees from all perspectives. It obviates the righteous mind and sees only human beings, confused by a labyrinth of unexamined beliefs, who suffer the consequences of those beliefs. But they are always human beings. There are in truth no enemies; only people who have forgotten their common humanity.

* * * *

One day, I hope my brother and all Jews will realize that Judaism's most sacred tenets extol reverence for human life more than an emotional attachment to land, no matter how holy they believe that land to be. Rabbi Schlomo Yitchaki (better known by the acronym Rashi), the most famous Biblical commentator of the Middle Ages, taught:

> Where the Torah tells about the creation of the first human being . . . the earth from which Adam was formed was not taken from one spot but from various parts of the globe. Thus, human dignity does not depend on the place of one's birth nor is it limited to one region.[11]*

---

* Rashi lived from 1040-1105 A.D. The quotation is not a direct quote from Rashi but G. Neuburger's explanation of his teaching.

Breakthrough

– 6 –

Abraham Foxman and Jimmy Carter

The Governments of the States Parties to this Constitution on behalf of their peoples declare: That since wars begin in the minds of men, it is in the minds of men that the defenses of peace must be constructed. UNESCO Constitution, adopted November 16, 1945.

Apartheid is Afrikaans for "separation" or "apartness." The dictionary definition is: "any system or practice that separates people according to race, caste, etc."[1] The United Nations has declared apartheid to be a crime against humanity. To many pro-Israelis any language that compares Israel's policies in the Occupied Territories with South Africa's past policies toward its indigenous population is an outrageous expression of anti-Semitism. The comparison was thrust into the light of public discourse with the release in 2006 of former President Jimmy Carter's book *Palestine Peace Not Apartheid*. The backlash against Carter for his use of *Apartheid* was immediate and furious. He was accused of smearing and demonizing Israel, of ignoring the facts and of being a propagandist for the Palestinians. Articles in the media portrayed him as an extremist, a liar, a Nazi sympathizer, a bigot and an anti-Semite.

* * * *

Abraham Foxman has been one of Carter's most vocal critics. Currently the National Director of the Anti-Defamation League, Foxman was born in Poland in 1940 at a time when the Nazi juggernaut was making its way through Europe. In 1941, with his family about to be forced into a ghetto, he was entrusted into the care of his nursemaid, who passed herself off as his mother, baptizing and raising him a Catholic. Foxman was reunited with his parents in 1944. Six years later the family immigrated to the United States. After graduating from the Yeshiva of Flatbush in Brooklyn, Foxman earned his bachelor's degree from the City College of New York and his law degree from the New York University Law School.

In 1965 Foxman joined the Anti-Defamation League, where he worked in the international affairs and civil rights divisions before becoming the ADL's associate director. Upon the death of longtime leader Nathan Perlmutter in 1987, the ADL Board appointed Foxman its National Director. Over the years Foxman has been recognized for his battles on behalf of equality and civil rights. In 1997 the *National Center for Black-Jewish Relations* of Dillard University, a historically black university in New Orleans, named Foxman co-recipient of the first Annual Martin Luther King, Jr. – Donald R. Mintz Freedom and Justice Award. In 1998 he received the Interfaith Committee of Remembrance Lifetime Achievement award "as a leader in the fight against anti-Semitism, bigotry and discrimination."[2] In 2002 he received the Raoul Wallenberg Humanitarian Leadership Award from the Center for Holocaust and Genocide Studies, and in 2006 French President Jacques Chirac named him a knight of the Legion of Honor, France's highest civilian tribute.

Describing itself as "the nation's premier civil rights/human relations agency," the Anti-Defamation League's charter states:

> The immediate object of the League is to stop, by appeals to reason and conscience and, if necessary, by appeals to law, the defamation of the Jewish people. Its ultimate purpose is to secure justice and fair treatment to all citizens alike and to put an end forever to unjust and unfair discrimination against and ridicule of any sect or body of citizens.

On both federal and state levels the ADL has been a champion of hate crimes legislation. The League has also spoken out in support of gay rights, an unpopular position with many of its Orthodox Jewish supporters.

The ADL draws a distinction between what it regards as anti-Semitic and legitimate criticism of Zionism and Israel:

> Criticism of particular Israeli actions or policies in and of itself does not constitute anti-Semitism. Certainly the sovereign State of Israel can be legitimately criticized just like any other country in the world.[3]

The League has sometimes struggled to reconcile the aims of its charter with its support of Israel. In 2007 the ADL (and Foxman in particular) drew criticism for its opposition to a congressional resolution acknowledging the Armenian Holocaust of 1915, probably the first genocide of the twentieth century. Between 500,000 and 1.5 million Armenians were exterminated by the Ottoman Empire. The Republic of Turkey, the Empire's successor and a secular Muslim state, has never publicly admitted to the genocide. Turkey and Israel have been political and military allies for many years.

* * * *

During his presidency Jimmy Carter gained the appreciation of world Jewry for his leadership in brokering the Camp David Accords, which established peace between Israel and Egypt.[*] Historian Douglas Brinkley, Carter's unauthorized biographer, said:

> There will never be a history of the Middle East written without Jimmy Carter's name in the index, Camp David is the beginning of a process that still goes on. And a hundred years from now, two hundred years from now, people will be talking about the Camp David process that began in those Maryland mountains.[4]

After leaving office, Carter and his wife Rosalynn founded The Carter Center. Through its partnership with Emory University in Atlanta, the Center has developed numerous peace programs dealing with democracy, human rights, conflict resolution and economic and social development.

In 2002 the Norwegian Nobel Committee awarded Carter the Nobel Peace Prize. In announcing their decision, the Committee praised him

> [F]or his decades of untiring effort to find peaceful solutions to international conflicts, to advance democracy and human rights, and to promote economic and social development. . . . At a time when the cold war between East and West was still predominant, he placed renewed emphasis on the place of human rights in international politics . . . . In a situation currently marked by threats of the use of power, Carter has stood by the principles that conflicts must as far as possible be resolved through

---

[*] On September 17, 1978, Israeli Prime Minister Menachem Begin and Egyptian President Anwar Sadat signed the *Camp David Accords: The Framework for Peace in the Middle East*.

Breakthrough

mediation and international co-operation based on international law, respect for human rights, and economic development.[5]

In his acceptance speech Carter spoke about the Middle East:

> For more than half a century, following the founding of the State of Israel in 1948, the Middle East conflict has been a source of worldwide tension. At Camp David in 1978 and in Oslo in 1993, Israelis, Egyptians, and Palestinians have endorsed the only reasonable prescription for peace: United Nations Resolution 242. It condemns the acquisition of territory by force, calls for withdrawal of Israel from the occupied territories, and provides for Israelis to live securely and in harmony with their neighbors. There is no other mandate whose implementation could more profoundly improve international relationships.[*]

Carter ended his speech with:

> War may sometimes be a necessary evil. But no matter how necessary, it is always an evil, never a good. We will not learn how to live together in peace by killing each other's children. The bond of our common humanity is stronger than the divisiveness of our fears and prejudices. God gives us the capacity for choice. We can choose to alleviate suffering. We can choose to work together for peace. We can make these changes – and we must.

* * * *

Soon after the publication of *Palestine Peace Not Apartheid*, Abraham Foxman posted a book review on the ADL website. Foxman's review is instructive and I am going to examine it in some detail. The review illustrates how unexamined fear and prejudice occlude natural intelligence. It also illustrates how insensitive to the suffering of others a man can become when faced with an issue that directly challenges his identity, even when that man has been an undeniable champion of human rights in other areas of his life.

---

[*] UN Security Council Resolution 242 was passed by the United Nations Security Council. Security Council Resolutions are binding. General Assembly resolutions are not.

Foxman begins with:

> One should never judge a book by its cover, but in the case of former President Jimmy Carter's latest work, 'Palestine Peace Not Apartheid', we should make an exception. All one really needs to know about this biased account is found in the title.[6*]

Foxman's statement is illogical. What is "found" in the title *Palestine Peace Not Apartheid* is Carter's contention that the occupation imposed on the Palestinian people is a form of apartheid, that apartheid is the principle obstacle to a peaceful resolution of the Israel-Palestine conflict. Apparently Foxman finds this thesis so provocative as to be presumptively dismissed, but there is nothing about it that warrants such a conclusion. The word apartheid in conjunction with Palestine has been recognized by numerous scholars, human rights organizations and Nelson Mandela as an accurate description of the situation in the Occupied Territories. Certainly a prospective reader is ill served by Foxman's statement. The reader wants to know if Carter has written something that can add to his understanding of the Israel-Palestine conflict. The reader wants to know if Carter has made his case; can the title be supported by the *evidence* Carter presents.

The second paragraph in Foxman's review is:

> It is truly shocking, at a time of Islamic extremism running rampant, of suicide bombs polluting cities in Europe, Asia and the Middle East, of Iran publicly stating its desire to wipe Israel off the map and building nuclear weapons to achieve that end, of the missile and rocket attacks by Hezbollah and Hamas on Israel, that Jimmy Carter can to a large degree only see Israel as the party responsible for conflict between Israel and the Palestinians.

Here too, Foxman proceeds illogically. Whatever the truth to Foxman's depiction of the state of Islamic extremism, there is nothing "shocking" in the fact that Carter sees Israel as the principle party responsible for the Israel-Palestine conflict. The Israel-Palestine conflict

---

* For Foxman's full review see Appendix IV.

is the subject of Carter's book, not Iran, not suicide bombings in Europe and not Hezbollah – that much *is* clear from the title. Carter has chosen the area he wants to examine, and it is within that area that he should be judged.

More interesting is how Foxman shifts the focus away from an examination of the evidence Carter presents. Foxman is essentially saying that even to write the book is a betrayal of the exigent needs of the times. He does this in a clever way. He uses a broad swath of big nouns and adjectives about events that presumably no one can ignore, and then he imputes to Carter a willful blindness about them. All of this is projection on Foxman's part. First it is a projection of a point of view that Carter undoubtedly does not possess. Does Foxman *really* think that Jimmy Carter does not know of such events and their importance? That is absurd. Foxman is projecting what is not true because it serves his purpose of diverting attention away from the evidence in Carter's book. Throughout the book Carter repeatedly calls for an end to violence:

> There is no place for sustained violence, which tends to subvert peace initiatives and perpetuate hatred and combat. Some Palestinians have responded to political and military occupation by launching terrorist attacks against Israeli civilians, a course that is both morally reprehensible and politically counterproductive.[7]

> Israel's right to exist within recognized borders – and to live in peace – must be accepted by Palestinians and all other neighbors. [p. 17]

> The Arabs must acknowledge openly and specifically that Israel is a reality and has a right to live in peace, behind secure and recognized borders, and with a firm Arab pledge to terminate any further acts of violence against the legally constituted nation of Israel. [p. 207]

Foxman is projecting in another way: he is projecting his fear. When I read the second paragraph of the review, I see a mirror image of myself talking to Bill and Westley. During my conversations with my two friends I constantly diverted the discussion away from what they were trying to tell me. Bill and Westley were presenting their straightforward assessment of the situation: that the Palestinians were the indigenous people of Palestine, that they had in large part been ethnically cleansed by Zionists, and that they continued to suffer a brutal and repressive occupation – these are the principle causes of the conflict. My reaction was to talk about pogroms and the Holocaust. I was stuck in the past. I was also conflating Arabs and Palestinians and painting all with the same brush: as irredeemable terrorists, basically as a pack of lying sub-humans.

Conversely, I passionately defended the IDF – how it fights with restraint, how it risks the lives of its own soldiers in order to limit civilian loss and how it mourns the deaths of the innocent on both sides. Today I see that thinking as an attempt to morally justify Israel's occupation and ethnic cleansing of the Palestinian people. The image of the Israeli military as beyond reproach was an obstruction that prevented me from recognizing the role I was playing in prolonging this unrelenting conflict.

My idealism about Israel was so insistent that I never asked a single relevant question of my friends. Not once did I say something as simple as "Are you sure? I mean, I find this almost impossible to believe. Can you give me some examples of what you are talking about?" And these were my best friends, men I had known for years and had the greatest respect for. Yet I refused to hear them. Why? Because I was afraid; I was afraid of what I might find out about Israel and about myself if I enquired of them.

I don't see any difference between what I was doing and what Foxman is doing. Foxman, after all, is talking about a book written by the single greatest friend Israel has ever had *without a doubt*. After the Yom Kippur War, which lasted three weeks, Israel was desperate for peace. The Jewish State had suffered casualties that on a per capita basis were equivalent to three times the losses suffered by the United States during the entire Vietnam conflict, which lasted more than a decade. Potentially more deadly than Vietnam was Israeli Prime Minister Golda Meir's decision on October 8, 1973, two days after the start of the war, to authorize preparations for the possible launch of atomic bombs against targets in Egypt and Syria. Thirteen twenty-kiloton bombs were assembled, and Jericho missiles and nuclear strike F-4's were armed and readied for action.[8]

The Soviet Union and the United States were also ready to resort to desperate measures. For the only time in their histories, each placed their nuclear arsenals on high alert.[9] There is no way to fathom the short or long-term consequences for the Middle East, or for the world, if even a single atomic bomb had been launched.

Traumatized by their losses, aware that Egypt was the greatest power in the Arab world with one of the strongest armies in the entire world, and wanting to avoid another possible nuclear scenario, Israel had collectively awakened to the fact that it had to negotiate a lasting peace with the Egyptians. Israel was also keenly aware that it was powerless to bring about such a peace. So, it turned to the United States and to Jimmy Carter in particular.

And Carter did not disappoint. Without his skill and hard work in mediating between two lifelong enemies, Anwar Sadat and Menachem Begin, peace would not have been possible and Israel might not even exist today, surely not in its present form. Carter's resolve to keep Sadat and Begin at Camp David until they reached an agreement was critical to the success of the talks. On many occasions one or the other leader wanted to abandon negotiations, only to be reasoned with, cajoled, or threatened back to the negotiating table by Carter. The animosity between Begin and Sadat was so great that they were seldom in the same room. Carter had to shuttle between the two just to keep the talks alive. Shlomo Ben-Ami:

> That the dramatic encounter between two extraordinary political figures like Begin and Sadat should not have been allowed to decline into another failure had much to do with the leadership of President Carter and with the concept of peace developed by his administration. . . . His was a bold, simplistic, yet at the same time extremely effective, approach that shocked his Israeli interlocutors with the revolutionary peace recipes that he put forward without even bothering to consult them. Others might have tried to untie carefully and laboriously the Gordian knot of the conflict; Carter preferred to cut it pure and simple.[10]

The Camp David Accords involved two separate agreements: *A Framework for Peace in the Middle East* and *A Framework for the Conclusion of a Peace Treaty between Egypt and Israel*. The first of these dealt principally with the end of Israel's occupation of the West Bank and Gaza and full autonomy[*] for the Palestinians, in accordance with U.N. Security Council Resolutions 242 and 338 (it is this section of the Accords that has not been realized – in large part because of its violation by a succession of Israeli governments).[+] The second agreement addressed Israel's pressing need for peace with Egypt and the future of the Sinai Peninsula, but its eventual outcome ran into numerous stumbling blocks until Carter flew to both countries, where he helped iron out the final status details. This peace treaty has not been violated to this day.

Many Israelis are grateful to Carter for what he accomplished at Camp David and for how peace has enriched their lives. Carter describes an incident that occurred while he and his wife were in Egypt:

> One morning in the early 1980s, as we were approaching the entrance to the tomb of Tutankhamen, a group of Israelis saw me and began to sing "*Hayvenu Shalom Aleichem* – Peace Be with You." We stopped to listen, and I noticed that my eyes were not the only ones that glistened. I went over to talk to them, and they thanked me "for giving us the opportunity to visit our friends in Egypt."[11]

A 2001 poll taken by the Israel-based Jaffee Center for Strategic Studies reveals that 85% of Israelis support the Camp David Accords.[12] Many of these supporters continue to understand that Carter is just as concerned for Israel's welfare today as he was thirty years ago. They know that Carter's criticism is not based in bigotry but in love and the disappointment that comes when a friend acts so hurtfully toward another. There is something else, then, to notice about Foxman's review:

---

* In his book Carter tells how he was surprised when Begin himself insisted on changing a preliminary wording of the agreement from "autonomy" to "full autonomy" for the Palestinians.

+ Ben-Ami [p. 161] points out that it was Begin's "lack of willingness to enforce Palestinian autonomy. . . in Gaza and the West Bank, which would lead two of his closest collaborators to resign, the Minister of Foreign Affairs Moshe Dayan and Defense Minister Ezer Weizman."

the feeling to it. Is this the way Foxman treats a friend of the Jewish nation?

What if there were no Camp David Accords? What if the president of the United States at the time hadn't been Jimmy Carter? The likelihood that Israel and Egypt (and Syria) would have fought another war would have been far greater. The possibility that nuclear weapons would have been used cannot be discounted. The likelihood that Israel would have eventually made peace with Jordan would have been far less. In any of these scenarios how many more soldiers and civilians would Israel have had to bury? The potential suffering that the Camp David Accords almost certainly prevented is one of the great victories in human history. The world and Israel are forever in debt to Jimmy Carter for what he accomplished in those thirteen days of peace negotiations. No other American president has done as much to protect Israel and ensure its security. Other leaders and diplomats have devoted enormous time and energy to bringing peace to the Middle East, but it is safe to say that the situation today is the worst it has ever been, *except* that the Camp David Accords are honored and there has been no further armed conflict between Egypt and Israel.

Foxman has devoted his life to protecting his people. He is *ipso facto* a professional in the field, yet he does not recognize a true friend of Israel even when that friend is standing before him and speaking his truth. What is a friend for if not to speak the truth when he sees someone he cares for acting irresponsibly and self-destructively? A difficult truth from a friend has unique value because it often addresses a blind spot that one otherwise cannot see. Bill and Westley were speaking their truth to me. I was too emotionally attached to my perspective to value their perspective. I resisted, raised my voice and even asked Bill if he was an anti-Semite. My passion and anger were avoidance – not really a way to avoid my friends' communication but to avoid my fear.

I remember the feelings I had just before my awakening: primarily righteous fury and then deep sadness. These were nothing at all like the passion I had displayed defending Israel. These feelings were more internal and contemplative, provoked by real information, not by fear. I knew that if I was going to confront my uncertainty I had to marshal every ounce of free attention and work my way through *Beyond*

Chutzpah. I no longer could choose passion and anger. In their place something chose me. I became taken over by real feeling. The sadness especially enveloped me; indeed, there was already very little "me" left. A great burden was being lifted: that I was beholden to an exclusive identity; that my identity was created out of certain beliefs; that its existence was dependent upon my "enemy's" existence.

When I awoke as myself what was revealed was non-separation, without disturbance and beyond fear. Then, surprisingly, a new range of feeling was available. Compassion was effortless. It flowed from my own intrinsic nature. It was an instinctive response to the recognition of that same nature in others. How could I not feel compassion? How could I not feel in the "other" the same inner yearning for freedom from confusion that I'd once had.

Foxman is as capable of transcending his fear and awakening to compassion as I was. Perhaps his burden is greater than mine, for in addition to his identification with the Jewish people and their history, he is also staunchly identified with his role as an international leader in the fight for human rights. He knows his influence can affect lives. His attachment to and melding of both identities distorts his vision, obliging him to favor one people over another. None of this is necessary, but to go beyond it Foxman will have to formulate the intention to find the truth, and he will need to look deeply within himself. He will have to speak and write with care and intelligence; otherwise, his words – as in this review – will remain an artifice that mask fear and betray a refusal to face that fear.

The third paragraph of Foxman's review is the following:

> In some ways, Carter's book reminds me of the outlandish paper on *The Israel Lobby and U.S. Foreign Policy* by professors John Mearsheimer and Stephen Walt, though he doesn't go to their extremes. Like them, his examination of almost every issue concerning the conflict results in blaming Israel for most or all of what has gone wrong.

One of the fruits of my transformation is sensitivity to the language used in the Israel-Palestine debate. Because I recognize that my past use of hyperbole helped propagate self-deception, I take notice when Foxman calls *The Israel Lobby and U.S. Foreign Policy* "outlandish." The paper (a book by the same name was subsequently published by the authors) was written by two well-respected professors, one from the University of Chicago, the other from Harvard. Their work has been extensively praised as a long-needed examination of the influence of the Israel Lobby in American politics. For example, Daniel Levy, former advisor to Israeli Prime Minister Ehud Barak, said the paper "should serve as a wakeup call, on both sides of the ocean."[13] In an article for *Haaretz*, Levy wrote:

> Yet their case is a potent one: that identification of American with Israeli interests can be principally explained via the impact of the pro-Israel lobby in Washington, and in limiting the parameters of public debate, rather than by virtue of Israel being a vital strategic asset or having a uniquely compelling moral case for support (beyond, as the authors point out, the right to exist, which is anyway not in jeopardy) . . . . The bottom line might read as follows: that defending the Israeli occupation of Arab territory has done to the American pro-Israel community what living as an occupier has done to Israel – muddied both its moral compass and its rational self-interest compass.[14]

Zbigniew Brzezinski, Carter's former National Security Adviser, said:

> Mearsheimer and Walt adduce a great deal of factual evidence that over the years Israel has been the beneficiary of privileged – indeed, highly preferential – financial assistance, out of all proportion to what the United States extends to any other country. . . . Money being fungible, that aid also pays for the very settlements that America opposes and that impede the peace process.[15]

The Israel Lobby and U.S. Foreign Policy has also been criticized by scholars and politicians covering a wide range of the political spectrum. Noam Chomsky for example, finds that the authors "have a highly selective use of evidence (and much of the evidence is assertion)."[16]

The only things definitive about the paper are: 1) it cannot be dismissed out of hand but it is controversial; 2) it received the same type of slurs from many of the same parties that Carter's book received; and 3) Foxman himself criticized the paper with language similar to his critique of Carter's book.

So what exactly is Foxman saying? An accurate translation is: "Carter's book is a lot like another controversial work I criticized (but not quite as bad); therefore, it too can be dismissed." This is clumsy reasoning: Foxman has not shown that Mearsheimer and Walt's paper can be dismissed as biased, nor has he shown that Carter's book is similarly biased.

Establishing equivalence between the paper and the book is virtually impossible. The paper is an academic exposition, with the language and sourcing that characterize such a work. Carter's book is a personal account, written largely as a product of more than thirty years experience in the peace process. He does not use an academic style nor does he attempt to rigorously document his facts. Moreover, whereas Mearsheimer and Walt focus on the relatively narrow issue of the Israel lobby, of which they are highly critical, Carter covers a vast body of history; and for the first eleven chapters he is remarkably neutral. There is not a single negative assessment of any of the historical figures who appear in these chapters. The book portrays all of the figures as human, with the complexities and paradoxes any human being can display. If anything, the feeling Carter develops in his book is one of considerable sympathy for those involved. It is true that for the last six chapters he concentrates on material related to the title of the book (it is not until the Sixteenth Chapter that the word apartheid is examined for the first time), and his narrative becomes increasingly critical of Israeli policies.* But even here the book builds on what has come beforehand.

It is impossible to read the book without recognizing that Carter in fact loves Israel. His descriptions of the land and the people are filled with warmth; his reminiscences of his visits to the holy sites and the hospitality he and his wife received seem to be some of the most precious memories of his life. And so, when he does become critical of Israeli

---

* The book contains sixteen chapters plus a "Summary." In referring to the last six chapters I regard the summary as a chapter.

policies, one knows immediately that he is doing so out of real need; that he must communicate the primary obstruction to peace as he sees it; that to do otherwise would be a betrayal of what his life is about, and of the land with which he feels such connection.

Foxman's purpose in writing the third paragraph of his review is to prod the reader into prejudging Carter's book. To accomplish this he diverts the reader's attention toward Mearsheimer and Walt so he can discredit the book through guilt by association. Foxman's diversion is as clumsy as his sophomoric repudiation of the two professors. When I read the sections of the review where he rebukes the three men, I knew that there must be real import to what Carter has written. Why else would Foxman be so defensive and treat their works so superficially and unfairly?

How a man as educated as Foxman can write as he does is puzzling until one understands his emotional attachment to his cause, the State of Israel. His attachment dictates his thought processes; it tells him to defend his cause, and to do it any way he can. But there is nothing to defend because Carter is not an enemy, he is a friend. And Foxman's attachment is not really to Israel, at least not the Israel that actually exists with its five-and-a-half million Jewish inhabitants. His real attachment is to an identity into which he has never enquired and the beliefs and images that flow from and reinforce that identity.

Foxman continues with his review:

> Listen to his conclusions: "Israel's continued control and colonization of Palestinian land have been the primary obstacles to a comprehensive peace agreement in the Holy Land." And, "The bottom line is this: Peace will come to Israel and the Middle East only when the Israeli government is willing to comply with international law, with the road map for peace..."

Foxman truncates the quotes he uses. The first sentence in full (along with the two sentences that follow) is:

> Regardless of whether Palestinians had no formalized government, one headed by Yasir Arafat or Mahmoud Abbas, or one with Abbas as president and Hamas controlling the parliament and cabinet, **Israel's continued control and**

colonization of Palestinian land have been the primary obstacles to a comprehensive peace agreement in the Holy Land. In order to perpetuate the occupation, Israeli forces have deprived their unwilling subjects of basic human rights. No objective person could personally observe existing conditions in the West Bank and dispute these statements.[17]

[Note: I have highlighted the part Foxman quotes.]

An unbiased reader will recognize that Carter supports his claims with pages of evidence and personal experience. The parts of the quote referring to human rights, which Foxman excludes, are supported by material especially difficult to acknowledge by someone convinced of the righteousness of the Israeli cause.

Carter details the colonization of Palestine in a particular way. Instead of using graphic language and illustrating the most egregious actions of the Israeli Government, the IDF and the settlers, he chooses understatement. He writes as if he is still at the negotiating table, speaking with the least inflammatory language possible. He steadily builds his case, principally through his own experience and the voices of the Palestinians (both Muslim and Christian), as well as the voices of Israeli leaders. The statements of the latter are particularly damning:

Speaking officially for the Likud coalition . . . Foreign Minister Yitzhak Shamir expressed his belief that the root of the Middle East conflict had nothing to do with Israel and that a solution of the Arab-Israeli conflict was not likely to affect regional stability. He minimized the importance of the Palestinian problem and considered Jews to be the natural rulers of Israel, the West Bank, and Gaza, with a right and obligation to continue populating the area. The proper homeland for Palestinian Arabs was to be found in Jordan, and the pre-1967 borders of Israel were of no consequence. Ariel Sharon went further, having called for the overthrow of King Hussein in favor of a Palestinian regime in Jordan, even if headed by Yasir Arafat. He added that the east bank of the Jordan is "ours but not in our hands, just as East Jerusalem had been until the Six-Day War."[18]

Every U.S. president of the past sixty years would immediately recognize the danger in the views espoused by both Shamir and Sharon; yet Carter does not take either man to task, he simply states their views and allows the reader to come to his own conclusions. There is more from Sharon:

> Foreign Minister Ariel Sharon declared the Oslo Agreement to be "national suicide" and stated, "everybody has to move, run and grab as many hilltops as they can to enlarge the settlements because everything we take now will stay ours. . . . Everything we don't grab will go to them."[19]

When Carter alleges that the Israelis have deprived the Palestinians of basic human rights and that "No objective person could personally observe existing conditions in the West Bank and dispute these statements," the reader knows that Carter has walked his talk. In Chapter Seven he relates his personal experiences in the Occupied Territories. In 1983 he spent time with the Palestinians and documented their grievances, which continue to this day. Carter states that, although he had "promoted the legal and political status of the Palestinians during the Camp David negotiations," till then he'd had little personal experience with them. The chapter is a testament to his commitment to discover the facts for himself. He immersed himself among the Palestinians:

> Our meetings took place in private homes, municipal offices, hospitals, vacant classrooms, the backs of shops or stores, and churches and mosques. . . . At first there would be considerable reticence about broaching any subject that was sharply focused or controversial, but soon the constraints would be dropped and a more lively discussion would develop, often with bystanders and even children participating. In the larger meetings, several people could speak both English and Arabic and sometimes competed as translators.[20]

Carter also met with Palestinian community leaders and professionals at the American consulate. During the various meetings he was introduced to a world of oppression, yet the language he uses to share his experiences with his reader shows remarkable restraint. Carter learned about the bulldozing of Palestinian homes; the taking of their land, water and crops; the strangulation of their economy; denial of medical needs such as the use of ambulances for the hospital in Gaza; the torture and killing of detainees; and the denial of almost all basic human rights such as the right to assemble peaceably, to travel without restriction, to own land without the threat of it being taken capriciously by the government, the right to be free from detention without specific charges, the right to a fair trial, and the right not to be imprisoned indefinitely. The Palestinians also complained that Israel often intercepted foreign aid that was destined for specific humanitarian projects in Palestine. Sometimes these funds were used by the Israelis to further the construction of settlements.

Carter did not simply take the Palestinians at their word; he questioned them further to see if they were taking advantage of any legal remedies open to them. He checked with Israeli authorities and official documentation of the time (all the sources are Israeli) to verify that the grievances were accurate and representative of the overall situation. The fact check in the book is not exhaustive, but the reader understands that it easily could be if Carter had wanted to write a different, more meticulous account.

Especially revealing is Carter's depiction of the maze that confronts Palestinians when they seek redress for their grievances from the legal system. He describes the situation:

> They claimed that their people were arrested and held without trial for extended periods, some tortured in attempts to force confessions, a number executed, and their trials often held with their accusers acting as judges. Their own lawyers were not permitted to defend them in the Israeli courts . . . .
>
> Once incarcerated, they had little hope for a fair trial and often had no access to their families or legal counsel . . . . Most of the cases were tried in military tribunals, but ninety percent of the inmates were being held in civilian jails . . . .
>
> I urged them to take the strongest case to the Israeli Supreme Court and tried to assure them that they would get a fair hearing and perhaps set precedents that would be beneficial in similar cases. One of the attorneys responded strongly: "At great expense we have tried this. It just does not work. It is not like the American system, where one ruling in the top courts is followed by all the subordinate courts. Here there is one system under civil judges and another under the military. Most of our

cases, no matter what the subject might be, fall under the military. They are our accusers, judges, and juries, and they all seem the same to us. When a rare civilian court decision is made in our favor, to protect a small parcel of land, for instance, it is not looked on as a precedent. By administrative decision or decree a new procedure is born to accomplish the same Israeli goals in a different fashion. Besides," he added, "we cannot take our client's case out of the West Bank into an Israeli court. We are not permitted to practice there."

I asked, "Then why don't you employ an Israeli lawyer?"

He responded, "Sometimes we do, but few of them will take our cases. Those who will do so are heavily overworked with their own Arab clients who live in Israel."[21]

Carter then has a conversation with Aharon Barak, a former Israeli attorney-general and chief justice of the Israeli Supreme Court, whom he describes as "one of the heroes" of the Camp David negotiations:

[Barak] explained that the judiciary had to walk a tight line between what was appropriate under the special circumstances of a military occupation and protecting the rights of people in the West Bank and Gaza. Also, the courts could deal only with cases brought before them. He admitted that it was not easy for aggrieved Palestinians to find their way through this tortuous legal path . . . .

I asked the chief justice if he considered the treatment of Palestinians to be fair, and he replied that he dealt fairly with every case brought before him in the high court but he did not have the power to initiate legal action. I asked him if he felt a responsibility to investigate the overall situation, and he replied that he had all he could do in deciding individual matters that were brought before the court. Barak said there were special legal provisions related to the occupied territories and acknowledged that many of the more sensitive issues were turned over to military courts. When I requested his personal assessment of the situation in the West Bank and Gaza, he said that he had not been in the area for many years and had no plans to visit there. I remarked that if he was to make decisions that affected the lives of people in the occupied areas, he should know more about how they lived. He answered with a smile, "I am a judge, not an investigator."[22]

Barak's statements are more disturbing to me than Shamir and Sharon's. The latter do not equivocate; their truth is undisguised, there for all to see. Yes, there is madness to their statements but at least one is under no illusions. Barak is the personification of illusion. His words seem reasonable, he discusses the constraints he is under, he smiles – but he is numb to the suffering Carter tries to get him to look at. He is only doing his job, but an entire people for whom he is the last bastion of hope are being betrayed by him. And that Barak can say these things to Jimmy Carter, whom he knew personally and who had gone the last mile for Israel – when I read this passage, I cannot help but see a man going unconscious before my eyes.

Barak told Carter "that he had not been in the area for many years and had no plans to visit there" and "I am a judge, not an investigator." The final scene in *Judgment at Nuremburg* takes place in a jail cell. German judge Herr Janning – played by Burt Lancaster – has been convicted of using his legal authority to enable the dispossession of Jews and others of their property, their humanity and, ultimately, their lives. At his request the chief judge at the Nuremberg trials – played by Spencer Tracy – has come to visit him. Herr Janning expresses his respect for the chief judge's competence and fairness. Then he says: "Those people, those millions of people. I never knew it would come to that. You must believe it. You must believe it." The chief judge replies: "Herr Janning, it came to that the first time you sentenced a man to death you knew to be innocent."

Natural intelligence is the ability to look and to feel. Where a man cannot look, he cannot feel; and where a man cannot feel, he has not really looked. Without both he will never understand. Throughout *Palestine Peace Not Apartheid*, Carter records the statements of Israeli leaders, officials, soldiers, and custom officers. Theirs is an almost continual revelation of the refusal to look and to feel. The book – precisely because it is written in an understated way – has a certain nightmarish quality. On the surface something somewhat justifiable is being communicated by the Israelis, but it is only equivocation; it is the verbal mind standing atop the truth, the living truth, trying to keep it from surfacing, recoiling from its core communication that one's fellow man is being humiliated and destroyed.

In *Eichmann in Jerusalem: A Report on the Banality of Evil* Hannah Arendt, one of the most influential political theorists of the twentieth century, says:

> The trouble with Eichmann was precisely that so many were like him, and that the many were neither perverted nor sadistic, that they were, and still are, terribly and terrifyingly normal. From the viewpoint of our legal institutions and of our moral standards of justice, this normality was much more terrifying than all the atrocities put together, for it implied – as had been said at Nuremberg over and over again by the defendants and their counsels – that this new type of criminal, who is in actual fact *hostis generis humani* [enemy of mankind], commits his crimes under circumstances that make it well-nigh impossible for him to know or to feel that he is doing wrong.[23]

I remember what it took for me to feel what I was doing. I didn't go smiling into the project. I felt oppressed. There was finally nowhere to turn but to the truth. It became obvious that this was the only option left. And still I had to take the process in steps; my senses could only absorb what I was learning in measured amounts. But my intention to discover what was true and what was false was my guide. My discovery was that my presumed identity was an illusion, a mental construct built of beliefs and images that manifested as emotional recoil from humanity. When I was released from the ordeal of that separation I was able to feel the other, to understand his pain, to empathize with it, to see myself in his place.

A separative identity superimposes its beliefs and images onto the world. The images that fit within the boundaries of one's identity are associated with positive beliefs; the images that fall outside the boundaries are associated with negative beliefs. The latter is what led me to believe that Muslims grow up in a culture of hatred. A separative identity is not a philosophy that exists abstracted from daily life; it incarnates in very concrete ways. This unconscious process is what allows Americans to give billions of dollars in aid to arm the Israeli military and enable it to incinerate innocents in the latest assault on Gaza; it is what allows millions of Jews to claim the Holy Land for themselves without any sense of responsibility for the inhabitants whose lands and homes they have seized. It is what allows Aharon Barak to smile away the implications of his participation in a legal system that justifies the dispossession of an entire people; and it is what allows Abraham Foxman not to see the humanity in Jimmy Carter and the millions of Palestinians whose lives mean so much to Carter.

Foxman's review is an embarrassment. That it has been written by the executive director of the leading Jewish human rights group makes it especially an embarrassment. Foxman is an expert in documenting human rights violations. He is expert at seeing through the ruses of official government pronouncements that attempt to justify and explain away the subjugation of others. The only explanation for the review is that he has in fact not looked. I doubt very much he even read the book. Even if he read it, he never *read* it. How could he? His attachment to idealistic images of Israel is so great that it is the functional equivalent of blindness.

I don't see good reason to be optimistic about the situation in Israel/Palestine. Reason most often supports the opposite conclusion. In Chapter Sixteen, *The Wall as a Prison*, Carter continues with his description of the deprivations Palestinians are subjected to, going into greater detail than in Chapter Seven. Here he deals with the current situation, and it *is* a nightmare. The unconscious process illustrated in his conversation with Aharon Barak has borne full fruit. How could it not? The fact that the process is unconscious does not diminish its gravity, nor does it exonerate its participants. It is a living process with a momentum of its own, and that momentum will continue until it is interrupted by some superior and opposite force. Carter often punctuates his narrative by showing the disconnect that exists between Israel's leaders and the majority of its citizens, who support the two-state solution even though the various Israeli governments have acted to frustrate that solution. But it is questionable if his assertion is still valid. Israel's invasion of Gaza from December 2008 to January 2009 left over 1,300 dead, mostly civilians; nearly 400 were children. More than 5,300 people were injured of which at least 1,606 were children.[24] In excess of 21,000 homes were destroyed, tens of thousands made homeless and 400,000 left without running water. Yet, the campaign was supported by ninety percent of the Israeli population.

* * * *

Returning to the final sentence in the fourth paragraph of the review:

> And, "The bottom line is this: Peace will come to Israel and the Middle East only when the Israeli government is willing to comply with international law, with the road map for peace…". (ellipse in original)

The full passage in Carter's book reads:

> The bottom line is this: Peace will come to Israel and the Middle East only when the Israeli government is willing to comply with international law, with the Roadmap for peace, with official American policy, with the wishes of a majority of its own citizens – and honor its own previous commitments – by accepting its legal borders. All Arab neighbors must pledge to honor Israel's right to live in peace under these conditions.[25]

When the entire sentence is displayed along with the sentence that follows, quite a different light is shed on Carter's motivation. Carter is not playing favorites. He is stating the necessary conditions for peace to have a chance; his aspirations for the Palestinians are balanced by his aspirations for the Israelis.

Foxman's fourth paragraph cannot be fully understood without looking at his next paragraph:

> In order to reach such a simplistic and distorted view of the region, Carter has to ignore or downplay the continuing examples of Palestinian rejection of Israel and terrorism, which have been part of the equation from the beginning and which are strong as ever today. He has to minimize or condemn all the instances of Israel's peace offers and withdrawals, most particularly former Israeli Prime Minister Ehud Barak's initiative at Camp David in 2000, Prime Minister Ariel Sharon's disengagement from Gaza in 2005 and current Prime Minister Ehud Olmert's campaign pledge to withdraw from the West Bank. And he has to frame every example of Palestinian distress

as simply the product of Israeli repression instead of Palestinian extremism, e.g., the economic condition of the Palestinians, which has much to do with the continued terrorism against Israel.

There is of course nothing "simplistic and distorted" in Carter's view of the region, except the way Foxman has simplified and distorted it.[*] Furthermore, declaring that prospects for peace would be enhanced through compliance with international law is an eminently reasonable position to take. Isn't this the common understanding of the world community? Is Israel somehow an exception?

Foxman makes three claims: 1) Carter ignores or minimizes Palestinian terrorism; 2) He ignores or minimizes Israeli peace proposals, especially Ehud Barak's initiative at Camp David in 2000, Ariel Sharon's disengagement from Gaza in 2005, and Prime Minister Ehud Olmert's campaign pledge to withdraw from the West Bank; and 3) Carter misapprehends the cause of Palestinian distress, ignoring Palestinian extremism as a causative factor. I am going to start by looking at Foxman's second argument.

Like Foxman, I also relied on Barak's Camp David initiative to defend the belief that Israel had gone to great lengths to come to terms with the Palestinians. I used those failed negotiations as a way to portray the Palestinians as obstructionist. My view that the Palestinians rejected an historic opportunity for peace was much like Foxman's. In his book, Carter does not detail the substance of the Camp David talks. He bypasses them and instead discusses the final proposal that President Clinton presented to both sides at the end of his presidency, a few months after the Camp David breakdown.

Carter explains that the Clinton proposal (commonly referred to as the Clinton Parameters) was "the best offer to the Palestinians," better

---

[*] A revealing exercise is to take each categorical statement in the review and see if it could apply to Foxman instead of to the book, Carter, or the Palestinians. When defending a position with which a person is strongly identified, the mind attributes motives or behavior to the other that the person himself is animating. The mind is at its crudest this way and the accompanying language is invariably strong and categorical. When the subject and object are reversed in the statement, the new statement often better reveals where the truth lies.

than anything Barak had offered at Camp David. Under its terms, Israel would maintain control of portions of East Jerusalem and the Jordan River valley and Palestinians would have no "direct access eastward into Jordan."[26] The West Bank would be split "into at least two non-contiguous areas and multiple fragments," some of which would be uninhabitable or unreachable.[27] And eighty percent of Jewish settlers would remain in 209 settlements on about ten percent of West Bank land.[28*] Carter further explains that "the percentage figure is misleading" because it does not take into account zones with radii of about four hundred meters that surround each settlement and are inaccessible to Palestinians; roadways connecting one settlement to the next and to Jerusalem; "life arteries," ranging in width from five hundred to four thousand meters, that provide sewage, water, communications and electricity; about one hundred military checkpoints that "block routes going into or between Palestinian communities, combined with an uncountable number of other roads that are permanently closed with large concrete cubes or mounds of earth and rocks."[29] Even with these inducements, Barak "stated that Israel had twenty pages of reservations."[30]

---

* Carter's use of about ten percent of West Bank land for eighty percent of the settlements is confusing. The Clinton Parameters (under *Territory*) state: "I believe that you should work on the basis of a solution that provides between 94 and 96 percent of West Bank territory to the Palestinian State with a land swap of 1 to 3 percent. . . . As you work out the territorial arrangements, you might also consider the swap of leased land to meet your respective needs." The Taba negotiations (see notation * on next page) dealt with the issues presented in the Clinton Parameters in greater detail.

Complicating matters further, chief U.S. negotiator Dennis Ross [*The Missing Peace: The Inside Story of the Fight for Middle East Peace*] published a "Map Reflecting Actual Proposal at Camp David." The text which accompanies the map states: "While no map was presented during the final rounds at Camp David, this map represents the parameters of what President Clinton proposed and what Arafat rejected: Palestinian control over 91% of the West Bank in contiguous territory and an Israeli security presence along 15% of the border with Jordan. This map actually understates the final Camp David proposal because it does not depict the additional 1% territorial swap that was offered from Israeli territory."

Carter sums up:

> There was no possibility that any Palestinian leader could accept
> such terms and survive, but official statements from Washington
> and Jerusalem were successful in placing the entire onus for
> failure on Yasir Arafat.[31]

The most revealing assessment of Israel's intentions at the time is by their own leader. On January 21, 2001, one day after Bill Clinton left office, Israeli and Palestinian officials gathered for the Taba Summit in Egypt. The declared basis for the Summit was the Clinton Parameters. When the talks ended on January 27, the Israelis announced that the Palestinians had rejected Prime Minister Barak's "generous offer" of ninety-five percent of the West Bank. Carter quotes Barak: "The only thing that took place at Taba were non-binding contacts between senior Israelis and senior Palestinians."[32*]

---

* Former Israeli Chief-of-Staff, General Amnon Lipkin-Shahak: "Taba was bullshit. . . . Taba was not aimed to reach an agreement. Taba was aimed to convince the Israeli Arabs to vote." Quoted in Swisher, p. 403, interview with Lipkin-Shahak, January 21, 2003. Lipkin-Shahak was suggesting that Taba was Barak's last chance to salvage the forthcoming Israeli elections in hopes that by appealing to the Israeli-Arab vote he could defeat Ariel Sharon.

Shlomo Ben-Ami, the head of the Israeli delegation at Taba voiced a more nuanced understanding: "Political constraints and electoral concerns would later cause Barak to dismiss Taba as a meaningless exercise aimed to placate the Israeli Left. But the truth of the matter was that, in real time, he did his utmost to encourage the Israeli team to reach an agreement [Ben-Ami, p. 274]."

Although there were points of agreement at Taba there were major issues that remained unresolved. *The "Moratinos Report" on the Israeli-Palestinian Talks at Taba (January 27, 2001)* was prepared after consultation with representatives from the Israeli and Palestinian sides; both sides acknowledged the fairness of the Report. Some of the issues the Report touches on are: "differences of interpretations regarding the scope and meaning of the parameters . . . . The Palestinian side stated that it had accepted the Clinton proposals but with reservations. The Israeli side stated that the Clinton proposals provide for annexation of settlement blocs. The Palestinian side did not agree that the parameters included blocs, and did not accept proposals to annex blocs. The Palestinian side stated that blocs would cause significant harm to the Palestinian interests and rights, particularly to the Palestinians residing in areas Israel seeks to annex. The Israeli side maintained that it is entitled to contiguity between and among their settlements. The Palestinian side stated that Palestinian needs take

The fact is that *Palestine: Peace Not Apartheid* covers virtually every peace initiative since 1977 and, other than the Camp David Accords, Israel's record is one of refusal and obfuscation. Carter notes peace proposals made by Secretary of State George Schultz and rejected by Israel during the Reagan years; peace discussions held in Madrid with Secretary James Baker during the George H.W. Bush years, in which Israel refused to curtail its settlement activity as a condition of peace; the Oslo Agreement and Wye River Memorandum during the Clinton presidency; the 2002 Saudi Arabian proposal, which Israel has never responded to, and the Roadmap for Peace, which the Palestinians fully accepted, the latter two during the George W. Bush years.[*]

Rather than focusing on the Camp David talks, Carter made a sensible choice to simply address the "best offer to the Palestinians." The Clinton proposal was, after all, a continuation of the Camp David talks with basically the same participants.

---

priority over settlements. The Israeli maps included plans for future development of Israeli settlements in the West Bank. The Palestinian side did not agree to the principle of allowing further development of settlements in the West Bank. Any growth must occur inside Israel. . . . The Palestinian side maintained that the 'No-Man's-Land' (Latrun area) is part of the West Bank. The Israelis did not agree. The Israeli side requested an additional 2 percent of land under a lease arrangement to which the Palestinians responded that the subject of lease can only be discussed after the establishment of a Palestinian state and the transfer of land to Palestinian sovereignty." There were other differences that were not resolved including the status of Jerusalem and the right of return for Palestinian refugees.

[*] The Saudi Proposal was adopted by the U.N. Security Council as Resolution 1397. The Roadmap was proposed by the quartet – the United Nations, Russia, the European Union and the United States – and outlined by President George W. Bush during a speech he gave in 2002. Israel put forward fourteen prerequisites and caveats that rendered any peace impossible. One of the provisos called for the "cessation of incitement against Israel, but the Roadmap cannot state that Israel must cease violence and incitement against the Palestinians." A few others: "The waiver of any right of return of refugees to Israel; No discussion of Israeli settlement in Judea, Samaria, and Gaza or the status of the Palestinian Authority and its institutions in Jerusalem; No reference to the key provisions of U.N. Resolution 242." Carter, p. 160.

* * * *

The Camp David talks are a source of confusion for most people. Like Carter, I remember President Clinton and Dennis Ross, the chief U.S. negotiator, blaming Palestinian Authority leader Arafat for their failure. A number of accounts came out later that partially cleared up the confusion by explaining that Ross and Clinton were trying to help Barak get re-elected in his election battle against Ariel Sharon, whom they did not think of as a potential partner for peace.*

Egyptian American translator and diplomat Gamal Helal has worked for every U.S. administration from George H.W. Bush to Barack Obama. Greatly valued by Dennis Ross and Bill Clinton, he was a member of the American team at Camp David. In a September 2002 interview with author Clayton Swisher, he said:

> Right before Camp David, Barak kept saying that this is the time to sit down and get to it. But in reality, they never sat down and got to it! Except for one dinner, this never happened, and even at dinner you could not discuss. The point was to go [to the Camp David Summit] because of the leaders. Once there, however, Barak locked himself up in the room. He didn't have one single gathering with Arafat except for tea with the condition not to discuss things of substance. Barak didn't play the role he said he wanted to play, which was to sit down and look Arafat in the eye. He did the same damn thing with the Syrians in Shepherdstown.[33+]

---

* In "Israel's Lawyer" (*Washington Post*, May 23, 2005) Aaron David Miller, who served as a deputy to Ross, wrote: "For far too long, many American officials involved in Arab-Israeli peacemaking, myself included, have acted as Israel's attorney, catering and coordinating with the Israelis at the expense of successful peace negotiations."

On page 768 of *The Missing Peace* (2004), Ross credits the Palestinian negotiators at Camp David and afterwards with making concessions on permanent status issues, Israeli early warning sites, three Israeli settlement blocs in the West Bank, and Jewish neighborhoods in East Jerusalem becoming part of Israel.

+ Swisher is a former federal investigator. He was a VIP security guard at Camp David.

Aaron David Miller was another member of the U.S. team. Currently a public policy fellow at the Woodrow Wilson International Center for scholars, he served as an advisor to six Secretaries of State on U.S. policy in the Middle East and the Arab-Israeli peace process. Here he quotes Barak's chief negotiator at Camp David, Shlomo Ben-Ami:

> [I]n the words of . . . Schlomo Ben-Ami, the prime minister's idea of the concessions required of Israel for such a sweeping accord "fell far short of even modest Palestinian expectations."[34]*

Miller also said:

> There was not a formalized, written proposal that covered the four core issues [refugees, security, borders, Jerusalem]. There was no deal on the table. None of the issues were explained enough in detail to make an agreement, though the Israelis made an interesting argument on Jerusalem.[35]

Former ambassador to Israel Ned Walker, who was also part of the U.S. team, said: "Of the ideas discussed at Camp David . . . there is no way in hell the Palestinian people would have accepted this thing."[36]+

* * * *

With regard to Ariel Sharon's 2005 Gaza disengagement, Carter says:

---

* Author's note: In a February 14, 2006 appearance on Democracy Now, Ben-Ami said: "[I]f I were a Palestinian I would have rejected Camp David, as well."

+ In *A Quiet Revolution: The First Palestinian Intifada and Nonviolent Resistance*, Mary Elizabeth King, p. 328, cites James L. Gelvin, scholar of Middle Eastern History at UCLA, *The Israel-Palestine Conflict: One Hundred Years of War*, p. 240: "Barak offered a non-negotiable package and immediately dubbed it an extraordinarily generous offer. 'Given the choice of taking it or leaving it, Arafat left it . . . 'Palestinian negotiators noted that Israel had not lived up to its previous commitments to redeploy its forces or halt settlement growth. Now Palestinian negotiators were asked to set aside what they had already negotiated and accept Israeli assurances of good faith. And Barak's refusal to put his offer on paper (lest it give ammunition to his opponents at home) certainly did little to reassure Palestinians. Rightly or wrongly, Palestinians smelled a rat.'"

They [the Palestinian population of Gaza] are being strangled since the Israeli "withdrawal," surrounded by a separation barrier that is penetrated only by Israeli-controlled checkpoints, with just a single opening (for personnel only) into Egypt's Sinai as their access to the outside world. There have been no moves by Israel to permit transportation by sea or by air. . . . Per capita income has decreased 40 percent during the last three years, and the poverty rate has reached 70 percent. The U.N. Special Rapporteur on the Right to Food has stated that acute malnutrition in Gaza is already on the same scale as that seen in the poorer countries of the Southern Sahara, with more than half of all Palestinian families eating only one meal a day.[37]*

Alvaro de Soto, United Nations Special Coordinator for the Middle East Peace Process, wrote about the legal ramifications of Sharon's disengagement from Gaza in his *End of Mission Report*:

Since, as I recall, the test of occupation in international law is effective control of the population, few international lawyers contest the assessment that Gaza remains occupied, with its connections to the outside world by land, sea and air remaining in the hands of Israel. The only thing that has really changed is that there are no settlers and no more Israeli boots on the ground – at least not based there.[38]

Little need be said about Ehud Olmert's promise to withdraw from the West Bank. Olmert is no longer prime minister, three years have passed, and Israel still occupies the West Bank. During Olmert's tenure Israel continued to construct settlements.

* * * *

The crux of the problem in reaching an Israeli/Palestinian peace accord is explained by Benny Morris, journalist Akiva Eldar, former Israeli Chief of Military Intelligence, General Yehoshofat Harkabi and Ze'ev Maoz, an expert on Israeli security. First, Morris:

For decades Ben-Gurion, and successive administrations after his, lied to the Israeli public about the post-1948 peace overtures

---

* Carter's book was written before Israel's 2008-2009 invasion of Gaza.

and about Arab interest in a deal. The Arab leaders (with the possible exception of Abdullah) were presented, one and all, as a recalcitrant collection of warmongers, hell-bent on Israel's destruction. The recent opening of the Israeli archives offers a far more complex picture.[39]*

Akiva Eldar:

Without lies, it would be impossible to talk about peace with the Palestinians for 36 years while at the same time seizing more and more Palestinian land. Without lies, it would be impossible to claim that there is no partner for the road map, while at the same time injecting more and more money into outposts that the road map calls for dismantling. Without lies, it would be impossible to promise "painful concessions" in exchange for peace, while at the same time terming people who concluded such an agreement "traitors."[40]

Harkabi:

We must define our position and lay down basic principles for a settlement. Our demands should be moderate and balanced, and appear to be reasonable. But in fact they must involve such conditions as to ensure that the enemy rejects them. Then we should manoeuvre and allow him to define his own position, and reject a settlement on the basis of a compromise position. We should then publish his demands as embodying unreasonable extremism.[41]

Zeev Maoz served as a soldier in three Israeli wars and spent significant periods of time in Occupied Territory. Currently Professor of Political Science at the University of California at Davis, Maoz is former head of the Jaffee Center for Strategic Studies at Tel Aviv University and former director of the M.A. Program at the Israeli Defense Forces' National Defense College.

First, Israel's decision makers were as reluctant and risk averse when it came to making peace as they were daring and trigger happy when it came to making war. Second, the official Israeli

---

* Abdullah was king of Jordan.

decision makers typically did not initiate peace overtures; most of the peace initiatives in the Arab-Israeli conflict came either from the Arab world, from the international community, or from grass-roots and informal channels. Third, when Israel was willing to take risks for peace, these usually paid off. The Arabs generally showed a remarkable tendency for compliance with their treaty obligations. In quite a few cases, it was Israel – rather than the Arabs – that violated formal and informal agreements.[42]*

Carter is a serious man who has operated at the most important levels of international negotiations. He is not interested in sophistry, he is interested in substance. Perhaps Foxman's only valid perception of Carter is that the latter knows what to minimize and what not to. The book's title directly addresses the salient issue: the subjugation of an entire people by apartheid – that is where the obstacle to peace is at the present time. Carter's argument is so simple yet so obvious: How can you take a people's land, deny them their rights, subject them to a brutal economic and political repression, and then claim that you have any concern for a real and just peace?

* * * *

And how can you expect them not to fight back? Foxman asserts that Carter ignores or minimizes Palestinian extremism. Foxman is correct that Carter does not explicitly explore the subject, but his explanation of Palestinian resistance is implicit throughout the book. Carter relies on a reader whose natural intelligence is not occluded, who can look and feel in human terms. For such a reader Carter does not minimize, he *explains*, and in a compelling way.

Although I do not believe Foxman is entirely ignorant of the history of Palestinian resistance, because he chooses to stigmatize it as terrorism, I want to lay out some basic facts. Despite their history of violent struggle, the Palestinians have a more extensive history of nonviolent struggle. For example, the First Intifada, which began in 1987, was primarily an organized nonviolent protest. This was after twenty years of

---

* Ben-Ami (p. 317) concurs with Maoz: "Peace breakthroughs in the Arab-Israeli conflict began almost invariably thanks to Arab, not Israeli, moves."

occupation, and four years after the abuses Carter documents in his 1983 visit. Often referred to as the "war of the stones," the First Intifada started in a refugee camp when an Israeli army tank transporter ran into a group of Palestinians, killing four and injuring seven.[*]

Highly organized throughout all strata of society, the Intifada was a popular uprising led, at first, by local leaders. It included all of the classic nonviolent strategies of civil disobedience, including: the boycotting of Israeli products, non-payment of taxes, general and local strikes and work stoppages, graffiti, the raising of the Palestinian flag, symbolic funerals, renaming streets and schools, ringing of church bells, and community based schooling. The latter was a creative response to the forced closure of Palestinian schools by the Israeli authorities. Community based schooling, however, was seen by Israeli authorities as a grave threat to their control over the Palestinian population because they could not determine the nature of the education that Palestinian children would receive. To discourage this practice, Israel instituted ten-year prison sentences for anyone caught participating.

The Palestinians also made widespread and effective use of leaflets which provided instruction and organization in their struggle against their oppressor. The vast majority of leaflets advocated peaceful resistance and called for a two-state solution to the conflict.

A number of incidents occurred where Palestinian "villagers would disarm Israeli soldiers, strip them, and then return their clothing and guns to Israeli military authorities."[43]

Professor Mary Elizabeth King, an expert on collective nonviolent action who worked with Jimmy Carter and Martin Luther King Jr. (no

---

[*] Intifada is Arabic for "shaking off." A common English translation is "uprising," but the term intifada "carries no implication of violence" and was deliberately chosen to "replace the confrontational vocabulary of the 1950s and 1960s, which implied ruin, damage, or downfall [King, p. 208]." The First Intifada began in December 1987. According to King (p. 295), it ended prior to 1992 "by which time armed 'strike forces' had appointed themselves or been propelled into action by competing factions that rejected the nonviolent strategy of the uprising." Because the First Intifada focused the world's attention on the legitimacy of the Palestinian cause, Israel was compelled to sit down with the PLO and negotiate an agreement that came to be embodied in the Oslo Accords of 1993.

relation), quotes Palestinian human rights monitoring group, Al Haq (Law in the Service of Man), which concluded that "'not a single Israeli soldier . . . [was] killed in the first year of the uprising. . . .'"[44] King then points out:

> IDF sources officially reported the following: Four Israeli soldiers killed in the West Bank and none in Gaza in 1988; two soldiers killed in the West Bank and one in Gaza in 1990; and one soldier killed in the West Bank and none in Gaza in 1991. . . . [T]he IDF spokesperson said, Israelis killed 706 Palestinian civilians.[45]

Despite the restraint practiced by Palestinians, in the first nine months of the Intifada, Israeli soldiers:

> killed more than two hundred Palestinians, seriously wounded (by beating, tear-gassing and shooting) many thousands more, locked up some seven thousand people with hardly a semblance of judicial procedure (including nearly two thousand under 'administration detention') . . . blown up houses, and enforced prolonged curfews on hundreds of thousands of people in villages and refugee camps . . . . Beating up people in their homes, breaking their limbs, clubbing them unconscious, shooting unarmed demonstrators in the back . . . .[46]

In 1989 Gene Sharp, an influential scholar of nonviolent action, made the following observation:

> Specific instructions . . . [were] issued by the . . . [PLO] and the leadership in the territories *not* to use firearms; with few exceptions, the order has been respected. The 15 percent or so of the uprising that is constituted by low-level violence involves chiefly stone throwing.[47]*

Regardless of Palestinian restraint, Israel did not view the PLO as a suitable partner for peace. Yet, it had imprisoned most of the Palestinian

---

* Sharp is founder of the Albert Einstein Institution, which promotes nonviolent methods in conflicts throughout the world. His work has been studied and applied by movements in Eastern Europe as well as the Palestinian Territories. His best known book is *The Politics of Nonviolent Action* (1973).

nonviolent activists – Radwan Abu Ayash, Ziad Abu Zayyad, Feisel Husseini, Muhammad Jaradat, Zahira Kamal, Ghassan Khatib, and Sari Nusseibeh.[48] Nusseibeh was prophetic:

> It was also territorial, that is, about land, and without understanding its lessons and securing a durable settlement based on justice . . . the conflict could become one of race and religion and, therefore, much worse.[49]

According to Professor King:

> An unfettered intifada would have been the most potent countervailing force to the PLO, a known Israeli objective. Yet Israel compromised those who were pressing for dissociation from the PLO and expelled Mubarak Awad – among the keenest advocates for nonviolent struggle not dependent of the PLO.[50*]

The same year the Israeli government expelled Awad it allowed Sheik Ahmed Yassin, the spiritual leader of Hamas, to distribute anti-Jewish hate literature as well as literature calling for the violent overthrow of the State of Israel.[51] Why would Israel suppress a nonviolent movement in favor of a violent one? Can it be that Israel needs to rely on claims of self-defense against a violent people to justify both the occupation and its methods? Israeli journalist Daniel Rubinstein observes:

> To Israelis it really doesn't make any difference if the *intifada* is violent or nonviolent, the problem is the goal of the Palestinians and not the means.[52]

Israeli authorities helped facilitate the birth of Hamas in 1987, going so far as to arm the group. Israel's goal was to develop a religious force to counter the influence of the PLO. Over time Hamas became more extreme in its methods, eventually turning in 1994 to suicide bombings. A number of Knesset members blamed Hamas's growth on Menachem Begin and Yitzhak Shamir's refusal to negotiate with the PLO. The irony is that both prime ministers had themselves been leaders of terrorist

---

* Author's note: Awad, a Christian pacifist who advocated peaceful resistance, was greatly influenced by Mohandas K. Gandhi.

organizations during the British Mandate: Begin led the Irgun (IZL) and Shamir led the smaller Stern Gang (LEHI).* The two groups were ruthless in their methods. They hijacked British military vehicles and lynched, kidnapped and murdered soldiers and officials of various rank. Before Hezbollah, Hamas or al-Qaeda existed,

> the dissident right-wing organizations, the IZL and LHI, introduced into the arena (in 1937-38 and 1947-48) what is now the standard equipment of modern terrorism, the camouflaged bomb in the market place and bus station, the car- and truck-bomb, and the drive-by shooting with automatic weapons . . . .[53]

Many people in the West have the mistaken notion that religious beliefs, such as the kind espoused by Hamas, are at the root of terrorism and, more specifically, suicide terrorism. University of Chicago Professor Robert Pape has collected the world's most extensive database of every suicide attack between 1980 and 2003. He explains: "there is little connection between suicide terrorism and Islamic fundamentalism, or any one of the world's religions . . . ."[54]

> Rather what nearly all suicide terrorist attacks have in common is a specific secular and strategic goal: to compel modern democracies to withdraw military forces from territory that the terrorists consider to be their homeland. Religion is rarely the root cause, although it is often used as a tool by terrorist

---

* IZL is an acronym for Irgun Zvai Le'umi, the National Military Organization. LEHI (also referred to as LHI) is an acronym for Lohamei Herut Yisr'el, Fighters for the Freedom of Israel. In 1940 a faction of Irgun (IZL) members broke away to form the Stern Gang when the Irgun decided to suspend their attacks against the British. The Stern Gang concentrated their efforts on defeating the British, whom they considered the primary obstacle to a Jewish State. "At the end of 1940, the LHI tried to establish an 'alliance' with Nazi Germany for the 'common' struggle against Britain. An operative named Naftali Lubinczik was sent to Beirut, where he made contact with Otto Werner von Hentzig, a German Foreign Ministry official and intelligence officer, and explicitly offered a 'military, political and intelligence' cooperation. But Berlin was uninterested [Benny Morris, *1948: The First Arab-Israeli War*, p. 29]." Whereas the Irgun membership was in the thousands, the Stern Gang never numbered more than a few hundred.

organizations in recruiting and in other efforts in service of the broader strategic objective.[55*]

By 1994 officials from Israel's Ministry of Foreign Affairs admitted collusion between their government and the Muslim Brotherhood of Egypt:[+]

> The Israeli government was anti-PLO. We tried ten to fifteen years ago to encourage the Islamic movements. . . . We *helped* this reaction to establish a power base in the West Bank and Gaza. In retrospect, we should have talked to the PLO in 1964, when it was first established, but fifteen years ago, we were trying to destroy the power base of the PLO.[56]

* * * *

Although personally I do not condone violence, I find it hard to judge. Never having lived under the conditions the Palestinians are subjected to, I can only speculate on the methods I would adopt to assert my rights in the face of decades of repression. Human beings want to be free. If oppressed too long and pushed too far, people will rebel, even when they know death is their likely destiny. During his 1998 campaign for prime minister, Ehud Barak outraged Israel's right wing when he said that if he had been born a Palestinian, "at the right age, at some stage I would have entered one of the terror organizations and have fought from there, and later certainly have tried to influence from within the political system."[57] Barak also "said he heard similar comments from the late Moshe Dayan and even from Yitzhak Shamir, Likud prime minister from 1986 to 1992."[58]

Barak implicitly authenticates the legitimacy of the Palestinian cause. Yet, in whatever position he serves in Israel's government, he also

---

* Pape points out that "the leading instigators of suicide attacks are the Tamil Tigers in Sri Lanka, a Marxist-Leninist group whose members are from Hindu families but who are adamantly opposed to religion. This group committed 76 of the 315 incidents [from 1980 through 2003], more suicide attacks than Hamas."

+ Hamas was formed by members of the Egyptian-based Muslim Brotherhood in December 1987. Founded in 1928, the Muslim Brotherhood is the world's oldest and largest Islamic political group. With the exception of Yasser Arafat, the founding members of Fatah were also members of the Muslim Brotherhood.

seeks to officially justify his country's actions against the Palestinians. He recognizes the grievances of the Palestinians yet foments their character assassination by Israelis, Americans, Jews and Christians who do not understand the history of this conflict. Like Aharon Barak, he is numb to the consequences of his actions upon generations of human beings, including his own people.

Throughout history the oppressed have inevitably risen up to challenge their oppressors. The second century B.C. Maccabean Revolt against the Seleucid dynasty of Antiochus IV, and the Jewish rebellions against the Roman Empire in the first and second centuries A.D., are among countless examples of this innate need for self-determination.

For decades these groups committed murder on a daily basis. They instigated the bloody Jewish War of A.D. 66, which lasted four years, ending in the destruction of the Temple in Jerusalem. The Zealots and Sicarii died at Masada in A.D. 70, where they carried out history's most famous mass suicide – men, women and children – rather than submit to Roman rule.[59*]

The Warsaw Ghetto Uprising of 1943 is another example of Jewish resistance. Foxman, who is considered an expert on the Holocaust, knows that Jewish resistance fighters preferred death to domination. If, in addition to the abuses perpetrated by the Werhmacht and SS, 400,000 German settlers were aggressively confiscating property belonging to Jews, perhaps the resistance fighters would have resorted to suicide attacks involving civilians, something which Foxman would undoubtedly have approved of.

Is Palestinian resistance unique? Are the Jewish people and the Zionist state uniquely irreproachable? Or is Foxman's need to defend his people from criticism so overwhelming that he cannot acknowledge that

---

* Author's note: Duke University religion professors Carol and Eric Meyers are skeptical as to the accuracy of the common description of the events at Masada. Eric Meyers points out that according to Jewish law suicide is "the ultimate affront." Equally compelling is "the absence of physical evidence, namely skeletal remains." Eric Meyers has directed archaeological digs in Israel for almost forty years. He is director of the Center for Jewish Studies at Duke. Carol Meyers is author of a number of books on women in Jewish and Christian scriptures. *Duke Magazine*, March–April 2010, pp. 29-30, 34.

like the Romans, Seleucids and Germans before them, Jews too can become oppressors. As long as Foxman holds onto myths, he will have to invent enemy images of the Palestinian people – probably seeing theirs as an incorrigibly violent, lawless society – so that he can rationalize Israel's policies as necessary responses to extremism.

* * * *

Foxman's review is a pretext to project his pain onto Carter and others who expose the dark side of Israel's behavior. It is a way to create one more enemy of the Jewish people to justify the belief that Israel is besieged from all sides by insensitive critics and anti-Semites. In later paragraphs Foxman uses more emotionally charged language: that Carter's views "give comfort to extremists," that "he unjustly encourages Israel bashers," and that he "will be used by elements that want to undermine support for Israel in this country." Because he cannot quarrel with – or even look at – the evidence in Carter's book, Foxman can only react. He can only see Carter as a threat. And when he reacts, he exposes himself. Bias and anguish inform every paragraph, telling the reader that there is something in the book and within himself that Foxman is not facing.

Former Israeli Minister of Education and past leader of the Meretz party, Shulamit Aloni in Carter's defense:

> The U.S. Jewish establishment's onslaught on former President Jimmy Carter is based on him daring to tell the truth which is *known to all*: through its army, the Israeli government practices a brutal form of Apartheid in the occupied territories. Its army has turned every Palestinian village or town into a fenced-in, or blocked-in, detention camp.[60]

One month after Foxman's review was published he was interviewed by the *New York Times*. In response to a question about Carter's book, Foxman said: "The title is to de-legitimize Israel, because if Israel is like South Africa, it doesn't really deserve to be a democratic state. He's provoking, he's outrageous, and he's bigoted."[61] Again, this is the reactive mind. There is nothing in Carter's book that can honestly be construed as de-legitimizing Israel. He simply criticizes Israeli policies that are obstructing the peace process. Several times Carter states that one of the key requirements for a just peace is that the Palestinians and neighboring states in fact *legitimize* Israel.

Notice how emotionally charged Foxman's words are: first there is "provoking" (an accurate adjective – Carter himself has admitted that one of the purposes of the book was to provoke a more forthright look at the subject); but then there is "outrageous" (such hyperbole is simply not justified by a reading of the book), and finally "bigoted" (clearly untrue, a character assassination that is absurd when applied to Jimmy Carter). This is the type of rhetorical progression that becomes habitual in those who won't look and feel, whose words serve their prejudices. The only de-legitimization taking place is Foxman's attempt to de-legitimize Jimmy Carter.

That Carter has dedicated much of his life to bringing peace to the Middle East and that he has had personal relationships with many of Israel's highest ranking political and military leaders, including Moshe Dayan, Golda Meir, Yitzhak Rabin, Abba Eban, Ezer Weizman and, of course, Menachem Begin, was not enough to persuade Foxman to at least consider the possibility that Carter had arrived at his conclusions through a serious study of the Israel-Palestine conflict.[*]

If Foxman could step away from his pain for a moment, he would recognize that the reason Carter has spoken out on behalf of an oppressed people is exactly because he is *not* bigoted. The *American Heritage Dictionary* defines a bigot as "one who is strongly partial to one's own group, religion, race, or politics and is intolerant of those who differ." With all due respect, to whom does Foxman honestly think this definition applies?

Foxman might also recognize what millions of people already know: that Carter's reverence for Christian values such as tolerance and compassion influenced his decision to write his book. If there had been more citizens in mid-twentieth century Eastern Europe as dedicated to ending human suffering as Carter is, more Jews undoubtedly would have survived the Holocaust. The caring expressed by Carter through words

---

[*] Abba Eban (1915-2002) served Israel as Foreign Minister and Ambassador to the United Nations. In addition to serving as Minister of Defense, Ezer Weizman (1924-2005) was Commander of the Air Force and Israel's seventh President.

and deeds brings to mind Raoul Wallenberg and Oskar Schindler, two Christians who risked their lives to protect Jews from the Nazis. It is a shame that Foxman's shortsightedness prevents him from seeing the comparison.

* * * *

Palestine Peace Not Apartheid is one of the most popular books ever published on the Israel-Palestine conflict. Carter has achieved what no other writer has: he has written a strong, provocative account of the conflict, while all the time presenting his evidence and conforming his language to reach the maximum audience possible. I believe he carefully chose material that would not alienate the reader, while it could still educate and awaken. For example, Carter probably considered a more detailed explanation of the roots of Palestinian "extremism," but there are only so many issues that can be dealt with in one book, especially one that is meant primarily for an American audience that has been weighed down since 9/11 with enemy images of Arabs and Muslims.

* * * *

In December 2006, shortly after his book was published, President Carter made a visit to Arizona where he met with rabbis who were angered by his use of the word apartheid in the book's title. According to the news account, Carter prayed with the rabbis but was unable to change their minds.[62]

What were the rabbis praying for? Assuming they were praying for peace, their prayers will be answered when they open themselves to the divine, when there is connection to God; but connection can only be awakened through feeling. And real feeling cannot be reawakened until one discovers what is obstructing it. A core insight of my transformation is that the primary obstruction to feeling is the illusion of a separate and exclusive identity and its necessary philosophy of us against them, as well as the dehumanizing judgments that accompany that philosophy. The identification is not limited to the verbal mind; it is primarily a constriction on the heart. Much of the compassion and luminous ease I enjoyed after awakening was because feeling had released my heart from servitude to a false identity.

The rabbis may have convinced themselves that they were praying for peace, but without an impulse to understand the pain of their "enemy" and the reality of his history, peace is not possible. If the rabbis deny that impulse and disavow that reality and, instead, continue to cling to unexamined beliefs and images, their intentions will never be aligned with their prayers and their devotion will never be to God but to their separative ego-identities. Only when the rabbis and their congregations remove the veil of denial and actually look at the baneful effects of Israel's domination of the Palestinian people, will they finally begin a process that can lead to the peace they have been helplessly praying for since 1948.

* * * *

Foxman ends his review with the expectation that Americans are as objective as he is:

> Ultimately, we have faith in the good sense, fairness and understanding of the American people. They know that life in the Middle East is much more complicated and will require seeing all sides of the issue, something President Carter doesn't seem to be interested in doing.

I have faith in an *educated* American public, one well served by influential Jewish Americans like Abraham Foxman, who, instead of indulging in fear and prejudice, take the time to consider deeply *Palestine Peace Not Apartheid* and inform the prospective reader that he too can gain a more comprehensive understanding of the conflict by reading and considering the difficult truths Carter communicates.

* * * *

Everyone has an innate capacity to affect the world in constructive or destructive ways. Foxman is in an uncommon position to influence the thinking of many Jews throughout the United States and Israel. His life has mostly been a testament to equality and human rights. When he is not feeling threatened he must have a great capacity for compassion. If he begins to look and to feel, he will gain a deeper understanding of the roots of the Israel/Palestine problem. The energy released through this revelation could initiate a process of healing – for himself, his people, the Palestinians and, ultimately, the world.

If I can say anything to Abraham Foxman, it is that fear is the principal threat to peace; it is fear that creates confusion and conflict.

Going beyond fear will give you the freedom to see all perspectives, to understand your role in the suffering of the other and to elicit from the other that same compassion. I too believed that Israel was threatened by a host of enemies; I too resorted to reactivity to defend Israel. I too claimed I wanted peace, when all the time my mind was filled with fear and prejudice. My point of view seemed so necessary and justifiable; only after waking up did I fathom how unnecessary and unjustifiable it had been. I wish – as with Odysseus and the Sirens – that there were a way to bind you to a mast so that you would listen to the cries of the Palestinian people. Then you would understand that there is no security but the commitment to truth itself. For me that commitment was enough. It was the doorway to the end of ignorance and fear. I urge you to make the same commitment.

– 7 –

Reflections of a Palestinian Refugee:
Interview with Ali

I am certain the world will judge the Jewish state by how it will treat the Arabs.[1] Chaim Weizmann.

Ali is a Palestinian refugee who recently completed his undergraduate college degree in the United States. He plans to attend medical school. Ali and I met at a human rights gathering. I found him to be very intelligent. Most of all, I was impressed with how informed and interested he is about world events. Ali's is an important voice that especially needs to be heard amidst an atmosphere that is frequently characterized by enemy images and an inability to understand the needs and hopes of the other.

Rich: Ali, how old are you?

Ali: Twenty-two.

Rich: Where were you born?

Ali: In Beit Jala, a Palestinian town near Bethlehem, about ten minutes from Jerusalem. I grew up in Dheisheh Refugee Camp, which is near Bethlehem in the Occupied Palestinian Territories.

Rich: How long have you been in the United States?

Ali: Almost four years. I came here for college when I was nineteen.

Rich: Did you come after graduating high school?

Ali: I came here one year after graduating high school.

Rich: A few weeks ago you told me how much you had learned in school before coming here. What did you study?

Ali: Physics, calculus, chemistry, Arabic, English, history, religions.

Rich: Did you go to public school?

Ali: Yes. The way it works for most students from Dheisheh is that from first through ninth grade we attend a United Nations school. After that, most students go to public school in Bethlehem, which has many schools. In my case, I went to a private high school.

When you enter a UN school new aspects of suffering emerge. Classes are crowded with forty to fifty students in each room. The buildings are so old that sections of walls sometimes fall down. Space is limited with thousands of students packed together in small yards. In the summer students have only extremely hot water to drink. There is no ventilation other than the windows, which bring in hot air. In the winter kids have to wear layers of clothing just to be able to sit in class.

Rich: Do most Palestinians continue on to college?

Ali: Yes we do. We don't have many tools. Our mentality is that education allows us to express ourselves and let the world know about us. In the United States, after finishing high school many kids travel; but we don't have much money, so instead of traveling we get more education. Palestinians from Dheisheh have more college degrees than Israelis from West Jerusalem. I believe that education will enable us to build a generation that will continue the struggle for Palestinian rights. We want a generation that can reach out to the world. At the same time we want to work on the ground to support our people. I wasn't taught to accept things as they are. I was taught to be involved in improving the living conditions of my people. Whether it's through communicating with the world, dancing, or development of our community, education is an essential need along with the experience that comes from daily life.

Rich: How easy was it for you to come to the United States?

Ali: There are many obstacles. First of all, you can't get around if you're Palestinian. One of the hardest things about my application to come to the U.S. was getting to the American consulate in West Jerusalem. The consulate gives you an appointment date for an interview. But they don't give you an official paper to give to the Israelis to tell them you have an appointment. And you need a pass from the Israelis to go to Jerusalem, which is almost impossible for a young guy.

When I had my appointment the wall hadn't been completed so I was able to sneak into Jerusalem. It was one of the scariest days of my life. I went with my sister. When we got to West Jerusalem, as we were walking the streets we made a turn and before us was a group of Israeli soldiers, standing right there. It was frustrating because I saw my future in front of me. I had already been accepted to college in the U.S. I couldn't start college in the Palestinian territories that year. I realized I had two options: If they stopped us, I could tell the soldiers I was under sixteen and didn't have an I.D. (you get an I.D. when you turn sixteen) or I could explain that I know I'm not supposed to be in Jerusalem but I came in illegally because I needed to go to the consulate. Who knows what they would have done. Luckily the soldiers didn't seem to notice us. My interview went alright since I had a lot of supporting documents. But the consulate told me they had to do a security check. That took about six months so I missed the spring semester. I arrived here in the summer of 2005.

Rich: Did you have an easy time coming to the United States?

Ali: Ironically, traveling thousands of miles to the US was easier than traveling the short distance from Bethlehem to Jordan. First, before I had even left the Bethlehem area our car was stopped by soldiers. I had no idea what was going on but as a Palestinian I knew to expect anything. The soldiers checked us and harassed the driver. Fifteen minutes later we faced another checkpoint, which is one of the biggest in the West Bank. As we waited in line we watched soldiers stopping and harassing people of all different ages. Some were made to stand aside for long periods of time and some were taken away to be searched. At the border Israeli soldiers took their time searching my bags. They also questioned me about all sorts of things. I had no choice but to answer. After getting through the Israeli side of the border we had to go through Jordanian checks and answer more questions.

Rich: Is traveling much different now than when you were young? With the continued growth of settlements and a larger military presence it must have gotten harder for Palestinians to travel to and from Israel.

Ali: Yes, it's even hard to travel in the West Bank. Now there is the wall, checkpoints, settlements and settler-only bypass roads. Bethlehem is surrounded by settlements and getting choked from all directions. The wall and checkpoints make it difficult. If you're driving your car in

Bethlehem, you can't go for more than fifteen to twenty-five minutes without running into a settlement, a checkpoint, or the wall.

Rich: Do the settlements have Jewish only roads?

Ali: Yes. That's one way of taking our land. Sometimes they build wide roads for Jews only. They try to avoid using land from the settlements so they take it from us. It's all about land. And it's another means of separation. It's similar to the apartheid system that South Africa had; certain people are treated better. They have more rights and greater opportunity. If you look at this from an unbiased point-of-view it's very clear what is happening.

Rich: What are Palestinian roads like?

Ali: You rarely go for more than one hundred meters without construction or damaged streets; the water pipes are broken. We don't have the money to fix the roads. Even when we do, Israel might not allow us to fix them. Many times, Israeli tanks have purposely destroyed our roads and infrastructure. During the invasion of Bethlehem they destroyed a big part of the old city, which had gone through extensive renovations in 2000 for the new millennium.

Rich: What does your culture teach Palestinian kids about Jews? And what about your text books in school? I've read studies that conclude that very little is taught that is anti-Jewish? Many Americans, however, believe that Palestinians teach children to hate Jews.

Ali: Before the Oslo agreement our curricula were subject to Israeli censorship. For example, you could not find the word *Palestine* in any of our schoolbooks. Israel may have controlled our education but they couldn't hide our daily suffering. More importantly, we don't teach our kids to hate. On the other hand, we can't lie to them and tell them they're not being occupied, not when they see a soldier in front of them holding a gun. We can't tell them their lives are similar to people who live in Israel or who live nearby in the settlements they can see from their village. There are always differences in the way people react to any situation. There will always be some who learn to hate. I can't deny that, but they are rare. And, as a matter of fact, the military occupation is affecting the education and creating reactions among Palestinians. But we try to make it clear that it's not about Jews. It's about people who came and took our land. It's as simple as that. And it's not Muslims against Jews. Christians are suffering as well and their land has been taken and their churches have been damaged. We teach our kids about our history and our struggle to regain our rights. We teach them the history of other nations and other conflicts.

As the kids grow up, they begin to understand the situation from their own experience. They learn to be active and effective in their communities. There is no propaganda for anything, but you have to tell the history. I don't want to be biased. I want to include the least amount of opinion when I speak to kids. We have been under occupation for over forty years. We can't lie about that because we would lose our credibility as teachers, friends, or parents. So, when the kids ask why we are here living in these conditions, we can't ignore their questions. They learn that it wasn't our choice to live in a refugee camp, to have this lifestyle. No, we were forced to grow up in the camps. We have to tell our story. Hate is probably in the mind of a soldier when he is killing a very young child, or a pilot whose job it is to bomb people's houses. Israeli soldiers killed my brother when I was five. I would like to know what school that soldier went to and what they taught him.

Rich: How old was your brother when he died?

Ali: Twelve.

Rich: How was he killed?

Ali: He was taking goats up a hill. There were people in the vicinity throwing stones. He got shot in his heart with an explosive bullet.

Rich: Was he alone?

Ali: He was with some friends.

Rich: Was he near the stone throwers?

Ali: No, he was a clear distance from them, just walking with the goats. It was a sniper's shot.

Rich: There must be other situations like your brother's.

Ali: Yes. Sometimes babies at home resting in their mothers' arms get shot. No one is safe from Israeli guns in Palestine and the bullets don't discriminate according to age. Many babies have been killed while playing with their milk bottles and many children have been killed on the way to or from school. Since 2000 more than nine-hundred children under the age of eighteen have been killed by the Israeli military. My brother's death was not a random killing.

Rich: I'm not excusing their behavior but most of the soldiers are young. I imagine they are immature and impulsive. Some must think it's a game of shooting a gun. Sometimes they don't consider the consequences.

Ali: When they are growing up, most have never seen a Palestinian. They generally only see Palestinians on TV or when they're standing at a checkpoint, harassing people or breaking into people's homes while they're asleep. They're told that they are defending their country from the Palestinians. Who are they defending it from? Mostly from babies, women, and unarmed men who are working to provide food for their families. I believe that each soldier knows exactly what he is doing. I don't think it's hard to tell that a child is not going to harm them. A gun is not a toy or a joke. When soldiers come into people's houses, they know exactly what they're using their guns for.

Rich: As you were growing up, when did you start noticing that your camp was under Israeli military control?

Ali: When I was just a few years old, I noticed that soldiers were around, but it takes a couple of years to understand what is really going on. I was born in 1986, the year before the First Intifada started. I remember seeing Israeli soldiers many times and I remember the curfew. I will never forget one time during curfew when I was in the neighborhood and the soldiers saw me. I started running toward my house. They followed me into the house. I don't remember why I ran or why they followed me but I still remember how scared I was. Fear is a feeling we grow up with. We feel it and sense it through our parents and older siblings. Also, my brother was killed in 1991 and a few other brothers were in prison in the late eighties and early nineties.

Rich: Why were they in prison?

Ali: For nothing really. One time my brothers were working on the roof when Israeli soldiers passed by. A soldier accused one of my brothers of throwing blocks at him. That's ridiculous. Are we supposed to have our hands up when the soldiers walk by? I'm just making a point, which is that the soldiers don't need a reason to arrest us. When they have the power they can do whatever they want. What are we supposed to do? The soldiers can come and take you from your house for any reason, regardless of age. They want to know who you are. Even if you spend a lot of time at home, minding your own business, the soldiers will come get you because they want to know more about you.

Rich: If the soldiers want to arrest someone do they usually go to their home?

Ali: They have many ways to get you. They can go to schools or workplaces. Often, they use checkpoints. That's where they get you.

Rich: What if you don't go by a checkpoint?

Ali: Then they'll come to your house.

Rich: Do they knock before entering?

Ali: Soldiers who bomb houses and kill innocent people don't need permission to enter someone's house. When they knock on doors, they do it for a reason: to uphold a military occupation. A soldier's knock is unforgettable; the whole neighborhood knows about it. Many times soldiers enter houses in the middle of night. Before they leave, they destroy everything inside the house and scare everyone. They don't seem to respect human rights or even their own families. If they did, they wouldn't take fathers and mothers from their children or children from their schools. Their behavior doesn't differentiate as to age or gender. They insult the young and old, males and females.

Rich: Now that you're living in the United States, how often do you return to Dheisheh to visit?

Ali: I went back the first year for a month-and-a-half. Six months later my Dad passed away, so I returned for two more weeks. That was it. I haven't seen my family in two-and-a-half years. I need to go back soon.

If it was easy to visit I would go home every year. Anyway, even when I'm here, I'm always thinking of Palestine and Dheisheh and my family.

Rich: Does Israel make it difficult for Palestinians to return to see their families?

Ali: Of course. Once people leave, Israel doesn't want them back. Their goal is not necessarily to prevent us from returning but to make it so miserable for us when we do return that we won't want to go back again. For example, when I come home I can't fly to Israel. I have to go to Jordan and then the Palestinian territories, which is a crazy experience. Coming or going, they can interrogate me and harass me on the borders. Then, when I go into the territories, I have to pass through checkpoints and undergo hours of security checks.

Rich: What did your father do for a living?

Ali: My father was a teacher. My mom was a housewife. I had a large family, seven brothers and four sisters. I was the next to last child. My father taught history and geography, and then he taught third grade.

Rich: Tell me about sanitation. I spoke with another Palestinian who also lived in a refugee camp. He told me that there were only a few toilets in the entire camp.

Ali: Until the 1970s every twenty-five families had to share two toilets. On average there are about six people per family.

Rich: That works out to one toilet for every seventy-five people.

Ali: Yes, that sounds right.

Rich: Tell me more about your living conditions.

Ali: People lived in tents for awhile. That changed when the United Nations built ten foot wide by ten foot long rooms, which housed entire families. Nowadays some people have added to their rooms or built new houses but that takes money, which is not so easy to come by because of the occupation's effect on our economy. Houses are so crowded together that the walls of neighboring houses touch each other. About twelve thousand people share an area of less than one square mile. This overcrowding creates a lot of health problems. But we only have a single medical clinic in the camp, which is run by the UN. And there is only one part-time doctor available to administer to thousands of people living under these conditions.

Rich: It is hard to imagine living like that. It must have been very difficult.

Ali: When you live in a refugee camp the first thing you see when you wake up in the morning is the house next door, which often blocks the sunlight. When you look out you can see Jewish settlements. They are higher up; big houses with lots of space, security, green lawns.

Growing up in Dheisheh we never had places to play. We had to create our own games since we didn't have resources. It's not just our houses that are crowded. The schools were also crowded. Every class had forty or more students. And because of invasions and curfews we weren't always able to go to school. For years during the First Intifada, our camp was surrounded by a nine-meter fence that had one entrance/exit controlled by Israeli soldiers. So you could say that we have been prisoners since we were born. We didn't have a choice. We didn't have basic needs such as utilities, a decent health system, and decent school buildings.

One of the biggest problems was and still is water. Often, we don't have enough water for our daily needs, even for drinking at times. When I was very young, I used to go with my mom to the nearby village to get some water. Since we lived on top of a hill, by the time we got home we had spilled most of the water. It is easy to notice the many water tanks on top of houses in our camp. Lack of water was one of the main problems in the summer; electricity was the biggest problem in the winter. Many of our heaters are electrical and there were a lot of days when we got no electricity. Living without heat in the cold winter increased the suffering. It was hard to study or do most things at night.

Overall, living in a refugee camp meant that our lifestyle was different than many people in the world. We had to adapt to survive. We didn't have a lot of means but we had the determination to live. We love life and our main goal is to have a respectful life with equality where we can enjoy our days and raise our children without fear.

Rich: How does it feel to be a refugee in your own country?

Ali: It's hard to describe. But imagine living in a small, crowded camp all your life, yet you can see how much space and potential your country has. Our grandfathers lived in peace with plenty of space for planting. It's hard to see how others live around the world and then compare it to what we have to face every day. We are not asking to dominate the world, we just want to dominate our own lives and have a choice. It is hard for me to travel and have a taste of freedom and security, then go back and see my people living in fear and being treated worse than animals are treated in other countries.

Someone asked me if I was proud to be a refugee. There is nothing to be proud of regarding the bare fact of being a refugee. I'm proud of what I learned growing up in a refugee camp, and I'm proud of the community I grew up in. I'm proud of my people and their struggle but I'm not proud of being a refugee. I'm proud of the person I came to be through the small streets of the camp. The camp played a role in making me who I am today. The camp taught me to stand for life and human rights, to be optimistic about the future, to create hope even when hope is hard to find, and to help those in need even if I need help. It taught me to keep going even with limited resources. If I had the opportunity, I would be proud of living in my hometown and having a choice where I wanted to live and being able to choose the conditions I wanted to live in. I would be proud if my people didn't have to face a hard life every day of every year.

Rich: Why do you think Israel treats your people the way you describe?

Ali: Because they want to kick the Palestinians out of Palestine. The reason they treat us so badly is to encourage us to leave. We are aware of that, but it will never work. The issue between Israelis and Palestinians is not about anything but land. I think that a system built upon the taking of our land and punishing us is dependent upon racism. The Israelis don't care where my people go. It's not about religion, it's about land. We have nothing against Jews or any other religion. The problem is the military occupation, which serves a Zionist ideology that has created an apartheid-like system. The media make it seem like we want to drive the Jews into the sea. They describe us in all kinds of ways that make us look scary and inhuman to the world. But that's all propaganda.

Rich: Would it be true to say that every family has a close relative in prison?

Ali: Most families have had someone killed, injured or imprisoned. Everyone is affected by the occupation. You're affected as a student, a housewife, a teacher, even a child playing in the streets because occupation affects every part of life. It's all there. As a Palestinian you don't have to look for suffering in people's lives. You don't need anyone to tell you stories or teach it to you in school because you're living it. You see the occupation reflected in your daily suffering. The moment you realize what occupation is, you notice that someone in your family is in prison, that someone in the neighborhood was killed by a soldier, that one of your relatives has a permanent disability because of the occupation, and that you can expect a five-hour wait at checkpoints in order to go to the next city.

Since 1967 more than 700,000 Palestinians have been in jail at least once, some of them many times. A million-and-a-half Palestinians in Gaza are controlled from land, sea and sky, which makes Gaza a big prison. This is collective punishment. The West Bank is not much different. The wall separates us from the outside world. Some areas are completely surrounded so that the only access is through a door that opens and closes at certain times. Tell me if you think that's any different than a prison!

Rich: Most people in the U.S. are not very aware of what's really going on in the Middle East. Let's talk about Hamas. Most Americans see Hamas as a terrorist organization that attacks Israel with suicide and rocket attacks. The last suicide attack was 2004. But I'd like to know about the political sympathies of the people in the refugee camps. What groups are they aligned with?

Ali: You see all kinds of combinations of people and the political movements they prefer. Everyone is trying to understand the conflict and do something about it. Depending on their mentality, they choose a political movement that best fits their ideas; some don't join any movement. They are all just trying to live normally. I don't want to defend or attack any group.

Again and again, I go back to the reasons why all this has happened. If you want to explain the Palestinian issue you can't just start with 2001 or 2002. You can't just start when Israel began building the wall. It didn't start there. It didn't start in 1948. It didn't even start in the twentieth century. I try to understand what leads some people to act violently. I try to understand the reasoning of soldiers who come and control us, occupy us and make us suffer. I ask myself why these people had to have such military force. I try to think how they might answer. The answer might be that they have a strong need to defend themselves. If you are born Jewish and you learn how often throughout history others were trying to kill you, trying to kill your children, you want to defend them.

Sometimes the way I explain this is that the Palestinians are also defending themselves. They are defending themselves for the sake of life. It is the opposite of what many people say: that we want death. If my people wanted to die, it would be so easy. We could just sit in our homes and the bombs would come and kill us. Living is hard but it is precious. You have to defend life. That's what all these people are doing, but everyone is different. You can't tell people how to think. You can't tell them the right way to struggle because they are the ones under pressure. These people want life just like all other people in the world.

The Israelis try to convince the world that Palestinians don't care about life. No. The Palestinians are struggling with the occupation for the sake of life. My people suffer from the moment they are born. They don't have enough water, they don't have enough electricity, they can't go to school all the time; they probably have been to prison or their brothers or some of their family members may have been killed. And then some people are angry at us for defending our rights. Of course there are Palestinians who believe violence is the only option, but most of us have other options. It's not just Palestinians who react whenever they feel their life is in danger. All humans and all creatures do. When someone is under stress they fight back. When one cell is under stress it changes its structure and tries to protect itself. It might choose to produce defensive mechanisms or it might attack. This is the way things are in nature.

Before 1987 there was no Hamas; there was the PLO. Did the Palestinians have peace? No, it was just the same. The world used to consider the PLO a terrorist organization and now they support it. They used to consider Nelson Mandela a terrorist. Now he's an international symbol for peaceful struggle. Years ago in the United States, blacks were not considered human. Why? Because those with the power wanted to justify slavery; they wanted to justify killing them. Whoever has the power decides who is right and who is wrong, who the terrorist is and who the defender is. The Israelis change the history because they have the power, and everyone accepts their version of what happened. I hope to see the day when everyone lives in peace, loving and respecting each others' existence and rights.

Rich: Many people are terrified of suicide bombings or another al-Qaeda attack in the U.S. They think most Muslims or Arabs are terrorists who want to kill every Jew, Israeli or American. So they demonize Muslims and Arabs. They want to incapacitate them or kill them because they don't want to be scared. They generalize al-Qaeda and suicide bombers onto the whole population. But it is not like that. Hamas, for example provides social services.

Ali: Yes, Hamas helps with educational projects and social services. They are a social, educational, military, political and financial system. They are part of the Palestinian community. The discussion here shouldn't be about Hamas. Israel will try to shut down any resistance movement, whether it is Hamas or not. We can spend a long time talking about Hamas and what they try to do to the Israeli military; whether violence is good or bad. What about before 1987, before Hamas existed? Some people say Palestine was a land without a people for a people without a land. Unless you deny the Palestinians' humanity you could never make such a statement. That is the worst of all terrorist acts. When you see them as not human you are taking away every right they have. That statement has terrorized and uprooted an entire population from their land. The problem is not about which Palestinian group is active. Israel wants to shut down any resistance movement, secular or religious. And the US continues to turn a blind eye to Israeli oppression.

Before 1948 Jews could go to Palestine but Zionists wanted the land. They had their reasons. Their ideology was about power and control, so they invented excuses to justify their actions. They dehumanized the native population, killed many of them, and kicked most of them out. When you say the Palestinian people do not exist, unless you consider them animals you couldn't make that statement. I ask you what could be more racist or prejudiced than that?

Rich: President Obama is telling Israel to stop building settlements and he is calling for a two-state solution. What do you think is realistic?

Ali: The tone of his speeches is so much better than eight years of Bush, but we haven't seen anything on the ground yet so we can't judge. But again, many mainstream politicians argue for a two-state solution. Some say that making two populations live in peace makes sense, and I think these people are sincere. But if you live there, it is different. I really cannot see a two-state solution. How can you do it? If you look at the map you cannot see a Palestinian state.

Rich: Because of the settlements?

Ali: Because of everything: the settlements, the wall, checkpoints, and military areas, because of the ideology. Without even talking about a solution you first have to acknowledge the rights of both peoples. You first have to accept the other as someone who has the same rights as you. That's the main problem. If we can get to that point, the two-state solution wouldn't be so difficult. But personally, I disagree with it. If you end up with a country that is just for Jews and other religions or races aren't welcome, or don't have the same rights, you are promoting a certain mentality. In twenty years you might get another generation that says, "These people don't have the right to the land, so why don't we take over?" It's not a complete solution; it's not a balanced solution; and it doesn't end the story. In my opinion, it will only end when people on both sides believe in equal rights for everyone. I think that can only happen in a one-state solution. You can't just give people the right to move to a country and live there because they happen to be Muslim, Christian or Jewish. If you manage to achieve a two-state solution, it won't last because it doesn't address the origin of the problem. Wherever there is exclusion there is pressure. A two-state solution might last five, ten, fifteen years but eventually it will fail. Nothing can take pressure forever.

Rich: And you think a one-state solution would last?

Ali: I do, because in a one-state solution everyone has equal rights and can live a nice life. I think that in a single state if people have equal rights they'll respect each other. The United States didn't reach its potential until everyone had equal rights.

Rich: That took nearly two hundred years.

Ali: Hopefully it won't take anywhere near that long. I think we're living in a completely different era. I know a one-state solution will be hard to achieve. It's a challenge. I say it's the ultimate solution to have equal rights. But acknowledging is the key. A one-state solution is really hard but a two-state solution is impossible. So which do you choose? Do you want to choose running and running and getting nowhere? Or run along and eventually get somewhere.

Rich: I prefer a one-state solution but what concerns me is that Jewish Israelis would be afraid of losing the Jewish character of their country. I'm afraid the ideological settlers and the right wing, the Avigdor Lieberman-type people, would form vigilante groups and there would be a lot of violence and death. On the other hand, the only way a two-state solution could work would be to dismantle some of the Jewish settlements. The 2002 Saudi plan calls for Israel to go back to the 1967 border. Israel would return the West Bank and Gaza to the Palestinians, and have full diplomatic relations with the Arab states.

Ali: For peace to have a chance, people like Lieberman cannot be in charge. If they are going to be in charge, then you're still not there. So you cannot accept the justifications of such people because they cannot be leaders if there is to be any solution. As I said, the one-state solution is not easy. It is going to take time, but when we get there it is going to be a stable situation.

I just don't think Israel will kick their people out of the settlements. Practically speaking, Israel has killed any possibility for a two-state solution. There are more than two hundred Jewish settlements in the West Bank and more than five hundred checkpoints and numerous military areas that cut the West Bank into small isolated areas. Israel has taken most of the water and a great deal of our agricultural lands. Looking at these facts, we can see that Israel hasn't left enough space for two states. They've killed the chances for a two-state solution.

There are many empty areas in Israel. With a one-state solution, Palestinians who were kicked out of their homes in Israel can live in those areas. On the other hand, if you kick people out of the Jewish settlements you create conflict. And if hundreds of thousands of people are angry, a large percentage would prevent the country from being stable. But if you give people land where no one is living, there is the potential for a solution. Honestly, I don't want to live in a country where there are no Jews, blacks or Christians. I wouldn't be comfortable. I enjoy interacting with people of different cultures and beliefs, and I think a community cannot function well if it is not open to cultural interaction.

We have to get to a point where people really want to end it. If you want to end it, you have to accept that Jews, Muslims and Christians are no different. You cannot build a country on racism. If something is wrong it cannot work. As a Palestinian refugee I cannot accept any solution that does not give me and other refugees the right to choose where I want to live. That is a basic thing.

Rich: Are you talking about a Palestinian right of return?

Ali: Yes, the right of return is critical. It's the key that would lead to any viable solution. You can't prevent people from living in their own country while others who come from Russia or Germany are always welcome. So how do you do it? It's about acknowledgment. The other side has to acknowledge our right of return because the Palestinian population is mainly a refugee population. So you're talking about sixty to seventy percent of Palestinians. How can you make a solution without satisfying these people? Most of them are not going to go back to their homes in Israel. But you have to give them the right to choose. That's how we define the right of return. Right of return means I have the choice, the opportunity and the chance to choose where I want to live, how I want to live and with whom I want to live. I want to have control over my life. All refugees have that right.[*]

Rich: When Clinton was president he suggested the right of return mostly applied to a return of refugees to the Palestinian Territories, with a limited number allowed to return to Israel proper. So, for example, Palestinian refugees from Lebanon and Syria could return to the West Bank or Gaza.

Ali: The right of return is individual *and* collective. No one can decide for Palestinian refugees that they want or don't want to return to their homeland. I don't know why some people try to make this seem unrealistic. Many Israelis have dual citizenship. They can live anywhere in the world and return to Palestine whenever they want. Every year new Jewish immigrants come to Palestine. At the same time, native Palestinians who are suffering inside and outside Palestine are not allowed to go to their homeland. By what kind of logic or law is that fair? Even though Palestinian refugees live in many countries they have kept their identity, just like the Jews did. They refuse to assimilate and they insist on keeping their culture alive.

U.N. Resolution 194 acknowledges the right of return.[+] Palestinian

---

[*] In their August 10, 2009 *New York Times* article, "The Two-State Solution Doesn't Solve Anything," Hussein Agha and Robert Malley succinctly describe the Palestinian position on the right of return: "In their [the Palestinian people] eyes, to accept Israel as a Jewish state would legitimize the Zionist enterprise that brought about their tragedy. It would render the Palestinian national struggle at best meaningless, at worst criminal. Their firmness on the principle of their right of return flows from the belief that the 1948 war led to unjust displacement and that, whether or not refugees choose or are allowed to return to their homes, they can never be deprived of that natural right. The modern Palestinian national movement, embodied in the Palestine Liberation Organization, has been, above all, a refugee movement — led by refugees and focused on their plight." Agha and Malley coauthored *The New York Review of Books* article, "Camp David: The Tragedy of Errors." Malley served Bill Clinton as Special Assistant on Arab-Israeli Affairs and was part of the U.S. negotiating team at the 2000 Camp David summit. Agha is a Senior Associate member of St. Anthony's College, Oxford.

[+] UNGA Resolution 194: "Resolves that the refugees wishing to return to their homes and live at peace with their neighbours should be permitted to do so at the earliest

refugees want to leave Lebanon and Syria. I don't think Palestinians in Europe and America are going to return home. It's about knowing you have the right to choose. I'm talking from personal experience. It's emotional. It's about acknowledgment first. The problem is not implementing the solution. The problem is getting the Israelis to acknowledge that we have the same rights, that we are equal.

I'm optimistic about the future. Despite all the suffering Palestinians have never given up. I gain hope when I look at the history of other nations. Oppression can't last and people won't stop until they get their rights. It's just a matter of time. There are many examples from all over the globe: South Africa, Algeria, and Vietnam to name a few. Eventually people will achieve their rights.

Hope is something we will never give up. My people want the world community to give us more support. They don't have to be pro-Palestinian; they just need to be pro-human rights. We don't want to replace or be replaced, and we don't want to treat the Israelis the way they treat us. We just want peace and equality. I just want my rights as a human being and as a Palestinian refugee. I want my dad to be resting in peace, not worried about our future and the future of our kids. If someone helps me or gives me the chance to achieve my rights I would be more than willing to be their best neighbor and friend.

Rich: Thank you for sharing your story.

Ali: You're welcome.

---

practicable date, and that compensation should be paid for the property of those choosing not to return and for loss of or damage to property which, under principles of international law or in equity, should be made good by the Governments or authorities responsible."

– 8 –
Purity of Arms

A rogue state habitually violates international law, possesses weapons of mass destruction and practises terrorism – the use of violence against civilians for political purposes. Israel fulfils all of these three criteria; the cap fits and it must wear it. Israel's real aim is not peaceful coexistence with its Palestinian neighbours but military domination.[1] Avi Shlaim

The image of Israel as a nation built upon integrity and humanity is articulated in the Israeli army's Code of Ethics. Known as the *Spirit of the IDF*, the code enumerates a set of values that form the cornerstone of a soldier's behavior. A particularly celebrated value is *purity of arms* (Tohar Haneshek):

> The IDF servicemen and women will use their weapons and force only for the purpose of their mission, only to the necessary extent and will maintain their humanity even during combat. IDF soldiers will not use their weapons and force to harm human beings who are not combatants or prisoners of war, and will do all in their power to avoid causing harm to their lives, bodies, dignity and property.[2]

Purity of arms has its roots in the Arab riots and attacks on Jewish civilians of the 1930s when "the Haganah refrained from armed reprisals against 'innocent Arabs' . . . and kept their weapons 'pure' by preserving them only for clear self-defense."[3]

By the time the United Nations General Assembly passed Resolution 181 on November 30, 1947, the methods of the Haganah were about to change.[*] Benny Morris:

---

* Resolution 181, the UN Partition Plan, divided Palestine into Jewish and Palestinian states and called for the termination of the British Mandate as of May 14, 1948. Fifty-six percent of Palestine was designated for the Jews (who represented 37% of Palestine's population and owned about 7% of Palestine's land) and 43% for the Arabs. Jerusalem and Bethlehem, the remaining 1%, were to form an international zone under UN administration. The resolution called for the two states to enter into an economic union with, among other stipulations, "Joint economic development, especially in respect of irrigation, land reclamation and soil conservation." [UNGA

As early as mid-December [1947], pure defense had already given way to an "active" or "aggressive" defense; restraint (*havlaga*), as practiced through most of 1936-39, was not to be the Haganah's way this time. Moreover, its reprisal raids tended to be disproportionate to the original Arab offense. This strategy

---

Res. 181, Part 1 Chapter 4, section D]. It also stated that "No expropriation of land owned by an Arab in the Jewish State (by a Jew in the Arab State) shall be allowed except for public purposes. In all cases of expropriation full compensation as fixed by the Supreme Court shall be paid previous to dispossession" [Part 1, Chapter 2/8].

Ben-Ami, pp. 32-34: "However satisfied they might have been with the vital international legitimacy accorded to the principle of a Jewish state in Palestine, it is hardly conceivable that the leaders of the Yishuv [the pre-state Jewish community in Palestine] thought of the minuscule state that was now created as the final territorial stage in the Zionist enterprise. . . . The 'partitioned' Jewish state as defined by the Resolution consisted of an Arab 'minority' of 49 per cent of the total population. In a memorandum it addressed to the UN, the Jewish Agency even made an explicit pledge to the effect that the new state 'will not be Jewish in the sense ... that the Jewish community will be superior in status to other communities'. . . . The endorsement of partition along the lines of Resolution 181 by Ben-Gurion was essentially a tactical move. 'Does anybody really think that the original meaning of the Balfour Declaration and the Mandate, and indeed, that of the millenarian yearning of the Jewish people, was not that of establishing a Jewish state in the whole of Eretz-Israel?' he had asked rhetorically in a speech to the People's Council on 22 May 1947. His acceptance of the principle of partition . . . was an attempt to gain time until the Jews were strong enough to fight the Arab majority. And in early December 1947 . . . he chose to hide his views behind philosophical reflections: 'There are no final settlements in history, there are no eternal borders, and no political demands are final. . . . A week later he pledged to Mapai's Central Committee that the borders of Jewish independence as defined by Resolution 181 were by no means final. It was then that Yigal Allon, who in the 1948 war was to be the most influential general and one whose impact in the definition of the objectives of the war was especially vital, said that 'the borders of partition cannot be for us the final borders ... the partition plan is a compromise plan that is unjust to the Jews. . . . We are entitled to decide our borders according to our defence needs.'"

Cypel, p. 53 [citing Flapan, p. 58], quoting Ben-Gurion speaking to U.N. representatives two months before the resolution was passed: "We are inclined to accept the creation of a Jewish state on a significant portion of Palestine, even as we confirm our right to all of Palestine." Cypel also quotes Ben-Gurion as saying: "As soon as we gain power, once our state is established, we'll annul [the partition] and will spread out over all the territory of Israel."

tended to spread the conflagration to areas that had so far been untroubled by the hostilities. From the first, the IZL and LHI, and to a lesser degree the Haganah, used terror attacks against civilian and militia centers. The Arabs responded by planting large bombs in Jewish civilian centers, especially in Jerusalem."[4*]

The passage of Resolution 181 marked the beginning of the civil war stage of the Arab-Israeli War, which lasted until Israel's declaration of statehood on May 14, 1948. Morris:

> [B]oth sides paid little heed to the possible injury or death of civilians as battle raged in the mixed cities and rural landscape of Palestine, though Haganah operational orders frequently specifically cautioned against harming women and children. But the IZL and LHI seem to have indulged in little discrimination, and the Palestinian Arab militias often deliberately targeted civilians. Moreover, the disorganization of the two sides coupled with the continued presence and nominal rule of the Mandate government obviated the establishment by either side of regular POW camps. This meant that both sides refrained from taking prisoners. When the civil war gave way to conventional war, as the Jewish militias – the Haganah, IZL, and LHI – changed into the IDF and as the Arab militias were replaced by more or less disciplined regular armies, the killing of civilians and prisoners of war almost stopped, except for the series of atrocities committed by IDF troops in Lydda in July and in the Galilee at the end of October and beginning of November 1948.[5+]

---

* The 1936–1939 Arab Revolt was against British colonial rule and the mass immigration of Jews into Palestine. Morris, *Righteous Victims*, p. 159, explains that between 3,000 and 6,000 Arabs died. By 1939 most of the Palestinian leadership, including potential leaders, were dead, incarcerated or in exile. In *1948* Morris, p. 21, says: "[The Arabs] had prematurely expended their military power against the wrong enemy and had been dealt a mortal blow in advance of the battle with the real enemy, Zionism. The damage to their war effort in 1947 – 1948 was incalculable"

+ Author's Note: The conventional war, or War of Independence, began May 15, 1948 and ended on July 20, 1949 with an armistice agreement between Israel and Syria. Yigal Allon and his second in command, Yitzhak Rabin, ordered the

Morris states that "the Jews committed far more atrocities than the Arabs and killed far more civilians and POWs in deliberate acts of

---

bombardment of Lydda, followed by an infantry attack in the center of the city. Israeli forces massacred 426 men, women and children. The following day, soldiers looted Arab homes, robbed the civilians and sent about 50,000 people on a march to the West Bank [see Pappe, pp. 166-7]. Referring to the residents of Lydda, Ben-Gurion instructed Allon to "Drive them out! [Ben-Ami, p. 44, based on Yitzhak Rabin's 1979 memoirs]."

In October, massacres took place in many villages. Morris: "There was an unusually high concentration of executions of people against a wall or next to a well in an orderly fashion. That can't be chance. It's a pattern [cited by Cypel, p. 149]."

By October 31, the Galilee was completely occupied by the Israeli army. Villagers who didn't run away were expelled. In Safsaf, four women and a girl were raped and a pregnant woman bayoneted [Pappe, p. 184, cites oral history posted at www.palestineremembered.com by Mohammed Abdallah Edghaim on 25 April 2001; archival evidence is in Hashomer Ha-Tza'ir Archives, Aharon Cohen, private collection, a memo from 11 November, 1948]; seventy men were blindfolded and shot [Pappe, pp.184-185, cites Nazzal, The Palestinian Exodus, pp. 95-6, Morris, *The Birth of the Palestinian Refugee Problem*, pp. 230-1, and Khalidi, (ed.) All That Remains, p. 497].

Morris: "During the takeover of the Lebanese border strip, Carmeli troops committed a major atrocity in the village of Hule [in the Galilee]. On 1 November [1948], after conquest, they rounded up local males and POWs, crowded them into a house, shot them, and then blew up the building. Altogether thirty-four to fifty-eight persons died. The company commander involved was tried, convicted, and sentenced by an Israeli court to a seven-year prison term, which he never actually served ['Khirbet Lahis,' *Ha'olam Hazeh*, 1 March 1978; Reuven Erlich, The Lebanon Triangle (Hebrew). Tel Aviv: Defense Ministry Press, 2000]. Hule was just one of a series of atrocities committed by the Golani, Seventh, and Carmeli brigades, and auxiliary units . . . Altogether, some two hundred civilians and POWs were murdered in about a dozen locations . . . . The main massacres, aside from Hule, occurred in Saliha, where sixty to eighty persons were blown up in the village mosque; Jish, where a dozen or more Moroccan or Syrian POWs and civilians were killed; and Safsaf, where fifty to seventy civilians and POWs were murdered (all three by the Seventh Brigade). 'Eilabun, where twelve (Christians) were executed (Golani Brigade); and 'Arab al-Mawasi, where another fourteen were executed (102nd Battalion). . . . No Israeli perpetrators were tried or jailed for the atrocities (except in the case of Hule), despite a string of internal IDF and civilian investigations authorized by the General Staff and the Cabinet [Morris, *Birth of Palestine Refugee Problem Revisited*, pp. 486-489];" cited by Morris, *1948: The First Arab-Israeli War*, p. 344-45.

brutality in the course of 1948."[6] His explanation for the disparity between the two sides is that the Arabs had less opportunity to commit atrocities because they captured fewer towns and villages. Morris does acknowledge that:

> The Arab regular armies committed few atrocities and no large-scale massacres of POWs and civilians in the conventional war – even though they conquered the Jewish Quarter of the Old City of Jerusalem and a number of rural settlements . . . .[7]

Morris also writes that when the Jewish Quarter of Old Jerusalem surrendered to the Arab legion on May 28, 1948,

> The [Arab] legionnaires deployed in force and protected the Jews from the wrath of the gathering Arab mob. The soldiers shot dead at least two Arabs and wounded others as they guarded the Jews. One POW recalled: "We were all surprised by the Legion's behavior toward us. We all thought that of the soldiers [that is, Haganah men] none would remain alive. . . . [We feared a massacre. But] the legion protected us even from the mob, they helped us take out the wounded, they themselves carried the stretchers. . . . They gave us food, their attitude was gracious and civil."[8]

* * * *

On the night of December 18, 1947, Jewish troops attacked the Palestinian village of Khisas in the Eastern Galilee. Their purpose was to avenge the murder of a Jewish cart driver from Kibbutz Ma'ayan Baruch, whose death was itself revenge for the killing of an Arab a few days earlier. Without any warning the soldiers began blowing up houses. Villagers were sleeping in their beds. Fifteen people, including five children, lost their lives and many took flight.[9] At a meeting between Ben-Gurion and some of his advisers, Eliyahu Sasson complained that the atrocities at Khisas were unprovoked:

> Actions such as the one in Khisas will prompt quiet Arabs to act against us. In all the areas where we committed no provocative actions – in the coastal plain and the Negev – the atmosphere is calm, but not in the Galilee.[10]

Moshe Dayan replied to Sasson: "Our actions against Khisas ignited the Galilee and this was a good thing."[11] Ben-Gurion and the other advisers agreed with Dayan. Ben-Gurion wrote in his diary the words of Palmach (the guerrilla strike force of the Haganah) commander, General Yigal Allon:

> There is a need now for strong and brutal reaction. . . . If we accuse a family – we need to harm them without mercy, women and children included. Otherwise this is not an effective reaction. During the operation there is no need to distinguish between guilty and not guilty.[12*]

Allon's words did not go unheeded. Late at night on December 31, Palmach soldiers snuck into the village of Balad ash Sheikh. Their orders from the Haganah were to "kill as many men as possible."[13] They were also warned to spare the women. Into the early morning hours of January 1, 1948 the troops moved from house to house taking the men outside and executing them. They also threw grenades and fired automatic weapons into the houses. Dozens died including women and children.[+]

A month later, in February, Yigael Yadin, chief-of-staff of the Haganah and Allon's superior, ordered deep incursions into Palestinian territory; the goal was to destroy villages.[⊥] On February 13 soldiers entered Jaffa, where they randomly dynamited houses with the inhabitants still inside. The next night, Palmach troops, under orders from Allon, attacked the Palestinian village of Sa'sa. They blew up about thirty-five houses while the inhabitants were still sleeping. Afterwards, many children were found among the sixty to eighty dead bodies. The *New York Times* reported that the village had offered no resistance.[14]

Four days after the Sa'sa massacre, Ben-Gurion again met with his advisers, two of whom, Josh Palmon and Ezra Danin, said that the

---

* Allon (1918 – 1980) was the general who won the Negev during the 1948 war. He later served as Israeli Deputy Prime Minister.

+ Pappe, p. 60, places the number of dead at over sixty. He also says that future military operations did not order troops to distinguish between men and women, as is suggested by Ben-Gurion's diary entry above.

⊥ Yadin went on to become the second chief-of-staff of the IDF, serving from 1949 to 1952.

Palestinians did not want to fight. They also reminded Ben-Gurion that the ALA (Arab Liberation Army) was only fighting in areas designated by the UN partition plan for a future Palestinian state. Ben-Gurion, who wanted the Israeli army to expand its intimidation of Palestinian villages, with the goal of driving the residents from their homes, said: "A small reaction to [Arab hostility] does not impress anyone. A destroyed house – nothing. Destroy a neighborhood and you begin to make an impression."[15] A month later, it was Yigal Allon's turn to echo Ben-Gurion's words: "If we destroy whole neighborhoods or many houses in the village, as we did in Sa'sa, we make an impression."[16]

Leaders of the Zionist left were uncomfortable with the methods employed by the Israeli troops. Aharon Cohen, director of Mapam's Arab department, admitted to feeling "'ashamed and afraid' at the 'deliberate eviction' of the Arabs."[17]* In July 1948, Yaacov Hazan, Cohen's superior, said: "the robbery, killing, expulsion and rape of the Arabs could reach such proportions that we would no longer be able to stand."[18]

* * * *

On December 4, 1948 the *New York Times* published a letter to the editor, the combined effort of twenty-eight prominent Jews.[19] Among the signatories were Albert Einstein and Hannah Arendt. The stimulus for the letter was Menachem Begin's forthcoming visit to the United States. Begin, the former leader of the Irgun, was head of the newly formed Herut (Freedom) Party, the political offspring of the Irgun. Earlier in 1948 the Irgun, along with the Haganah and Stern Gang, had been merged into the Israeli Defense Forces.

Einstein and the others compared Herut to the Nazi and Fascist parties and referred to the Irgun as a "terrorist, right-wing, chauvinistic organization in Palestine." The letter admonished Herut's potential financial and political backers about the dangers of supporting a party that had recently "preached the doctrine of the Fascist state." Then it warned: "It is in its actions that the terrorist party betrays its real character; from its past actions we can judge what it may be expected to do in the future."

---

* In 1997 Mapam, the United Workers Party, merged with other Israeli political parties to form what is now the Meretz party.

Although the signatories were aware of the Irgun's history of terrorism, the specific action to which the letter referred was the April 1948 massacre at the Palestinian village of Deir Yassin:

> This village, off the main roads and surrounded by Jewish lands, had taken no part in the war, and had even fought off Arab bands who wanted to use the village as their base. On April 9 . . . terrorist bands attacked this peaceful village, which was not a military objective in the fighting, killed most of its inhabitants – 240 men, women, and children – and kept a few of them alive to parade as captives through the streets of Jerusalem.

According to Israeli historian Ilan Pappe, recent research has lowered the number of victims at Deir Yassin to ninety-three, which includes the slaughter of thirty babies but does not include those killed in the actual battle.[20] In his book, *1948: The First Arab-Israeli War*, Benny Morris places the number at 100 to 120, which does include combatants.[21] Morris:

> Deir Yassin is remembered not as a military operation, but rather for the atrocities committed by the IZL and LHI troops during and immediately after the drawn-out battle: Whole families were riddled with bullets and grenade fragments and buried when houses were blown up on top of them; men, women, and children were mowed down as they emerged from houses; individuals were taken aside and shot.[22]

Morris explains that the "IZL, Haganah, Arab officials, and the British almost immediately inflated the number to '254' (or '245'), each for their own propagandistic reasons."[23] The Palestinians publicized the massacre to alert the international community to the brutality the Zionist forces were willing to resort to in order to achieve their goal of ethnically cleansing Palestine for a Jewish state. The Zionists, in this solitary case of admitting to war crimes committed during Israel's War of Independence, publicized Deir Yassin to instill fear in the hearts of Palestinians so they would abandon their villages.

I.F. Stone:

> Jewish terrorism, not only by the Irgun, in such savage massacres as Deir Yassin . . . "encouraged" Arabs to leave the

areas the Jews wished to take over for strategic or demographic reasons. They tried to make as much of Israel as free of Arabs as possible.[24*]

Menachem Begin:

[The massacre at Deir Yassin had] unexpected and momentous consequences. Arabs throughout the country . . . were seized with limitless panic and started to flee for their lives. This mass flight soon developed into a maddened, uncontrollable stampede. Of the about 800,000 Arabs who lived on the present territory of the State of Israel, only some 165,000 are still there. The political and economic significance of this development can hardly be overestimated.[25]

Begin also said: "The massacre was not only justified, but there would not have been a state of Israel without the 'victory' at Deir Yassin."[26] Although Israeli Prime Minister Ben-Gurion laid the blame for the massacre at the feet of both the Irgun and Stern Gang, it was the Haganah (the Jewish defense forces) that had coordinated the attacks with those groups.

Tsvi Ankori, a Haganah official, admitted that when he entered the homes of some of the victims he "saw genitals that had been cut off and women's bellies crushed."[27] Morris:

According to Jerusalem Shai [Haganah Intelligence Service] commander Levy (reporting on April 12), "the conquest of the village was carried out with great cruelty. Whole families – women, old people, children – were killed, and there were piles of dead [in various places]. Some of the prisoners moved to places of incarceration, including women and children, were murdered viciously by their captors." In a report the following day, he added: "LHI members tell of the barbaric behavior [*Hitnahagut Barbarit*] of the IZL toward the prisoners and the

---

* Stone (1907–1989), an investigative journalist, was well-known as the publisher of I.F. Stone's Weekly. In the 1950s he challenged McCarthyism and in 1964 was the only American journalist to challenge President Lyndon Johnson's misleading account of the Gulf of Tonkin incident. www.wikipedia.org.

dead. They also relate that the IZL men raped a number of Arab girls and murdered them afterward (we don't know if this is true)."[28]

A Stern Gang intelligence officer testified that a soldier "took two Arabs, tied them back to back, and placed a dynamite 'finger' between their heads, then shot at the dynamite and their heads exploded."[29]

On April 4, 1972 Israeli newspaper *Yediot Aharonot* published an eyewitness report of the massacre that had originally been sent by a Palmach commando to Israel Galili, head of the Haganah command. The commando, Meir Pael, had waited twenty-four years before allowing his report to be made public. Here is an excerpt:

> They [Irgun and Stern Gang soldiers] fired with all the arms they had, and threw explosives into the houses. They also shot everyone they saw in the houses, including women and children – indeed the commanders made no attempt to check the disgraceful acts of slaughter. I myself and a number of inhabitants begged the commanders to give orders to their men to stop shooting, but our efforts were unsuccessful. In the meantime some twenty-five men had been brought out of the houses: they were loaded into a freight truck and led in a 'victory parade', like a Roman triumph, through to Mhaneh Yahuda and Zakhron Yosef quarters [of Jerusalem]. At the end of the parade they were taken to a stone quarry between Giv'at Sha'ul and Deir Yassin and shot in cold blood.[30]

When they originally planned their attack the Irgun and Stern Gang commanders rejected the idea of killing prisoners, deciding instead to expel Deir Yassin's inhabitants.[31] Irgun deputy commander Yehuda Lapidot stated that his troops were ordered not to kill POWs, women or children.[32] But Shai operative, Mordechai Gichon, admitted:

> "In the afternoon [of April 9], the order was changed and became to kill all the prisoners. . . . The adult males were taken to town in trucks and paraded in the city streets, then taken back to the site and killed with rifle and machine-gun fire. Before they were put on the trucks, the IZL and LHI men searched the women, men, and children [and] took from them all the jewelry

and stole their money. The behavior toward them was especially barbaric . . . ."[3]

According to Israeli military historian, Aryeh Itzhaki, director of the IDF archives in the 1960s:

> The time has come; a generation has gone by and it is now possible to face up to the ocean of lies in which we were brought up. In almost every town conquered in the War of Independence acts were committed that are defined as war crimes, such as blind killings, massacres, and even rapes.[34*]

Israeli archives are not the only sources that document the Deir Yassin tragedy; the survivors also bear witness. One Palestinian resident of Deir Yassin spoke of the carnage that day:

> Me, my children and my brother, were hiding in this house. . . . They threw bombs at our home and my children and I got wounded. When things calmed down the Jews broke the door down and took us out. They started to beat up my brother Musa severely. I gave a soldier some money so that he wouldn't kill Musa. He took the money and said: "you are kind-hearted. I will show you what I will do to your brother." He threw him to the ground and my brother fell down . . . . The soldier then pointed his gun to Musa's head and shot him five times.[35]

Fahimi Zidan, who was twelve at the time, also survived the atrocities:

> The Jews ordered all our family to line up against the wall and they started shooting us. I was hit in the side, but most of us children were saved because we hid behind our parents. The bullets hit my sister Kadri (four) in the head, my sister Sameh (eight) in the cheek, my brother Mohammad (seven) in the chest. But all the others with us against the wall were killed: my father, my mother, my grandfather and grandmother, my uncles and

---

* Itzhaki defines a massacre as the "deliberate killing of between 50 and 250 victims in a single episode, whether these are civilians, including old people, women, and children (often by blowing up houses with the occupants locked inside), or civilians and Palestinian soldiers who had been taken prisoner and were killed with a bullet to the back of the head before being thrown into a common ditch" [Cypel, p. 68].

aunts, and some of their children. Halim Eid saw a "a man shoot a bullet into the neck of my sister Salhiyeh who was nine months pregnant." Then he cut her stomach open with a butcher's knife.[36]

Richard Catling, the British Assistant-Inspector General who interrogated witnesses after the massacre, included the following in his report:

> There is . . . no doubt that many sexual atrocities were committed by the attacking Jews. Many young school girls were raped and later slaughtered. Old women were also molested. One story is current concerning a case in which a young girl was literally torn in two. Many infants were also butchered and killed. I also saw one old woman . . . who had been severely beaten about the head with rifle butts. Women had bracelets torn from their arms and rings from their fingers, and parts of some of the women's ears were severed in order to remove the earrings.[37]

* * * *

The Haganah was particularly concerned with "males between the ages of ten and fifty."[38] That was how they defined "men." In the villages of Nasr al-Din, Tirat Haifa and Ayn al-Zaytun, executions took place in keeping with the Yishuv's (the Yishuv was the pre-state Jewish community in Palestine) policy of making an impression. Ayn al-Zaytun, with its mineral pools and flowing stream, was coveted by Jewish settlers only a mile away in Safad. They had begun buying land in the surrounding area of the village. This aroused suspicion among some of the Palestinians and contributed to an air of unease and hostility between the two populations. At dawn on May 2, 1948 Jewish troops began shelling the village and throwing hand grenades. By noon Palmach soldiers entered the village, where they were met by women, children, old people and young men who had not already fled. The residents were waving a white flag. The soldiers herded them into the town center. Men whose names appeared on a pre-prepared list were immediately shot dead. If a man not on the list happened to protest, he too was shot. Yusuf Ahmad Hajjar told the soldiers that he "expected to be treated humanely." As punishment for his insolence he was forced to pick out thirty-seven teenage males, who were shot with their hands tied behind their backs. The rest of the villagers were taken to the outskirts of the village, robbed of their possessions and ordered to leave. Homes were burned to the ground and the village was cleansed of its inhabitants.[39] There is no consensus on the number of people killed that day. *The Palmach Book* cites seventy. Other sources believe that figure is too low.

A few weeks later Hans Lebrecht was ordered by the commander of his military unit to build a pump station and divert the deserted village's stream in order to supply water to his battalion. He described what he saw:

> The village had been totally destroyed, and among the debris there were many bodies. In particular, we found many bodies of women, children and babies near the local mosque. I convinced the army to burn the bodies.[40]

Today Ayn al-Zaytun, along with other forgotten villages, is hidden beneath the Birya Forest. The JNF (Jewish National Fund) welcomes visitors to the area:

> Ein Zeitun has become one of the most attractive spots within the recreational ground as it harbors large picnic tables and ample parking for the disabled. It is located where once stood the settlement Ein Zeitun, where Jews used to live ever since the medieval times and until the 18th century. There were four abortive [Jewish] settlement attempts. The parking lot has biological toilets and playgrounds. Next to the parking lot, a memorial stands in memory of the soldiers who fell in the Six-Day War.[41]

Pappe replies to the JNF's description:

> Fancifully meshing history and tourist tips, the text totally erases from Israel's collective memory the thriving Palestinian community Jewish troops wiped out within a few hours.[42]

* * * *

Dawaymeh is a Palestinian village a few miles west of Hebron. By late 1948, due to the flight of refugees, its population had swelled from 2,000 to 6,000. On October 28 Battalion 89 of Brigade Eight entered the village in twenty armored cars. Their order from Chief of Staff Yadin was: "Your preparations should include psychological warfare and 'treatment' (*tipul*) of citizens as an integral part of the operation."[43] The soldiers' aim was to expel the entire population in one hour. When that failed, they began to indiscriminately fire their automatic weapons. By the time they were finished, hundreds of dead bodies were piled in the village mosque and on the streets. Jewish soldiers who participated in the atrocities "reported horrific scenes: babies whose skulls were cracked open, women raped or burned alive in houses, and men stabbed to death."[44]

* * * *

Ariel Sharon, as a young military leader of special commando Unit 101, was involved in a number of raids against Palestinian targets. In 1953 Sharon obtained permission from his superiors to attack the Palestinian refugee camp of al-Burg, which was alleged to be a base for infiltrators. When he described the operation to his soldiers, one of them protested that Sharon's purpose seemed to be to kill as many civilians as possible. The *Paratroopers' Book*:

> As an ex-Palmach who believed in the purity of arms he refused to participate in an expedition directed not against enemy soldiers but against the civilian population. Arik [Sharon's nickname] did not force him to take part. In a heated discussion, Shlomo Baum [Sharon's adjutant] hurled a remark at him: "There are no pure or impure arms; there are only clean weapons that work when you need them and dirty weapons that jam the moment you fire."[45]

Sharon rejected the soldier's argument and told his men that the women of the camp were whores who served the infiltrators. Fifteen people, mostly women and children, were subsequently killed.[46]

"Infiltrator" was a deliberately misleading term, meant to mischaracterize a group of people as having deadly intentions toward Jews. In reality, they were primarily *fellaheen* (peasants) who had been driven from their villages. Poor and hungry, they were attempting to return to their homes to recover possessions left behind, to harvest their crops or graze their flocks of sheep.[*] IDF orders to front line units,

---

[*] Morris, *Righteous Victims*, p. 260: "In the summer of 1948, refugees – propelled by

however, beginning in 1949 and lasting until 1956, were "at night to fire at anything that moved, no questions asked, and during daylight hours to fire at every adult male."[47] The troops also had permission to fire from distances of hundreds of yards even though their targets could not be distinguished as to age or gender. Soldiers often took advantage of this liberal policy by shooting at farmers and shepherds in no-man's land or across the border with Jordan. The Jordanians continually complained to the Israelis that Jewish soldiers were injuring or killing the innocent. Foreign Minister Moshe Sharett also criticized Israel's unforgiving policy. Moshe Dayan, at the time the head of the IDF Southern Command, responded to Sharett with the following explanation:

> Are [we justified] in opening fire on the Arabs who cross [the border] to reap the crops they planted in our territory; they, their women, and their children? Will this stand up to moral scrutiny . . .? We shoot at those from among the 200,000 hungry Arabs who cross the line [to graze their flocks] – will this stand up to moral review? Arabs cross to collect the grain that they left in the abandoned villages and we set mines for them and they go back without an arm or a leg. . . . [it may be that this] cannot pass review, but I know of no other method of guarding the borders. If the Arab shepherds and harvesters are allowed to cross the borders, then tomorrow the State of Israel will have no borders.[48]

During these years, between 2,700 and 5,000 Arabs were killed. Most were unarmed.[49]

---

poverty, homesickness or the desire for revenge – began to infiltrate in large numbers into Israel." P. 269: "During 1948-9, most of the infiltrators crossed the borders to harvest crops left behind, to plant new crops in their abandoned lands, or to retrieve goods. Many others came to resettle in their old villages or elsewhere inside Israel, or to visit relatives, or simply to get a glimpse of their abandoned homes and fields." P. 270: "Most of the infiltrators were unarmed individuals, though it appears that the proportion who came armed and in groups steadily increased after 1950, largely in reaction to the IDF's violent measures. . . . Only a very small proportion, certainly far less than 10 percent, of the infiltrators came with the express purpose of attacking people or sabotaging Israeli targets."

* * * *

Another opportunity for Sharon to terrorize civilians occurred when he decided to avenge the deaths of a woman and two children from the Jewish settlement of Yehuda, near Tel Aviv. The three had been killed on October 12, 1953 when a grenade was lobbed into their house. The government of Jordan condemned the murders and offered to open their borders to Israeli police so they could track down the criminals. Israel declined. Late at night on October 14, Unit 101 crossed the border into Jordan (the West Bank) and entered the Palestinian village of Qibya. They booby-trapped about forty-five houses with dynamite and began firing their weapons into the homes. When they were finished, sixty-seven people, mostly women and children, were dead. No casualties were sustained by the Israelis.[50]

U.N. observers arrived at the scene within hours of the killings. They reported:

> Bullet-riddled bodies near the doorways and multiple bullet hits on the doors of the demolished houses indicated that the inhabitants had been forced to remain inside until their homes were blown up over them. . . . Witnesses were uniform in describing their experience as a night of horror, during which Israeli soldiers moved about in their village blowing up buildings, firing into doorways and windows with automatic weapons and throwing hand grenades.[51]

In the investigation that followed, Sharon claimed that he had given orders to his soldiers to check each house and warn the occupants to leave. The soldiers denied receiving such an order.[52] The Israeli Defense Forces Archives:

> Sharon and the IDF subsequently claimed the villagers had hidden in cellars and attics and the troops had been unaware of this when they blew up the buildings. But in truth the troops had moved from house to house, firing through windows and doorways, and Jordanian pathologists reported that most of the dead had been killed by bullets and shrapnel rather than by falling masonry or explosions. In any event, the operational orders, from CO Central Command to the units involved, dated

October 13, had explicitly ordered "destruction and maximum killing."[53]

On November 24 the United Nations passed Security Council Resolution 101, which expressed "the strongest censure of that action." The *New York Post*, a decidedly pro-Israel newspaper, compared the massacre at Qibya to that at Lidice.[54*]

Prime Minister Ben-Gurion offered a fictionalized account of what had happened, claiming that a thorough investigation by his government had determined that Israeli soldiers could not have committed the massacre because none were absent from their barracks the night in question. He blamed angry frontier settlers for the attack at Qibya. Most of them were "Jewish refugees from Arab countries or survivors of Nazi concentration camps. . . ."[55]

The Israeli public and military took great pride in their accomplishment and Ben-Gurion, after meeting with Sharon, was "satisfied to discover that Sharon and his family belonged to the 'correct' political stream (the Laborite one). . . ."[56] Henceforward, Ben-Gurion "gave Sharon his personal protection and maintained a special relationship with him, which Sharon used every time he got into trouble following one of his adventurous and unauthorized military operations."[57]

In 1955 the Israeli government admitted that "there had been nothing reckless or impulsive about the lethal raids across the borders. On the contrary, the policy of reprisals is the fruit of cold, unemotional political and psychological reasoning."[58]

* * * *

The establishment of Israel in 1948 brought military rule into the lives of its Arab citizens, who were looked upon as security risks. Arab villages near the Jordanian border were subject to a permanent 9 PM to 6

---

* On June 4, 1942 SS Officer Reinhard Heydrich died of mortal wounds incurred in Prague on May 27. The assassins were Free Czech agents who had been trained in England. In retaliation, the Nazis hunted down the Czechs, murdering them and 1,000 others suspected of involvement. As a further reprisal, Hitler falsely charged that the Czechoslovakian village of Lidice was complicit in Heydrich's assassination. The village was completely leveled, building by building, and its existence removed from maps. All 172 males over the age of 16 were killed, and the women and younger children were deported to concentration camps.

AM curfew. On October 29, 1956, the first day of the Suez War, the starting time was moved back to 5 PM.* The mukhtar (headman) of one of the border villages, Kfar Qassem, told the Israeli commander in charge that he had only been informed about the new curfew time at four-thirty in the afternoon; and that the fellaheen working in the fields had not been informed at all, nor was there a way to inform them. As the workers trickled back to the village, the Israeli border police gathered each group together, lined up the men, women and children and shot them dead. Everyone received the same treatment. In total, the police shot forty-seven people. There was no ambiguity about the instructions they had received: "Cut them down."[59] Afterwards, Moshe Sharett – at the time not a member of the cabinet – exclaimed: "My God, what will become of our little country!"[60] The Israeli government unsuccessfully tried to hide the massacre from the media and the public. *Davar* editorialized:

> How can it be, then, that normal people, our own boys, would commit a criminal act of this sort? There is no escaping the truth: not enough has been done to inoculate this nation against the dulling of the moral sense, against the tendency to ignore the holiness of human life when speaking of an enemy or a potential enemy.[61+]

Six weeks later, forced to make a statement, Ben-Gurion spoke to the Knesset: "There is no people in the world that values human life more than does the Jewish people . . . . We have learned that man was created in the image of God and no one knows what color skin Adam had."[62⊥] Many throughout Israel compared Kfar Qassem to Nazi atrocities. This was not the first time such a comparison was made. In a 1948 cabinet meeting agriculture minister Aharon Zisling had said:

---

* Israel, Britain and France attacked Egyptian forces in the Sinai in retaliation for the nationalization of the Suez Canal and blockade of the Straits of Tiran by Egypt.

+ *Davar* was a Hebrew daily newspaper that was published in Palestine/Israel between 1925 and 1996.

⊥ Author's note: That the statement by Ben-Gurion was purely political can be inferred from how he often referred to Jews from Arab countries: "Avak-Adam," which means subhuman. Giladi, p. 17.

I have not always agreed when the term *Nazi* was applied to the British. I would not want to use that expression with regard to them, even though they committed Nazi acts. But Nazi acts have been committed by Jews as well, and I am deeply shocked.[63]

Placed on trial, the soldiers received sentences of seven to seventeen years, which were reduced on appeal. Within three years of the Kfar Qassem murders, as a result of pardons, every soldier was free.[64] Some went on to hold high ranking positions in the IDF.[65] The soldiers' commander, Colonel Yisachar Shadmi was acquitted of murder but found guilty of having overstepped his authority. For his punishment he was fined one grush, equal to a penny in the old Israeli currency.[66] In rendering his verdict, Judge Benyamin Halevy stated:

> The hallmark of manifest illegality is that it must wave like a black flag over the given order, a warning that says: "forbidden.". . . Illegality that pierces the eye and revolts the heart, if the eye is not blind and the heart is not impenetrable or corrupt – this is the measure of manifest illegality needed to override the soldier's duty to obey and to impose on him criminal liability for his action.[67]

After Kfar Qassem, *Purity of Arms* became formalized into the *Spirit of the IDF*. Remembering Kfar Qassem, author and journalist Tom Segev wrote in 2006:

> But not every soldier hears during the course of his service that there are orders that must not be carried out; the IDF does its best to wear down any conscientious objection; soldiers shoot at Palestinians as part of the routine of the occupation; police officers working in Arab communities in Israel sometimes have a light hand on the trigger; Avigdor Lieberman is in the government.[68]

* * * *

A few weeks after Israel's victory in the 1967 Six-Day War, Amos Oz and Avraham Shapira began visiting kibbutzim, where they interviewed soldiers who had fought in the war. In all, they interviewed 140 people, most of whom were officers. Some of the interviews were made into a book titled *Soldiers Talk*. Their work struck a nerve in Israel and became a bestseller, so successful that it was translated into several languages and adapted for the stage in New York City. Tom Segev explains that "*Soldiers Talk* reflected an emotional need to talk about the experience of war and to expose feelings and thoughts. The interview participants seemed gentle, peace-loving, awkward, thoughtful, sad, sensitive to human rights, and tormented about the necessity of war and the cost of victory. . . ."[69] The soldiers spoke of their initial enthusiasm for war and how their enthusiasm turned to hate; of fear and how they overcame it; how they had become part of a war machine; how they denied their feelings and how they devalued human life; and how the soldiers who, together, face death, develop a brotherhood with each other. Golda Meir called *Soldiers Talk* a "holy book" and said "We have been blessed to have such sons as these."[70]

Later it was revealed that "'extremely graphic' testimony about war crimes had been omitted" and that the words of some of the soldiers had been altered. For example, "Some terribly negative things are revealed. When you see soldiers shooting at defenseless civilians . . . elderly people" became "Some very negative things are revealed." And "Unleashing that really bordered on cruelty . . . I know that one squad commander . . . some guy, around forty, put his hands up – so he shot a round into his stomach. . . . There was a kind of unleashing . . . grenades in all the houses . . . just burning houses for no reason" became "And there was a kind of unleashing . . . unbelievable, really. . . ."

"We had to take really drastic measures . . . blowing up houses and searching houses . . . and extreme things. . . .There was a situation where human life played no role. You could kill. There was no law" became "There was no law."

With regard to Arabs attempting to cross the Jordan River, the book's editors changed the words "to kill" to "to prevent the crossing of." "There was an explicit, written order . . . as of today, whoever crosses the Jordan – shoot. Doesn't matter who he is, what he is, how or why" became "There was an order not to allow anyone to cross the Jordan except over the bridges. I know that we carried out the spirit of the order, without hurting people."

A soldier described an incident where his unit came upon a wounded Syrian soldier. While they were arguing over what to do one of the soldiers shot the Syrian in the head. The book changed the story to read: "One guy suggested killing him. Of course we wouldn't allow it." The book omitted another excerpt where a soldier, when asked how he could kill said "just like I kill flies on a screen."[71] Comparisons to the Gestapo or S.S. did not make their way into the final draft of *Soldiers Talk*.

The power of literature such as *Soldiers Talk* cannot be overestimated. After the Six-Day War, the IDF was highly revered by the Israeli public. With almost mythic power and speed, triumphant on the battlefield, the armed forces had rescued their country from a peril many feared would lead to another Holocaust. *Soldiers Talk* demonstrated that the soldiers were not only courageous, they were humane, fair and innocent; they treated their enemy with respect. *Soldiers Talk* showed the world how moral Israel's armed forces were, that they were beyond reproach.

* * * *

Aharon Bachar, a former columnist for *Yediot Aharonot*, recounts a meeting that took place in 1982 between Labor Party leaders ("including some of the most noted hawks, such as Golda Meir's adviser Israel Galili") and Prime Minister Begin.[72] The laborites provided Begin with "detailed accounts of terrorist acts [against Arabs] in the conquered territories."[73] They described the collective punishment that had taken place in the Palestinian town of Halhul in 1979:

> The men were taken from their houses beginning at midnight in pajamas, in the cold. The notables and other men were concentrated in the square of the mosque and held there until morning. Meanwhile men of the Border Guards [noted for their cruelty] broke into houses; beating people with shouts and curses. During the many hours that hundreds of people were kept in the mosque square, they were ordered to urinate and excrete on one another and also to sing Hatikva [The "Hope," the national anthem of Israel] and to call out "Long Live the State of Israel." Several times people were beaten and ordered to crawl on the ground. Some were even ordered to lick the earth. .

On Holocaust day, the 27 of Nissan [the date in the Jewish calendar], the people who were arrested were ordered to write numbers on their hands with their own hands, in memory of the Jews in the extermination camps.[74]

Peace Now reported an incident in which young recruits were given clubs and told: "Boys, off you go to assault the locals."[75] The Labor Party leaders' report also discussed the beatings, torture and humiliation of prisoners and how settlers were allowed into prisons to participate in those abuses; it described "how the settlers brutalize the local inhabitants with impunity, even in the case of a settler who killed an Arab, whose identity is known but who is not arrested."[76] In another of a myriad of incidents, "settlers caught an old man who had protested when his lands were taken and shaved off his beard – just what Polish anti-Semites did to Jews."[77] An article in *Davar* said: "Some of us Israelis behave like the worst kind of anti-Semites, whose name cannot be mentioned here, like the very people who painted a picture of the Jew as a sub-human creature . . ."[78]

* * * *

Pulitzer prize-winning reporter and former *New York Times* Middle East bureau chief, Chris Hedges interviewed a Jewish woman who was born in Long Island, New York to a "Zionist-oriented family." Allegra Pacheco attended Barnard College before earning a law degree from Columbia University. She practiced law for a few years in the United States before immigrating to Israel. After passing the national bar exam, she moved to Bethlehem, where she became the first Israeli attorney ever to have a law office in Palestinian Territory. The cases she dealt with focused on the injustices Palestinians are routinely subjected to: home demolition, land confiscation, torture, and imprisonment without charge.

One of her clients was Palestinian human rights activist Abed al-Rahman al-Ahmar. Abed had recently been interrogated and tortured. Soon after their meeting in 1996 he was sent to prison for two-and-a-half years. After his release Abed and Allegra fell in love and married. Allegra became pregnant. Eight months into the pregnancy Abed was arrested and sent to prison for the thirteenth time. As of the summer of 2006, he was still incarcerated, cramped into a tent in the desert with twenty other men. His captors do not provide heat for the cold winters or cooling for the hot summers. Since prisoner health is not a priority for the Israelis, nothing is done about the open sewer or the disease-carrying mosquitoes. Abed does not know what he is charged with. That is a secret the Israelis keep to themselves.

Allegra gave birth to their first child while Abed was in captivity. She has not been able to mail photographs of their son to Abed because the Israelis have told her the prison has no mailing address. At the time of the interview Abed's imprisonment had recently been extended for a second six-month period (Israeli law permits incarceration to be extended for six months at a time without charge or explanation).

Abed has been tortured during four of his prison stays. When he was sixteen he was arrested for throwing stones at Israeli soldiers. While in detention he was forced to sit in contorted, painful positions with his head covered by a bag soaked in urine. Amnesty International has designated him a prisoner of conscience. He has filed a lawsuit against the Israeli government, which is pending. The Israelis have told Allegra that if Abed drops the lawsuit he will be released. The couple has refused the offer.[79]

Because Allegra is Jewish and has American citizenship she is more fortunate than other women. Sometimes, when Israeli authorities want to force a confession from an uncooperative Palestinian prisoner, they threaten or even arrest his wife. This tactic is a violation of the International Covenant on Civil and Political Rights, which stipulates in Article 7 that: "*No one shall be subjected to torture or to cruel, inhuman or degrading treatment or punishment...,*" and the Fourth Geneva Convention, which forbids: "*outrages upon personal dignity, in particular humiliating and degrading treatment* [Article 3(1)(c):]."[80]

* * * *

Purity of Arms is an attempt to integrate the ideal of morality into the social and legal framework of a people whose history bears the scars of arguably the greatest immorality known to man. But the ideal is not reality. Of all the massacres and atrocities only Deir Yassin was willingly acknowledged by Israel's leaders and only for tactical reasons intended to aid in the dispossession of another people. In general, events that contradict *purity of arms* are rejected as lies, ignored or explained away. The belief that one's tradition is rooted in moral behavior is a critical aspect of identity that must be preserved. Journalist and author Sylvain Cypel:

> The concept of purity of arms . . . led to the ignoring of the new expulsion in 1967, later totally banished from collective memory, of some 250,000 additional Palestinians and the Arab population of the Golan, and it enabled public opinion to remain indifferent during the bombing of Beirut in 1982. Ultimately, the concept of the purity of the Israeli army served as a constant, astonishing self-justification in the two intifadas.[81*]

* * * *

During the 2006 month-long war that ravaged Lebanon, seven-thousand Israeli bomb and missile strikes, supplemented by sea and infantry attacks, killed over 1,100 Lebanese and wounded about 4,400. The dead and wounded were predominantly civilians. Tens of thousands of homes were destroyed and one million people displaced. On the Israeli side, Hezbollah rocket attacks killed forty-three Israeli civilians and twelve IDF soldiers, and hundreds of civilians were wounded.[82]

Amnesty International described the effects on Lebanon:

> [T]he country's infrastructure suffered destruction on a catastrophic scale. Israeli forces pounded buildings into the ground, reducing entire neighborhoods to rubble and turning villages and towns into ghost towns, as their inhabitants fled the bombardments. Main roads, bridges and petrol stations were blown to bits. Entire families were killed in air strikes on their homes or in their vehicles while fleeing the aerial assaults on their villages. Scores lay buried beneath the rubble of their houses for weeks, as the Red Cross and other rescue workers were prevented from accessing the areas by continuing Israeli strikes.[83]

Israel claimed that the destruction throughout Lebanon was a consequence of the enemy's use of human shields to camouflage rocket launches. The IDF argued – and I enthusiastically agreed – that by embedding themselves within the civilian population Hezbollah had

---

* Author's note: more than 100,000 people fled the Golan Heights and 11,000 fled the Gaza Strip in the wake of the 1967 war.

committed war crimes. Therefore, they were the ones responsible for the civilian deaths, not the Israeli infantry or air force, which are taught not to target defenseless citizens.

Human Rights Watch conducted a detailed study on the basis of investigations by researchers who stayed in Lebanon during the war and others who joined them at war's end. They concluded:

> We did not find . . . that Hezbollah routinely located its rockets inside or near civilian homes. Rather, we found strong evidence that Hezbollah had stored most of its rockets in bunkers and weapon storage facilities located in uninhabited fields and valleys. Similarly, while we found that Hezbollah fighters launched rockets from villages on some occasions . . . when it purposefully and repeatedly fired rockets from the vicinity of UN observer posts with the possible intent of deterring Israeli counterfire, we did not find evidence that Hezbollah otherwise fired its rockets from populated areas. The available evidence indicates that in the vast majority of cases Hezbollah fighters left populated civilian areas as soon as the fighting started and fired the majority of their rockets from pre-prepared positions in largely unpopulated valleys and fields outside villages.[84]

The report also found:

> [T]he primary reason for the high Lebanese civilian death toll during the conflict was Israel's frequent failure to abide by a fundamental obligation of the laws of war, the duty to distinguish at all times between military targets that can be legitimately attacked, and civilians, who are not subject to attack. This was compounded by Israel's failure to take adequate safeguards to prevent civilian casualties.[85]*

HRW also refuted the Israeli assertion that their bombardment was carried out only after civilians had evacuated their homes:

---

* Israel refused to cooperate with HRW's repeated requests for information that would clarify the specific causes of civilian casualties. In contrast, NATO, the U.S. and coalition military personnel did provide HRW with relevant information for Kosovo (1999), Afghanistan (2001) and Iraq (2003); HRW, "Why They Died," Part VII.

It is questionable whether Israeli officials really believed the assumption that there were no Lebanese civilians left in southern Lebanon, or simply adopted such a formal assumption to defend their actions. Evidence suggests that Israeli officials knew that the assertion that all civilians had fled was erroneous. At the time of the Israeli attacks in southern Lebanon, stories about Lebanese civilians dying in Israeli strikes or trapped in southern Lebanon filled the Israeli and international media. In addition, foreign embassies were in regular contact with Israeli diplomats with requests to assist with the evacuation of their nationals caught in the fighting in southern Lebanon. And in some instances, Israel seemed to know exactly how many people remained in a village. . . . Israel must have known from its past conflicts in southern Lebanon that a civilian population is rarely able or willing to leave its homes according to timetables laid down by a belligerent military.[86]

The Israeli military did warn the population when it was about to bomb their neighborhoods, but HRW determined that the population was not given sufficient time to leave the area. They also determined that the warning flyers were too ambiguous to be helpful.[87*] Additionally, despite appeals from the U.N., Israel failed to create safe passage corridors in southern Lebanon. Making matters worse, Israeli forces attacked fleeing civilians.[+]

On August 11, 2006, the United Nations passed Security Council Resolution 1701, the permanent ceasefire, which called for an end to

---

* The following flyer was dropped over Lebanon on July 25 and also broadcast over the radio: "To the People of Lebanon Pay Attention to these instructions! The IDF will intensify its activities and will heavily bomb the entire area from which rockets are being launched against the State of Israel. Anyone present in these areas is endangering his life! In addition, any pickup truck or truck traveling south of the Litani River will be suspected of transporting rockets and weapons and may be bombed. You must know that anyone traveling in a pickup truck or truck is endangering his life. The State of Israel." Cited by HRW, "Why They Died," Part VII.

+ Israeli Justice Minister Haim Ramon said: "Anyone left in South Lebanon is a terrorist." David Wearing, "Britain's Role in the Israeli-Hezbollah War," *The Democrat's Diary*, September 7, 2006; cited by Sultan, p. 40.

hostilities as of the morning of August 14. Israel took advantage of the seventy-two hour period that followed to drop hundreds of thousands of cluster bombs onto the countryside. Each cluster bomb contains hundreds of bomblets that can cover areas as wide as one square kilometer.[88] Thirty to forty percent of the bomblets fail to detonate on impact, which makes them ticking time bombs. If someone passing by has the misfortune to kick or pick up one of these inconspicuous objects, which are about the size of a soda can, they are likely to set off an explosion. Since the ceasefire began, more than two hundred Lebanese have been maimed and thirty killed.[89] The UN and Lebanese army have been clearing areas throughout Lebanon but the bomblets are so spread out and in such abundance that the UN estimates it will be years before Lebanon is free of them.[90*] According to the *American Task Force for Lebanon*:

> The UN has been "screaming" for information on where Israel fired cluster bombs. Israel is reluctant to give up battlefield information that would provide the dates and coordinates, because this would leave them open to international and humanitarian scrutiny on its use of cluster bombs in civilian areas.[91]

U.N. aid official, Jan Egeland called Israel's use of cluster bombs "shocking and completely immoral."[92]

* * * *

Hezbollah enjoyed substantial popular support from the Shiite quarter of Dahiya, in the southern part of Beirut. Israeli war planes, equipped with American-made GBU-28 bunker-busting bombs, utterly destroyed the quarter.[+] The events at Dahiya have become a model for Israeli military planning. In 2008, *Haaretz*, *Yedioth Aharonot* and the *Jerusalem Post* all reported on Israel's newly named Dahiya doctrine (or strategy). *Haaretz* quoted IDF Northern Command Chief Gadi Eisenkot:

---

* On January 20, 2007, the U.S. State Department acknowledged that Israel had violated the U.S. Arms Export Control Act by blanketing Lebanon with these American-made munitions. Sultan, p. 127.

+ The U.S. also provided Israel with $300 million in aviation fuel that enabled Israel to destroy more of Lebanon's infrastructure. Patrick Seale, "Why is Israel Destroying Lebanon?" *Al-Hayat*, July 21, 2006; cited by Sultan, pp. 113-4.

Breakthrough

What happened in the Beirut suburb of Dahiya in 2006 will happen in every village from which shots are fired in the direction of Israel. . . . We will wield disproportionate power against every village from which shots are fired on Israel, and cause immense damage and destruction. From our perspective, these are military bases. This isn't a suggestion. This is a plan that has already been authorized.[93]

YNetNews, operated by *Yedioth Aharanot*, reported:

IDF Northern Command Chief Gadi Eisenkot uttered clear words that essentially mean the following: In the next clash with Hizbullah we won't bother to hunt for tens of thousands of rocket launchers and we won't spill our soldiers' blood in attempts to overtake fortified Hizbullah positions. Rather, we shall destroy Lebanon and won't be deterred by the protests of the "world. . . ." This strategy is not a threat uttered by an impassioned officer, but rather, an approved plan. . . . In practical terms, the Palestinians in Gaza are all Khaled Mashaal, the Lebanese are all Nasrallah, and the Iranians are all Ahmadinejad.[94]*

The *Jerusalem Post*:

In any future conflict with Hizbullah, Israel will likely cite the Shi'ite group's increasing influence within the Lebanese cabinet as a legitimate reason to target Lebanon's entire infrastructure, government sources have told The Jerusalem Post.[95]

While ignoring the fact that Hezbollah's existence is a direct outgrowth of Israel's 1982 invasion of Lebanon, the Dahiya doctrine enunciates a philosophy that is commonly characterized as terrorism: the targeting of non-combatant civilian populations, including women and children.

Moshe Dayan said: "Israel must be like a mad dog, too dangerous to bother."[96] Moshe Sharett, while Prime Minister, wrote of his Defense Minister Pinhas Lavon: "'[He] constantly preached for acts of madness'

---

* Khaled Mashaal, the leader of Hamas, is currently in exile in Syria. Hassan Nasrallah is the leader of Hezbollah.

[or] 'going crazy' if Israel were ever crossed."[97] Dayan and Lavon were advocates of the idea that the most effective way to subdue resistance was to instill fear in the minds of the enemy. If Lebanon was a new model for deterrence, *Operation Cast Lead*, which began on December 27, 2008, was its advanced implementation.

Breakthrough

– 9 –

Gaza

*Everything we're doing, everything, everything, is shameful;
we're humiliating the Palestinians as individuals and as a
collectivity. None of us could endure what we're making them go
through.*[1] Avraham Shalom, former head of Shin Bet (ISA or
Israeli Security Agency)

The Gaza Strip, approximately one hundred forty square miles in size, is
home to one and a half million people, more than fifty percent of whom
are under the age of sixteen. It is one-eleventh the size of Rhode Island,
the smallest state in the United States, but has fifty percent more
inhabitants. The Gaza Strip is one of the most densely populated places
on Earth.

When World War I came to an end and the Ottoman Empire began
to break apart, Gaza was taken over by the British Mandate. In 1948,
when the Mandate ended and the Arab-Israeli war began, Gaza became
home to large numbers of Palestinian refugees. The area fell under the
control of Egypt in 1949, when the Cairo government signed an armistice
agreement with Israel that ended hostilities between the two countries.
Seven years later, Israel's victory in the Suez War gave it control over
Gaza (and the Sinai). Constrained by the Soviet Union and the United
States, it returned the land to the Egyptians. The Jewish State regained
control over Gaza with its overwhelming victory in the 1967 war. Gaza
became a closed military area. Anyone wishing to leave needed to first
obtain a permit from Israeli administrators.

In the 1970s Israeli Jews began to establish settlements in Gaza. In
1981, obliged to honor the terms of the Egypt-Israel peace treaty, Israel
ordered the removal of all settlements from the Sinai Peninsula. Some of
the dislocated settlers moved to Gaza. To make way for the growth of the
illegal Jewish settlements, Gazan families were forced to move, greatly
increasing the population density of the remainder of the Gaza Strip. By
2005, twenty-five percent of Gaza's land and most of its water resources
had been expropriated by eight thousand Jewish settlers. In August of that
year Israeli prime minister Ariel Sharon, under international pressure,
followed through with his disengagement plan and the settlers were

relocated. This was supposed to have marked an end to Gaza's status as a closed military area.

Many point to the Gaza disengagement as an example of Israel's sincerity in trying to make peace with the Palestinians. Some claim that, as far as Gaza is concerned, the occupation ended with the withdrawal of Israeli troops. If this were true, it would be an enormous relief to the citizens of Gaza, who have endured years of brutal oppression. In 1996 Samir Quota, the director of the Gaza Community Mental Health Programme (GCMHP), described the suffering of Gaza's children:

> You have to remember that 90 percent of children two years old or more have experienced – some many, many times – the [Israeli] army breaking into the home, beating relatives, destroying things. Many were beaten themselves, had bones broken, were shot, tear gassed, or had these things happen to siblings and neighbors.... The emotional aspect of the child is affected by the [lack of] security. He needs to feel safe. We see the consequences later if he does not. In our research, we have found that children who are exposed to trauma tend to be more extreme in their behaviors and, later, in their political beliefs.[2]*

Israel's defenders' trust that the disengagement signified the Jewish state's peaceful intentions as well as an end to the occupation of Gaza was belied by the actual terms of the disengagement plan and by the statements of ranking Israeli officials. From the *Disengagement Plan of Prime Minister Ariel Sharon – Revised, May 28, 2004*:

> Israel will guard and monitor the external land perimeter of the Gaza Strip, will continue to maintain exclusive authority in Gaza air space, and will continue to exercise security activity in the sea off the coast of the Gaza Strip.[3]

In speaking about the disengagement with Ari Shavit of *Haaretz*, Dov Weisglass, Ariel Sharon's chief adviser, said:

---

* GCMHP was established in 1990 "to provide comprehensive community mental health services - therapy, training and research - to the population of the Gaza Strip."

The disengagement is actually formaldehyde. It supplies the amount of formaldehyde that's necessary so that there will not be a political process with the Palestinians.[4]

To Shavit's question: "So you have carried out the maneuver of the century? And all of it with authority and permission," Weisglass answered:

When you say 'maneuver,' it doesn't sound nice. It sounds like you said one thing and something else came out. But that's the whole point. After all, what have I been shouting for the past year? That I found a device, in cooperation with the management of the world, to ensure that there will be no stopwatch here. That there will be no timetable to implement the [West Bank] settlers' nightmare. I have postponed that nightmare indefinitely. Because what I effectively agreed to with the Americans was that part of the settlements would not be dealt with at all, and the rest will not be dealt with until the Palestinians turn into Finns. That is the significance of what we did. The significance is the freezing of the political process. And when you freeze that process you prevent the establishment of a Palestinian state and you prevent a discussion about the refugees, the borders and Jerusalem. Effectively, this whole package that is called the Palestinian state, with all that it entails, has been removed from our agenda indefinitely. And all this with authority and permission. All with a presidential blessing and the ratification of both houses of Congress.[5]

In his conversation with Shavit, Weisglass couched his comments within the context of terrorism, that the freezing of the political process was necessary to prevent a Palestinian terrorist state. Whether Weisglass actually believed his own rhetoric is questionable. What is not questionable is that treating human beings with no regard for their welfare, collectively punishing them and denying them opportunities for a decent livelihood are guaranteed to produce the type of frustration and despair that lead to violence.

In accord with Weisglass's thesis, Alvaro de Soto said:

Sharon used the disengagement to gain vital concessions from the U.S. – including the Bush letter of assurances on retention of settlement blocs and non-return of refugees to Israel – while proceeding with the construction of the [separation] barrier and the implantation of more settlers in the West Bank.[6]

Currently professor of international relations at Oxford University, Avi Shlaim is a former Israeli soldier who served in the 1960s and is widely regarded as one of the leading authorities on the Israel-Palestinian conflict. His view of the Gaza pullout:

> Ariel Sharon decided to withdraw from Gaza unilaterally, not as a contribution, as he claimed, to a two-state solution. The withdrawal from Gaza took place in the context of unilateral Israeli action in what was seen as Israeli national interest. There were no negotiations with the Palestinian Authority on an overall settlement. The withdrawal from Gaza was not a prelude to further withdrawals from the other occupied territories, but a prelude to further expansion, further consolidation of Israel's control over the West Bank. In the year after the withdrawal from Gaza, 12,000 new settlers went to live on the West Bank. So I see the withdrawal from Gaza in the summer of 2005 as part of a unilateral Israeli attempt to redraw the borders of Greater Israel and to shun any negotiations and compromise with the Palestinian Authority.[7]

Tanya Reinhart:

> There is no doubt that Sharon openly used the Gaza disengagement plan to expand and strengthen Israel's grip of the West Bank . . . . and even in the eyes of the most committed Israeli expansionists, it is clear that Israel does not benefit from this piece of land, one of the most densely populated areas in the world, and (unlike the West Bank) lacking any natural resources.[8]

In addition to putting an end to the political process, the disengagement was calculated to extricate Israel from its responsibility for the lives of Gaza's residents. Articles 55 and 56 of the Fourth Geneva Convention confer responsibility for the well being of the occupied population on the occupying power, including "ensuring the food and medical supplies of the population" as well as health and hygiene. Ariel Sharon:

> There are today 1.8 million Palestinians supported solely by aid from various international organizations. These organizations told us clearly that if we continue to hold on to the territories and run everything, they can't give that aid.[9]

The disengagement solved this problem for Sharon: "the disengagement move will obviate the claims about Israel with regard to its responsibility for the Palestinians in the Gaza Strip."[10]

The Jewish settlements in the Gaza Strip had served as natural security zones, which prevented Palestinians from launching homemade rockets deeper into Israeli territory. Once the evacuation was complete the IDF decided to create buffer zones near the Gaza-Israel border. The residents of two Palestinian towns were forced to relocate. Palestinians who entered the zones would be risking their lives. In the five months following the disengagement IDF soldiers killed nine unarmed civilians, including an eight year-old child and four other minors. The victims were in the area of a perimeter fence. Four were shot trying to cross the fence and enter Israel to find work. The others were between one hundred and five hundred meters away and had no intention of coming any closer. The IDF admitted that the civilians had no weapons and that their soldiers did not issue any warnings before the deadly shots were fired. The failure to distinguish between combatants and non-combatants is illegal under international law.[11]

Buffer zones were not enough to satisfy Israel. It decided to encourage Gaza's civilian population to pressure Hamas to end its rocket attacks. In September 2005, one month after the evacuation of the settlers, Israeli air force jets began flying over Gaza at high speeds and low altitudes. Their purpose was to create "sound bombs" by breaking the sound barrier. Chris McGreal of the *Guardian* reported twenty-nine sound bombs, or sonic booms, over five days in late September and twenty-eight over a week-long period in late October-early November. The bombs induce widespread fear among the population, especially children, who are often traumatized. Other symptoms include nosebleeds, miscarriages, anxiety attacks, muscle spasms, temporary loss of hearing, and breathing and heart problems.[12]

Dr. Eyad El-Sarraj, founder of the Gaza Community Mental Health Programme, gave a firsthand account of the terror inflicted on Gaza's citizens, especially the most vulnerable:

> Gaza was awakened from its dreams of liberation with horrible explosions which have shattered our skies, shaken our buildings, broken our windows, and thrown the place into panic. We have been bombed since Friday 23 September, day and night. Usually between 2:00-4:00am, between 6:30-8:00 in the morning during the time children go to school, and in the afternoon or early evening . . . Gaza is in a state of panic, children are restless, crying, frightened and many are wetting their beds. Some children are afraid to leave home and refuse to go to school. Many are dazed, pale, insomniac and have a poor appetite. Some pregnant women reported colics and some were admitted to the hospital with precipitated labour. Many people complain of ear pressure. All are stunned. Israel's new method of creating intentional sonic booms in our skies was never used before the disengagement, so as not to alarm the Israeli settlers and their children. Israel is inducing learned helplessness to the Palestinians in Gaza with the aim of making the whole population captive to fear and paralysis.[13]

U.N. Middle East Envoy de Soto told Israel that he was "deeply concerned at the impact on children, particularly infants, of the use of sonic booms."[14] He also emphasized the United Nations' call for Israel to stop its deafening assault. Israeli army intelligence issued a public response:

> We are trying to send a message in a way that doesn't harm people. . . . What are the alternatives? We are not like the terrorists who shoot civilians. We are cautious. We make sure nobody is really hurt.[15]

* * * *

On January 25, 2006 elections were held throughout the Palestinian territories – Gaza, the West Bank and East Jerusalem. Voters were asked to choose representatives to the Palestinian Legislative Council (PLC). The turnout was an impressive display of democracy at work: more than three-quarters of eligible voters cast ballots. International monitors ensured that the elections were peaceful and transparent. When the votes were counted Hamas had won a resounding and unexpected victory. Of the one hundred thirty-two seats available Hamas had taken seventy-six, while Fatah, Mahmoud Abbas's party, had taken forty-three.[16] The remaining seats were split among other parties. Ismail Haniyeh became the new Prime Minister of the Palestinian Authority (PA).

The results were disconcerting to the Israeli government, which had tried to stall the election and prevent Hamas's participation. The United States, however, had insisted that the elections take place and Israel had reluctantly gone along with its powerful ally. Both the U.S. and Israel were well aware of the reasons for Hamas's strong showing: the Palestinian people were fed up with the corruption that permeated the ranks of Fatah; they wanted a government that would be more responsive to the needs of the people it represented than to Israel; and they expected their government to negotiate on their behalf for a just peace. Under Yasser Arafat the Jewish settler population on Palestinian land in the West Bank had grown from just over 100,000 at the time of the Oslo Accords to nearly 300,000 at the time of the election, a thirteen-year period. Arafat and his party Fatah had failed to prevent the continued appropriation of their people's land, water and civil rights.

The Israeli public, unlike their government, did not seem overly concerned about the results of the Palestinian election. In polls taken a few days after Election Day about half the public indicated they thought that Hamas "[would] moderate its involvement in terror attacks, and ... [that] it is now the Palestinian people's legitimate representative in every way and that negotiations should be conducted even with a Palestinian government that it forms."[17] A few days before the election, *Haaretz* reported senior IDF sources as saying that, although Hamas would keep its military wing if it did well in the election, it was "likely to maintain the calm it agreed to about a year ago." And: "Since the understanding it reached with the Palestinian Authority at the end of January 2005, Hamas has generally avoided perpetrating attacks."[18]

The Sharon government, however, was not interested in a Palestinian democracy whose policymakers did not collaborate with its plans for the Occupied Territories. And it was not hospitable to the replacement by a new ruling structure of one that had established a network of control throughout the West Bank that functioned according to the dictates of Israel.[19] Neither was the United States interested in a democratically elected Hamas government, despite George W. Bush's claim that he wanted to bring democracy to the Middle East.

The U.S. and Israel were unwilling to deal with Hamas even though a number of American and Israeli analysts, including former National Security Adviser and former head of Mossad Ephraim Halevy, believed that the two countries had the ability to strengthen Hamas's moderate wing and engage them in a peace process.

The Bush administration directly set in motion a plan that would lead to civil war between Hamas and Fatah. First, the U.S. and its quartet allies (Russia, the European Union and the United Nations) spelled out that Hamas's only option if it wanted to stay in power was to recognize Israel's right to exist, comply with all prior agreements and renounce the use of violence. When Hamas refused, the quartet countered by discontinuing aid to the PA. Insofar as their militias were concerned, the lack of assistance harmed Fatah more than Hamas. Whereas Fatah was dependent for aid on the U.S. and Israel, Hamas was the recipient of millions of dollars in aid from Iran. Consequently, Fatah was unable to pay its soldiers while Hamas had no such problem. Simultaneously, Israel detained or imprisoned sixty-four members of Hamas, including government ministers and officials from the Legislative Council. Avi Shlaim:

> America and the EU shamelessly joined Israel in ostracizing and demonizing the Hamas government and in trying to bring it down by withholding tax revenues and foreign aid. A surreal situation thus developed with a significant part of the international community imposing economic sanctions not against the occupier but against the occupied, not against the oppressor but against the oppressed.[20]

On June 24, 2006 Israeli soldiers crossed the border and abducted the Muammar brothers, two civilians from Gaza City.[21] The next day,

Hamas captured Israeli soldier Gilad Shalit near the Gaza border. Israel retaliated three days later by launching *Operation Summer Rains*. The operation's stated goals were to free Shalit and stop the Qassam rocket attacks on towns, such as Sderot and Ashkelon, in the western Negev. The IDF targeted civilian infrastructure including bridges and the Gaza Strip's only power plant. Hundreds of thousands of Gaza's residents were left without electricity and there was a shortage of water. An underreported fact is that Israel had fired 7,700 shells into Gaza in the nine months that elapsed between Sharon's evacuation of the settlers and Shalit's abduction.[22]*

B'Tselem's Status Report of September 2006 concluded:

> The attack did not impede the capability of Palestinian organizations to fire rockets into Israeli territory. Presumably, it also was not intended to achieve that purpose. Possibly, the objective was to collectively punish the entire Palestinian population by transmitting a "message of deterrence" to those responsible for making and launching the rockets. It may also simply be that the primary motive was revenge for the abduction of the IDF soldier. Whatever the case, it was forbidden and was a war crime.[23]

Gideon Levy reported that in July and August alone "Israel killed 224 Palestinians, 62 of them children and 25 of them women."[24]+ He wrote:

> [Israel] bombed and assassinated, destroyed and shelled, and no one stopped it. No Qassam cell or smuggling tunnel justifies such wide-scale killing. A day doesn't go by without deaths, most of them innocent civilians. . . . Families have been killed in

---

* Author's Note: in contrast, during the nine years between 2000 and 2008 Palestinian groups fired a total of 8,088 far more primitive mortar and rocket shells into Southern Israel: Intelligence and Terrorism Information Center at the Israel Intelligence Heritage and Commemoration Center (IICC), "Summary of Rocket Fire and Mortar Shelling in 2008," 2009, p. 5.

+ "In 2005 – 2007 alone the IDF killed 1,290 Palestinians in Gaza including 222 children," Shlaim: "How Israel brought Gaza to the brink of humanitarian catastrophe."

their sleep, while riding on donkeys or working in fields. Frightened children, traumatized by what they have seen, huddle in their homes with a horror in their eyes that is difficult to describe in words. A journalist from Spain who spent time in Gaza recently, a veteran of war and disaster zones around the world, said he had never been exposed to scenes as horrific as the ones he saw and documented over the last two months.[25]

The air force also resumed its practice of low-flying jets and sonic booms. From late June till late July 2006 Israeli pilots flew three-four sonic-boom sorties night after night.[26]

At the end of 2006 the U.S. arranged for arms shipments to be sent to Fatah. On February 1, 2007 Fatah attacked the Islamic University of Gaza, setting buildings on fire. The following day Hamas attacked a number of police stations. President Abbas, in a difficult position and realizing that a civil war had begun, convened talks with Hamas in hopes of creating a unity government. He and Haniyeh agreed that in exchange for Fatah holding certain influential governmental positions, Haniyeh would stay on as prime minister. The reconciliation between the two factions filled the streets of Gaza with Hamas and Fatah loyalists, whose differences were momentarily forgotten as they celebrated together.

The reconciliation was unacceptable to the American government. Secretary of State Condoleezza Rice flew to Ramallah where she made it clear to Abbas that she wanted him to vacate the January vote and hold new elections. Abbas agreed to Rice's demand but never implemented it.

The U.S. decided to increase the number of Fatah soldiers by almost 5,000, train them and provide more equipment, all to the tune of $1.27 billion over a five-year period. Hamas got wind of this development and launched a pre-emptive attack against Fatah in June 2007. The unity government collapsed. Within five days the fighting was over and Hamas had taken complete control of Gaza. It also took possession of most of the weapons that had been provided to Fatah.

In July 2007 David Wurmser resigned his post as Vice-President Dick Cheney's chief Middle East adviser. *Vanity Fair* reports that Wurmser accused the Bush administration of "engaging in a dirty war in an effort to provide a corrupt dictatorship [led by Abbas] with victory" and that Wurmser did not think Hamas had any intention of taking over the Gaza Strip. Wurmser: "It looks to me that what happened wasn't so much a coup by Hamas but an attempted coup by Fatah that was pre-empted before it could happen."[27]

Following Hamas's takeover, Israel, with U.S. approval, decided to punish the residents of Gaza. All land and water borders between Gaza and the outside world were sealed and a total blockade was imposed. Israel again contended that the Qassam rocket attacks necessitated this action. Trucks carrying supplies into Gaza dropped from five hundred to six hundred per day to around seventy.[28] Early in 2008, as part of their campaign to intimidate the residents of Gaza, former Israeli general and Deputy Defense Minister Matan Vilnai warned the Palestinians they faced a possible "Shoah."*

The blockade remained in force for about a year until Israel and Hamas agreed to a six-month ceasefire, or "lull," to begin on June 19, 2008. In return for a cessation of rocket attacks Israel agreed to end its incursions and military strikes into Gaza and open the border crossings. The two sides agreed to discuss the Gilad Shalit situation separately. The people of Gaza would finally have access to food, fuel, building materials, appliances and medical supplies. A humanitarian catastrophe had, presumably, been averted.

Hamas expected the number of trucks entering Gaza to return to pre-blockade levels, but traffic only increased to about ninety per day.[29+] The lack of a good faith effort by Israel strongly suggested an ulterior motive: that it was continuing to punish the population for their support of Hamas. Avi Shlaim: "Israel's objective is not just the defense of its population but the eventual overthrow of the Hamas government in Gaza by turning the people against their rulers."[30]

---

* Shoah (Disaster) is the Hebrew term for the Holocaust. Its literal definition is "burnt offering."

+ The Intelligence and Terrorism Information Center at the Israel Intelligence Heritage and Commemoration Center (IICC) has a different understanding ["The Six Months of the Lull Arrangement," December 2008, p. 3]: "Hamas leaders admitted that there was an improvement in the supply of goods and that civilian life was returning to normal."

Israel expected Hamas to ensure that rocket attacks into Israeli territory would cease. The Intelligence and Terrorism Information Center at the Israel Intelligence Heritage and Commemoration Center (IICC) calculated the total number of rockets and mortar fired by Palestinian groups from January 1 through June 18, 2008 to be 2,278, a monthly average of three hundred and eighty.[31] From the time the lull took effect on June 19 until November 4 the number of rocket firings totaled twenty (three of which landed in Gaza); mortar firings totaled eighteen (five of which landed in Gaza).[32] No Israelis were killed during this phase of the ceasefire. The IICC reported:

> The lull was sporadically violated by rocket and mortar shell fire, carried out by rogue terrorist organizations, in some instance in defiance of Hamas (especially by Fatah and Al-Qaeda supporters). Hamas was careful to maintain the ceasefire.[33]

Although Hamas was not perfect, Israeli officials knew that it had acted in good faith. But on November 4, 2008 IDF troops entered Gaza and killed six Hamas soldiers because they were allegedly digging a tunnel for the purpose of kidnapping Israeli soldiers.[34] Hamas said its members had been digging the tunnel for defensive purposes. Israel's critics accused it of using that day's U.S. presidential election between Barack Obama and John McCain as cover for its incursion, based on the expectation that the U.S. and other nations would be too distracted to pay much attention to another act of violence. Hamas responded by launching a wave of rocket attacks.

The next day, Israel sealed all crossing points into Gaza. Food, medical supplies, spare parts and other necessary items were not allowed in. Once again Israel had decided to collectively punish the civilian population for violating the same ceasefire that it had just violated. It is inconceivable that Israeli strategists did not know that Hamas's response to Israel's violation of the ceasefire would be a resumption of rocket attacks. From November 4 until December 19, the day the ceasefire was set to expire, Palestinian groups launched 171 rockets and 120 mortars.[35] Foreign Minister and Kadima party leader Tzipi Livni blamed Hamas for the failure of Gaza to return to normal:

In order to create a vision of hope, we took out our forces and settlements, but instead of Gaza being the beginning of a Palestinian state, Hamas established an extreme Islamic rule.[36]

By maintaining its stranglehold on the availability of food and other supplies, not only did Israel deprive the Palestinians of any possibility their lives could return to some degree of normalcy, it also fostered more poverty and a climate of hopelessness and anxiety. PLO legal counselor and negotiator Diana Buttu:

When the Israelis pulled out, we expected that the Palestinians in Gaza would at least be able to lead some sort of free life. We expected that the crossing points would be open. We didn't expect that we would have to beg to allow food in. . . .[37]

In truth, Israel was motivated by its obsession with rendering Hamas powerless. Israel pretended the rocket attacks were solely Hamas's responsibility. Its leaders lacked the fortitude to inquire within. Had they done so they would have discovered the obvious: policies that intimidate an entire population are likely to become deadly incentives to a people who have lost so much they have nothing left to lose. Yossi Alpher, former Mossad official and former adviser to then Prime Minister Ehud Barak:

[The blockade is] collective punishment, humanitarian suffering. It has not caused Palestinians in Gaza to behave the way we want them to, so why do it. . . . I think people really believed that, if you starved Gazans, they will get Hamas to stop the attacks. It's repeating a failed policy, mindlessly.[38]

Israel could have followed the advice of its own and American analysts by helping Hamas improve its enforcement efforts. It could have allowed more trucks carrying humanitarian supplies into Gaza as a show of good faith. But its intention to replace the democratically elected Hamas with the more collaborative Fatah led the Israeli government to expose its citizens in the south to a massive acceleration of rocket attacks. Ephraim Halevy: "If Israel's goal were to remove the threat of rockets from the residents of southern Israel, opening the border crossings would have ensured such quiet for a generation."[39]

172

* * * *

On December 14 a high-level Hamas delegation met with Egyptian Minister of Intelligence Omar Suleiman who, as mediator, had helped negotiate the ceasefire between Hamas and Israel, which was set to expire in just five days. Hamas offered to end all rocket attacks in return for Israel ending its raids into Gaza and re-opening the border crossings. Suleiman conveyed Hamas's proposal to Israeli authorities. On December 19, Robert Pastor, a senior adviser at the Carter Center and professor at American University, met with Hamas leader Khaled Mashaal, who made the same offer. The next day Pastor passed Mashaal's offer on to a "senior official" in the IDF, who told Pastor he would get back to him. He never did. As for the Egyptian offer, it is unclear whether Israel ignored the offer or rejected it outright. At an Israeli cabinet meeting on December 21, Yuval Diskin, head of Shin Bet (Israeli Security Agency), said: "Make no mistake, Hamas is interested in maintaining the truce."[40] Diskin said that if Israel ended the blockade, Hamas would restore the ceasefire.[41]

On Saturday, December 27, Israel decided to violate the Jewish Sabbath by launching an air offensive against the Gaza Strip. The streets were crowded as the bombing began at 11:30 AM.* Operation Cast Lead was set in motion. Two hundred twenty-nine people were killed that first day and more than 700 were wounded.[42] Four police stations were hit. Ninety-nine policemen died.[43] Among the dead were dozens of rookie traffic cops who had recently completed their training and were attending a graduation ceremony in their honor.

Two weeks later, on Sabbath day, Israel blocked UNRWA (United Nations Relief and Works Agency) from receiving desperately needed humanitarian supplies.[44] The reason the Israeli government gave for its lack of cooperation in providing food and other necessities to the starving Palestinians was that it was not willing to violate the Sabbath.

---

* *Human Rights in Palestine and Other Occupied Arab Territories, Report of the United Nations Fact Finding Mission on the Gaza Conflict*, p. 524, found that the timing of the initial attack "appears to have been calculated to create the greatest disruption and widespread panic among the civilian population."

During the next twenty-two days (until Israel withdrew its forces on January 18, 2009) Israel waged an air, land and sea offensive that was spectacular in its devastation. Hospitals, clinics, concrete factories, water and wastewater treatment facilities, ministries, fishing harbors, agricultural lands, mosques and schools were bombed, medical aid was denied to the wounded, ambulances were prevented from passing through checkpoints to reach the wounded, sixteen ambulance workers and doctors were killed trying to assist the wounded, and Palestinian children were used as human shields by Israeli soldiers. When threatened with violence, civilians in most of the world have the option of finding shelter in neighboring countries. Living in a closed military area, their borders sealed, the citizens of Gaza had nowhere to go.

The IAF (Israeli Air Force) said that eighty percent of the bombs that struck Gaza were precision guided with ninety-nine percent hitting their targets.* The operators of these weapons have the ability to detect small details of the objects in their sights and to strike fast moving vehicles.[45]

B'Tselem reported:

> Whole families were killed; parents saw their children shot before their very eyes; relatives watched their loved ones bleed to death; and entire neighborhoods were obliterated.[46]

A United Nations General Assembly report quoted the ICRC (International Committee of the Red Cross): "The Israeli military '*failed to meet its obligation under international humanitarian law to care for and evacuate the wounded.*' Israel made no effort to allow civilians to escape the fighting."[47] From the same report, UNICEF Director Ann M. Veneman:

> The crisis in Gaza is singular in that children and their families have nowhere to escape, no refuge. The very thought of being

---

* Cited by Jeffrey White, "Examining the Conduct of IDF Operations in Gaza," March 27, 2009, Policy Watch 1497, the Washington Institute for Near East Policy. Among the institute's board of advisers are Henry Kissinger, Richard Perle, Martin Peretz, Mortimer Zuckerman, George P. Schultz and Warren Christopher. WINEP was founded in the mid 1980s by Martin Indyk and Dennis Ross and sponsored by AIPAC.

trapped in a closed area is disturbing for adults in peace times. What then goes through the mind of a child who is trapped in such relentless violence? [48]

The General Assembly report ends as follows: "No more children – should ever, in Gaza or anywhere, have to live without their mothers and no more mothers – ever, anywhere again – have to be told that they too, have lost their children to such atrocities."[49]

The National Lawyers Guild investigated:

Israel's destruction of civilian homes also appears to have been unnecessary and wanton. In all of the cases documented by the Delegation, the interviewees reported that there was no Palestinian fighting from in or around the homes. Furthermore, many of the instances of home demolition took place after the Israeli military took control of an area, meaning that there remained little or no Palestinian fighting from the locale. Consequently a military necessity argument is diminished. Therefore, it is more likely that Israeli soldiers engaged in willful attacks on civilian homes and thus are guilty of war crimes.[50]

Amnesty International:

Much of the destruction was wanton and resulted from direct attacks on civilian objects as well as indiscriminate attacks that failed to distinguish between legitimate military targets and civilian objects. . . . Hundreds of civilians were killed in attacks carried out using high-precision weapons – air-delivered bombs and missiles, and tank shells. Others, including women and children, were shot at short range when posing no threat to the lives of the Israeli soldiers. Aerial bombardments launched from Israeli F-16 combat aircraft targeted and destroyed civilian homes without warning, killing and injuring scores of their inhabitants, often while they slept. Children playing on the roofs of their homes or in the street and other civilians going about their daily business, as well as medical staff attending the wounded were killed in broad daylight by Hellfire and other highly accurate missiles launched from helicopters and unmanned aerial vehicles (UAVs), or drones, and by precision projectiles fired from tanks.[51]

Amnesty also explained that by forcing Palestinian civilians to remain inside their homes and on the ground floors, Israeli soldiers had effectively turned them into human shields. Exacerbating the danger to the civilians was the fact that the soldiers did not provide the residents with any kind of protective wear, let alone the body armor and helmets they wore for their own protection. And the soldiers shielded themselves behind sandbags but provided no such protection for the civilians.[52]

Another example of human shields was described by soldiers who testified that they forced civilians to walk into houses with the soldiers following behind, their rifle barrels resting on the civilians' shoulders.[53]

* * * *

White phosphorus was used as an incendiary against Hamas military targets. Other typical purposes for this compound are screening and signaling. None of these uses are in violation of international law. Israel, however, repeatedly utilized white phosphorus in densely populated areas, which does violate international law. White phosphorus burns on contact with oxygen, reaching 1500 degrees Fahrenheit. Its effects are extremely painful and often fatal. The Israeli Ministry of Health:

> [w]hite phosphorus can cause serious injury and death when it comes into contact with the skin, is inhaled or is swallowed. . . . Because it is very soluble in fat, it quickly penetrates the skin from the surface or from an embedded fragment.[54]

Burns covering as little as ten percent of the body can be fatal because of their effect on the heart, liver and kidneys.[55] Human Rights Watch criticized the IDF for using white phosphorus even when its troops weren't in the area and when safer smoke shells were available. HRW: "As a result, civilians needlessly suffered and died."[56]

* * * *

HRW also investigated seven incidents where a total of eleven civilians were killed, nine of whom were women and children; eight civilians were wounded:

> In each case, the victims were standing, walking, or in a slowly moving vehicle with other unarmed civilians who were trying to

convey their noncombatant status by waving a white flag. All available evidence indicates that Israeli forces had control of the areas in question, no fighting was taking place there at the time, and Palestinian fighters were not hiding among the civilians who were shot. Whether waving a white flag or not, these people were civilians not taking an active part in hostilities, and therefore should not have been attacked, according to international humanitarian law (the laws of war).[57]

Desmond Tutu visited Gaza as part of a U.N. fact-finding team. He met a woman who told him how in the space of a few minutes she had witnessed the deaths of her husband, baby and son: "Her son was on the floor, struggling to push back his bowels, which had been disemboweled, trying to shove them back into his abdomen, and she said that she said to him 'no, my son, go and join your brother and your father.'"[58]

Israeli soldiers admitted to "cold-blooded murder."[59] A mother and her two children were shot dead when, after being released from their house and told to turn right, they turned left. One NCO described how his commanding officer ordered snipers to go up to a rooftop and kill an old lady who was crossing the street below. A squad leader said:

> What's great about Gaza – you see a person on a path, he doesn't have to be armed, you can simply shoot him. In our case it was an old woman on whom I did not see any weapon when I looked. The order was to take down the person, this woman, the minute you see her. There are always warnings, there is always the saying, "Maybe he's a terrorist." What I felt was, there was a lot of thirst for blood.[60]

Soldiers wrote "Death to the Arabs" on walls and spat on family photographs. They destroyed property and threw furniture out into the streets. Commanders told their soldiers it was acceptable to shoot at anyone they came across "because everyone left in the city is culpable because they didn't run away." Soldiers decided: "we should kill everyone (in the center of Gaza); everyone there is a terrorist."*

---

* Among the many sources that have reported these incidents is the *Times Online*, "Israeli soldiers admit to deliberate killing of Gaza civilians," March 20, 2009 and Stephen Lendman, "Incriminating Evidence of Israeli War Crimes in Gaza," March

In all of their actions the soldiers were on firm theological ground. They had been instructed by the army's chief rabbi, Avichai Rontzky: "When there is a clash between...the Ethical Code and the Halakha (religious law), certainly the Halakha must be followed."[61] The military rabbinate also distributed a brochure to the soldiers. In it were these words: "Exercising mercy towards a cruel enemy means being cruel towards innocent and honest soldiers."[62] The young soldiers were also told that they were "conducting a war of 'the sons of light against the sons of darkness.'"[63] The soldiers took to heart the words of the rabbis. One popular tee shirt worn by Israeli soldiers had the image of a pregnant woman's belly on the back with the caption: "1 shot 2 kills."[64]

The minarets of many mosques were specifically targeted. These structures were not large enough to hold people, nor did they have stairs to accommodate sniper fire.[65] Perhaps their destruction was a thinly veiled message that the Jewish state has no tolerance for Islam.

By permitting the rabbinate to administer advice to its military, the IDF was liable for having substituted Halakha for International Law.

The National Lawyers Guild:

> The Delegation found more than ample evidence to establish a *prima facie* case that the Israeli military committed significant violations of international law in Gaza from December 27, 2008, to January 18, 2009. Specifically, the delegation found that Israeli forces appear to have violated:
> - the principle of distinction by engaging in the willful killing of . . . Palestinian civilians;
> - the principle of proportionality by carrying out a number of attacks where the "collateral damage" that resulted was vastly disproportionate to the direct military advantage that could have been achieved by Israel;
> - customary international law on the use of weapons by misusing certain weapons, including the use of indiscriminate weaponry in residential and other heavily populated civilian areas;

- the obligation to provide medical care to the wounded by deliberately denying or delaying access to medical care for wounded people; and the prohibition on attacking medical facilities and personnel. [66]

* * * *

Israel's government and its defenders rejected the criticism leveled by the various human rights groups, calling their authors anti-Semitic, accusing them of libel or claiming they were guilty of inadequate research or incompetent analysis. An Israeli army spokesman said:

> The Israeli Defense Forces does not target innocents or civilians, and during the operation the army has been fighting an enemy that does not hesitate to fire from within civilian targets. . . .[67]

Defense Minister Ehud Barak claimed that any human rights abuses were exceptions and not the rule. He also said:

> The Israeli Army is the most moral in the world, and I know what I'm talking about because I know what took place in the former Yugoslavia, in Iraq.[68]

The lives of Israelis and Palestinians are often dependent on the judgments of high ranking officials within Israel's government and military. One would hope that these officials do not weigh the preciousness of human life against the relative behavior of leaders and warmongers. If Barak were to be exonerated of possible war crimes on the grounds that he is not as immoral as Slobodan Milosevic or Saddam Hussein, then the latter two ought to have been exonerated on the grounds that they were not as immoral as Adolf Hitler or Joseph Stalin. Does Barak really mean to argue that war crimes (actually, *numerous, specific, well-documented* war crimes) are to be forgiven because it is possible to find even worse historical examples? No objective person can review the history of the IDF without concluding that, at best, its morality is equally balanced by its propensity for massacre. Barak's statement is mere sophistry. It turns the history of international law on its head, and if accepted it would return the community of nations to a time of savagery unchecked by any meaningful judicial review.

Israel cannot have it both ways. It cannot put in place its Dahiya doctrine, which is designed to inflict maximum damage upon a population, and then deny responsibility for its predetermined consequences with the excuse that its army was merely defending itself. It cannot threaten a Shoah, associate all Gazans with Khaled Mashaal and then, after killing nearly one-thousand civilians, including hundreds of children, deny it did so with premeditation or that its actions constituted war crimes.*

Journalist Ethan Bronner, in a *New York Times* article that was published on the final day of Operation Cast Lead, stirred up old memories of Pinhas Lavon and Moshe Dayan and new ones of Gadi Eisenkot:

> The Israeli theory of what it tried to do here is summed up in a Hebrew phrase heard across Israel and throughout the military in the past weeks: "baal habayit hishtageya," or "the boss has lost it." It evokes the image of a madman who cannot be controlled. "This phrase means that if our civilians are attacked by you, we are not going to respond in proportion but will use all means we have to cause you such damage that you will think twice in the future," said Giora Eiland, a former national security adviser.[69]

The fact is, as Zeev Schiff, one of Israel's most eminent military analysts, once said: "the Israeli Army has always struck civilian populations, purposely and consciously... the Army . . . has never distinguished civilian [from military] targets ... [but] purposely attacked civilian targets."[70+]

---

* Israel continues to betray its intentions. For example, Prime Minister Netanyahu vowed to hold all of Lebanon responsible for acts of provocation by Hezbollah. Andrew Lee Butters, "Israel vs. Hizballah: Drumbeats of War," August 14, 2009, Time.com.

+ Schiff (1932-2007), author, military analyst and defense editor for *Haaretz*, was senior associate at the Carnegie Endowment for Peace, a fellow at the Washington Institute for Near East Policy, and Brochstein Fellow in Peace and Security at the James A. Baker III Institute for Public Policy at Rice University. "The most respected military analyst in Israel," praised by many Israeli leaders, including Benjamin Netanyahu and Ehud Barak, former Israeli Defense Minister Moshe Arens said of Schiff: "Not on the right or the left, because he was above political disputes, objective as only he knew how to be. Nor among the many writers and analysts and the Israeli press. As professional and sharp-eyed as they come, he was superior to them all. His

Mordecai (Motta) Gur, IDF Chief-of-Staff during Operation Litani, Israel's 1978 invasion of Southern Lebanon, was once asked: "You maintain that the civilian population should be punished?" Gur, a member of the Labor Party and generally considered a moderate, replied:[*]

> And how! I am using Sabra language: and how! I never doubted it, not for one moment. When I said . . . bring in the tanks as quickly as possible and hit them from far off before the boys reach a face-to-face battle, didn't I know what I was doing? I gave that order. Of course, that was not the first time that I had given that order. For thirty years, from the War of Independence to this day, we have been fighting against a population that lives in villages and in towns and the question that accompanies us endlessly each time from the beginning is whether or not to hit the civilians. . . .[71]

Gur eventually modified his position: "This was the great political and strategic mistake – the reliance on force as the almost exclusive factor in the formulation of policy."[72]

* * * *

On January 12, 2009, the Human Rights Council (HRC) of the U.N. General Assembly passed Resolution S-9/1. The resolution requested a report on the Gaza conflict through an "urgent, independent international fact-finding mission." On September 15, 2009 the *Report of the United Nations Fact-Finding Mission on the Gaza Conflict* was released. Entitled *Human Rights in Palestine and Other Occupied Arab Territories*, the 575 page document is the most definitive of the many studies that have come out since the end of Operation Cast Lead.

The U.N. fact-finding mission was led by Richard Goldstone, a respected Jewish South African judge and former war crimes prosecutor for Rwanda and Yugoslavia. A Zionist and long-time supporter of Israel, Goldstone is a trustee and board member of the Hebrew University in

---

articles were read by statesmen and politicians, generals and reservists, and they knew that he wrote the stark truth and how to listen to his views." *Haaretz*, "Hundreds pay their final respects to Haaretz reporter Ze'ev Schiff," June 21, 2007.

* Gur (1930 – 1995) served as Chief-of-Staff from 1974 to 1978.

Jerusalem as well as president emeritus of the World ORT school system.[73] His mother was a Zionist activist. The HRC originally asked Goldstone to investigate possible war crimes and crimes against humanity by Israel but not by Hamas. Goldstone demurred until the Council altered its mandate to include possible violations by Hamas.*

After the report was made public Goldstone's daughter gave an interview on Israeli Army Radio. Speaking in Hebrew, she said "her father wrestled with the decision to take on the task" and that he "did not expect to see and hear what he saw and heard." Nicole Goldstone, who has made aliyah to Israel, also said: "Israel is more important to me than anything. I'm not there at the moment, but my heart is always there."[74]

Among its conclusions the report states:

> While the Israeli Government has sought to portray its operations as essentially a response to rocket attacks in the exercise of its right to self defence, the Mission considers the plan to have been directed, at least in part, at a different target: the people of Gaza as a whole.[75]

The investigation focused on thirty-six cases that were "illustrative of the main patterns of violations."[76] In eleven of the cases the Israeli military deliberately targeted civilians, some of whom were shot "trying to leave their homes to walk to a safer place, waving white flags and, in some of the cases, following an injunction by the Israeli armed forces to do so."[77] Regarding these cases, the report stated: "There appears to have been no justifiable military objective pursued in any of them."[78]

After reviewing evidence related to the Hamas policemen who were killed on the first day of the offensive, the Mission determined that they

---

* The original HRC mandate authorized a "'fact-finding mission' regarding Israel's conduct of Operation Cast Lead against violent militants in the Gaza Strip between December 27, 2008, and January 18, 2009." The mandate was changed to: ". . . to investigate all violations of international human rights law and international humanitarian law that might have been committed at any time in the context of the military operations that were conducted in Gaza during the period from 27 December 2008 and 18 January 2009, whether before, during or after." Richard Goldstone letter to Representatives Howard Berman and Ileana Ros-Lehtinen of the U.S. House Committee on Foreign Affairs, October 29, 2009.

were "deliberately targeted." The authors clarified that the Israeli view was that the police were "part of the Palestinian military forces in Gaza."[79] The Mission disputed that contention:

> The Mission finds that, while a great number of the Gaza policemen were recruited among Hamas supporters or members of Palestinian armed groups, the Gaza police were a civilian law-enforcement agency. The Mission also concludes that the policemen killed on 27 December 2008 cannot be said to have been taking a direct part in hostilities and thus did not lose their civilian immunity from direct attack as civilians on this ground.[80]

Goldstone and his colleagues alleged that Israel's military liaison ignored repeated pleas from U.N. officials to halt the use of white phosphorus and to stop shelling the UNRWA compound, which contained a large fuel depot and where nearly seven hundred civilians took shelter.

The Mission accused the Israelis of deliberately destroying "food supply installations, water sanitation systems, concrete factories and residential houses. . . ." and of a "systematic destruction of the economic capacity of the Gaza Strip."[81] It described the actions of the Israeli military as disregarding "basic international humanitarian law and human rights norms"[82] and as "an assault on the dignity of the people."[83]

The Mission found that Israeli soldiers "herded" people together and detained them in "open spaces" where they were "exposed to extreme weather conditions:"

> The soldiers deliberately subjected civilians, including women and children, to cruel, inhuman and degrading treatment throughout their ordeal in order to terrorize, intimidate and humiliate them. The men were made to strip, sometimes naked, at different stages of their detention. All the men were handcuffed in a most painful manner and blindfolded, increasing their sense of fear and helplessness;
>
> Men, women and children were held close to artillery and tank positions, where constant shelling and firing was taking place, thus not only exposing them to danger, but increasing their fear and terror. This was deliberate, as is apparent from the

fact that the sandpits to which they were taken were specially prepared and surrounded by barbed wire;

During their detention in the Gaza Strip, whether in the open or in houses, the detainees were subjected to beatings and other physical abuse that amounts to torture. This continued systematically throughout their detention. . . .

The methods of interrogation amounted not only to torture in some of the cases, but also to physical and moral coercion of civilians to obtain information;

These persons were subjected to torture, maltreatment and foul conditions in the prisons. They were deprived of food and water for several hours at a time and any food they did receive was inadequate and inedible;

While in detention in Israel they were denied due process.[84]

The report concluded that these actions were "a grave breach under article 147 of the Fourth Geneva Convention and a violation of the Convention against Torture and Other Cruel, Inhuman or Degrading Treatment or Punishment."[85] Other actions deemed in violation of the Fourth Geneva Convention were "willful killing, torture or inhuman treatment, willfully causing great suffering or serious injury to body or health, and extensive destruction of property, not justified by military necessity and carried out unlawfully and wantonly."[86]

In summary, the Mission pointed out the following:

The operations were carefully planned in all their phases. Legal opinions and advice were given throughout the planning stages and at certain operational levels during the campaign. There were almost no mistakes made according to the Government of Israel. It is in these circumstances that the Mission concludes that what occurred in just over three weeks at the end of 2008 and the beginning of 2009 was a deliberately disproportionate attack designed to punish, humiliate and terrorize a civilian population, radically diminish its local economic capacity both to work and to provide for itself, and to force upon it an ever increasing sense of dependency and vulnerability.[87]

The evidence uncovered and analyzed by the fact-finding mission led the authors to conclude that "serious violations of international human rights and humanitarian law were committed by Israel during the Gaza conflict, and that Israel committed actions amounting to war crimes, and possibly crimes against humanity."[88] They warned:

> Furthermore, the harsh and unlawful practices of occupation, far from quelling resistance, breed it, including its violent manifestations. The Mission is of the view that ending occupation is a prerequisite for the return of a dignified life for Palestinians, as well as development and a peaceful solution to the conflict.[89]

Not surprised by the report's conclusions, Israeli journalist Amira Hass said: "The Goldstone Commission's findings are in line with what anyone who didn't shut his or her eyes and ears to witness testimony already knows." Describing the state of mind of the blind and the deaf, Hass also said: "There is only [one] thing worse than denial – the admission that the IDF indeed acted as has been described, but that these actions are both normal and appropriate."[90]

Echoing Hass, Gideon Levy didn't mince words:

> Cast Lead was an unrestrained assault on a besieged, totally unprotected civilian population which showed almost no signs of resistance during this operation. . . . There was no need to wait for Goldstone to understand that a terrible thing had occurred between the Palestinian David and the Israeli Goliath. But the Israelis preferred to look away, or stand with their children on the hills around Gaza and cheer on the carnage-causing bombs. Under the cover of the committed media, and criminally-biased analysts and experts – all of whom kept information from coming out – and with brainwashed and complacent public opinion, Israel behaved as if nothing had happened. Goldstone has put an end to that, for which we should thank him.[91]

Levy's use of "criminally-biased analysts and experts" may have been in reference to the conclusions of five investigations into Operation Cast Lead ordered by the IDF. The issues the IDF looked into were:

- claims regarding incidents where UN and international facilities were fired upon and damaged;

- incidents involving shooting at medical facilities, buildings, vehicles and crews;
- claims regarding incidents in which many uninvolved civilians were harmed;
- the use of weaponry containing phosphorus;
- damage to infrastructure and the destruction of buildings by ground forces.[92]

On April 22, 2009 IDF Chief of the General Staff, Lt. General Gabi Ashkenazi, made the results of these investigations available. As expected, the IDF exonerated itself, concluding that it had "operated in accordance with international law," and had "maintained a high professional and moral level." The IDF admitted to "a very small number of incidents in which intelligence or operational errors took place" but called them "unavoidable" and occurring "in all combat situations."[93]

Amnesty International criticized the IDF investigations:

> The information made public only refers to a handful of cases and lacks crucial details. It mostly repeats claims made by the army and the authorities many times since the early days of Operation "Cast Lead . . . . It does not even attempt to explain the overwhelming majority of civilian deaths nor the massive destruction caused to civilian buildings in Gaza. . . . [T]he army's claims appear to be more an attempt to shirk its responsibilities than a genuine process to establish the truth. Such an approach lacks credibility.[94]

The Goldstone report also expressed "serious doubts about the willingness of Israel to carry out genuine investigations in an impartial, independent, prompt and effective way as required by international law."[95]

As it did with the various NGO reports, Israel's government severely criticized the HRC report. The Foreign Ministry labeled it "biased from the start." President Shimon Peres said "[the report] makes a mockery of history and fails to distinguish between aggressor and those acting in self-defense."[96*] Ehud Barak, who faces possible indictment by

---

* Author's note: The ratio of Palestinians killed during Operation Cast Lead

the International Criminal Court for war crimes and crimes against humanity, called the investigation a "kangaroo court" and said: "If the U.N. or anyone else has complaints, they should direct them to the Israeli government."[97]

Goldstone did in fact direct numerous inquiries to the Israeli Government. Beginning in April 2009 and over a three-month period, he corresponded with Ambassador Aharon Leshno-Yaar, Israel's permanent representative to the Human Rights Council in Geneva. The correspondence between the two men included Prime Minister Netanyahu.[98] Goldstone repeatedly asked to consult with the government and to meet with "relevant" government and military officials. Leshno-Yaar acknowledged his and his government's respect for Goldstone's record of impartiality but refused to cooperate with the fact-finding mission, arguing that the Human Rights Council was incapable of conducting an unbiased investigation.

The truth, as Israeli war veteran and former Knesset member Uri Avnery explained, is that the Israeli government boycotted the mission because "they knew full well that the commission, any commission, would have to reach the conclusions it did reach."[99]

Goldstone tried to allay Leshno-Yaar's fears:

> [T]he Mission has been requested and established by the President of the UN HRC to "investigate all violations of International Human Rights Law and International Humanitarian Law that might have been committed at any time in the context of the military operations that were conducted in Gaza during the period from 27 December 2008 and 18 January 2009, whether before, during or after." As such, the scope of the Mission's investigation is not the result of its own deliberations

---

compared to Israelis was over one hundred fifty to one. The death toll of Palestinian children alone is thirty-five times higher than all the Israeli fatalities. B'Tselem determined that nine Israelis were killed by Palestinians during Cast Lead. Three were civilians, one was a member of the security forces and five were IDF soldiers. An additional four Israeli soldiers were killed by friendly fire. According to B'Tselem, the total number of Palestinians killed was 1,387 of which 320 were minors. "9 Sept. 2009: B'Tselem publishes complete fatality figures from Operation Cast Lead."

or personal convictions, however legitimate or authoritative. It is a clear mandate, legally and formally given to it.[100]

Leshno-Yaar, on behalf of the Israeli government, was not persuaded. For example, he alleged that "members of the Mission were accompanied at every stage of their visit to Gaza by Hamas officials." Goldstone "categorically" denied Leshno-Yaar's claim and stated that no Hamas member had ever accompanied anyone from the Mission.[101]

* * * *

The report did not ignore possible war crimes by Hamas, accusing the Palestinian group of either deliberately firing rockets at Israeli civilians or failing to recognize that the inaccuracy of the rockets left civilian populations in jeopardy. Hamas was also held responsible for the widespread "psychological trauma" and "feelings of insecurity"[102] caused by the rocket fire. Hamas retorted that its rocket attacks were acts of self-defense that were not aimed at civilians "but rather at IDF artillery and other positions from which attacks at Gaza were launched."[103]

The mission also pointed out that the Israeli government had taken measures to protect its Jewish citizens from mortar and rocket fire, including fortifying public buildings and schools and constructing shelters. But it noted that Israel did not provide the same level of protection to its Palestinian citizens, whose villages were also in the line of fire.[104]

Additionally, the Mission chastised Palestinian security services for "a pattern of organized violence directed mainly at Fatah affiliates and supporters."[105] Some of the alleged human-rights abuses against Palestinians included torture, illegal detention, denial of family visits and warrantless searches of homes.[106] The HRC Mission charged that between December 19, 2008 and February 27, 2009, unidentified gunmen and members of the Palestinian security services killed between twenty-nine and thirty-two residents of Gaza.[107] However, it found no evidence to support Israel's claim that Palestinian armed groups made use of civilians as human shields; that they forced people to stay in areas under attack; that hospitals were used as shelters for Palestinian combatants; or that ambulances were used to transport armed men.[108]

Without question, criticism of Israel dominates the HRC report, whose findings are consistent with the conclusions of Amnesty

International, the International Red Cross, the National Lawyers Guild, Human Rights Watch, B'Tselem, Breaking the Silence and others. Such uniformity among internationally respected organizations is compelling. Nonetheless, the addition to the consensus of the world's preeminent human rights watchdog has had no effect on the prevailing attitude of the Israeli establishment. For example, Finance Minister Yuval Steinitz called Goldstone an "anti-Semite."[109] And current Minister of the Interior Eliyahu Yishai who, as Deputy Prime Minister during Operation Cast Lead, had urged the IDF to "bomb thousands of houses, to destroy Gaza," slandered Goldstone as an "abominable anti-Semite."[110]*

* * * *

With near universal condemnation of the Jewish state, Israel's government and its defenders will have to invent an anti-Semitic conspiracy. Their logic is upside down. The condemnation of Israel is not a product of anti-Semitism. Rather, the behavior that elicited the condemnation fans the flames of anti-Semitism worldwide.

In an interview with *Tikkun*, Goldstone explained how he dealt with one woman's accusation that he was betraying his own people:

> I said I wasn't going to dignify her remarks with a response, but they call to mind the attacks made on me as a white South African for going against the interest of whites during the Apartheid era. And I said having regard to the terrible history of the Jewish people, of over 2,000 years of persecution, I found it difficult to understand how Jews wouldn't respond in protecting the human rights of others. And I talked about that as being a fundamental Jewish value.[111]

Israel has been maintaining an illegal occupation, replete with land seizure, collective punishment and settler-instigated and military-enabled violence for over forty years. Yet, it continues to deny that it has violated international humanitarian law. By persisting in "acts of madness" Israel will alienate itself more and more from the global community. The sad likelihood is that the world's disapproval will impel the Israeli establishment to become even more inured against and contemptuous of world opinion than in the past. Israeli society will likely ignore pleas

---

* Yishai is leader of the Ultra-Orthodox Shas Party.

from every corner of the globe to abide by international law and end the occupation and make peace. Campaigns urging boycott, divestment and sanctions will proliferate as will worldwide growth in anti-Semitism. More lives, including Jewish lives, will be lost. Eventually the United States will be blamed for enabling Israel's behavior and be pressured to minimize its support for the Jewish state. Large numbers of Israeli citizens will flee their country. All of this will not only make Israel less secure, but also fuel its self-destructive certainty that the world is insensitive to Jewish suffering. That belief has been at the heart of Zionism since the days of Theodore Herzl. At one time it was necessary for survival but it has become self-deceiving and self-fulfilling. It creates isolation and an exaggerated need for security, resulting in harsh and pre-emptive reaction to any perceived threat. In turn, non-Jews living under Israeli control and facing institutionalized discrimination become convinced that Israel is insensitive to their suffering. And, like any other people, they resist, usually with nonviolence but sometimes with violence.

The Israeli position is that its soldiers do not target civilians. Government spokespersons contend that the "regrettable" deaths of civilians are the fault of the enemy for embedding its fighters within urban centers. This is the same argument Israel used with respect to Hezbollah during the Second Lebanon War. If they actually believed that argument, Israeli military strategists surely planned for the possibility that Hamas, too, would embed its fighters within civilian populations. If, as Israel contends, Hamas used civilians as human shields, then clearly these strategists made little attempt to distinguish between the target and the shield. The statistics bear this out: nearly eighty percent of the fatally wounded were civilians.

* * * *

One Israeli who supported Cast Lead, probably speaking for the overwhelming majority in Israel, said: "We do feel bad about it, but we don't feel guilty . . . The most ethical moral imperative is for Israel to prevail in this conflict over an immoral Islamist philosophy."[112] I would ask: how many children must die before Israelis feel responsible enough to demand an end to their country's relentless onslaught upon the Palestinians? Before my transformation I too expressed regret at the deaths of the innocent, but looking back I can see that I was merely trying to prove to myself that I had not lost my humanity.

Israel's real moral imperative is to acknowledge the historical reasons for the conflict with the Palestinian people and to sit down with their democratically elected leaders and find a way to avert further bloodshed. But this is anathema to Israel's leaders. They are too beholden to the religious right, and to the goal of a Greater Israel, to take that step. Their public excuse is Hamas's refusal to recognize Israel and its call for its eradication, but the real reason is that they want to extract more concessions from the Palestinians.* They are trying to conceal their impatience to possess as much of the West Bank as possible before they sit down to negotiate in good faith. The fact is that Hamas has stated its willingness to negotiate on the basis of the 1967 borders and has also agreed to accept the will of the Palestinian people. But the Israeli government refuses to recognize Hamas as the duly elected government of the Palestinian people; it would like nothing more than to eradicate Hamas. At one time the PLO, too, called for the eradication of the Jewish State, yet Israel's failure to engage the PLO in dialogue hindered prospects for peace. In 2007 U.N. Envoy de Soto said:

> A good cause can and has been made by the peace camps in Israel that the whole idea to require the Palestinians to recognize up front, as a pre-condition to talks, that Israel has the right to exist is bogus. Israel has never been asked to recognize up front that the Palestinians have a right to a state – all Israel has ever done is recognize the PLO as a valid interlocutor (the equivalent would be if the Palestinians recognized the Israeli government as a legitimate representative of the Jewish people living in historic Palestine). For all these reasons, this precondition is seen in such circles as imbalanced and an excuse not to engage in negotiation. When Hamas members are asked about the recognition demand, they respond with a rhetorical question: "What are the borders of this Israel you would have us recognize?" The pragmatists in Hamas argue that recognition

---

* Neither Egypt nor Jordan was required to recognize Israel as a precondition to peace negotiations. Sultan, p. 27.

amounts to acceptance of the occupation, and that only if Israel recognizes the right of the Palestinians to a state in the 1967 borders would the question arise whether Hamas should recognize Israel.[113]

Hamas's willingness to accept a two-state solution with borders based on the 1967 Green Line is not a ploy. A report published by the Strategic Studies Institute of the U.S. Army War College stated:

> HAMAS' initial strategy of armed resistance and popular uprising against Israel has been tamed as it has instead pursued political participation, accepted the notion of a limited area of an envisioned Palestinian state, and in its calmings and truces which acknowledge (and therefore "recognize") Israel in a *de facto* manner.* It was severely criticized for this change in strategy by [al-Qaeda leader] Ayman Zawahiri.[114]

On June 3, 2009, Hamas sent U.S. President Obama a letter, which said in part:

> We in the Hamas Government are committed to pursuing a just resolution to the conflict not in contradiction with the international community and enlightened opinion as expressed in the International Court of Justice, the United Nations General Assembly, and leading human rights organizations. We are prepared to engage all parties on the basis of mutual respect and without preconditions.[115]

Yuval Diskin has acknowledged that Hamas is willing to accept a long-term ceasefire on the 1967 borders.[116] Amira Hass reported: "The Hamas leader in Gaza, Ismail Haniyeh, said on Saturday his government was willing to accept a Palestinian state within the 1967 borders."[117]

Jimmy Carter:

> But one of the things that they [Hamas] committed to me that was very significant, and they announced it publicly, by the way,

---

* The following is footnoted in the text of the report: "To the assertion that HAMAS continued rocket attacks on Israel: first, these were quieted, by and large, since June 2008, and even prior, many of these attacks are not launched by HAMAS but by Palestinian Islamic Jihad and other groups."

to Al Jazeera and others, was that they would accept any agreement that's negotiated between the Israelis and the Palestinians if it's submitted to a referendum in the West Bank and Gaza, and the Palestinians approve it. That means they would accept Israel's right to exist if that's in the agreement and so forth.[118]

Roger Cohen of the *New York Times*:

Henry Siegman, the president of the U.S./Middle East Project, whose chairman is [Brent] Scowcroft . . . told me that he met recently with Khaled Meshal, the political director of Hamas in Damascus. Meshal told him, and put in writing, that although Hamas would not recognize Israel, it would remain in a Palestinian national unity government that reached a referendum-endorsed peace settlement with Israel.[119]

If Hamas's goal is to convince Israel to end the occupation, its rocket attacks against Israel have been counterproductive. And if Israel's goal is a lasting peace, its punitive actions have also proven counterproductive. There are elements within Hamas that are determined to continue their armed struggle against Israel. Virtually all counterterrorism experts acknowledge that in a guerrilla-type war, where one side employs terrorist tactics, the other side's conventional military superiority loses its advantage. Israel can continue to fight Hamas and other armed Palestinian organizations, as it has for decades, but if it does it will be punishing an entire population and radicalizing future generations of young Palestinians. Alternatively, a faster approach to ending the violence would be for Israel to end the occupation. Most Palestinians are tired of violence, tired of seeing their children grow up without a future, tired of seeing them maimed or killed. Like all people, they want peace. Ending the occupation (with security guarantees) would go a long way toward alleviating the poverty and despair that foster extremism. Ending the occupation would enable Palestinian children to have safe drinking water instead of contaminated and brackish water, which causes serious health problems. When schoolchildren in Bureij Refugee Camp held an election to choose the *"one thing they most wanted* for their school: *They chose to have drinking water."*[120] Would even a single child in Israel conceive of such an yearning if offered the same choice?

Israel is unwavering in its accusation that Hamas is an irredeemable terrorist organization that seeks Israel's destruction. To the public that accusation is reinforced whenever Hamas perpetrates acts of violence. Israel's public has been taught to see their nation as an innocent victim of an implacable enemy. These automatic and unexamined assumptions provide Israel the motive to perpetrate its own acts of violence in the name of self-defense, while avoiding any real peace process.* Israel's ability to posit itself as a constant casualty of unprovoked attack and anti-Semitism obscures the fundamental reasons for the conflict. These are the lack of self-determination by a group of people who happen not to be Jewish, and the brutal occupation of their land. Waging war is not a path to peace, unless the enemy can be permanently vanquished.

Prominent Israeli officials have begun to openly acknowledge the futility of the occupation. Shlomo Ben-Ami:

> Internationally legitimised borders will offer Israel more deterrence power than F-16 raids on terrorist targets that end up killing innocent civilians without deterring the terrorists. . . [T]his is an era where power without legitimacy only breeds chaos, and military supremacy without legitimate international consent for the use of force does not offer security.[121]

In September 2008, as his term as Prime Minister was nearing its end, Ehud Olmert said that if Israel wanted peace it had to withdraw from East Jerusalem and the West Bank. He reprimanded "traditional Israeli defense strategists" who "had learned nothing from past experiences," and "seemed stuck in the considerations of the 1948 war of independence." Olmert admitted that for thirty-five years he had supported Israeli sovereignty over all of Jerusalem and said: "For a large portion of these years, I was unwilling to look at reality in all its depth." While recognizing that Israel had a "difficult" and "terrible" decision to make, one "that contradicts our natural instincts, our innermost desires,

---

* In May 2007 Ismail Haniyeh offered Israel a ten-year truce in return for an end to the siege of Gaza. Israel ignored the offer. Sultan, pp. 24-5.

our collective memories, the prayers of the Jewish people for 2,000 years," Olmert said:

> We have to reach an agreement with the Palestinians, the meaning of which is that in practice we will withdraw from almost all the territories, if not all the territories. We will leave a percentage of these territories in our hands, but will have to give the Palestinians a similar percentage, because without that there will be no peace.[122]

In a written statement submitted to the United Nations Secretary-General, the International Organization for the Elimination of all Forms of Racial Discrimination (EAFORD) quoted Jordan's Queen Rania Al Abdullah who, in the aftermath of the Gaza invasion, asked what the citizens of the world could say:

> "To the mothers watching their children cry in pain, huddle in fear, and deal with more trauma than any of us will experience in an entire lifetime? That they are collateral damage? That their lives don't matter? That their deaths don't count? That the children of Gaza do not have the right to life, liberty and security?"[123]

EAFORD's response to the Queen: "The blood of Gaza's children is on all our hands, it is the world's collective responsibility."

– 10 –
Collapse of a Society: Interview with Fatima

When a Palestinian child paints a picture of the sky, there's always an Israeli helicopter there, too.[1] Avi Dichter, former Minister of Internal Security, May 31, 2005

Rich: Fatima, can you tell me a little about yourself? How old are you and were you born in the United States?

Fatima: I am twenty-four years old and an American citizen. I was born in the United States to an American Muslim family.

Rich: I know that your education through high school took place in the United States. Did you attend public or private school and did you go to college in the United States?

Fatima: I went to both public and non-denominational private school through high school. For university I moved to London where I did my undergraduate work in Arabic and Development Studies at SOAS (the School of Oriental and African Studies). I am now completing my graduate degree at SOAS. When I finish I will have a MS (Master of Science) in Globalization and Development.

Rich: What do you plan to do with your degree?

Fatima: I'd like to work on global problems, possibly for an NGO; or work for the U.N. if that would be possible.

Rich: Can you tell me the dates you went with the *Codepink* delegation to Gaza?[*]

Fatima: We left Cairo and entered Gaza on Friday, May 29, 2009.

---

[*] From Codepinkalert.org: "Codepink is a women-initiated grassroots peace and social justice movement working to end the wars in Iraq and Afghanistan, stop new wars, and redirect our resources into healthcare, education, green jobs and other life-affirming activities. Codepink rejects foreign policies based on domination and aggression, and instead calls for policies based on diplomacy, compassion and a commitment to international law. With an emphasis on joy and humor, Codepink women and men seek to activate, amplify and inspire a community of peacemakers through creative campaigns and a commitment to non-violence."

Rich: How many of you were in the delegation?

Fatima: Close to seventy. I think the actual number was sixty-six.

Rich: What did your group hope to achieve?

Fatima: Our goal was to provide toys and support for the children of Gaza. We went to a lot of children's rehabilitation centers. We also built playgrounds for the children.

Rich: What did you see and what conclusions did you draw?

Fatima: We saw the absolute decimation that occurred as a result of the incursion of late December to mid-January. In addition to rehabilitation centers, we visited universities and hospitals. We met with various government officials and different political activists and groups. We tried to get a contextual feel for what is going on in Gaza.

Rich: Did you meet with John Ging of the United Nations?[*]

Fatima: Our first day in Gaza, John Ging welcomed us to the U.N. compound and gave a speech about the situation in Gaza since the incursion. He explained the humanitarian conditions and the needs of the Palestinian people there. In no uncertain terms, he stated that the siege was completely contrary to international law, and he categorically stated that the siege needs to end now. He also referred to the bombing of schools, hospitals and mosques during Israel's invasion earlier in the year.

Rich: When you say siege, you are referring to Israel's blockade?

Fatima: Yes. The stated purpose of the blockade is to prevent weapons and luxury goods from entering Gaza. "Luxury" is a very arbitrary term. Israel doesn't even allow food in that meets basic nutritional requirements. In terms of fruits and vegetables, what enters Gaza is actually the excess from Israel and that is determined by the Israel farmers lobby. So the food that is allowed into Gaza is not based on the nutritional needs of the population but on what the farmers have no use

---

[*] John Ging has been head of the United Nations Relief and Works Agency (UNRWA) in the Gaza Strip since 2006.

for. Also, the list of items changes every day; it is very arbitrary and not based on basic needs, but decided by a few people. One day there might be a large amount of melons, the next day there might be something else. Shampoo might be allowed in but not conditioner. Ketchup is not allowed because it is considered a luxury good. The people need tunnels because these things would be completely inaccessible were it not for the tunnels.

Rich: Jimmy Carter said the Israelis even designated crayons and paper as security hazards. When he met with Israeli officials and asked them to explain how they could come to such conclusions, they offered no explanation. What you just described is more evidence of what I consider to be irrational thinking and a disregard for the welfare of an entire people. It reminds me of something Dov Weisglass said at a Kadima party meeting a few months after the Jewish settlers were evacuated from Gaza: "We will put the Palestinians on a diet, but not make them die of hunger."[2]

Fatima: Yes, we have heard similar comments coming out of Israel. They are rather common.

Rich: Did you meet with any of Gaza's citizens while you were there?

Fatima: We had the honor and pleasure of meeting a lot of local people. We had some friends and a lot of contacts that we set up before we went. My sister and I went to Rafah where we stayed with friends a night or two. One friend and his family are 1948 refugees. His parents live in the Rafah refugee camp. Our friend moved out and bought his own home.

Rich: Isn't Rafah on the border with Egypt?

Fatima: Yes, the crossing to Egypt is at Rafah. Our friend's home was only 700 meters from the border. We asked him about his experience during the invasion. He said his youngest two children clung to him the whole time. The bombs shook the house so violently that on the first day of the invasion the windows broke; and it was the middle of winter.

His house had been freshly painted just before the incursion. Now there were cracks on every wall where every brick was. He kept apologizing to us for the appearance of the house. But the important thing is that his house had survived. Paint is another item that isn't allowed in;

neither is glass. When he replaced the windows of his house he used whatever glass was available. Each pane is a different color and a different kind of glass. Some panes are car glass, some are fogged shower glass, and some are even stained glass.

Rich: What else did you see?

Fatima: We saw some of the blown-up Israeli settlements. As you know, the Israelis pulled out in 2005. Before they left, the settlers blew up all of their buildings including greenhouses, which were used to grow vegetables. There were a couple of buildings that survived, which European organizations bought and gave back to the Palestinians. Some of these were bombed in the invasion.

Prior to the disengagement in 2005, the Gaza Strip was divided into three distinct sections and there was no freedom of movement, so it was similar to the West Bank. Nowadays, everyone is constantly on the beach. We asked our friends about that and they explained that prior to 2005 people had very little access to the beach because that is where the settlers were. Since 2005 there has been freedom of movement within the Gaza Strip itself.

Rich: So, before the settlers left in 2005 the Palestinians lived in one of three sections and could only move within the section they lived in?

Fatima: Like the West Bank, they could move to other sections but there were checkpoints where they would have to wait an indeterminate period of time, or be detained and then imprisoned. In terms of freedom of movement it was very limited. The only real access to the sea was further north, so if you were from Rafah or somewhere in the South a trip to the beach wasn't worth it because by the time you passed through each checkpoint and got to the beach it could be evening. Keep in mind: we're talking about a very short distance. Gaza is about fifty kilometers in length and about twelve kilometers at its widest. On average it is about six or seven kilometers wide, so it's really a tiny area.

Rich: And the entire western edge of Gaza is on the Mediterranean, so there is nobody in Gaza who lives more than twelve kilometers from the sea. Is it accurate to say that the Israeli settlements were like a fourth section of Gaza to which the Palestinians had no access?

Fatima: That's right. And considering Gaza is the third most densely populated area on Earth you can imagine how packed it must have been when the settlers lived there.

Rich: When the settlers left they blew up their homes and buildings and shops?

Fatima: Yes.

Rich: Why do you think they did that?

Fatima: My first reaction is that I have no idea. When I think about it logically and as a compassionate human being, there is no reason why they would do that. However, in light of Israel's policies it is easy to come to the conclusion that the settlers didn't want the Palestinians to benefit from the buildings. It is clear from the blockade that making life as miserable as possible for Palestinians of Gaza is pretty standard.

Rich: What else did you do while you were in Gaza?

Fatima: We visited the Gaza airport. It was actually bombed before this latest incursion, in 2002. It's a beautiful building. It was designed by a Moroccan architect from Casablanca. The entire airport was shelled. I think it was only in operation for a year or two.

Rich: Were the building and runways all bombed in 2002?

Fatima: Yes, so it is no longer being used.

Rich: Were schools bombed in Operation Cast Lead?

Fatima: John Ging said that over a hundred, maybe two hundred schools had been hit and those were U.N. schools. I believe that most schools in Gaza are administered by the U.N.

Rich: Wasn't there an American school that was bombed?

Fatima: The American school was destroyed. It was quite a large institution.

Rich: Was it a college or high school?

Fatima: I think it was a primary or secondary school.

Rich: When Israel bombed it were there children in the school?

Fatima: I don't think children were there when it was bombed. They stopped coming once the bombing started. There was one school where people were taking shelter and it was bombed. I'm not sure how many people died or were injured.

Rich: What did the streets look like?

Fatima: The devastation was terrible. Everything was bombed. Nothing got away unscathed. The landscape consists mainly of destroyed houses and rubble. You can't go anywhere really and not see something destroyed. Some neighborhoods fared better than others but every neighborhood has destroyed buildings or bombed roads.

Rich: Can you tell me about the hospitals and rehabilitation clinics you visited?

Fatima: You hear about how 1,400 people died, and many were children. But it's important to realize how many people who were injured have died since the invasion from lack of medical care; and how many people who did not have serious injuries have died due to the blockade because they were not able to get the medicine they needed. A number of doctors told us, "We have all the equipment we need to administer chemotherapy but we don't have the chemicals" or "We have most of the equipment for a particular type of surgery but we might be missing one instrument." At the rehabilitation center we saw a lot of people who lost limbs and we saw many deaf children. At one hospital I visited, there was a woman with two beautiful little girls sitting on each side of her, her daughters, and she said, "Well, this one is deaf but she smiles; and this one can hear but she never smiles anymore."

You hear these types of stories. We met a man who lost both of his arms and he broke down and said "I can no longer hug my children." Through newspapers and television we hear about the loss of life but we don't see an entire generation of people who have no arms or legs or who have been burned by phosphorus or something else.

Some of the places we visited, for example the Wafaa hospital, aren't more than a couple of kilometers from the Israeli border. This hospital was very badly shelled. They had recently added a brand new rehabilitation wing for the elderly. They were moving patients in when it was bombed. The whole front is covered in shell holes. It was also a teaching hospital. In the brand new auditorium the plastic hadn't even been removed from the chairs. The head doctor showed us around. He pointed to the side of the building where a shell had entered and knocked out about half the wall and ripped through three more walls. The holes were several meters wide. Some of the members of the delegation asked about rebuilding. The doctor shrugged and explained that there were no supplies. "And even if there were," he said, "what happens when they bomb us again tomorrow?"

Rich: Israel claims that hospitals and the other targets were hiding places for Hamas militants.

Fatima: When you see the destruction in Gaza, their claim is ludicrous. When you see hundreds of schools, when you see hospitals and neighborhood after neighborhood of residences that have been destroyed, you know that it just isn't possible. How many militants would there have to have been to hide in all these places along with the civilian population? Is every house in every neighborhood a haven for Hamas fighters? We spoke with a woman who is studying physical science at the university. She told us, "They weren't in our homes, they weren't in our mosques. That's ridiculous." When you see the devastation you know that Israel did not just target Hamas; they targeted the entire population.

And many U.N. workers throughout Gaza died or were injured. The U.N. headquarters compound and U.N. schools were bombed. We spoke to a few Europeans who were working for UNRWA and they told us that foreign U.N. workers were not permitted to leave the compound because of U.N. guidelines; or they were physically removed and evacuated from the compound by the U.N. However, you have to understand that there are 10,000 people working under John Ging. That includes Palestinians. These people continued their work throughout the incursion and many died as a result. We spoke to a Dutch woman who works for UNRWA who was really upset about this. She told us you don't hear about Palestinian U.N. employees dying because they are not foreigners. The U.N. headquarters compound and U.N. schools were also bombed. The warehouses that stored tons of humanitarian relief supplies were set ablaze and their contents incinerated. We saw bombed U.N. cars and bombed convoy trucks.

Rich: I remember that in 1967, prior to the Six-Day War, Nasser ordered the U.N. peacekeeping force out of the Sinai and Gaza. Did the Israeli government notify the U.N. that it was about to invade Gaza and that it intended to bomb U.N. buildings?

Fatima: I don't know the answer to that question but it is possible that Israel alerted the U.N. to the invasion, but surely not that they were going to bomb U.N. buildings. We did speak with another woman who works for UNRWA. When Israel began their bombing she was with an Israeli official, reminding him of the GPS coordinates to the compound and asking him to make sure that Israeli warplanes avoid bombing those coordinates, but as she was sitting with him, Israel bombed the compound.*

Rich: Were she and the official in Gaza at the time?

Fatima: No, they were in Israel, but not far from Gaza.

Rich: I want to know more about the children. Did you spend much time with them?

Fatima: We went to several children's centers. The children were very well behaved but they were shell-shocked. Some of them were too quiet. They weren't just shy. They should have been more outgoing. In one of the children's centers the content of the pictures they were drawing was really disturbing. They were painted in primary colors and awkward shapes, but the content was unmistakable. "This is my mother screaming;" "this is my best friend who died." And the pictures had blood in them. It was really disturbing.

Rich: In the documentary *Occupation 101*, the filmmakers mention a psychological study of the children of Gaza that was conducted before this latest incursion. The study revealed how many of them have been traumatized by witnessing the beatings of their fathers by Israeli troops

---

* Israel maintains a list of GPS coordinates and had the coordinates for the UN compound before the invasion began.

and how many have given up the will to live. The filmmakers also interviewed a Palestinian woman who spoke about the terror her young children experience, how frightened they are when Israeli soldiers suddenly appear in the dark, yelling for the mother's ID; and how the children cannot sleep at night. The woman also told the filmmakers how her daughter tried to hang herself from a tree. When the woman asked her child why she tried to kill herself the girl said: "I don't want to live; I'd rather die." Were you able to speak with the children about their feelings?

Fatima: I would have loved to talk to them about their feelings but what we were really only able to do was observe their behavior. The children acted out in various ways. They were either really confused or withdrawn or – I don't want to say violent – but they definitely were more aggressive. The head of the Palestinian Center for Human Rights explained that many children see that their parents are no longer able to protect them and that causes them to lose faith in the world around them; they no longer feel safe. In some cases they idolize their aggressor. That is very detrimental for their development.

Rich: What is the state of mind of the Gazans in general?

Fatima: Of course human beings have different ways of dealing with their experiences and their trauma. In terms of adults, there is a tremendous amount of fortitude and patience and forbearance. However, at the same time people have been oppressed for so long that it is difficult to maintain much hope. There is sort of an abnormal normalcy that pervades their society.

I can tell you a little story that really affected me. One of our friends was a wonderful man who showed us all around Gaza and took us to various centers. He wasn't affiliated with *Codepink*. This man had spent a significant amount of time in Israeli prisons. He said between the late 1980s and about 1993 he was imprisoned three to nine months every year as a result of "administrative arrests" that the Israelis carry out. He sent me an email a few days after we left. He said: "I've had this feeling since you and your group left and I couldn't put my finger on it, but this morning I woke up and realized what the feeling was." He said it was "the same feeling I used to get when my mom would come to visit me in prison and then leave, or one of the other prisoners would leave and I would still be in prison. I realized that you left us in prison." That was really powerful.

Rich: How did the Gazans treat you? What was their reaction to your mission?

Fatima: They were so hospitable. They loved that we were there. They said: "You came for us?"

Rich: Is there any light in this situation? I mean, a friend of mine in India emailed me recently with a beautiful story about the surfers in Gaza. He is an old surfer himself from California and he told me that a Jewish American from Hawaii had learned of the beaches and waves in Gaza and had managed to have fifteen surfboards sent to the Gazans, and now they have a surf club. The donor said that his hope is that someday Israeli and Gazan surfers will have competitions on those beaches. So is there any sense of real hope or is the situation just grim and hopeless?

Fatima: It is grim. However, there are wonderful things that come out. The people of Gaza are indicative of the incredible way people can behave when faced with hardship; in terms of their hospitality and what they do to help their neighbors. We heard story after story that during the bombing there would be thirty or so people in one room because everyone in the neighborhood would congregate in one house, five or ten families in one place, so there is a collective sense in the way people do take care of each other. And in spite of having nothing, their generosity is unbelievable.

In terms of stories like surfing, this is going to sound harsh, but I wouldn't honestly want to focus on positive stories too much. They are important to focus on so as not to lose hope, but in the broader scheme the people in Gaza told us what they want from us: "While we appreciate your help, we don't need it; what we need and what we want is a stance from individuals and governments and a change in U.S. policy." We heard this over and over again. "If you give us medicine or a cash donation today, tomorrow we are going to be bombed and again the next day and probably again the next year until there is nothing left." It's almost like what's the point. Send a surfboard today, but the recipient might need a prosthetic leg tomorrow. So there are simple, redeeming things and small incredible projects that are happening but it is difficult without a comprehensive shift occurring.

Rich: Is there something else you would like to say?

Fatima: We often hear that Gaza is the world's largest open air prison and it is really true. It's on the Mediterranean. When the sun sets out on the horizon you see what looks like a city out at sea. There are so many lights from the Israeli warships that are lined up along the Gaza coast. Throughout the night they practice exercises, so you hear the sound of constant shelling. Under international law there is a range of about twelve to thirteen kilometers from shore where people have the right to fish, but Israel limits the Gaza fishermen to two or three kilometers.

Also, when we were there the Israelis instituted a three-hundred meter rule, which means if you were within three hundred meters of the Israeli border you would likely be shot. This is one of the richest farm areas. Formally, the Israelis do not allow farmers to come within three-hundred meters of the border but in actuality they shoot at farmers within seven-hundred meters of the border. They shoot at farmers trying to plant their fields. Farmers were complaining to us: "I used to have the whole field but now I only have up to that furrow. I can no longer use the rest of the field to grow vegetables."

Rich: Wouldn't Israel say that it imposed the three hundred meter rule to protect its border?

Fatima: Precisely, its security. On one side Israeli warships are lined up along the coast. On each of the two sides of Gaza that border Israel is an Israeli imposed three hundred meter no-man's land. The southern border is shared with Egypt and it is militarized. Access to and from Egypt is only available periodically when the crossing is open. That is why there are so many tunnels. The tunnels, by the way, are frequently bombed by Israel and gassed by Egypt.

Rich: During the Nazi occupation of Poland, the Jewish Resistance in the Warsaw Ghetto built tunnels, which enabled them to smuggle weapons and communicate with the outside world. In the case of Gazans, even though the tunnels can be used to smuggle weapons, I would guess that their main purpose is to bring in food and medical supplies and other necessities.

Fatima: That's right. On the Gazan side the tunnels are not even hidden.

Rich: Did you speak with anyone who is a member of Hamas? What did you learn or hear about Hamas?

Fatima: They are the government and like any government they have a political wing, an army, social services, all sorts of programs. The main Hamas representative we met with reminded us that they were democratically elected. The primary message he kept repeating, the thing he really emphasized, was that they were democratically elected: "We were elected because Fatah is corrupt; we were elected because our people wanted transparency. Regardless of your opinion of us, don't forget that we were elected by the people, don't forget that."

Rich: What about opposition to Hamas? There were people who voted against them. Does Hamas suppress dissent?

Fatima: We saw a large demonstration in broad daylight in Gaza City that was organized by the PFLP (Popular Front for the Liberation of Palestine), which is a secular movement. The demonstrators were highlighting the need for unity. So there is some opposition and it is in the open.

Rich: Are there refugee camps in Gaza?

Fatima: There were originally about 70,000 Gazans. Today the population is about 1.5 million. If you take into account population growth, about 1,000,000 are 1948 refugees. I think it is important for people to know that the vast majority of Gaza's population consists of 1948 refugees. When we talk about most of the towns in Gaza we are talking about refugee camps. Most of the camps are from 1948. Nowadays, they look like ramshackle towns.

Rich: Because Operation Cast Lead destroyed so many neighborhoods there must be more camps in Gaza than previous to the invasion.

Fatima: Yes, there are substantial-sized tent camps since Operation Cast Lead. There is a blockade on all building supplies – wood, concrete, and metals – so nothing has been rebuilt. The people who are living in tents are stuck there until Israel gives them permission to rebuild their homes.

Rich: Are there other places they can live?

Fatima: Some people have moved into unfinished housing blocks. They don't have running water or electricity. Other people move in with their families. Some people rent but we were told that rent prices have trebled so if you don't have the economic means or the support structure of a large family you end up in a tent. Also, in towns like Rafah, there are no more places to rent.

Rich: When you talk to people in the United States and England about what you saw in Gaza, do many of them blame the Palestinians? Do they claim that the rocket attacks into Israel were the reason Israel invaded in the first place?

Fatima: People ask me, "What about Sderot, what about Ashkelon and other Israeli towns, what about the rockets?"* I explain to them that Sderot used to be a village named Najd: a Palestinian village where people lived and worked and died and were driven out in 1948. And Ashkelon sits on the remains of a Palestinian village once called al-Majdal. So, to only start with the story from now, with rockets being lobbed over the wall, is very shortsighted. There are people in Gaza who are from Najd and al-Majdal. Those towns are so close the people can almost see them, yet they have no access. Regardless of your standpoint we all know that bombing schools, places of worship, or hospitals is contrary to international law, yet it was highly prevalent.

Rich: Did you see any Israelis while you were in Gaza?

Fatima: No.

Rich: Fatima, I really appreciate your taking the time to talk with me.

Fatima: Thank you.

---

* Sderot and Ashkelon are cities in Southern Israel. Sderot is one kilometer and Ashkelon is fifteen kilometers from Israel's border with Gaza.

Breakthrough

– 11 –

Hebron

It's he, the other, always the other, who puts us in a situation in which we use force. Excuse me, where we are obliged to use force. For ultimately he's clearly the one who started it. All we did was react. Maybe another time, when they've understood – forced into it, by force, because force is all they understand – we'll be able to talk with them. If there's anyone to talk with. That's what we say. That's exactly what 'they' say also. Not only can't we see the other and talk to him, but it's absolutely forbidden to do so. He's not allowed to have a name, the other, or a past, a history, plans, descendants, dreams, suffering, loves, and misfortunes. Because if we understood his history, if we saw his loves and his fears, if we knew his plans and his dreams, maybe, God forbid, we would discover how much he's like us – almost the spitting image. And then we would no longer be able to hit him so hard. Yaakov Raz, University of Tel Aviv Professor of Asian Studies[1]

Thirty kilometers south of Jerusalem, with a present-day population of 160,000 Palestinians, Hebron is the second largest city in the West Bank. Only Nablus is larger. Hebron is also the second most sacred city to Jews, after Jerusalem, and one of the most sacred cities to Muslims.

According to the *Book of Genesis*, Abraham, the first patriarch of Judaism and Islam, purchased the Cave of Machpelah (Sanctuary of Abraham) from Ephron the Hittite for a family burial site after the death of his wife Sarah. Located in the heart of Hebron (al-Khalil), Machpelah is also known as the Cave (or Tomb) of the Patriarchs. Besides Abraham and Sarah, Isaac and his wife Rebekah and Jacob and his first wife Leah are also believed to be buried there. In Judaism, only the Temple Mount in the Old City of Jerusalem surpasses the Cave of the Patriarchs in holiness. All three major Abrahamic religions – Judaism, Christianity and Islam – believe that the remains of Adam and Eve are entombed in the Cave. Some Jewish sources claim that the skull of Jacob's brother, Esau, lies buried at the site, while some Islamic sources maintain that the grave of Jacob's son, Joseph, is in Machpelah.

Since the first century B.C., when Herod the Great enclosed the Cave behind large walls, Machpelah has gone through a number of reconstruction projects. In the seventh century, the Muslims built a roof over the Cave and refashioned it into the Ibrahimi Mosque. Around 1100 A.D. the area was conquered by the Crusaders. Hebron's significance for Christians was that Mary's cousin Elizabeth, the mother of John the Baptist, lived there. The Crusaders added gabled roofs and clerestory windows to the Cave's enclosure and transformed the mosque into a church. In 1188 A.D. Salah al-Din threw out the Christians and restored the church to a mosque. He then constructed minarets on the four corners of the enclosures, two of which survive to this day. Two entrances were later added by the Muslim Mameluks at the end of the fourteenth century.

Given its importance to their respective religions, Hebron has remained a bone of contention between Jews and Muslims for centuries. In 1929 an ongoing dispute between Palestinians and Israelis erupted into violent anti-Jewish riots throughout Palestine. Each side had been railing about the other's disrespect for its religious sites. On August twenty-third, Palestinian Arabs murdered sixty-seven of Hebron's Jews. Some of the victims were raped and tortured. According to Zionist archives, four hundred and thirty-five Jews found safety in the homes of twenty-eight Palestinian families. Following the riots Jewish residents abandoned their homes and moved away from Hebron, leaving it without a Jewish presence for the first time in eight hundred years.

The British government appointed Sir Walter Shaw to lead an investigation into the source of the riots. In March 1930 his board of inquiry reported:

> ...If there was in Palestine in August last a widespread feeling of resentment amongst the Arabs at the failure of His Majesty's Government to grant them some measure of self-government, it is at least probable that this resentment would show itself against the Jews, whose presence in Palestine would be regarded by the Arabs as the obstacle to the fulfilment [sic] of their aspirations.
> . . . It is our belief that a feeling of resentment among the Arab people of Palestine consequent upon their disappointment at the continued failure to obtain any measure of self-government ... was a contributory cause to the recent outbreak and is a factor

which cannot be ignored in the consideration of the steps to be taken to avoid such outbreaks in the future.[2]

The Shaw Commission also said:

> In less than 10 years three serious attacks have been made by Arabs on Jews. For 80 years before the first of these attacks there is no recorded instance of any similar incidents. It is obvious then that the relations between the two races during the past decade must have differed in some material respect from those which previously obtained. Of this we found ample evidence. The reports of the Military Court and of the local Commission which, in 1920 and in 1921 respectively, enquired into the disturbances of those years, drew attention to the change in the attitude of the Arab population towards the Jews in Palestine. This was borne out by the evidence tendered during our inquiry when representatives of all parties told us that before the War the Jews and Arabs lived side by side if not in amity, at least with tolerance, a quality which to-day is almost unknown in Palestine.[3]

In 1968, nearly forty years after the bloodshed, Rabbis Moshe Levinger and Eliezer Waldman and a group of families decided the time had come for Jews to repopulate this ancient city. Levinger's contingent of eighty-eight people moved into the Nahar al-Khalid hotel, allegedly to celebrate the Jewish holiday of Pesach (Passover). Levinger had assured Israeli General Uzi Narkiss that his group only wanted to hold a traditional Seder in Hebron and would return to Israel the following day. Having deceived the general, the group stayed at the hotel for six weeks before agreeing to Defense Minister Moshe Dayan's proposal that they move to an abandoned military compound east of and overlooking the city. For more than two years the group lived in temporary housing while constructing their new settlement on the outskirts of Hebron. They named their settlement Kiryat Arba. According to the Hebrew Bible, Kiryat Arba is another name for Hebron.

In 1979 ten women, including Rabbi Levinger's wife Miriam, and forty children left Kiryat Arba in the middle of the night and expropriated a large, vacant building in the center of Hebron. The building, known as Beit Hadassah, had been a charity institute and medical clinic prior to the

1929 riots. With its new residents, Beit Hadassah became the first of four small settlements in the city, making Hebron the only Palestinian city with an organized Jewish presence inside its urban boundaries.[*] Today, the city's total settler population numbers about six hundred. An impermanent group of two to three hundred yeshiva students also resides in the settlements. Fifteen hundred to several thousand IDF soldiers control Hebron and protect the Jewish population.[+]

According to the United Nations Office for the Coordination of Humanitarian Affairs (OCHA), these urban settlements and the Cave of the Patriarchs are connected to Kiryat Arba "by a corridor lined with eighty-seven obstacles that physically prevent access by the local Palestinian population."[4]

Kiryat Arba is now home to 7,000 settlers, most of whom are members of *Gush Emunim* (Bloc of the Faithful), a right wing religious/political/nationalistic movement that believes the coming of the Messiah will be hastened by Jewish settlement in the Holy Land. One of their favorite slogans is "Arabs out!"

Gush Emunim was founded in 1974, following the national trauma of the 1973 Yom Kippur War. Their mandate is: "The Land of Israel, for the people of Israel, according to the Torah of Israel."[5] For Gush Emunim, "[t]he entire Land of Israel is the Promised Land to be 'conquered, possessed and settled.'"[6] They view the Arab-Israeli conflict

---

[*] The other Jewish settlements are Avraham Avinu, Tel Rumeida, and Beit Romano. In March 2007 settlers raided a house in the a-Ras Palestinian neighborhood of Hebron and established a fifth settlement. Soon afterwards, the Defense Ministry decided to evacuate this settlement. Despite the Ministry's decision, however, the settlement continued to grow over the next year. B'Tselem reports that Palestinians in this area are now faced with daily abuse at the hands of settlers and IDF soldiers. B'Tselem, "19 March '08, Hebron: The Settlement in the a-Ras neighborhood is one-year old."

[+] In 1997, the PLO and Israeli government agreed to the Hebron Protocol, which divided the city into sectors labeled H-1 and H-2. H-1 is home to 120,000 to 130,000 Palestinians and is under the control of the Palestinian Authority. H-2 contains Hebron's Jewish settlements and is under the control of the Israeli army whose primary mission is to protect the Jewish settlers. About 30,000 Palestinians live in H-2, but their numbers have been decreasing due to harassment and violence by Jewish settlers and the effects of the settlers' behavior on their economy.

as an eternal struggle between the forces of good and evil. Accordingly, war is necessary to redeem the Promised Land. Gush Emunim also believes that "Arab hostility springs, as does all anti-Semitism, from the world's recalcitrance in the face of Israel's mission to save it."[7] And "Humane treatment is appropriate . . . 'only for those Arabs ready to accept the sovereignty of the people of Israel.'"[8] They stress that "Thou shalt not kill" is an incorrect translation of the Sixth Commandment. The correct translation is: "Thou shalt not commit murder." The distinction as applied to Arabs is stark: since the killing of an Arab is an act of self-defense, not murder, Jews cannot be accused of violating the Sixth Commandment.[9] In his memoirs, Yitzhak Rabin referred to Gush Emunim as a "cancer in the body of Israeli democracy."[10]

* * * *

On the grounds of the Meir Kahane Memorial Park in Kiryat Arba lies the burial place of Baruch Goldstein. His grave, like the Cave of the Patriarchs, is a pilgrimage site for many Jews. Goldstein was a follower of Kahane and a member of his ultra-nationalist political party, Kach, as well as the Jewish Defense League. The JDL was founded by Kahane in Brooklyn, New York in 1968 to protect Ultra-Orthodox Jews from harassment by the local population.

During the Muslim holy month of Ramadan, at dawn on the day of the Jewish festival of Purim, February 25, 1994, the American born and trained physician, wearing his army reservist uniform, walked into the Ibrahimi Mosque and proceeded to the back of one its rooms. Goldstein waited for the worshippers to begin their prayers, whereupon he threw a hand grenade into the crowd and opened fire with his automatic weapon, slaughtering twenty-nine Muslims and wounding one hundred and fifty. Before he could complete his executions, he was subdued and beaten to death with iron bars. Witnesses say that more than one gunman fired on the Muslim worshippers and that Israeli soldiers witnessed what was happening but did nothing to stop the massacre. In the chaotic days that followed, an additional twenty-six Palestinians and nine Jews were killed and many more were injured.

Purim commemorates the success of Queen Esther and her uncle Mordechai in foiling Haman's evil plot to murder all the Jews of Persia. As recounted in the *Book of Esther*, Haman was royal vizier to the court of King Ahasuerus. He is one of the greatest villains in the *Tanakh* and often considered the embodiment of evil.* For his intended crime, he was put to death.

There are some who speculate that Goldstein chose to carry out his mass killings on Purim day because he believed, like other members of Gush Emunim, that all Arabs shared Haman's ambition to eradicate the Jewish people from the face of the earth. Goldstein's friends say he acted preemptively because he thought an attack against Hebron's Jewish population was imminent. They also claim that about thirty of his closest friends in the Hebron-Kiryat Arba area had lost their lives in violent incidents in the few years leading up to the Purim day massacre. One of the fatalities was the son of Goldstein's best friend. When Goldstein arrived at the scene of the hostilities, the young man was still alive. Goldstein tried to administer medical care but was held back by Arab men and the boy died. Goldstein must have been profoundly angered that he was unable to save the life of a fellow Jew, especially one whom he knew and cared so much about. Throughout his career, however, Goldstein consistently refused to dispense medical assistance to any non-Jew. He declared: "I am not willing to treat any non-Jew. I recognize as legitimate only two [religious] authorities: Maimonides and [Meir] Kahane."+

Goldstein's death certificate lists homicide as the cause of his death. Reportedly, his wife wanted the Israeli government to file charges against his "murderers." The government declined.

A shrine honoring Goldstein was built next to his gravesite, but was destroyed by the Israeli government in 2000. A plaque remains. It reads:

> Here lies the saint, Dr. Baruch Kappel Goldstein, blessed be the
> memory of the righteous and holy man, may the Lord avenge his

---

* The Tanakh is the Hebrew Bible. It consists of the Torah (Five Books of Moses), Nevi'im (Prophets) and Ketuvim (Writings). The Book of Esther comes from Ketuvim.

+ Moses Maimonides (1135 – 1204), also known as the Rambam, is considered one of the greatest Torah scholars in Jewish history. He is the author of the Mishneh Torah, a code of Jewish law, and *The Guide for the Perplexed*. Maimonides taught that "it is forbidden to save them [Gentiles] at the point of death [Kovel, p. 30.]"

blood, who devoted his soul to the Jews, Jewish religion and Jewish land. His hands are innocent and his heart is pure. He was killed as a martyr of God on the 14th of Adar, Purim, in the year 5754 (1994).[11]

Following Goldstein's death, on March 18, 1994, the United Nations passed Security Council Resolution 904 which:

Calls upon Israel, the occupying Power, to continue to take and implement measures, including, *inter alia*, confiscation of arms, with the aim of preventing illegal acts of violence by Israeli settlers.

The Israeli security forces enacted strict measures, not, as UNSC 904 stipulated, to protect the Palestinian population from further acts of violence, but to prevent retaliation against Goldstein's fellow settlers. These measures set the stage for a new era of oppressive control over Hebron's Palestinian citizens.

* * * *

For hundreds of years the Old Suq (market) in the heart of Hebron was a thriving area of shops and businesses. But with the encroachment of Jewish settlements, many establishments have been forced to close their doors. OCHA reports that only ten percent of the shops in the Old Suq are still functioning.[12] Most of the Old City's residents have left and only twenty percent of those who remain are employed. Seventy-five percent of the population lives below the poverty line and the average per capita income of the area is $160 per month, far less than the meager $405 per capita monthly income in the entire West Bank.[13]

When I visited Hebron in June 2010 as part of an InterFaith Peace-Builders (IFPB) delegation, young teenagers and old men begged us to buy their goods. They were so desperate that they were offering the items for a quarter or fifth of the cost to buy them in other areas of the West Bank.

Jewish settlers now occupy the second stories of buildings on both sides of the streets within the Old Suq area. They frequently show their feelings for Palestinians by throwing human excrement, garbage and solid objects at the passers-by below.[14] The shopkeepers have had to install wire mesh above the open air walkways of the streets to shield their customers. Settlers also express themselves with graffiti. Sylvain Cypel traveled to Hebron in December 2002. While exploring the old city, he saw abandoned shops with their walls and metal curtains covered in "biblical phrases accompanied by slurs: 'The Arabs are pigs, Death to Arabs' and the like."[15] Someone even wrote "Arabs to the gas chamber."[16] That particular slogan was, apparently, more than the authorities could condone, so they made sure it was erased. Walking around the old city of Hebron, I too saw shocking expressions of hatred.

In a joint report with the Association for Civil Rights in Israel, B'Tselem concluded: "Israeli law enforcement authorities and security forces have made the entire Palestinian population pay the price for protecting Israeli settlement in the city."[17] Among the groups' findings were that "severe and extensive restrictions on Palestinian movement" and "the authorities' systematic failure to enforce law and order on violent settlers attacking Palestinians" have caused an "economic collapse" in Hebron's Old City. More than 1,000 housing units and 1,800 commercial establishments have been abandoned as a result of Israeli policies.[18]

Documented cases of violence and criminal activity include physical assaults by settlers, destruction of shops, the cutting down of fruit trees, poisoning of water wells, severing of electricity lines and water pipes, burglary, attempts to run people over, breaking and entering, throwing vegetables and bags filled with urine at Palestinians, stoning Palestinians, spilling hot liquid on the face of a Palestinian, and the killing of a young Palestinian girl.

Even though soldiers can be found on every corner, they do nothing to stop the settlers.[19] Their role, apparently, is to provide cover and to give the settlers enough confidence to know they can get away with just about anything, as long as it is directed at a Palestinian. The settlers have become a de facto vigilante organization quasi-deputized by their government to punish anyone who is guilty of the crime of not being Jewish.

With soldiers showing little inclination to deter inhuman behavior on the part of settlers and settlers applauding the inhuman behavior of the soldiers, the Palestinian residents have become near-defenseless casualties of the kind of savagery that can only be born of fear and hatred. One soldier described the power the settlers have in this holy city:

> Jews did as they pleased there, there are no laws. No traffic laws. Nothing. Whatever they do there is done in the name of religion, and anything goes – breaking into shops, that's allowed....[20]

B'Tselem recorded eyewitness testimonies of Israeli soldiers. Here is a typical account of a soldier's experience:

> "I saw a group of settlers, including men, women and children, going into the yards of Palestinian homes, destroying everything in their path. They broke windows, fences, and flower pots and damaged cars. At that stage, I saw a soldier who was on duty, standing near one of the Palestinian homes that came under attack. He did nothing. Four other soldiers arrived a little later. They didn't try to stop the settlers either."[21]

B'Tselem's full report includes eyewitness testimonies related to the killing of a fourteen-year-old boy, the stabbing of an eight-year-old boy, and the beating of a nine-year-old boy, all Palestinians.

* * * *

The fact that so few Jewish settlers can dictate the lives of so many Palestinians is evidence of the profoundly damaging effects that religious fervor and Zionist expansionism have had on a society that was thrown by circumstance into the role of Israel's enemy. Baruch Kimmerling describes this dynamic:

> These settlers behave like masters of the city, continually harassing the Arabs. An entire Israeli brigade of soldiers guarantees the security of this small handful of settlers. Because the settlement is close to the site known as the Ibrahamia Mosque . . . the Jewish community of Hebron regularly plays host to thousands of Jews for prayers that are more like political demonstrations. Thus, large numbers of the Arab inhabitants of the city are under curfew most of the time.[22]

Former President Carter is also troubled by the living conditions of Hebron's Palestinians:

About 450 extremely militant Jews have moved into the heart of the ancient part of the city, protected by several thousand Israeli troops. Heavily armed, these settlers attempt to drive the Palestinians away from the holy sites, often beating those they consider to be "trespassers," expanding their area by confiscating adjacent homes, and deliberately creating physical confrontations. When this occurs, the troops impose long curfews on the 150,000 Palestinian citizens of Hebron, prohibiting them from leaving their homes to go to school or shops or to participate in the normal life of an urban community.[23]

The soldiers also participate in terrorizing Hebron's residents. Human rights group Breaking the Silence (*Shovrim Shtika*) was formed by IDF veterans for the purpose of collecting testimonies of soldiers who have witnessed or participated in crimes and civil rights violations in Occupied Territory. The group's website states:

> Cases of abuse towards Palestinians, looting, and destruction of property have been the norm for years, but are still excused as military necessities, or explained as extreme and unique cases. Our testimonies portray a different and grim picture of questionable orders in many areas regarding Palestinian civilians. These demonstrate the depth of corruption which is spreading in the Israeli military. While this reality which is known to Israeli soldiers and commanders exists in Israel's back yard, Israeli society continues to turn a blind eye, and to deny that which happens in its name. Discharged soldiers who return to civilian life discover the gap between the reality which they encountered in the Territories, and the silence which they encounter at home. In order to become a civilian again, soldiers are forced to ignore their past experiences. Breaking the Silence voices the experiences of those soldiers, in order to force Israeli society to address the reality which it created.[24]

Here is an excerpt from the testimony of a soldier stationed in Hebron:

> We would go on these revenge missions.
> Against whom?
> Palestinians who threw stones at us.

But you don't really know who throws the stones?

Other kids inform on them. We catch them, beat them to a pulp, kids who were nearby, until they lead us to their homes.[25]

In addition to revenge missions, Israeli soldiers dispel their boredom by stopping vehicles just for fun, smashing windows and beating up the passengers, randomly beating up children on the streets, sticking loaded, cocked pistols inside the mouths of children while threatening to kill them, stealing a variety of items – stereo equipment, tobacco, etc. – from shops, using threats of violence to repeatedly extort money and goods from shop owners, stealing money from people's homes, throwing stun grenades into mosques during prayer services, firing at unarmed demonstrators, preventing people from going to the hospital, abusing corpses, randomly raiding houses late at night when people are sleeping, and lining people up and playing a game to see which soldiers can choke their victims and cause them to pass out the quickest. Sometimes, soldiers receive orders to look for and shoot at anyone they can find who is "armed" with stones. People, often children, are frequently shot in the arms, legs and abdomen during these assaults. According to B'Tselem "Cases of 'punishment' and abuse of Palestinians by IDF soldiers in the Occupied Territories occur daily."[26] Cypel expands upon the attitude of the military:

As for impunity, it is almost always taken for granted. When the commander of the Hebron garrison, returning from leave, found that his vehicle had been stolen, soldiers raided the Arab city, leaving thirteen dead; an investigation went nowhere. When border guards beat a 14-year-old Palestinian to death in the street, the soldiers of their unit signed a letter claiming that they had not left the base. Everyone knew that this was collective false testimony. Case closed.[27]

Routine checkpoints are areas where soldiers have free rein to exercise their power over the city's residents. They don't need even the slightest provocation to harass and detain anyone. If a bored soldier feels like playing with a line of cars waiting to pass, he might move a finger ever so slightly and direct the cars to move forward a little bit and backward a little bit, to the right and to the left. He can play conductor, with the cars his orchestra, and keep them waiting for no reason other than to bask in the feeling of control one small digit has over an entire population. He may make the cars wait until he tires of the game and begins to look for other creative ways to harass Palestinians. The soldiers have as much leeway in their behavior as the settlers. A patrol commander explained to a soldier: "Listen, you can do whatever you want, whatever you feel like doing."[28]

Ometz Lesarev (Courage to Refuse) is another group of army veterans who are attempting to raise the Israeli public's consciousness about the effects of occupation on both Palestinians and Israelis. The soldiers have begun to question the instructions of their leaders. Ami Kronfeld articulated a common point-of-view:

> But a growing number of soldiers fail to see why they are asked to shatter children's knees, shoot pregnant women in the back and in general subjugate a defenseless population (and still risk their own lives in the process) – all just in order to maintain absolute control over occupied people.[29]

One young soldier who served in Hebron "talked of 'losing the human condition'. Asked what he meant, he replied: 'To lose the human condition is to become an animal.'"[30]

How will Israeli soldiers sleep at night, burdened by memories of shooting pregnant women in the back or of shattering the knees of defenseless children? The unexamined beliefs and images they inherit, as the young soldier discovered, rob them of their humanity. Israel has made a Faustian bargain in which it has traded the soul of its people for unbridled power. Former soldier, Yonatan Boemfeld:

> It's hard to deal with this reality. It's hard to accept the price Israeli society pays for every soldier that is sent to serve in the Palestinian cities. The price is heavy; the destruction of basic values, of human codes of behavior, of humane norms. What thoughts pass through the head of an IDF warrior when he takes the chopped-off head of a terrorist, sticks it on a stake and pushes a cigarette in its mouth? My generation is smoking itself to death in India because they can't deal with the truth that only they know, that only they experienced as the horrible routine of the checkpoints . . . . We have sinned the sin of pride. We

thought we were the biggest, the strongest, the undefeated. Now we eat ourselves from the inside. And anybody who says different is like an alcoholic who denies his illness.[31]

Israel calls itself the Jewish State, but the conduct of its military and settler population reflects poorly on the farsightedness of Jewish law. Rabbi Gershon Winkler points out that up until the nineteenth century, of the world's civilizations only Jewish law prohibited violence to animals.[32] Winkler also emphasizes that while the Code of Hammurabi, the first known collection of laws to supersede even a king's authority, prescribed death to anyone who harbored a runaway slave, Deuteronomy (Devarim 23: 16-17) states:

> You shall not surrender to his master a slave who has escaped from his master to you; he shall dwell with you, in your midst, in the place which he shall choose within one of your villages, where it pleases him most; you shall not oppress him.[33]

Yet, in the twentieth and twenty-first centuries, the Palestinian inhabitants of Hebron spend their lives in the midst of daily oppression, not even afforded the same consideration as animals or escaped slaves. They are subject to settler violence and harassment at any time; they are often under curfew; and when they go out of their homes they face further humiliation.

Even little girls returning home from school are not exempt from the wrath of settlers. One volunteer from the *Ecumenical Accompaniment Programme in Palestine and Israel* (EAPPI) described what he witnessed at a Palestinian girls' school in Hebron:

> There were bars on the windows, but settlers came and stuck in pipes to break the glass. There was no money to fix them, so the girls shivered through the winter. After school, settler kids would hide and wait for the girls to walk by, throwing stones and eggs at them as they passed. The other EAPPI volunteers and I walked with them sometimes, trying to shield the attacks. Once as we were walking I saw the mother of a settler child that was throwing stones at the young girls. I pointed and said, "Look! Look what your child is doing!" Her eyes fixed on me and her expression said clearly that she approved of her son's

behavior. She hadn't come to discipline her child; she had come to watch.[34]

The undeveloped minds and bodies of Palestinian children, who grow up in surroundings saturated with the fear of violence and cruelty, are on alert twenty-four hours a day, not knowing when it will be their turn to have a gun shoved in their mouths, to be stoned, to be choked to the point of passing out, to be beaten up, to be shot in the abdomen or threatened with death by a Jewish fanatic. They can be accosted suddenly, while playing with friends or going to the store. Maybe while they are sleeping, a band of soldiers or settlers will burst into their homes and terrorize their families. Surely, they are terrified, angry and confused that they are treated this way just for being born Palestinian. How will they manage this merciless stress and what will become of them as adults? Their environment practically begs for them to act out their pain in violent ways. Yet, Israel does not seem to care, even though it is responsible for these conditions.

Jewish-American activist and author, Anna Baltzer, asks her readers to contemplate what the children go through under such oppressive circumstances:

> Think of a child, a very young child, who knows that his parents and siblings are never safe, and that none of them can keep him safe. Think of a two-year-old who shuffles his feet faster and lowers his head with fear at the sight of any settler. Think of a kid who watches his mother and father humiliated on a daily basis and can do nothing to protect them. Think about the shame, the feeling of powerlessness, the suppression of the normal, healthy instinct to fight back. These are the greatest crimes. Any day a Palestinian child dares to stand up to his oppressors is a small victory.[35]

The soldiers and settlers are also victims. The abuse they are subjected to, however, is generally not committed by their "enemies," but by their parents and their religious, political and military leaders, whose aggressive and fear-based exhortations are drilled into their impressionable minds from early childhood. These children, then, also become slaves to unexamined beliefs. And their education system, reflecting society's bias, influences and reinforces their conditioning. A former South African soldier told me that young soldiers don't realize until much later what a "trance" they were in while in the military; and that some of them develop a disdain for politicians and military leaders when they realize how "frivolously these leaders play with human life."

In 1985 well-known Israeli educator Adir Cohen conducted a study of 1,700 children's books, all of which had been published after 1967. He also interviewed pupils between the ages of ten and twelve at a Jewish school in Haifa. He concluded:

> Five-hundred twenty of the works studied presented a degraded and deeply negative view of the Arab: 66 percent portrayed him as violent, 52 percent as wicked, 37 percent as a pathological liar, and 28 percent as sly. Out of eighty-six books for young children, Cohen found twenty-one cases in which Arabs were described as lethal, thirteen in which they were called murderers. Terms like *animal*, *snake*, *bloodthirsty*, *warlike*, and *dirty* were recurrent. As for the replies of the young pupils to the five questions Cohen asked them, they merely reproduced these racist stereotypes. Seventy-five percent saw the Arab as a murderer, a kidnapper, and a terrorist. Eighty percent spontaneously described him as dirty. Ninety percent believed he had no right to the Land of Israel. Cohen concluded that the demonization of the Arabs as a disturbing and vile figure was part and parcel of a system of shared convictions perceived as legitimate in history books and children's books alike.[36*]

---

* On the other hand, it would be naïve to think that anti-Semitism does not exist among Palestinians. A *Haaretz* article from January 2, 2001 by Akiva Eldar ("What Did You Study in School Today, Palestinian Child?") acknowledges that Palestinian textbooks do contain some degree of anti-Semitism. However, the overall tone of the article is encouraging: "The Palestinians are being rebuked where they should in fact be praised. For this school year the Palestinian Authority has, for the first time ever, printed its own textbooks. A research team from the Harry S. Truman Research Institute for the Advancement of Peace, led by Dr. Ruth Firer, has established that the new books are 'freer of negative stereotypes of Jews and Israelis, compared to Jordanian and Egyptian books.' The defense establishment has investigated and confirmed this finding." Eldar quotes Dr. Firer: "We were surprised to find how

As part of their indoctrination into Israel's siege mentality, elementary-school children correspond with active duty soldiers. A few messages of support are: "Dear soldier, I have a favor to ask you. Please kill a lot of Arabs." "I'm praying that you return home safe and sound. Do this for me: kill at least ten of them." "You don't give a damn about laws: a good Arab is a dead Arab."[37]

When Abraham Burg visited a high school, the students – Israel's future leaders – told him: "'When we're soldiers, we'll kill old people, women, and children . . . . We'll drive them out, we'll put them on planes to Iraq. Hundreds of thousands of them, millions.'"[38*]

One IDF soldier talked about the feelings Jewish children in Hebron, some as young as three or four, have about Arabs:

> [T]his is what I note for myself: your mission is to protect Palestinian homes from little, vicious Jewish children. Period. That's the mission there on Saturdays. That's when they pass along, a whole bunch of about ten kids, and you have to be something like their adult accompanier. The kids are terrible, really. A horror. The parents know, okay? We couldn't do a thing. Somehow they instill such hatred in their kids . . . . I get down from one of my posts and there's this four-year old child asking, "Have you killed an Arab already?" A three-four-year old child plays in the sand and asks me this. I ask him: "Why child, what happened?" "Arabs beat me up" he answers. And I

---

moderate the anger directed toward Israelis in the Palestinian textbooks is, compared to the Palestinian predicament and suffering. . . . This surprise is doubled when you compare the Palestinian books to Israeli ones from the 1950s and 1960s, which mentioned gentiles [only] in the context of pogroms and the Holocaust."

Baltzer, p. 378, cites the *Israel/Palestine Center for Research and Information*, "Reviewing Palestinian Textbooks and Tolerance Education Program," submitted to the Public Affairs Offices US Consulate General (Jerusalem, 2003): "professional educators – Israeli, Palestinian and American . . . concluded: '[The Palestinian] textbooks do not incite against Israel or against peace' and 'the overall orientation of the curriculum is peaceful despite the harsh and violent realities on the ground . . . . Religious and political tolerance is emphasized.'"

* Burg is former Speaker of the Knesset and former chairman of the Jewish Agency and World Zionist Organization. His father, Joseph Burg, was chairman of the National Religious Party and member of the Knesset.

go, "What? Who hit you?" Then I understand that he wasn't actually hurt, but someone got it into his head that some Arab hurt him some time in history, something that didn't even happen. Where does so much hatred come from . . . They're being filled with so much hatred.[39]

Children are taught to resent Palestinians for living on land the Jews covet, are trained to throw stones and eggs at them, to revile them just for being Palestinian. Can anybody be surprised by their behavior when, as armed soldiers, they are placed in situations where the opportunity to externalize their hatred upon their peoples' enemy constantly presents itself? Can anybody be surprised if the moment they see a Palestinian they perceive a terrorist intent on killing them?

Israel's leading demographer, Arnon Soffer, professor of geography at Haifa University and architect of the separation barrier, has captured the mindset of Israel's leaders and its supporters: "If we don't [kill], we'll cease to exist."[40]

Paralleling the breeding of false ideas in the minds of Jewish children,

> The curriculum of public schools for Arabs in Israel was written with the aim of creating a new ethnic identity for them (much as the Hashemite educational policy tried to Jordanize the Palestinians). . . . The aim was to thwart the flowering of a Palestinian Arab national identity.[41]

Hence, not only have Israeli institutions established conditions needed to rob the Palestinians of their future, they have set out to erase the Palestinians' connection to their past. The Israeli establishment is attempting to shape the Palestinian historical narrative of the twentieth and twenty-first centuries so that it conforms to the Zionist narrative from the same period.

* * * *

> As a Jew, I was ashamed at the scenes of Jews opening fire at innocent Arabs in Hebron. There is no other definition than the term 'pogrom' to describe what I have seen. We are the sons of a nation who know what is meant by a pogrom, and I am using the word only after deep reflection.[42]

So said Israeli Prime Minister Ehud Olmert in reaction to settler-instigated violence, just weeks before he authorized Israel's crushing invasion of the Gaza Strip. The stimulus for the settlers' behavior was the Israeli security services' eviction of Jews from Beit HaShalom, Hebron's "House of Peace," in December 2008. Jewish soldiers stood by and watched the bloodshed. No charges were filed against the settlers.

Jewish settlers in Hebron and throughout the West Bank have spray painted mosques and businesses with the Star of David. "Do they not remember Kristallnacht? Or do they specifically remember Kristallnacht?" asks Hannah Mermelstein.[43*] Within seven years after Kristallnacht six million Jews had been exterminated. Does a similar fate await the Palestinians of Hebron, perhaps even the entire West Bank or Gaza? Perhaps not; genocide in the Holy Land would precipitate too great an outcry from the international community. Even the United States, Israel's most compliant ally, would have no choice but to join in the chorus of disapproval. But what if the religious right and their settler movement gain even more influence and control over the Israeli government? Then what?

Israeli journalist Gideon Spiro, a former paratrooper, was decorated for heroism in the 1956 Suez war. He was among a group of soldiers that took control of East Jerusalem in 1967. In the 1980s, inspired by Palestinian nonviolent activist Feisel Abd al-Qadir Husseini, Spiro joined the *Committee Confronting the Iron Fist* (Lajnat Muwajahat al-Qabda al-Hadidiyya).[+] The Committee practiced civil disobedience and other nonviolent methods to protest the occupation. The Committee's formation marked the beginning of "contemporary nonviolent action against the Israeli military occupation."[44] In 1982, in response to Israel's invasion of Lebanon, Spiro co-founded *Yesh Gvul* (There is a limit). The

---

* Mermelstein is co-founder of Birthright Unplugged, which organizes tours so young Jews can experience Israel. Kristallnacht (Crystal Night) occurred in Nazi Germany on November 9 to 10, 1938. Ninety-six Jews were murdered, hundreds injured, more than 1,000 synagogues burned, thousands of Jewish businesses destroyed, schools and cemeteries vandalized and 30,000 Jews rounded up and sent to concentration camps. See "Kristallnacht," at Jewishvirtuallibrary.org.

+ "Iron fist" was a term used by David Ben-Gurion, Yitzhak Rabin and Yitzhak Shamir. King, p. 165.

organization's mission was to support soldiers who refused "to enforce policies they deem[ed] illegal, immoral and ultimately harmful to Israeli interests."[45] The group declared that as "responsible citizens" they would "take no part in the continued oppression of the Palestinian people in the occupied territories . . . . There are things that decent people don't do."[46]

In a 2006 interview with Professor King, Spiro commented:

> Between 1933 and 1939 [even before the 'Final Solution'], Nazi Germany was a brutal, racist regime. I think that large numbers of Israeli society, and Israeli ruling circles, sometimes resemble those of Nazi Germany in the 1930s, especially in their adoption of racist principles.
>
> I am a survivor of crystalnacht, the night of shattered glass, when Germans in 1938 rampaged Jewish shops and synagogues. When I see Israeli soldiers and Jewish settlers in the occupied territories, they are very often acting more brutally [than] what was happening when I was a small child during that period [1933-39] in Nazi Germany. Israel is the classic example of a beaten child, who became a beating parent. Jewish racism and Jewish war crimes are not less ugly because they are Jewish.[47]

* * * *

A few months after the 1967 Six-Day War, French President Charles de Gaulle, chastened by his country's century-long occupation of Algeria, predicted: "Now Israel is organizing an occupation on the territories it seized, which can't go on without opposition, repression, and expulsions, and a resistance is becoming evident there that, in turn, it will call terrorism."[48]

As IDF Chief-of-Staff, Yitzhak Rabin was the architect of Israel's victory in 1967. At war's end he proposed the creation of a Palestinian state. He told Israeli Prime Minister Levi Eshkol that annexing the West Bank would be tantamount to the creation of a "South African situation."[49] Twenty-seven years later he said: "We are paying with blood for ruling over another people . . . . Ruling over another people has corrupted us."[50]

In 1969 Israeli philosopher and Zionist Yeshayahu Leibovitz, speaking about the Occupied Territories, predicted: "'concentration camps would be erected by the Israeli rulers . . . Israel would be a state that would not deserve to exist, and it will not be worthwhile to preserve it.'"[51] In the past few years, even before the Gaza invasion, reports by human rights organizations have begun to confirm Leibovitz's prophesy. Many have used the term "open air prison" to describe the living conditions of Palestinians throughout the Occupied Territories.

* * * *

Through indoctrination into a culture of hatred, Israel has attributed to the Palestinians the intentions of the evil Haman and of other persecutors throughout its people's history. Israel has transformed itself from a defender of the dispossessed into a perpetrator of dispossession, and the Palestinian people have been forced to assume the familiar role of scapegoat for the unresolved fear, confusion and trauma of a people once known for their commitment to justice. By placing militant, bigoted, fundamentalist settlers in the middle of Hebron – and Israeli police and soldiers to protect and enable them and even participate with them – Israel is not only promoting its own state-sanctioned form of terrorism, it is severely traumatizing an entire population, especially young children.

The Jewish State wants to cleanse Hebron and the West Bank of the scourge of Palestinian life. It is following the advice of Moshe Dayan, who said: "Let us approach them [the Palestinian refugees in the Occupied Territories] and say that we have no solution, that you shall continue to live like dogs, and whoever wants to can leave – and we will see where this process leads."[52]

– 12 –

Seizures, Settlements and the Security Fence

Ye shall not steal; neither shall ye deal falsely, nor lie one to another. Leviticus 19:11[1]

Israel's monument to more than sixty years of struggle with its Palestinian neighbor is the structure its government refers to as the "security fence." The Israeli media commonly refer to it as the "hafrada" (separation) barrier. Construction began in June 2002 with an expected completion date sometime in 2010. The Israeli Ministry of Defense states:

> The *sole purpose* of the Security Fence . . . is to provide security. The Security Fence is a central component in Israel's response to the horrific wave of terrorism emanating from the West Bank, resulting in suicide bombers who enter into Israel with the sole intention of killing innocent people.[2]

The greater part of the barrier consists of a series of electronic fences, razor wire as much as 70 meters wide, ditches and patrol roads. When construction is completed, the barrier will span a distance of 790 kilometers; the Green Line is 315 kilometers in length.[3] In some places the barrier is built of concrete and is nine meters high, making it twice as tall as the Berlin Wall. Nearly 75 percent of the barrier (525 of the 721 km) is situated inside the West Bank.[4]

In answer to the question, "What is the status of Palestinians who reside between the Security Fence and the Green Line," the Israeli Ministry of Defense replied:

> Only a small number of Palestinian villages will be included on the western side of the Security Fence. Their residents will not have to relocate and their legal status will remain unchanged.[5]

Challenging the Ministry's assessment, Amnesty International states:

> When completed the fence/wall will cut off more than 15% of West Bank land from the rest of the West Bank and some 270,000 Palestinians living in these areas will be trapped in closed military areas between the fence/wall and the Green Line or in enclaves encircled by the fence/wall. More than 200,000

Palestinian residents of East Jerusalem will also be cut off from the West Bank and hundreds of thousands of other Palestinians living in towns and villages east of the fence/wall will also be affected as they need access to areas on the other side of the fence/wall to reach their land and their workplaces, schools and health care facilities and other services, and to visit their relatives.[6]

The fifteen percent of the West Bank that Amnesty cites includes "some of the most agriculturally productive land and richest water resources in the West Bank."[7] In their July 2007 report on the impact of Israeli settlement on the Palestinian population, OCHA found that the majority of farming families on the west side of the barrier no longer had access to their land.[8] Trees and irrigation systems are also casualties of the barrier's construction.[9] Encircling sixty-nine Jewish settlements comprising 83% of the settler population, the barrier effectively annexes Palestinian land into the State of Israel.[10]

Within Jerusalem governorate, only five kilometers of the barrier's 162 kilometer length run along the Green Line. The rest of the barrier trespasses on and devours parts of the West Bank. By design, most of the Jewish-only settlements that surround East Jerusalem are located to the west of the barrier, connecting them to the city's boundaries and providing easy access to Jerusalem for Israeli settlers. The reverse is the case for about twenty-five percent of Palestinian residents who are cut off from their own city.[11]

The ICRC (International Committee of the Red Cross), in a confidential report that was leaked to the *New York Times*, accused Israel of isolating Palestinian Jerusalemites from the rest of the West Bank and of making it difficult for West Bank Palestinians from outside of Jerusalem to reach the city's schools and hospitals. The committee also explained that it was "virtually impossible" for Palestinians who were not born in Jerusalem to move to the city and that even visiting permits were hard to obtain.[12]

Residents of the West Bank town of Beit Jala, which is east of the barrier, asked the government to redraw the barrier's route so they would not have to pass through checkpoints to reach their land, which is situated between Jerusalem and the western side of the barrier. The authorities' response was to turn down their request and seize their entire one thousand acre parcel. As a result, two hundred families have lost their principal source of income.[13]

Since May 2008 residents of the West Bank village of Ni'lin have been demonstrating against the barrier's intrusion onto their land. In 1948 Ni'lin's land area was 57,000 dunams.[*] By 1967 the area had been reduced to 33,000 dunams. Subsequent to the 1967 Six-Day War, an additional 23,000 dunams were confiscated, some of it for Jewish settlements. By the time the barrier is completed another 2,500 dunams of Ni'lin's land will have been confiscated, leaving the village with a total of 7,500 dunams, or less than fifteen percent of its original area.[14]

Only five minutes away from Ni'lin is the village of Bil'in, where weekly protests have been going on for over five years. Here too, Israel has seized private property, separating villagers from more than fifty percent of their land. While in Bil'in I met with Mohamad Amireh, a member of the Popular Committee of Ni'lin, a group that is committed to nonviolent resistance. Mohamad had come to Bil'in to meet with our delegation. He was a farmer until the Israelis decided to build the separation wall in his village and separate him from his land. Mohamad teaches at his local elementary school. One day his student, ten-year old Ahmed Musa, drew a picture of two flags, one Israeli the other Palestinian. Mohamad asked Ahmed why he had drawn the picture. Ahmed answered: "Why can't we live together in peace?" Mohamad told the other students in the class what Ahmed had said and they all cheered.

On July 29, 2008, at a peaceful demonstration against the separation wall, Ahmed was playing with a camera. An Israeli border police officer shot him in the head. He died a few days later. On May 25, 2010, the police officer was indicted on a charge of negligent manslaughter. The indictment may be a small victory for a people who rarely see justice but it does not guarantee conviction. Of the small percentage of cases of violence toward Palestinians that are investigated, only a fraction is brought to trial. Since 2001 B'Tselem has handled thirty-five cases where Palestinians were injured or killed by Israeli fire. Only sixteen were

---

[*] A dunam is 1,000 square meters, slightly less than a quarter-acre.

investigated by Israeli authorities and only Ahmed's and one other resulted in indictments.

Despite the Ni'lin villagers' peaceful protests, nearly 200 residents have been injured, elderly women beaten, and three residents killed by Israeli soldiers and police.

I was deeply impressed by Mohamad's presence, by his sincerity and by his commitment to nonviolence. As we walked together this sturdy man described how he was trying to talk with an Israeli commander at one of the village's demonstrations. As Mohamad held his three-and-a-half year old son in his arms he pointed out to the commander that both men had children and for the sake of the children they should make peace. The commander responded by grabbing Mohamad's son from his arms and throwing him into the cactus. True to his principles, Mohamad did not retaliate.

His son has not recovered from the psychological damage borne of this violent act. He has become very angry toward the entire family. When he is old enough to understand what happened to him will his anger be directed toward Israelis?

Seventy-two year-old widow Zuheira Murshad owns land near the West Bank village of Falame. Mrs. Murshad is unfortunate in two respects: not only is her land separated from the rest of the West Bank by the security fence, it is also near the home of former Israeli Defense Minister Shaul Mofaz, whose estate straddles the Green Line. In September 2004, during Mofaz's tenure as head of the Defense Ministry, the Israeli army notified Mrs. Murshad that her trees would be cut down. She said:

> The army has fenced in my land and I have not been able to go to tend to it and now they want to cut down my trees, my livelihood. First the army said that I needed a permit to go to my land. The permit is difficult to obtain; to apply I have to go to the army base in the Israeli settlement of Kedumim and it is difficult and dangerous for me to get there. And if I get the permit it is only for me, but I cannot tend the land by myself and need people to help me but nobody else can get a permit and so I have not been able to tend to my land. My own trees are going to waste and I now have to work on someone else's land to pick

olives. I am an old woman, I don't cause any harm to the Israeli Defence Minister; but they have caused much harm to me, they have destroyed my life.[15]

In February 2005 Zuheira Murshad's petition to halt the destruction of her property was rejected by the Israeli Supreme Court.

* * * *

On July 9, 2004 the International Court of Justice (ICJ) in The Hague, in a near unanimous decision – of the fifteen judges on the court, only one dissented and he did so primarily on procedural grounds – ruled that the barrier was in violation of international law. In his concurring opinion, Judge El-Araby wrote:

> The magnitude of the damage and injury inflicted upon the civilian inhabitants in the course of building the wall and its associated régime is clearly prohibited under international humanitarian law. The destruction of homes, the demolition of the infrastructure, and the despoilment of land, orchards and olive groves that has accompanied the construction of the wall cannot be justified under any pretext whatsoever.[16]

The Ministry of Defense has acknowledged "that the construction of the Security Fence can introduce hardship into the lives of innocent Palestinians and *regrets* those hardships."[17] But when asked, "Why isn't the security fence built along the green line," the Ministry answered:

> On the practical level a fence along this line would create far greater humanitarian problems, arbitrarily dividing certain villages, and separating others from access to water and other basic services on a large scale. Moreover, it would ignore the aim of the fence, which is to frustrate acts of terrorism directed against Israeli population centers. It is the terrorists who, by their murderous attacks, have dictated the route, which seeks to protect as many civilians as possible, while seeking to minimize the humanitarian and environmental hardship.[18]

The construction of the barrier has caused changes to the lay of the land, redirecting not only rainwater but sewage as well.* Stories abound

---

* The problem of raw sewage is not just a phenomenon of the Wall's construction.

of village wells being contaminated and homes flooded. Shadia Mohammad Salih Jaradat lives in Zububa village in the Jenin district. She told journalists how sewage seeps under the door of her house, how her family must vacate the premises for three months of the year, and how her children cannot go to school because of all the foul-smelling mud. Her vegetable garden, chickens and pigeons have been lost. She feels hopeless because there is no one to turn to. Her husband says that at times the villagers have no choice but to drink the contaminated water; and he believes that Israel's actions are intentionally designed to force people to give up and leave.[19]

Imposition of sewage problems upon thousands of people and the wanton failure to correct those problems is callous, but insanitary living conditions serve the purpose of ethnic cleansing by encouraging emigration; and the resulting health problems will inevitably accelerate a decline in the growth rate of the Palestinian population, thanks to lowered life expectancy and infant mortality rates.

* * * *

The Defense Ministry claims that the barrier's route is meant to "frustrate acts of terrorism" and is "dictated" by the terrorists. Confiscating Palestinian land to build the barrier exacerbates the very frustration that leads to terrorism in the first place. If Israel knows anything, it knows that the confiscation of Palestinian land – which began in earnest prior to 1948 – is what created the conflict.

Destroying the livelihoods of tens of thousands of farmers and other wage earners cannot serve Israel's long-term security or the security of Jews worldwide. In any case, there is no consensus that the barrier is the most effective remedy to violence. The Strategic Studies Institute, U.S. Army War College:

> Reliance on perimeter control as through barriers has, along with years of constricting movement, curfews, and land acquisition policies, led to a terrible apartheid-like separation of the population and threatens any coherence to the West Bank. It may be impossible to convince Israel to dismantle the security

---

Many Jewish settlements do not have proper sewage plants. They spew their waste into Palestinian villages, causing health problems and ecological disaster.

fence, known as the Wall. But there would be a great benefit to doing so. The Jewish and Palestinian populations do not need to be herded into separate areas – they need to be reacquainted with each other, as segregation has bred hatred and fear.[20]

Nobel Peace Prize recipient, Archbishop Desmond Tutu, a recognized authority on institutionalized segregation:

> The lesson that Israel must learn . . . is that it can never get security through fences, walls and guns . . . . [I]n South Africa, they tried to get security from the barrel of a gun. They never got it. They got security when the human rights of all were recognized and respected.[21]

The United Nations:

> The continuation and even consolidation of Israeli settlements and related infrastructure on occupied land are the main reasons for the mistrust and frustration felt by ordinary Palestinians, which often find their outlet in violence of one form or another.[22]

If security really were Israel's cardinal concern it would be dedicated to making peace. Clearly, however, Israel is dedicated to land acquisition and settlement construction at the expense of peace. In its *Summary* of a December 2005 joint report with Israeli NGO, Bimkon (Planners for Planning Rights), B'Tselem stated:

> Israel contends that the Barrier's route is based solely on security considerations. This report disputes that contention and proves that one of the primary reasons for choosing the route of many sections of the Barrier was to place certain areas intended for settlement expansion on the 'Israeli' side of the Barrier. In some of the cases, for all intents and purposes the expansion constituted the establishment of a new settlement.[23]

OCHA notes: "The construction of the Barrier since 2002 has further fragmented the West Bank and reinforced the permanence of the settlements. *The route of the Barrier is determined by the settlements*." And: "Without the settlements, the Barrier could follow the Green Line with minimal disruption to Palestinian life."[24]

In an interview with *Haaretz*, Haggai Alon, past senior adviser to Amir Peretz, said: "[T]he IDF is setting a route for the fence that will not enable the establishment of a Palestinian state and is allowing itself to evade High Court orders to change the route."[25]* In December 2005, Tzipi Livni, leader of the opposition Kadima party, and at the time Israel's Justice Minister, contradicted the State Prosecutor's Office, which, in a hearing before the High Court, stated that the barrier's route was determined by security. Livni admitted that the barrier would be "the future border of the state of Israel" and "by means of its rulings on the separation fence the [Israeli] High Court was sketching the borders of the state."[26] Emphasizing her point, Livni said: "One does not have to be a genius to see that the fence will impact the future border."[27]

If, as Livni admits, the barrier's route was drawn to expand the borders of Israel, it is also true that Israel's intentions toward the Palestinians are not humanitarian but predatory. Particularly revealing is the Israeli government's statement that the barrier is a "*temporary security measure*" that "does not reflect a political or other kind of border."[28] If the barrier is temporary, why would Livni admit that it was the future border of Israel? If the barrier is temporary, when does Israel intend to return to its rightful owners in Beit Jala, Bil'in, Ni'lin and countless other communities the land it seized to build the barrier?

* * * *

The Bethlehem district, with a population of about 176,000, lies six miles south of Jerusalem in the West Bank. The city of Bethlehem is home to the oldest Christian community in the world and to the Church of the Nativity, the birthplace of Jesus of Nazareth. It is also the birthplace of David and the site where he was crowned Israel's second king. Just outside of Bethlehem is Rachel's Tomb, Judaism's third holiest site. Rachel was the second wife of the patriarch Jacob, and mother of Joseph. The area around Rachel's Tomb has been seized and is now surrounded by the barrier, which protects an illegal settlement that sits on land where Palestinians and their businesses once flourished. Members of some of the most militant, Ultra-Orthodox Jewish sects reside in the new

---

* Amir Peretz was Minister of Defense and leader of the Labor Party until 2007 when he was replaced by Ehud Barak.

settlement. According to OCHA, 86,000 Jewish settlers live in outposts and settlements in the Bethlehem area.[29]

Mundher Elias al-Bandak has lived near Rachel's Tomb his entire life. In April 2002, bulldozers suddenly appeared on his property. When he asked what they were doing, they shot at him. They took his property and built a thirty-meter-wide road. The barrier is only seventy-five feet from his bedroom. Mundher describes its effect on his life:

> You cannot measure the psychological impact of the wall. You can't capture it in words or images. Nor can you control it or be treated for it or push it away. This ghost never goes away, and it always controls your consciousness, even when you sleep, the nightmare grabs hold of you. When you are made to feel like an animal, confined by walls. . . . How can people treat their fellow brothers in ways worse than animals are treated?[30]

OCHA reports that the barrier, Israeli military zones, Jewish settlements and an Israeli-controlled nature reserve leave only thirteen percent of the Bethlehem area for use by the Palestinian population.[31] Bethlehem's tourism industry has been adversely affected. Tourists who come are now bussed to the holy places from Har Homa, an older Israeli settlement, and then bussed back. They do little shopping or dining anymore, so Bethlehem's economic base is diminishing. As a result, the few who are able to leave the city, mostly Christians, are doing so.

For over one thousand years, Christians and Muslims have lived peacefully in this venerated city. Now, if Hebron and other areas of the West Bank are any indication, they will be harassed and threatened by belligerent fundamentalists, their new neighbors. In all likelihood, the Israeli army will look the other way or assist the fundamentalists in their campaign of hatred and intimidation.

* * * *

Jewish settlers are mostly indifferent to the devastating impact of the barrier's construction. So far, they have dispossessed the Palestinians of thirty-eight percent of their West Bank property.[32]* According to official

---

* This figure includes roads, military bases and related infrastructure, but does not include private Palestinian land that has been confiscated for nature preserves, nor does it include land taken for future settlement expansion. In "Land Grab," B'Tselem

data provided by the Civil Administration, the majority of settlements are situated on privately owned Palestinian land. About eighty percent of the settlers are motivated by financial incentives. For economic settlers, who come from poorer backgrounds than most Israelis, cash rebates, housing subsidies and loan forgiveness are hard to ignore.

For the twenty percent of settlers who are inspired by religion, their purported God-given right to the land supersedes the rights of Palestinian people, whose claims of private ownership are irrelevant. On the basis of divine entitlement – which implies a divine abandonment of the Palestinian people – these settlers have misrepresented the meaning of old laws and contrived new ones; and they have nullified the legal – not just the moral – rights Palestinians have to their ancestral homes; all with the consent of the Israeli government. B'Tselem criticizes Israel's strategy:

> Particularly evident is Israel's manipulative use of legal tools in order to give the settlement enterprise an impression of legality. When Jordanian legislation served Israel's goals, Israel adhered to this legislation, arguing that international law obliges it to respect the legislation in effect prior to the occupation; in practice, this legislation was used in a cynical and biased manner. On the other hand, when this legislation interfered with Israel's plans, it was changed in a cavalier manner through military legislation and Israel established new rules to serve its interests. In so doing, Israel trampled on numerous restrictions and prohibitions established in the international conventions to which it is party, and which were intended to limit infringement of human rights and to protect populations under occupation.[33]

Tens of thousands of Palestinians have become destitute and homeless as a result of these discriminatory legal interpretations.[34]

One scheme the settlers devised to colonize the West Bank is the use of forged deeds. The Migron settler outpost, situated near Ramallah, was established by more than forty Jewish families. The "legal" basis for their

---

states: "Israel has used a complex legal and bureaucratic mechanism to take control of more than fifty percent of the land in the West Bank."

action was a deed signed in 2004 by the owner of the land. Recent investigation revealed that the "owner" died in 1961.[35]

Sheikh Jarrah, a Palestinian neighborhood in East Jerusalem, has been involved in a legal battle with Jewish settlers, who claim that the Sephardi Jewry Association purchased the neighborhood's land in the nineteenth century. The settlers want to evict the Palestinians, tear down their homes and replace them with apartments. Their scheme, however, has been exposed by the Turkish government's uncharacteristic cooperation with the Palestinians. For decades the Turks have maintained close military and political ties to Israel and have avoided antagonizing Tel Aviv. Recently, however, Ankara granted Palestinians access to the Ottoman land registry archives, which show that the Sephardi Association deeds are forgeries. Israeli courts, however, have yet to issue a ruling on the case.

Israel's security forces chose not to wait for the court's guidance. On August 2, 2009 they evicted two Palestinian families from their homes, one of whom had lived there continuously for fifty-three years. The properties – originally built for Palestinian refugees by the United Nations – had been given to the Palestinian families when East Jerusalem was under Jordanian rule. Jordan, however, never formally registered the properties in the inhabitants' names. When Israel gained control over East Jerusalem in 1967, the opportunity to do so was lost.

Referring to the evictions, Robert Serry, the UN Special Middle East Coordinator said: "These actions heighten tensions and undermine international efforts to create conditions for fruitful negotiations to achieve peace."[36] The British Consulate in East Jerusalem: "These actions are incompatible with the Israeli professed desire for peace. . . . We urge Israel not to allow the extremists to set the agenda."[37]

In November 2009, the Ministry of the Interior, after stalling for nearly two years, finally complied with an Israeli human-rights group's request for data regarding the residency status of Palestinians in East Jerusalem. The Ministry wrote to *HaMoked: Center for the Defence of the Individual*: "The status of 4,577 residents of East Jerusalem was revoked in 2008, of which 99 were children under 18 years of age."[38] According to Hamoked:

the total number of residency revocations in East Jerusalem in 2008 is equal to more than 50% of the total residency revocations performed by the Ministry of the Interior in East Jerusalem over the first 40 years of occupation: from the beginning of the occupation in 1967 until 2007, the Ministry of the Interior revoked the status of more than 8,500 residents of East Jerusalem.[39]

Prime Minister Netanyahu made clear Israel's intentions: "Our sovereignty over [a united Jerusalem] is unquestionable. . . . We cannot accept the idea that Jews will not have the right to live and buy [homes] anywhere in Jerusalem."[40] A few months later, the Netanyahu government announced its approval for the construction of 692 new apartments in East Jerusalem.[41] American and Palestinian officials immediately denounced these plans as an obstruction to peace. Israel, of course, will never publicly admit that it regards peace as secondary to the dispossession of Palestinians and the acquisition of land. It still insists that it is willing to make peace with the Palestinians. But Israel's idea of peace requires the Palestinian people to give up East Jerusalem as the capital of their state and the international community to give up its expectation that Israel abides by international law.

International Humanitarian Law and the Fourth Geneva Convention prohibit transfer of an occupying country's citizens to the territory it occupies, yet the Israeli government has designated more than one-third of East Jerusalem for Jewish settlement.* Since the occupation began in 1967, about 2,000 Palestinian homes in East Jerusalem have been demolished, 670 of them between 2000 and 2008 owing to a lack of permits.+ According to Israeli courts, the Palestinians are to blame

---

* Article 49 of the Fourth Geneva Convention: "The occupying power shall not deport or transfer parts of its own civilian population into the territory it occupies."

+ ICAHD (Israeli Committee Against House Demolitions) estimates that between 1967 and 2009, 24,245 Palestinian homes were demolished in the OPT [Internal Displacement Monitoring Centre (IDMC), "Global Figures 2009; last updated December 21, 2009]. In 2009 alone, 270 homes were demolished in the West Bank, displacing over 600 Palestinians; half were children. As of June 2010 4,800 demolition orders are pending [Amnesty International, "As Safe as Houses? Israel's demolition of Palestinian Homes," p. 3, March 10, 2010]. Homeowners receive no

because of their failure to abide by the law: if they obtained building permits they would be allowed to build homes.* But the legal system ignores a few salient points: 1) only thirteen percent of East Jerusalem is zoned for Palestinian home construction; 2) the zoned areas are too built-up to accommodate all the Palestinian families in need of housing; 3) the cost of obtaining a permit is prohibitive and the process is complicated. The UN Special Coordinator's Office estimates that Israel issues 1,100 fewer permits than are needed each year to meet Palestinian population growth.[42] The Office cautions:

> [T]hese actions harm ordinary Palestinians, heighten tensions in the city, undermine efforts to build trust and promote negotiations, and are contrary to international law and Israel's commitments.[43]

The *New York Times* reports that the ICRC accused "[Israel of a] general disregard [for] its obligations under international humanitarian law – and the law of occupation in particular." The ICRC said: "[Israel is using its rights as an occupying power under international law] in order to further its own interests or those of its own population to the detriment of the population of the occupied territory."[44]

While the State of Israel ignores international law, powerful interests within Israel ignore Israeli law. Israeli courts have ruled that outposts are illegal. Outposts are, for all intents and purposes, fledgling settlements that have been set up without proper authorization from the government. Talia Sasson, the former head of the State Prosecution Criminal Department conducted an inquiry on behalf of the Israeli Prime Minister's Bureau. She concluded that the IDF, along with the Civil Administration, the ministries of Defense, Construction and Housing, Interior Affairs and Agriculture, and the Settlement Division of the

---

compensation and are themselves forced to pay the cost of demolition.

* From January 2000 to September 2007 91 building permits were issued to Palestinians throughout the entire OPT while 18,472 permits were issued to Israelis. "The Civil Administration also indicated that, for every building permit issued to Palestinians, 55 demolition orders were issued, 18 of which were executed." B'Tselem, "Planning and Building," August 8, 2008; btselem.org/English/Planning_and_Building/20080805_al_Aqabeh_demolition_order s.asp.

World Zionist Organization, had allocated land, issued electricity and water permits and helped fund the outposts. Each of these agencies was a willing accomplice to the illegal behavior of settlers who failed to obtain the required building permits. According to *Peace Now*, by 2006 more than one hundred outposts, with a population of about 2,000 settlers, had been established.[45]

With respect to the lack of space for Palestinian housing, OCHA explains that the shortage is a result of Israel's "failure to provide Palestinian neighborhoods with adequate planning." Continuing:

> This shortage has been exacerbated in recent years by the reported influx of Palestinian Jerusalemites into the city due to Barrier construction and the threat of losing residency status in the city if they move outside the Israeli-defined municipal borders of Jerusalem.[46]

Causing even more hardship, Israel has invoked the onerous Absentees' Property Law to seize thousands of acres of privately owned land in and around East Jerusalem. The properties belong to Palestinians whose access is now blocked by the barrier. According to Chris McGreal, some of the land will be used to expand already existing Jewish settlements.[47] The hundreds of Palestinian landowners affected by this decision will receive no compensation from the State of Israel.

The Absentees' Property Law was first passed by the Knesset on March 14, 1950 in order to legalize Jewish ownership of Palestinian land. Reaching back in time, the law took advantage of the flight of Palestinians during the 1948 War by decreeing that any Arab property owner not living on his land during the period from November 29, 1947 – the date the Yishuv accepted the United Nations Partition Plan – to September 1, 1948, automatically forfeited his property to the State of Israel without compensation. According to Kimmerling and Migdal, the Israeli government used this law to confiscate "as much as forty percent of Arab lands (about two million dunams). . . ."[48]

At first glance, one would think the law applied only to those who abandoned their homes during wartime for safe haven in Arab lands; and that Palestinians who did not abandon their homes were exempt from the law's ramifications. Unfortunately, that would be an error of interpretation. The law punished anyone who:

(i) was a national or citizen of the Lebanon, Egypt, Syria, Saudi Arabia, Trans-Jordan, Iraq or the Yemen, or (ii) was in one of these countries or in any part of Palestine outside the area of Israel, or (iii) was a Palestinian citizen and left his ordinary place of residence in Palestine (a) for a place outside Palestine or (b) for a place in Palestine held at the time by forces which sought to prevent the establishment of the State of Israel or which fought against it after its establishment.[49]

Any Arab who met any of these stipulations was abruptly transformed from legal resident into potential illegal absentee. If an Israeli-Arab left his home to transact business in Lebanon or walked a mile to see relatives for a single afternoon in East Jerusalem or another village in Palestine deemed not yet under IDF control, he was (as of March 14, 1950) judged to be an absentee.* The fact that the Israeli-Arab never intended to abandon his property, and the fact that he may have returned to his property within hours or even minutes of his departure, was completely beside the point to the custodian of Absentees' Property.

Many of the "transgressors" were living on their properties within the State of Israel when the Absentees' Property Law was passed, but that, too, didn't matter. The Palestinians' inability to alter the physical universe by manipulating time was what ultimately incriminated them. Unlike Israeli politicians who, in their calculating minds, could travel backwards in time and manufacture violations, the Palestinians failure to foretell the future by traveling forward in time left them vulnerable to the State's decrees.

With such a cunning legal weapon, the custodian could seize the absentee's property – his home, business, bank accounts and all belongings – and give the fruits of the seizure to someone he considered more deserving, generally a European Jew who had just arrived in Israel. Or the custodian could simply turn the property over to the Jewish National Fund, which still owns most of the land in Israel. Palestinians who fled in 1948 – virtually all of whom thought they would be able to return when the war ended – were stripped of their heritage in this

---

* East Jerusalem was under Jordanian control until its annexation by Israel in the wake of the 1967 war.

inventive manner. The law even stipulated that any property or money owed to the absentee by another party was to be handed over to the custodian.[50] And to ensure that the law produced its desired result the Knesset indemnified the custodian from any obligation to produce evidence that proved his decision was based on accurate information. If the custodian erred in designating someone an absentee, his decision still stood.[51] In short, the law was a pretense that legalized the practice of ethnic cleansing.

Israel's Jordanian counterpart was legally responsible for Jewish-owned property under Jordanian control in East Jerusalem. In contrast to the actions of the Israeli custodian, however, the Jordanian actually protected Jewish property. Israeli lawyer Chaim Aron Valero found him to be quite reasonable:

> I don't know about all the properties, but I know quite a number
> of properties remained registered to this day in Jewish names as
> in Mandate times. They were not expropriated and their
> ownership did not pass to the Jordanian government.[52]

Israel's latest use of the Absentees' Property Law takes advantage once again of powerless Palestinians who have been separated from their properties not by choice but by the design of the Israeli government. The law states the conditions under which Israel can legally confiscate private land, while ignoring the fact that these conditions were imposed upon the "guilty" party by Israel itself. Israel, as mastermind of and accessory to this "crime," is also its judge, its enforcer and its beneficiary. In 2004, attorney Daniel Seidemann explained:

> The law states that, if you live in the West Bank but own land or
> property in Jerusalem, that you are an absentee, and that land
> becomes state property . . . . The law allows, basically, the
> taking of Palestinian private property and turning it into state
> land.[53]*

---

* Seidemann represents Arab families whose properties have been confiscated by Israel.

* * * *

Regarding the Israeli Ministry of Defense's statement implying that the barrier's route is necessary to ensure that Palestinians have reasonable "access to water and other basic services," Tanya Reinhart clarifies Israel's intentions:

> Sharon and the Israeli army designed the wall's route with a view to annexing as much West Bank land as possible. Yet it wasn't only territorial greed that drove Israel to send its bulldozers into the Palestinian lands of the northern West Bank, where the wall has now been completed. These lands are on the western part of the Mountain Groundwater Basin – the large reservoir in the West Bank whose waters flow underground to central Israel. Of the 600 million cubic metres of water that the Mountain reservoir provides annually, Israel takes about 500 million. Control over water resources has always been a primary motivation for Israel's occupation of Palestine.[54]

OCHA reports:

> Israeli water consumption is more than five times higher than that of West Bank Palestinians (350 litres per person per day in Israel compared to 60 litres per person per day in the West Bank, excluding East Jerusalem). West Bank Palestinian water consumption is 40 litres less than the minimum global standards set by the World Health Organization (WHO).[55]

While Jewish settlers have green lawns and swimming pools for their children to play in, Palestinian children often do not have enough clean water to drink. To add insult to injury, Palestinians have to pay four times as much per gallon of water as their Israeli neighbors.[56]

* * * *

The ability to travel freely within the West Bank is another issue the Palestinians deal with on a daily basis. In November 2005 *The Agreement on Movement and Access* was signed by Israel and the Palestinian Authority. Like many previous agreements, however, Israel did not abide by its promises. *Haaretz*:

> [T]he World Bank, the United Nations organization considered to be friendliest to Israel, published a harsh report, which

claimed that although Israel signed an agreement in 2005 to ease restrictions on movement in the territories, they have only become stricter. The report states that Israel prevents Palestinians access to about half the areas of the West Bank, and it claims that the restrictions on movement were designed to grant priority to the movement of the settlers and to help the expansion of the settlements at the expense of the Palestinian population.[57]

There are times when restrictions are so severe that Palestinians are confined to their towns; there are even times when they are confined to their homes:

Between June 19 to August 30, 2002, the inhabitants of Ramallah . . . were permitted to leave their homes for only fifty-one hours, that is, a total of four hours each week for ten weeks. There were hundreds of identical curfews.[58]

The Israeli authority further humiliates Palestinians by requiring those who are stuck between the security fence and the Green Line to obtain permits to live in their own homes. These permits must be renewed on a regular basis.

With their movement restricted, Palestinian businesses will continue to fail, poverty will dramatically increase, access to schools and social and medical services will be delayed or denied altogether, and the psychological and physical health of the population will suffer even more than it already has.

* * * *

James Akins, former United States ambassador to Saudi Arabia from 1973 to 1976 and a member of the Council on Foreign Relations said:

The daily humiliation of Palestinians living under occupation, the plummeting of their standard of living, the reduction of their lands to tiny enclaves divided from each other by Israeli roads connecting Israeli settlements and forbidden to Palestinians all make life miserable. President Ariel Sharon's plan is clearly to make life so difficult for Arabs that they will see no choice but emigration. Many have left. Those left behind have become embittered.[59]

– 13 –
The Self-Hating Jew

How to recognize an adherent of ethnic, communitarian, clannish thinking? The mechanism is always the same: mention to him any misdeeds whatsoever of his camp, and, in an almost Pavlovian reflex, he will speak of the misdeeds, the defects, the crimes, and the monstrousness of the opposite camp.[1] Sylvain Cypel

Jimmy Carter is representative of a growing chorus of human rights activists who are speaking out against the suffering of an occupied people. Their criticism of Israel is motivated by the understanding that everyone, regardless of religion or ethnicity, has inherent and equal rights to self-determination. Many pro-Israelis, however, are adamant in their belief that critics of Israel are, *ipso facto*, either anti-Semites or self-hating Jews. Alan Dershowitz made the following comment on Shalom TV:

> Jimmy Carter has literally become such an anti-Israel bigot that there's a kind of special place in Hell reserved for somebody like that. He has no sympathy or understanding for the suffering of the Jewish people, for the plight of the Jewish people. He loves every Muslim extremist he can find . . . . If you're an Israeli Carter doesn't like you and if you're an Arab or a Muslim he likes you.[2]

Dershowitz's characterization of Jimmy Carter is a common description of an anti-Semite. He attributes to the latter a lack of sympathy and understanding which, as regards the plight of the Palestinian people, is almost certainly true of himself.[*]

Because Carter's status gives him a unique ability to influence public perceptions of the Israel-Palestine conflict, he is mistakenly looked upon by pro-Israelis as a threat to the existence of the Jewish State. Since

---

[*] A "special place in Hell" is particularly revealing. I cannot help but wonder what is going on in Dershowitz's mind for him to make such an extreme statement. Hell is what Dershowitz experiences when his identity is threatened by a man whose willingness to speak truthfully about the occupation can neutralize enemy images of an entire culture of people.

my transformation I have spoken with Jewish friends, relatives and acquaintances about the conflict. All but a tiny minority has taken offense with my findings and one hundred percent of those who took offense denigrated the former president with slurs such as anti-Semite, Nazi sympathizer or bigot, yet only one had actually read *Palestine Peace Not Apartheid*.

One evening I had a telephone conversation with Meir Schneider, during which I described my transformation as well as my insights into conflict in general and the Israel-Palestine struggle in particular. I thought Meir would appreciate my experience and view it within the context of his own healing philosophy, seeing it as a moment "of grace or liberation" in which I had stepped outside of the world mind; and that in some very positive way I had changed and healed myself. Unfortunately that was not the case. Instead, Meir reacted by telling me my views were anti-Semitic. He then brought up Jimmy Carter, whom he called an anti-Semite. I tried to explain that Carter's and my own concern for the welfare of the Palestinians did not diminish our concern for Jews and Israelis, and that advocating equal rights for all people is not anti-Semitic or anti-Israel. Meir was too upset to hear me.

I then began to speak about peace. At that point, Meir said he would accept a two-state solution to the conflict as long as the major Jewish settlements surrounding Jerusalem were included within the internationally recognized borders of Israel. He went on to say that a major advantage of peace for Israel was that the Palestinians could be exploited for menial labor that Israelis were not interested in doing. As Meir was speaking, I could not detect any feeling for the Palestinians. Their lives were irrelevant. His voice projected utter certainty in the position he was putting forth. His interest in peace had nothing to do with the social, economic and educational opportunities the Palestinians would finally be able to enjoy. All that mattered was how Israelis would benefit. The essence of what Meir was saying seemed to be that it would be perfectly acceptable if a peace were established in which Palestinians were consigned to lives of poverty and second-class citizenship.

As the conversation wound down Meir suggested I read Alan Dershowitz's *The Case for Israel* and Dennis Ross's *The Missing Peace – The Inside Story of the Fight for Middle East Peace*. I agreed to do so, seeing no worthwhile reason to tell him that I had already read sections of

Dershowitz's book and found them unreliable. A few days later I obtained Ross's book and read it from cover to cover. Ross, Middle East envoy and chief peace negotiator during the presidencies of George H.W. Bush and Bill Clinton, provides an account of the Middle East peace process from 1988 to the end of the Clinton presidency in 2001. My primary interest in reading the book was Ross's explanation for the failure of the Camp David negotiations in the summer of 2000. While studying the book, I learned that Ross's account was disputed by a number of American, Israeli and Palestinian participants at Camp David; and that Ross, who is Jewish, was perceived as so biased in favor of Israel that President Clinton had to limit his involvement.

Eight months later a friend sent me an advertisement for a series of lectures on the Middle East, scheduled to take place in San Francisco. Well-known scholars from the University of California and other schools were among the speakers. They were Jews, Muslims and Christians. Unable to attend the lectures myself, I thought they might be of interest to Meir. I sent his office the following email:

> I've attached a flyer about a series of lectures being held in San Francisco about the Israel-Palestine peace process, all with outstanding internationally known lecturers. I thought Meir might be interested in attending. Rich

Meir replied:

> Rich,
>
> I think that it will be a waist [sic] of my time. I do not appreciate your anti Israel and anti Semitic view point as well as your rigid view point. I will go to the stupid lectures you send me too when you will read the books I suggest for you to read like *The Case for Israel* by Alan Dershowitz as well as meet the true Israelis. Thank you, Meir

Meir assumed I had not read the books he had recommended. He never contacted me to verify his assumption. He apparently did not consider the Israeli citizens I knew, including himself, to be "true Israelis." I responded to Meir's anger with a longer email in which I told him I was sorry he was upset. I also said:

Now [since the transformation] I see how our beliefs lead us to support policies that cause our own people harm in addition to the targets of the policies we support. Finally, accusations of anti-Semitism are a foil on the part of the accuser so he doesn't have to really inquire into his own views and their repercussions. I know you have a great capacity to do that. Is there anything wrong with that? You have always been about growth, no? I am telling you as your friend, they are really good speakers, not anti-Semites; and in your heart you know I am not an anti-Semite. If you don't want to go to any of the lectures but want more information, I can recommend some books by Jewish/Israeli authors based on the Israeli State archives and the Central Zionist archives. There is a lot going on about Israel/Palestine. I know you want to be informed. Look at both sides of the issue. Good luck. Rich

Meir replied with further accusations, among them that the "so-called experts" I was talking about "had no integrity," even though he had not bothered to look into their writings. The one "expert" he mentioned by name was someone whom he and I had never discussed and whom I had never even read. He also said he had no intention of backing off from his position. I found this statement interesting in light of his earlier statement that I was the one who had the rigid viewpoint. He ended his email:

I hate the extreme left position on Israel and I hate when Jews join them and want to annihilate their brothers with bullshit and bogus claims. I do not think that your view point is humane at all. Shame on you.

I wrote Meir a short response:

[My position] is humane to both Palestinians and Israelis, not favoring one at the expense of the other. . . . I was open enough to read your suggested books, just as I was open enough to read Avi Shlaim, Ilan Pappe, Benny Morris (a staunch Zionist), Baruch Kimmerling, Tanya Reinhart, and more; I've seen no such openness from you.

As I anticipated, Meir ignored that email and two subsequent longer emails in which I tried to respond to each of the concerns that he had expressed in his communications to me. He was not willing to discuss the issues either of us had brought up, apparently finding it easier to jettison a friendship and hurl unfair accusations at me and others who did not share his point of view.

* * * *

In the past the term self-hating Jew was associated with Jews who were ashamed of or hid their religious and cultural backgrounds. But as the debate over Israel's policies in the Occupied Territories has intensified, the use of the label to describe its Jewish critics has become common within Jewish culture. The idea that a three-word label can encapsulate the character of a person is problematic. A human being is far more than what a single phrase can say about him, and this particular phrase is so divisive that it makes tolerance and cooperation impossible.

For some, support for Israeli policy is unconditional, even as it conflicts with Jewish values; for others, Jewish values are unconditional, even as they conflict with support for Israeli policy. If pro-Israelis would make an effort to discover why some of their peers campaign for Palestinian equality, they would learn that their peers are making a conscious choice not to remain silent when witnessing one group's denial of basic human rights to another group. These critics see their people, like the rest of mankind, as complex beings, capable of acts of inhumanity as well as acts of kindness. They are able to concede that at times Israel does violate the rights of others, that it has used torture and mistreated and killed innocent people, and that its leaders do not always tell the truth about these acts. These critics believe the Israeli government has hijacked their heritage by replacing morality and brotherhood, so highly valued in Judaism, with bigotry and exclusion. They believe, therefore, that by opposing policies that relegate the Palestinians to second-class citizenship they are preserving the integrity of their own tradition. This begs the question: What exactly is self-hating in such a point-of-view?

In the course of writing this chapter, I asked a couple of pro-Israelis who have used the label self-hating Jew how they knew that the person they were labeling actually hated himself. All that either person was able to say was that his fellow Jew didn't support Israel's policies in the

Occupied Territories. Neither person could come right out and complete their train of thought by saying something like: "and that proves they hate Israel and their Jewish identity." Both became helplessly tongue-tied and embarrassed when given an opportunity to intelligently explain themselves. What became clear to me was that the use of the term self-hating Jew is an emotionally charged retaliatory mechanism, used to disgorge feelings of discomfort, anger or hatred that arise when a fellow Jew criticizes Israel. By refusing to take responsibility for these feelings – through an honest investigation into the understanding that motivates Israel's critics – these pro-Israelis transfer responsibility for their feelings onto the other and scapegoat him with the label self-hating Jew (or anti-Semite). By doing so, they eradicate the possibility for real understanding. Then they can go back to indulging in unconscious complacency.

The use of the label self-hating Jew is a cop-out. This near automatic reflex is the resource of someone who is too lazy and/or obstinately unwilling to try to understand a point of view that challenges his own beliefs and assumptions. Slurring the character of the critic is also a classic way of dismissing dissident points of view. It is similar to accusations that Americans who opposed the 2003 U.S. invasion of Iraq were unpatriotic.

Self-hating Jew implies that rational dialogue is impossible because a self-hater must be utterly confused. He is biased toward his very self and, therefore, unable to objectively discuss anything that relates to his heritage. But who is confused? Who in fact is incapable of a discussion about Israel and who is insecure with his own identity? Only one who is afraid of what he might find out about Israel or himself. In my conversation with the two people I mention above, both were uncomfortable with my questioning, even though I approached them in a way that did not threaten them. They saw that I obviously did not hate anything, least of all myself or Jewish culture. Because I was a real person, not some critic in the news, it was very difficult for them to justify the label self-hating Jew.

Whenever criticism of Israel reaches a sharp enough pitch, Israel's defenders react personally, as if it were they who were being criticized.

They fall victim to feelings of suffocation, as if the world were caving in upon them, and they attribute these feelings to anti-Semitism. They are, in fact, victims, but not of anti-Semitism. They are victims of an unexamined mind, which has no tolerance for negative images of Israel. But without examining the beliefs that give rise to their oppressive feelings, the defenders will project their self-created suffering out into the world and the world will suffer from their denial.

Formerly, whenever I was confronted with criticism of Israel, there was usually a moment when I recognized that the criticism might actually contain some truth. There was also the recognition that my perspective had more to do with how I wished to see my people than how they really are when looked at without prejudice. I saw that my attachment to certain beliefs and images was a defense designed to preserve a childlike faith in Israel as guardian of integrity and humanity. Somehow, I had to reconcile my treasured images with the reality that conflicted with them. However, rather than making use of the tension between these forces as a gateway to transformation, I rejected the latter and adhered to the safety of the former. Even when friends I normally trusted pointed to Israeli deeds that seemed out of character, I reacted by ignoring or rationalizing the suffering of the Palestinians.

Equating Palestinian freedom with Palestinian terrorism, I worried that if Israel relinquished strict control over its subjects, the lives of its citizens would be imperiled. I presumed that Jews who criticized Israel were willfully ignorant of the evil intentions of the Palestinians, and that their willfulness demonstrated support for the destruction of the Jewish state. Fearful of annihilation, I unconsciously superimposed Nazi images onto the Palestinian people, and then denied that the Jewish state could ever act indefensibly toward them. Fear prevented me from empathizing with the pain of the Palestinians and it blinded me to the possibility that a country in which I had invested so much faith could administer such brutal and deadly policies.

Complementing my stubbornness, I dealt with my suffocating feelings by projecting them onto Israel's critics. It never occurred to me to deal with my feelings in another way. Had I allowed them to guide me to a prudent consideration of the issues in dispute, I would have come across readily available research based on declassified documents from, among other reputable sources, the Israeli State Archives, IDF Archives, David Ben-Gurion Archives, and Central Zionist Archives.[*] Then I would no longer have needed to interpret Israel as a reflection of unexamined beliefs.

Fortunately, my feelings did eventually guide me to a more objective investigation of the modern history of my people; and they put me in touch with deep-seated beliefs and images that obstructed my native clarity and compassion. I discovered that my willfulness had led me to ignore reliable documentation – like the sources above – that proved how inhumane some Israeli policies are. And I realized that my belief in the purity of the Jewish nation was a form of denial that veiled the real Israel, an imperfect nation, whose policies do not always reflect the integrity and humanity I believe in. This new perspective showed me that by ignoring the suffering of others, I had sacrificed the very values Israel once personified.

Speaking as honestly as I can, criticism of Israel per se is not the primary concern of pro-Israelis. More provocative is the fear that the criticism may be warranted. The real conflict is the inability to integrate the hard-to-believe but inescapable awareness of the Jewish state's inhumane treatment of the other with unquestioned loyalty to the image of Israel as a nation that values equality for all. One consideration acknowledges the dark side of Israeli policy and behavior. The other denies the dark side exists. The unresolved struggle to reconcile awareness with loyalty is the source of the use of the label self-hating Jew and claims of anti-Semitism.

How is it that a person can be devoted to the well being of one group and be hostile to the well being of another? Is it true that there is an inherent difference between two peoples that justifies devotion to one and hostility towards the other? Are such feelings real or has something been added that distorts feeling? From my perspective, the determining factor is the labels that are applied to a people and the beliefs and images

---

[*] A group of Israeli scholars (referred to as new or revisionist historians) with access to these and other archives, have challenged the commonly accepted accounts of Israel's past history, including Israel's role in the flight of the Palestinians. They include Ilan Pappe, Benny Morris, Tom Segev, Avi Shlaim and Simha Flapan.

associated with the labels. These labels are the mind's attempt to resolve fear and gain security, but they occlude the very mechanism that can achieve these aims.

The ability to look and to feel is what achieves security. This ability is inherent and it functions perfectly when there is no recoil from the circumstances of existence. In simple practical situations it makes itself known. Everyone has experienced it. There is a moment when you just know there is danger, when you know that a person is not to be trusted. Then you act accordingly. You do not need one iota of belief about the situation. You have no preconceptions and you are not recoiled from the situation. You are simply being present. Then there is the real feeling that something is amiss.

Conversely, everyone has experienced ignoring this ability, over-riding it with the mind and suffering as a result. You meet a person and his presence is disturbing, his eyes are constantly shifting, he speaks too rapidly and is overly defensive. But instead of honoring the signs, you go to the mind: "Oh, he is just a little peculiar and I will rent him one of my apartments anyway." Three months later you are in court, trying to get him evicted for not paying the rent.

Before my transformation labels dominated my conversation about the Israel-Palestine conflict. I could say spiteful things about Arabs, yet I had spent very little time with them. I was living in my head, imagining that my labels were accurate and would bring security to Israel (and to myself). I had deceived myself into believing that my passionate feelings were justified by the conflict. By indulging these feelings I could remain oblivious to the reality that an entire society was being oppressed and mistreated by my people. The truth is that these feelings arose out of a frustration brought about by my refusal to calm down and examine the conflict and my reactions with honesty.

Because I recoiled from the situation I was confused. I was ignoring signs that under any other circumstance would have alerted me to danger. In my personal life I knew that anger and violence were destructive to a relationship. I knew that if I had an argument with my partner and then began to label her, the argument would explode and there would be a complete loss of intimacy and connection. I also knew that once I had calmed down and been restored to sanity the labels would be recognized as false.

Politically I was going against my instincts for fairness and equality. I had almost always found the United Nations to be just, but now I was angry with it because of its criticism of Israel. From the first time I saw George W. Bush, I had been deeply disturbed by the man. But I supported his unqualified support of Israel. During the Vietnam War I had quickly turned against U.S. policy because the war's horrific images were undeniable. I could never justify raining napalm down on the population of a third-world country. But now I was supporting Israel's merciless destruction of much of Lebanon.

What I am talking about is natural intelligence as the means for practical security. If we look and feel, then certain things become clear. But we have to renounce labels, we have to renounce the philosophy of us against them, and we have to end our recoil from the human reality of the conflict. There is nothing to fear; we needn't wait. Do we wait until we discover the nationality, race or origin of a person before we feel concern or neglect for him or her? If so, then there is no real feeling at all. Our concern and our neglect are false. Both are manifestations of fear and confusion. Our support for Israel is selfish, founded upon an attachment to a cause with which our identity is so inextricably bound that we have lost our connection to humanity. We may tell ourselves we support an end to conflict, but as bearers of inner conflict we constantly subvert our goals.

Beyond the mind lies a vast expanse of freedom, unqualified by our presumed mortality as a separate person. In this space of freedom true feeling arises; it flows from the heart. In the field of human relations its expression is compassion. Compassion is the expression of peace and the means of peace. When we know it then we also know that peace for the world is possible.

* * * *

I never used the term self-hating Jew. I am thankful that I didn't. I believe the label is a powerful barrier to understanding. The key to understanding is dispassionate intelligence. Fear and anger permeated every argument I made in defense of Israel. Invariably I moved from the quandary of fear to the apparent certainty of anger. But I never crossed over into hate. There is a special feeling that accompanies the words self-hating Jew. The key is in "hate." Characterizing someone in any way with this word introduces viciousness to the mind. This viciousness makes the mind utterly dualistic – and utterly obtuse. The subtle awareness that my ingrained perspective was perhaps incorrect would have been extinguished if I had described Israel's Jewish critics as self-hating. As it was, because I did not become involved in hate, I remained open to a dispassionate investigation of the Israel-Palestine conflict.

* * * *

Poet and essayist, Irina Klepfisz has been accused of self-hatred. In 1988, she was one of the organizers of the *Jewish Women's Committee to End the Occupation of the West Bank and Gaza*. Her father, Michal Klepfisz, belonged to the Jewish Fighters Organization in the Warsaw Ghetto. He was killed in 1943 while protecting other Jewish fighters who were trying to escape during an uprising against the Nazis.[3] Explaining why she was driven to seek justice for the Palestinians, Klepfisz said: "Knowing that the world was passive and indifferent while six million Jews died, I have always considered passivity and indifference the worst of evils. Those who do nothing, I believe, are good German collaborators. I do not want to be a collaborator."[4]

And what was the reaction to Klepfisz's efforts?

> [Klepfisz's committee's] proposal to end the violent repression of the Palestinian uprising and to support an international peace conference and a two-state solution was often greeted with hostility. Some Jews insisted that the Holocaust precluded such political action. One Jewish man told Klepfisz that he wished she were buried in Poland like his own parents. A few Jews wished another holocaust on the demonstrators. Still others felt that their actions would lead all Jews, including them, "back to the ovens."[5]

Klepfisz summarized the condemnation of her committee's vision of Palestinian and Jewish states living peacefully side by side: "We were told that to give the Palestinians a state was to give Hitler his final victory, that our behavior was desecrating the Holocaust of the 1940's and ensuring the Holocaust of the 1990's, perhaps even the 1980's."[6]

Sara Roy is Senior Research Scholar at the Center for Middle Eastern Studies at Harvard University. Roy too has been called a self-hating Jew. She describes what Judaism means to her:

> I grew up in a home where Judaism was defined and practiced not so much as a religion but as a system of ethics and culture. God was present but not central. Israel and the notion of a Jewish homeland were very important to my parents, who survived Auschwitz, Chelmno and Buchenwald. But unlike many of their friends, my parents were not uncritical of Israel. Obedience to a state was not a primary Jewish value, especially after the Holocaust. Judaism provided the context for Jewish life, for values and beliefs that were not dependent upon national or territorial boundaries, but transcended them to include the other, always the other. For my mother and father Judaism meant bearing witness, raging against injustice and refusing silence. It meant compassion, tolerance, and rescue. In the absence of these imperatives, they taught me, we cease to be Jews.[7]

One Jewish group, Masada2000, responded to Professor Roy's remarks:

> The crux of Sarah Roy's problem is that she's filthy Judenrat scum.* Despite the fact she lost over 100 members of her family in Nazi ghettoes and death camps, Roy committed her life to documenting the living conditions of the Palestinian people.+

Human rights activist, Daniela Fariba Vorburger is yet another compassionate Jew who has been slurred as self-hating by Masada2000:

---

* Judenrat were the Jewish councils formed in Poland at the behest of the German authorities. Their purpose was to serve as intermediaries and implement the repressive policies of the Nazi government. Masada2000 also refers to self-hating Jews as "dirty rats."

+ masada2000.org/list-QR.html. Masada2000 has compiled a list of approximately 8,000 "self-hating Jews," including Americans such as Thomas Friedman, Woody Allen, Ed Asner, Richard Gere and Israelis such as Shimon Peres, Ehud Olmert, and Tzipi Livni, and, of course, Noam Chomsky, Norman Finkelstein, Baruch Kimmerling, Benny Morris, Ilan Pappe and Tanya Reinhart.

This Executive Committee member of EJJP [European Jews for a Just Peace]. . . a network of eighteen Jewish peace groups in ten European countries. . . hopes to "speak to the greater public in the name of the large numbers of European Jews who are dissatisfied with Israeli policies towards the Palestinians. In particular, it hopes to demonstrate the diversity of opinion within the European Jewish community, which has lately seen anti-Semitic attacks launched not only by non-Jews, but also by 'mainstream' Jews against other Jews who have criticized Israeli policies." Translation: Suck up to and lick the boots of those Arabs/Muslims Nazi thugs who pace the streets of Europe looking for Jews to beat up or murder! [8]

Vorburger replied to the attack on her character:

The classification is absurd! . . . Why should I hate myself if I'm standing against injustice and for the dignity of other (non-Jewish) people? Why should I hate myself because I express criticism against a state's policy which "happens" to be Israel? [Jews] still have this ghetto mentality that everybody hates us and is against us. Whenever there is a criticism, we see it as anti-Semitism, as pure hate. With this mentality, it's even less acceptable if people "from within" criticize the club! I'm proud to be Jewish, but I also think that it's important to stand up and speak against injustice, crime, killings, etc., including when these crimes are committed by Jews. As long as the Israeli government is speaking in the name of all Jews, hence also in my name, I will also speak out against a policy, committed in my name, with which I do not agree. [9]

Masada2000 could easily be dismissed as an aberration, as one of countless websites that spew the most extreme language in support of their pet prejudice. But the use of rhetoric like Masada's permeates all levels of Jewish society. For example, Leon Wieseltier, the literary editor of *The New Republic*, has described Norman Finkelstein as "poison, he's a disgusting self-hating Jew, he's something you find under a rock." Israeli Prime Minister Benjamin Netanyahu recently called U.S. presidential adviser David Axelrod and White House Chief-of-Staff

Rahm Emmanuel self-hating Jews. And Abba Eban once categorized critics of Zionism as either anti-Semites or neurotic self-hating Jews.[10]

The assertion that Irina Klepfisz, Sara Roy, Daniela Vorburger or any Jew who is dedicated to equality for all people harbors self-hatred defies common sense. Given the self-esteem it takes to stand for justice amidst fierce disapprobation, a more accurate assessment is that Jews who protest the unfair treatment of the downtrodden are self-loving Jews.

– 14 –

Hope and Reconciliation: Interview with Leah

Security for Israel means hope for the Palestinians. Ami
Ayalon, J Street Conference, October 27, 2009[*]

Every Friday, my Hasidic brother emails his Jewish friends and relatives
an interesting interpretation of the *Torah* portion that corresponds to that
particular week in the Jewish calendar. Occasionally, he also sends
articles about the Israel-Palestine conflict that he considers important.
There have been times when I found an article so prejudiced that I
responded by emailing a forceful refutation to his email list.

About two years ago, my brother's friend Leah, who lives in the
Jewish settlement of Ma'ale Adumim outside of Jerusalem, decided to
play peacemaker between us. Her words were calming and
compassionate. That was the start of an occasional email friendship. I
learned from Leah that she is involved in a dialogue group whose
members are Palestinian and Israeli. Even though Leah never provided
details about how the group was formed, I was heartened to learn that a
friend of my brother even belongs to such a group.

In mid-October 2009, Leah emailed me a link to an article that had
just appeared in the *Jerusalem Post*. To my surprise, "Settling Their
Differences," was about her group.[1] The article even included a
photograph of her living room where the group often meets. By the time I
finished reading the article I knew I had to interview her for this book. To
me, Leah represents a future where people look beyond their
indoctrination to see the humanity in the other.

Rich: Leah, I know you live in Ma'ale Adumim but I'd like to know
about your background. Where did you grow up?

Leah: I grew up in the Bronx in New York City. My father was raised in
Austria as a secular Jew. When he realized what Hitler was planning to
do to the Jews of Europe he made a vow that if God saved him he would
become observant. He left Austria for New York in 1938. My mother was

---

[*] Ayalon is former commander-in-chief of the Israeli navy and former head of Shin
Bet.

born in Poland. Her grandparents were massacred in a pogrom in 1920. When my mother was around eight years old her mother died, so she moved to Romania to live with her aunt. When she was old enough she went to Vienna to work in a fur factory. That's where she met my dad, who was a furrier.

Rich: Were you brought up Orthodox, Conservative or Reform?

Leah: I was brought up Orthodox. As I grew older my parents became even more religious. I was rebellious. When I was twelve, my parents told me I could no longer wear trousers. They were also concerned that a lot of my Jewish friends were not religious. They wanted to make sure I hung out with the right crowd. So, even though I never wanted to give up Orthodoxy, they sent me to live with my Ultra-Orthodox sister in Montreal. After three months, though, I returned home. I attended synagogue every week. The community I grew up in – the Kingsbridge Heights Jewish Center – was warm and wonderful. The members of the congregation were like family. Every Shabbat morning after tefillah my dad invited guests over to our house for Kiddush and then the men would study *Torah* together.[*]

Rich: What was your parents' attitude about Israel and the Arabs?

Leah: My parents were Zionists. They were very pro-Israel. So were the rest of our community and synagogue. But my parents were never anti-Arab, although my dad was racist toward African-Americans, even to the point of changing the TV station when an African-American was on. He did tolerate Sammy Davis Jr., who had converted to Judaism. I often felt like I was growing up with a Jewish Archie Bunker.

Our first trip to Israel was in February 1973, when I was seventeen. For part of the trip my father hired an Arab driver to take us around Israel. The remainder of the time we rented a car. One day it was raining and the roads were muddy. Somewhere near Hebron or Bethlehem our car got stuck on a dirt path in an Arab village. We couldn't get it unstuck. An Arab man wearing a keffiyah took us by the hand and helped us up a

---

[*] Tefillah is the Hebrew word for prayer. Kiddush means sanctification and refers to blessings recited over a glass of wine.

steep hill.* He took us inside his home to call for help. I was surprised he was so friendly. At first I was really suspicious. I thought instead of helping us up the hill he was going to throw us off the cliff. Even when we were inside his house I was still scared. His wife served us mint tea. I had never had herbal tea before and I thought they were trying to poison us. After we left, my dad told me that Arabs had learned about hospitality from Abraham.

Rich: Did you go to college?

Leah: After graduating from high school in 1973, I attended college in Israel for one year. Then I returned to the United States where I went to work for the New York State Tax Department. Their offices were on the 65th floor of the World Trade Center. I was in the tax withholding unit. I was eighteen years old and this was my first job. After working there for two years I got promoted to supervisor. I stayed in that position for another three years. But when an opportunity came along to work in the entertainment industry I couldn't resist. So I quit my state job and worked for three years at Sire Records. Their clients included the Ramones, Talking Heads and the Pretenders. The pay was crap but it was probably my most interesting job, the ultimate glamour job. In the early 80s, I took courses at Hunter College. I was planning to get a Bachelor's Degree in Languages but I dropped out when I got married.

Rich: What was your job at Sire Records?

Leah: I was secretary to the Vice President of Legal Affairs.

Rich: Once you were on your own did you remain an observant Jew?

Leah: I became non-observant when I was nineteen. At twenty-one, I left home to live alone on the Upper West Side of Manhattan.

Rich: When did you meet my twin brother and sister-in-law?

Leah: After I was married in 1983, my husband and I moved to Toronto. We decided to become observant. We were drawn to the warmhearted

---

* A keffiyah is a traditional Arab headdress made of cloth.

Chabad community.* That is where we met your brother. My husband liked his very honest and no-bullshit attitude.

Rich: In the *Jerusalem Post* article you described yourself as a former militant Jew who was a member of Kach. What drew you to Kach? What did you think of Meir Kahane and his message?

Leah: I read some of Kahane's books, like *Listen World, Listen Jew*; and I read his articles in the *Jewish Press*, an Orthodox Jewish publication. His words resonated with me, especially when he criticized the hypocrisy among Orthodox Jews. He decried the fact that now that our people finally had a state they preferred a comfortable life in New York. Instead of moving to Israel, these Jews would buy luxury homes, designer clothes and wigs (for the women) and take expensive kosher vacations during Jewish holidays. He said that God giving us a state was a sign that we should move there. Kahane referred to Arabs as dogs; and he worried about Arab anger at the Jews and about Israel being a democracy. He believed our people would eventually become a minority and be in grave danger. That is why he advocated the transfer of Arabs to Jordan, which he called Arab Palestine.

Rich: At Kach gatherings what kinds of things did you hear? How did members talk about non-Jews and Arabs in particular?

Leah: In Toronto most of the focus was on the neo-Nazi movement in Canada. Some of the members used to come to the office in military fatigues, which I found quite amusing. When they did talk about Arabs they would say there were twenty-one Arab countries the Palestinians could move to. They were totally prejudiced. They thought all Arabs were terrorists and they also called Arabs dogs. I didn't like that kind of language.

After we moved to Israel in 1995, I went to a Kach Purim gathering, which was advertised as "Celebrate Purim in Deir Yassin." Deir Yassin was one of the Arab villages where massacres took place in 1948. It is

---

* Chabad-Lubavitch is a Hasidic movement that was founded in the 18th Century by Schneur Zalman, known as the *Alter Rebbe* (Yiddish for "Old Rebbe"). Originally headquartered in Lubavitch, Russia, it is now headquartered in Crown Heights, Brooklyn, NY.

now the Ultra-Orthodox neighborhood of Har Nof. The Kach members were singing songs and having fun, but in their discussions they expressed hatred for anyone who didn't think like them; and they spoke disrespectfully about the recently assassinated Yitzhak Rabin and other left-wingers they didn't like. I felt uncomfortable listening to them poking fun at the deceased Prime Minister. Even though I opposed Rabin's policies, I thought it would have been better to vote him out of office, not murder him. They didn't seem to think there was anything wrong with his murder.

Rich: Wasn't Kach outlawed in Israel before you moved there?

Leah: Yes.

Rich: Were you worried your association with Kach might get you into trouble with the Israeli authorities?

Leah: No. I was pretty discreet about my involvement.

Rich: As a member of Kach, you too must have been highly prejudiced toward the Arabs. How would you describe your feelings about them?

Leah: I mistrusted them and thought all Arabs wanted all Jews dead. I wished we didn't have to deal with that problem and wished they were transferred out of *our* land. After all, didn't they know that God had promised Israel to us and not to them? What were they doing on our land? What were they doing in Biblical towns like Shechem and Hebron and Bethlehem? I used to say that they were the ones who stole our land. Beit Jala was once the Biblical village of Gilo. Battir was once the village of Beitar. There are other examples.

Rich: I know my brother and sister-in-law were never members of Kach. What did they think of you being a member?

Leah: I don't remember.

Rich: How long were you a member?

Leah: I was a paying member for a year, but I felt a part of their organization for about fifteen years.

Rich: What caused you to leave their organization?

Leah: The last time I attended a Kach gathering was nine or ten years ago at a memorial for Kahane in a Jerusalem hotel. Teenagers were dancing in a circle and singing "All the Arabs Die" to the tune of *Am Yisrael Chai* ("The people of Israel live!"). If I hadn't known these people were Jews I would have thought they were Nazis. My husband and I just looked at each other and said: "This isn't normal." My husband was a renovator. His business was remodeling houses. He had gotten to know some Arabs because he regularly hired them to work for him. He wouldn't tolerate that kind of stuff. That was the last time I attended one of their events.

Rich: At the time of this Kach gathering, how long had your husband worked with Arabs? Was it his job as a renovator that first brought him into contact with them? Also, did you raise your children to hate or distrust Arabs? What do they think of Arabs now?

Leah: You're correct that my husband had never met Arabs before he started hiring them, which was a year before we went to the Kahane memorial. As far as my children are concerned, we did not raise them to hate anyone. Their distrust of Arabs comes from growing up in this society and from their peers. So even though I've changed, my kids haven't.

Rich: How old are your children?

Leah: I have five kids ranging in age from seventeen to twenty-five.

Rich: After you left Kach, what did you do? Did you feel there was something missing in your religious practice? Did you look for other groups that were more in tune with your way of thinking?

Leah: We certainly felt that something spiritual was missing from our lives. We looked for community but couldn't find anything we were really attracted to. One by one my kids became secular and, in the end, we did too. More accurately, though, you could say that although we are no longer Orthodox, we consider ourselves traditional with a strong belief in God.

Rich: What occurred in your life that caused you to become friends with Palestinians and end up in a dialogue group with them?

Leah: During the Second Intifada, the Israelis and Palestinians seemed to be playing a deadly game that reminded me of ping pong. The IDF would kill Palestinians and Palestinians would retaliate by killing Jews. My daughters had friends who were killed by suicide bombers. When things like this happen a person can either become more extreme in their views or try to understand why there is all this violence. I think most Israeli Jews tend to become more extreme, to hate even more. In my case, I felt terribly distressed because I couldn't see a real solution in sight. One day there was an article in the *Jerusalem Post* about an interfaith prayer group that was meeting across from the Western Wall. I decided to go. Once I was there I felt "this is it. This is my new community." One of the things I had learned in the Chabad community, whose goal is to bring the Messiah, was that if you want the Messiah bad enough you should act as if he is already here. Well this was it, wasn't it? To see Muslims, Jews and Christians praying together to one God and not fighting was remarkable. I was hooked.

Soon after this service I went to a weekend interfaith retreat that consisted of twenty-five Jews and twenty-five Palestinians from Nablus. The only Israelis these Palestinians had ever seen before this retreat were soldiers. At first, when I saw these young men from Nablus, I was terrified. My friends had often told me not to turn my back on Arabs, because you can't trust them: they would act friendly, but in the end they would stab and kill you. And they want to throw all the Jews into the sea. I spoke with these young Palestinians who showed me their bullet wounds. They told me that all they had done was to go outside after curfew in order to get medicine or to come home. I was shocked that "we" could do such things to other people. I thought, "Shit, that's not what we've been told." I broke down and started crying. In our heart-to-heart talks, I realized they had the exact same fears about us as we had about them. This also surprised me.

I met an artist from Ramallah whose studio was destroyed in a raid by the IDF. He wasn't a terrorist, he was an artist. He took a handful of earth and said to me: "I love this land" and I said: "I love this land too." Then I realized that I could not hate a people who love the same thing as passionately as I do; and that maybe it is possible to find common ground and live together on this beloved land. That weekend, my first encounter with Palestinians, was very emotional for me. I cried most of the weekend. I was so overwhelmed. Sometimes I cried for their pain and sorrow and sometimes I cried for the fact that we were never told anything about the other side, about their humanity. It was always only about us. It was as if they never existed. I felt betrayed by my own society. But now I had discovered some long lost cousins, a long lost family. I felt very close to them and I cried from happiness too. I overcame my fear that weekend. That weekend changed my life. From then on, I worried about my new family every time the IDF went into Nablus to conduct an "operation;" and they worried about me traveling on buses.

Rich: What you are saying is beautiful. I experienced something similar. I went through feelings of intense sorrow for those whom I had once feared and considered the enemy. But afterwards I knew great peace. It is such a relief to see all people as human beings. This process I am describing was one of the most valuable experiences of my life. It brought me closer to the purpose of my life, which is to fully realize my inherent oneness with all of life. Have your meetings with Palestinians affected your spiritual journey?

Leah: Yes, definitely; it is a relief to see the humanity in Arabs. My life has become enriched spiritually. I feel as if I'm doing *tikkun olam* by bringing people together. I feel that this is my true spiritual path and that our ultimate destiny is to be together. I am drawn to this view like a moth to fire. I believe God wants us to do anything we can to live in the Holy Land in peace. And He wants the children of his beloved Abraham to live together in harmony rather than discord. A Sufi friend said to me that Jerusalem is the heart of the world and if the heart is sick, so is the world.

Rich: Leah, I agree with your Sufi friend. I think he is pointing to the inter-connectedness of all beings. I believe that if the Israelis would make a fair peace with the Palestinians in which both sides recognize their shared humanity, confess to their acts of cruelty and acknowledge the other's acts of kindness, it would serve as a model for the world, encouraging other peoples to resolve their differences.

You said you once believed that all Arabs wanted all Jews dead. I think it is fair to say that you considered all Arabs terrorists and Jew haters. That is the way my brother thinks and is similar to how I once thought, though neither of us had ever actually spent much time with Arabs. Yet we were certain we understood their nature. Now that you are freed of these enemy images are you able to look back and see how fear induced your imagination to create a world of suffering for yourself and others?

Leah: Yes, it was fear of the unknown.

Rich: It appears to me that many Jews label Arabs as terrorists and Jew haters because they are afraid to seek a real path to peace. Is there anything you would like to say about that?

Leah: If you believe your life is in danger, why would you want to meet these people? People are always cautioning me about my friendships, but they have never had the first-hand experience of meeting with Arabs. I don't know what it would take to remove their fear, unless their *own* people (i.e. right wing, religious) begin to teach them differently. If a leader in their community has a change of heart, then there would be a change of heart in the community. Now there is a theory going around that Palestinians were originally Jews who always lived on the land and converted to Islam in the Seventh Century. Even Orthodox Jews are talking about this. If they are curious enough about this to start a conversation, that too might break down barriers.

Rich: I support anything that breaks down barriers between people. David Ben-Gurion believed that many Palestinian Muslims were converted Jews. And Shlomo Sand, professor of history at Tel Aviv University, is a proponent of the theory that the ancestors of today's Jews were mostly converts from other religions. His book, *The Invention of the Jewish People*, has created quite a stir. From my perspective, however, it doesn't matter what our genetic heritage is. At a deeper level we are all one people; we are all Palestinians and we are all Israelis; we are all Jews and we are all Muslims and Christians. Our true identity transcends any limitation.

Suppose the Jews in Israel became convinced that Palestinians and Jews are descended from the same source. And suppose they accepted Palestinians as equals and formed a single state. If they could do that on the basis of a common genealogy, why couldn't they do that on the basis of a common humanity? The barrier to that kind of tolerance and cooperation lies in the unexamined beliefs we are brought up with. These beliefs, which are associated with our presumed identity, foster intolerance and conflict. As long as we refuse to question our beliefs we will imagine the other doing or intending to do what, unbeknownst to our conscious minds, we are already doing to ourselves. And because we will always be imprisoned by these beliefs, we will never realize our full humanity.

Leah: I think Jews and Palestinians need to discover what they have in common in order to build trust. That is why I am happy with this historical theory, which raises the possibility that we come from the same genealogical tree. Without trust we will never be able to live together on the same land. Each of us has to brush away our fears as if they were like an annoying fly buzzing around our face. I don't think most people want to question their core beliefs, but if they come to believe that the Palestinians are *long lost Jews* they might think differently about them. This would break down some barriers.

Rich: After attending the weekend retreat did you continue to go to interfaith groups?

Leah: I attended many interfaith, nonpolitical gatherings from Interfaith Encounter Association and from Jerusalem Peacemakers. I had finally found my niche.

Rich: When did you start a dialogue group?

Leah: After being a member of one of the Interfaith Encounter Association's groups in Jerusalem, I was asked to be the Jewish coordinator in Jerusalem. I accepted and worked in that position for three years, but the group wasn't challenging enough for me so I left it and started a new group in my home. There is so much animosity between Jewish settlers and Arabs, so much mistrust and misinformation about religious Jews and Muslims that I thought: what if I could get them together? What if they would start to talk? That might change much of the negative dynamics between them. So I decided to begin with my own neighborhood, which is just over the green line and not an ideological settlement. That might be a good beginning for others to follow. My current group is now nearly three years old.

Interview with Leah

Rich: What do your husband, kids and father think about what you are doing? How do other Jews like my niece and her husband, who live in Jerusalem, view your activities?

Leah: My father died when I was still anti-Arab. My husband is supportive but rarely joins our group. My kids just wish they had a normal mother. Most people think I'm crazy. There are people who no longer speak to me but that's okay. Some people call me the Arab ambassador of Ma'ale Adumim – I really like that title. Your niece has friends who come from the violent Jewish settlements. But she has recently said there must be two sides to every story. So that is a step in the right direction.

Occasionally, though, something exciting happens. Just the other day I got a phone call from a friend who also lives in Ma'ale Adumim. She is a teacher at a local high school. She wanted to speak to me about an idea she has about arranging a meeting between her high school students and Israeli Arab students in Abu Ghosh. I was quite surprised, so I questioned her a few times to make sure I understood what she was saying, that her students really want this meeting. She said they did. I find this remarkable, since her husband once came with us to one of Rabbi Kahane's memorial gatherings. So it looks like another window is opening here.

Rich: This is good news. It could be the beginning of many more openings. I hope that after your friend and her students meet with the students at Abu Ghosh they tell their peers all about it. Maybe their meeting can influence other Jewish teachers and students to meet with their Arab contemporaries.

Leah: That is what I am hoping.

Rich: Leah, just one more question about the reactions other Jews have to your work. Have you received threats or hate mail? Has anybody called you an anti-Semite or self-hating Jew?

Leah: Sometimes I get emails telling me that by inviting Arabs into my home I'm supporting terror. Nobody has called me an anti-Semite or self-hating Jew to my face but people keep asking me if I have any friends left. They are terribly frightened.

Rich: What has the group taught you about yourself, about the Palestinians, about conflict and about your people?

Leah: The group has taught me that the popular belief among Israelis that Islam is a religion of violence is unfair. I think if you interpret religion in a certain way, Judaism and Christianity can be considered equally violent. We can see, for example, how the Biblical story of the conflict between Abraham's wife Sarah and her handmaiden Hagar has led to the present day conflict between brothers. Some Jews interpret this as: "you see, Sarah knew Isaac wouldn't be able to live with Ishmael, and it was good that she chased Hagar and Ishmael away." Others see it differently, that we are meant to repair this ancient conflict: "what if the brothers live like brothers? Isn't that a lot better than everlasting war within our family?"

I want to tell you about a small thing that happened recently. I walked into a restaurant with Arab waiters. I said a few words to them in Arabic and they literally were so moved by my trying to communicate with them in their own language that they gave me free baklava. I was stunned. I thought to myself: is this all it takes, just a small gesture to get to know them a little? What if we got to know them a lot? Just think what would happen then.

Rich: Leah, when did you learn Arabic? Did you learn it after you began attending interfaith groups?

Leah: Yes, but it's a difficult language. I am not yet at a conversational level.

Rich: Do you ever visit any of your Palestinian friends in their homes? If so, what do you experience and what are their homes and villages like?

Leah: Yes, I have been fortunate to visit. I've experienced only love and warmth and a ton of food. In that respect they're worse than Jewish mothers. And another thing: many people believe that Arabs are filthy people, but when I walk into their homes, rich or poor, their homes are spotless. Even Bedouin tents are kept clean. Their food is also delicious and I'm a big connoisseur of food. I feel totally safe when I'm in their villages and homes. My kids sometimes get frightened, thinking I'll be kidnapped, but that is a perception they haven't let go of yet.

Rich: In your talks with Palestinians, have you discussed the Jewish people and their history of persecution? Do they know of these things and what is their reaction?

Leah: The Palestinians I speak with are not really aware of our history. Unfortunately, they see us as usurpers and don't know about us being exiled from Biblical Israel 2,000 years ago, nor do they know about the Spanish Inquisition. I spoke to a very intelligent woman from Bethlehem who was an Arabic-English translator by profession. I asked her if she was aware that there were Jewish refugees from Arab countries. She didn't know anything about that. I tried to explain to her that these Jews came to Israel in 1948 because they were being persecuted by Arab countries. I told her that approximately eighty percent of the residents of Ma'ale Adumim are Sephardic Jews whose families fled Arab countries in 1948.

Rich: How did she respond?

Leah: She just said "I don't know." She felt the same way I once felt: that her people were the only refugees or victims.

Rich: When I had my transformation and began to see the horrors of the past sixty-plus years, I knew beyond any doubt that I could never live in Israel. I could never live on land that was once Palestine, except, of course, if it was necessary for me to be there to work for peace. You live in a Jewish settlement in the West Bank on land that Palestinians claim belongs to them. The international community considers the settlements illegal and basically agrees that the land you live on was stolen by Israel. How do you reconcile your willingness to hear the Palestinian point-of-view and see them as equals with your residing in an illegal Jewish settlement?

Leah: Ma'ale Adumim is on land that was barren before its construction; my father was ill and already lived here. It costs fifty percent less to live here than in West Jerusalem. Before 1967 this area belonged to Jordan and was not privately owned by *any* family, at least not in the new area where I live. There are some sections close to Azariah that may have been privately owned by Arab landowners from Abu Dis. I *would* feel much worse living in Tel Aviv's Ramat Aviv Gimmel neighborhood where an Arab village was destroyed in 1948 or in West Jerusalem where Arabs were chased out in 1948.

Rich: What about the separation barrier? Does it border your settlement? How do you feel about it, and how does it affect the lives of Palestinians in the area?

Leah: We don't have a security fence bordering Ma'ale Adumim. We do have a checkpoint at the entrance and a fence by the highway but not all around the settlement. I wish the fence didn't have to be there. It punishes an entire people instead of the few who want to commit terror acts. I think the fence actually creates more danger because it makes it harder to meet the other. If we can't come together we will never learn to coexist with each other. What I have learned is that if we don't come together and talk, stereotypes and fear will remain. On the other hand, there is a radical element among Palestinians that believes they'll become martyrs by killing Israelis, so it's good to have security checks. I am sure, however, that their radical views would change if they were given an opportunity to meet with Israelis.

Rich: Are you familiar with Ariel Sharon's statement that the Israelis must grab all the hilltops for settlements? Isn't Ma'ale Adumim on a hilltop?

Leah: Yes, it's built on a hill, but so are the Arab villages of A Tur and Issawiya.

Rich: Are you aware that per capita Israeli water consumption is five times that of Palestinians who live in the West Bank? Do you know that while Jews in Ma'ale Adumim and other settlements have swimming pools for their kids to play in, many Palestinians don't even have clean water to drink; that many families are forced to collect water in order to survive?

Leah: Yes, I am aware of this. I think it is very unfair. I found this out recently when I went on a study tour with Ir Amim (City of Nations). I don't understand this unfairness that the Israeli government is responsible for and I am embarrassed by it. The same unfairness trickles down to education. For example, the Jerusalem municipality doesn't allocate enough money to the Arab sector. This leaves many children without classrooms and schools. In turn, the kids go to private schools, which are funded by Islamic extremists. Israel is shooting itself in the foot by not funding enough education for the Arab population. There is a misconception by many Israelis that Arabs don't pay property taxes and therefore don't deserve these types of funding. But those that have residency (blue ID cards) definitely pay taxes and should receive the same services as Israeli Jews. Furthermore, there are no building permits given to Arab neighborhoods, so I can see why everyone is so livid when Jewish neighborhoods are being built up for "natural growth" purposes while natural growth for Arabs is ignored.

Rich: You've explained that Ma'ale Adumim is not an ideological settlement. Are there any religious Jews who live there?

Leah: There are secular and religious Jews. There are even a few Israeli Arabs living here but they keep it quiet.

Rich: Do you support a two-state solution? What would you like to see happen? What would you like to see the Israeli government do?

Leah: I would like to see one state where people live together in peace. One thing that Muslims would appreciate and that Israelis could easily do would be for Jewish employers in Israel to give their Muslim employees time off to celebrate the holidays of Eid al-Adha and Eid ul-Fitr.* Also, just as Israeli public television stations wish all of us a Happy New Year on Rosh Hashanah, and acknowledge other Jewish holidays, they could acknowledge Ramadan and wish all Moslems an *Eid Mubarak* ("May you enjoy a blessed festival").+ These are simple things that could have a profound effect.

I would also like to see the Israeli government provide building permits for Arabs to expand existing towns and build new ones, just as

---

* Eid al-Adha (the Great Festival) commemorates the willingness of Ibrahim to sacrifice his son Ismael. Eid ul-Fitr (the Minor Festival) is a holiday that marks an end to the month-long fasting period of Ramadan.

+ Ramadan is the ninth month of the Islamic calendar. From dawn to dusk devout Muslims fast and abstain from smoking, drinking and over-indulging in anything that distracts them from their spirituality.

they do for Jews. That would be fair. And in order to allay the fear of Arab expansion, people need to be educated about each other. This begins in early childhood. Both societies could commit to teaching all of their people the history and religion of the other. Monetary awards to schools that initiate peace projects could be established. Teach Arabic in elementary schools. Make it compulsory. Likewise, Hebrew should be compulsory in Arab schools. This is just for starters.

Rich: You would like to see a one-state solution to this conflict. Ideally, would you like to see a united country where Arabs and Jews live side-by-side in the same neighborhoods or would you prefer a country where Arabs and Jews are segregated, kind of like the American South up until the latter part of the twentieth century?

Leah: Personally, I want to see us living together, side-by-side. I think the fear of giving up a holy city, like Hebron, is frightening to Jews so some get violent towards anyone they think will take that away from them. If Jewish settlers in places like Hebron felt secure in the knowledge that they could stay where they are, their attitudes would change; and I don't think they would be as violent. Many problems stem from each side believing the land is *theirs only.* All of us need to learn that this is God's land, to be shared by all of his children. I've seen maps of Palestine in Arab homes and schools in the West Bank. Palestine is not just the West Bank and Gaza. It is all of Israel. Palestinians won't be satisfied being squished into a separate, tiny state. Let us all have the freedom to work and live where we wish; but this has to come with knowledge and respect for the other. *Both of us* have to recognize and respect the historical connection to this land that we each have, rather than one side accusing the other of fabricating a connection.

Rich: You are saying that you have found a common humanity with the Palestinians, just as they have with you. So, if it is possible for the people to discover this relationship, I am thinking that the obstruction to Peace is primarily with the leaders. Where do you think the obstruction to peace is now?

Leah: I agree with you. Leaders have the power to change the system – for example in education and in allocating money to projects where

Arabs and Jews can learn about one another. Also, the media – newspapers, radio, TV – can play big roles in educating people. They need to let people know that it is possible for Arabs and Jews to get along. They need to create a certain excitement about what is possible.

Rich: How would you feel if the Israeli government agreed to a peace treaty that required all settlers to leave Ma'ale Adumim and the Occupied Territories? Would you leave willingly with or without any compensation you might receive?

Leah: I don't know what I would do. I wouldn't be happy to leave, unless peace was totally guaranteed. However, again, look what happened when the settlers left Gaza. We had the opposite of peace. Everyone expected the Gazans to be happy. Many people point to that. I wonder if the Gaza disengagement was a test run to see how Palestinians would react when Israelis are evacuated.

Rich: Leah, I want to get back to Gaza in a minute, but I am curious about something. Generally I use the word *Palestinian* to refer to a particular group of Arab people who come from, or whose ancestors came from, Palestine, just as I refer to Arab people who come from Egypt as Egyptians. More than five million of these Palestinians live in Israel and the Occupied Territories. I know that many Israelis refer to them as *Arabs*. I am also aware that historically many Israelis do not differentiate Palestinian from Arab. That makes it easier to ignore the Palestinian claim to the Holy Land. So when you say Arab are you saying it out of habit or for another reason?

Leah: I use the terms interchangeably. So when I talk about Arabs, I am referring to their ethnicity not their nationality. Yes, right wingers are told never to define these people as Palestinians because there never was a Palestinian nation. This gets very complicated, no?

Rich: Leah, from my perspective, complications arise out of a refusal to conduct objective research so as to free ourselves of indoctrinated beliefs and learn, to the greatest extent possible, the real history of the Palestinian people and the Israel-Palestine conflict. I believe that if people were to take that step much of their prejudice would dissolve. In your case you were willing to meet with Palestinians, to listen to their experiences and to learn from them. As a result you have let go of a lot of your indoctrination and prejudice.

Leah: That is true.

Rich: What do you think of Operation Cast Lead in Gaza? Are you familiar with the Dahiya strategy, which deliberately ignores the distinction between civilians and militants? And what do you think about Netanyahu's denunciation of the Goldstone Report that was highly critical of both Hamas and Israel?

Leah: These are tough questions for me. First, I haven't had the time to read the Goldstone Report. I need to read it first before giving you my answer about Netanyahu's speech. As for Cast Lead, why did Hamas shoot missiles into Sderot after the disengagement? What were we to do? Another ping pong game happened. One can only speak when there is calm. I don't know what the solution is over there. I wish I knew.

Rich: Leah, I agree with you that when people feel threatened, as when they are faced with rocket attacks, they do whatever they feel is necessary to protect themselves and their children. Their fear leads them to ask what steps are necessary for protection. A typical response is to find a way to eliminate the threat as quickly as possible. But fear also usually prevents them from asking *why* the enemy is trying to harm them and what they might have done to incite the enemy to take such drastic action. The problem with fear is that as long as people are in its grip they will never understand the other and they will never resolve conflict. Having said that, and taking into account your question as to whether the Gaza disengagement was a test run to see how Gazans would react, I hope you will read my chapter on Gaza.

Leah: I would like to read your book.

Rich: Regarding your comment that you don't know what the solution is for Gaza and, really, the entire region, my transformative experience taught me that the only lasting solution is compassion, because compassion seeks to understand; compassion recognizes that we are all in this together, that no event happens by itself, that there are innumerable and mostly insignificant events that coalesce into one defining moment in the life of a person or a nation, that we are all responsible for each other and that the destiny of the world depends on each and every one of us. I am sure that this spontaneous understanding I experienced has parallels in Judaism. I know that you have studied our common heritage in greater depth than I have. Does my description of compassion remind you of any similar understanding within Judaism?

Leah: Yes, it reminds me of the saying, "Love your neighbor as yourself." According to the *Torah*, even if a neighbor treats you badly, you are obligated to love that person. Here is a true story: when we first moved to Israel we were neighbors with a Jewish Moroccan family. They were awful to us, always causing problems. One afternoon I decided to invite their daughter to my home to play with my kids. She had a good time and enjoyed the candies I gave her. Afterwards, the family was friendly to us. The same thing could happen on a larger scale.

Rich: Now that you have let go of your irrational fear of all Arabs, do you feel as if you see the world with a greater clarity?

Leah: Yes and with more hope, optimism and happiness.

Rich: Leah, if more people were willing to face themselves and grow as you have done there would be tolerance and peace in Israel/Palestine. Thank you for sharing your time with me.

Leah: Thank you.

– 15 –

Redemption

Demography and territory, the two pillars of the Zionist enterprise, cannot be reconciled unless Israel abandons her territorial ambitions and departs from the unrealistic, and morally corrupting, dream of possessing the biblical lands of Eretz-Israel. Shlomo Ben-Ami, p. 331

Throughout the writing of this book I have operated under the assumption that humankind is innately compassionate. From the beginning that assumption informed my decision to share my transformation in order to encourage readers, especially Jewish readers, to investigate the history of the Israel-Palestine conflict for themselves. Another intention was to provoke an inner debate in which the old indoctrination, undone by inquiry, would be replaced by a new, more conscious relationship to the world, where we take responsibility for our beliefs. With knowledge at its root, this relationship is available to all who have not lost touch with their innate compassion.

Notwithstanding my faith in humanity, I knew that my message would attract criticism from those who are reluctant to acknowledge the extensive body of research that has led to my conclusions. I was also aware that some would accuse me of overstating the positive qualities of one group – whose image has largely been perceived within my culture as negative – and the negative qualities of another group – whose image has largely been perceived within my culture as positive. There is a fine line between accurately presenting information that deconstructs beliefs and images that are crucial to our identities and dehumanizing any of the subjects of this book. Hopefully, I have not crossed that line. I trust that I have balanced the equation by demonstrating that Palestinians and Israelis are no more and no less human than any other group of people. To argue that one society is inherently evil and the other inherently innocent is merely the unexamined mind's attempt to deal with its confusion. But confusion can never be resolved in a world that is perceived in terms of black and white.

In order to mitigate the hurt and indignation that I fully expect some readers will feel, and to present my views as effectively as possible, I made every effort to match the most impeccable source material I could find to the primary audience I expect to attract, who are secular Jews and Americans. Thus, I endeavored to avoid, as much as possible, anything with an Arab thumbprint on it. My hope is that if readers can relate more comfortably to the Jewish, Israeli and American sources I use, they might seriously consider the information I present. Taking into consideration how I might have reacted at one time, there was no doubt in my mind that if I had relied even moderately on Arab sources many readers would judge this book as biased.

In a sense, though, this book *is* biased; it is biased in favor of human rights and a full accounting of the injustices that have denied millions of people the opportunities that most Jews and Israelis take for granted. Because Israel maintains a decidedly superior position in its relationship with the Palestinian people, it falls upon the Jewish state to assume the initiative. Without a genuine commitment on its part to heal the conflict, a fair peace will never be achieved.

True leaders recognize their responsibility to go beyond archaic social paradigms and raise the consciousness of their citizens. The government of Israel would be well advised to embrace this responsibility and begin to treat the Palestinians with the same consideration as it treats its own people. A commitment to fair treatment would generate respect between the two peoples and neutralize the idea that violence is the only way to solve disagreements. This would benefit Israel's citizens with a more dependable security.

The United States and Great Britain also have it within their power to spark an expansion of consciousness by confessing their roles in helping to create this situation in the first place. The United States can also act by giving human rights priority over its patronage of neo-con, Zionist and evangelical interests, which exert a destructive influence on its Middle Eastern policy. If Israel refuses to abide by international and humanitarian law, America's legislators must put an end to the loan guarantees and subsidies that provide it with the means to maintain the occupation.

* * * *

Theodore Herzl was the guiding light of the Zionist movement. He died in 1904 at the age of forty-four. In 1896, in the Conclusion to his book, *The Jewish State*, he said:

> The Jews who wish for a State will have it. We shall live at last as free men on our own soil, and die peacefully in our own homes. The world will be freed by our liberty, enriched by our wealth, magnified by our greatness. And whatever we attempt there to accomplish for our own welfare, will react powerfully and beneficially for the good of humanity.[1]

The idealism and hope expressed by Herzl preceded an unbroken trail of destruction for the Palestinian people. To the vast majority in the Middle East, Herzl's prophesy is an artifice. Increasing numbers of people, motivated by fury and despair, have joined extremist groups, finding in acts of terror the only means they know to focus the world's attention on the effects of Zionism.

At one time it might have been possible for European Jewish immigrants to settle a foreign land while developing positive relations with their Arab neighbors. But that would have taken a real sensitivity to the task at hand: the creation of a Jewish state in a land that had been populated for millennia by another people. The Palestinians had a fundamental entitlement to the land, which was born of living and dying there, of developing a culture and society. Establishing an unfamiliar society in Palestine while retaining the goodwill of their Palestinian hosts would have taken leaders with the intelligence to assess conditions as they really were and the wisdom to adapt to them accordingly. Instead, the Zionist movement based its assessment on the insensitive and misleading catchphrase: "a land without a people for a people without a land."

Zionism did have the advantage of wise leaders – Ahad Ha'am and Martin Buber, for example – but their criticism of Zionist attitudes went unheeded. In the late nineteenth century, Ahad Ha'am ('one of the people') said:

> Yet what do our brethren do in Palestine? Just the very opposite! Serfs they were in the lands of the Diaspora and suddenly they find themselves in unrestricted freedom and this change has awakened in them an inclination to despotism. They treat the Arabs with hostility and cruelty, deprive them of their rights, offend them without cause and even boast of these deeds; and

nobody among us opposes this despicable and dangerous inclination...[2*]

In 1914 Ahad Ha'am predicted:

> [The Zionists] wax angry towards those who remind them that there is still another people in Eretz Yisrael that has been living there and does not intend at all to leave its place. In a future when this illusion will have been torn from their hearts and they will look with open eyes upon the reality as it is, they will certainly understand how important this question is and how great our duty to work for its solution.[3]

Rejecting the ideas of Ahad Ha'am, Zionism embraced instead the views of those who advocated a brutal pragmatism. No less a hawk than Raphael Eitan (1929-2004), founder of the extreme-right, ultra-nationalist *Tzomet* (The Movement for Zionist Renewal) party, confessed to Israel's brutality in the following remark: "I don't believe in peace, because if they had done to us what we did to them we'd never agree to make peace."[4]

Eitan, who had been Ariel Sharon's second in command for years, was in charge of Israeli troops when they slaughtered hundreds of Egyptian POW's after the 1956 Sinai campaign, powerful evidence that he meant it when he said "the only good Arab is a dead Arab." In 1978, Eitan succeeded Mordecai Gur as IDF Chief-of-Staff. During his tenure, which lasted until 1983, he presided over Israel's destruction of Palestinian society in Lebanon. Eitan proposed that for each incident of stone-throwing by Palestinians ten settlements should be built: "When we have settled the land, all the Arabs will be able to do about it will be to scurry around like drugged roaches in a bottle."[5] He eventually admitted to having ordered soldiers to brutalize prisoners and impose collective punishment.

Shimon Peres once said there were two ways to confront conflict: "with the power of power or the power of wisdom."[6] Up until the present

---

* Ahad Ha'am is the pen name of Asher Ginzberg (1856-1927). Born in the Ukraine, Ginzberg was an essayist and founder of Cultural or Spiritual Zionism. He believed that Political Zionism, as formulated by Herzl, would fail because of the problems it would create in its dealings with the Arab population.

Israel has chosen the former; the time has come for it to choose the latter. Israel needs to be reminded of the text of its own *Declaration of the Establishment of the State of Israel*, which was born on May 14, 1948:

> [The State of Israel] will foster the development of the country for the benefit of all its inhabitants; it will be based on freedom, justice and peace as envisaged by the prophets of Israel; it will ensure complete equality of social and political rights to all its inhabitants irrespective of religion, race or sex; it will guarantee freedom of religion, conscience, language, education and culture; it will safeguard the Holy Places of all religions; and it will be faithful to the principles of the Charter of the United Nations.[7]

If Israel will not unequivocally respect the values it has espoused, then it is incumbent upon the international community to impose strict sanctions until its government awakens to the wisdom of taking those values seriously. The international community must expect nothing less than a sincere effort by all parties to end the conflict, not being satisfied until the two sides reach a just and equitable solution; one that confers equal rights on all citizens and resolves the core issues of refugees, security, borders and Jerusalem.

* * * *

In general, both sides of the debate view the Israel-Palestine conflict in simple and sharply polarized terms. Each assumes that the problem lies with the other, who is inherently unjust and violent. Complicating this mutual lack of trust, each side also sees itself as unfairly stereotyped by the outside world. An extraordinarily high emotional charge accompanies these views. The history of violence in the region and its direct impact on the lives of practically every individual makes for a collective mind that is filled with images of mortal enemies and destruction. Fear and anger directly inform every political decision in the region. Many Israelis and Palestinians doubt they will ever see peace in their lifetimes. After sixty years of Israeli statehood and endless negotiations, peace seems more like a mirage than an imminent reality.

Having studied this problem from a more enlightened perspective than was possible before my transformation, it has become clear to me that all of us have been creators of, and active participants in, a mass illusion. As Americans, Israelis, Palestinians or Arabs, we have unconsciously agreed not to venture outside the bounds of culturally indoctrinated beliefs and images. Our fear of breaking the taboo of blind loyalty to this indoctrination has caused us to ignore our own suffering and the suffering of others. Dennis Ross:

> Peacemaking can never succeed in an environment dominated by mythologies and untruths. One can decide that peace is not possible because the gap between the two sides is simply too great to overcome. But efforts to promote peace should not falter because one side or the other believes in myths that bear no relationship to reality. If ever there was a regional conflict that has been sustained by mythologies, by avoiding the unpleasantness of reality, by ignoring the need to see the world as it is, it is the Middle East.[8]

* * * *

One example of an untruth is the Zionist claim that Arab countries broadcast radio messages to encourage the exodus of Palestinians from villages in what is now Israel. Recited before the United Nations, this claim was calculated to minimize the world's sympathy for the plight of the Palestinian people and to deny them the right to return to homes left behind in the new nation of Israel.

In 1959, Professor Walid Khalidi proved that the claim was a fabrication. His findings were independently corroborated two years later by Irish scholar and U.N. diplomat, Erskine Childers. By examining the archives of Arab governments and newspapers and the reports of the CIA, as well as the BBC, which monitored every Arab radio broadcast in 1948, both men demonstrated that no such encouragement had occurred. To the contrary, the Arab broadcasts appealed to people *not* to leave their homes. When asked by the U.N. to account for its longstanding claim, Israel failed to produce one iota of evidence.[9] Misinformation like this has influenced generations of Jews to dismiss the Palestinian people's narrative and slander them as propagandists and liars.[*]

---

[*] Israel has established a National Information Directorate to deal with *hasbara*. Commonly used to refer to propaganda, spin or information, the literal meaning of *hasbara* is explanation. Yarden Vatikai, the Directorate's chief, said: "The hasbara

Redemption

* * * *

If Israelis and Palestinians want to end the bloodshed, they need to find the values they have in common and commit themselves to understanding the suffering of the other. Otherwise, by failing to understand why the other rejects its reality, each side will continue to cultivate conflict. The great need is for enough individuals to overcome their conditioning and reappraise their beliefs and images. By making that choice, they will gain a more powerful sense of themselves and a less restrictive identity. Then they will be able to redefine the boundaries of their *and* the other's awareness and improve the prospects for a lasting solution.

The alternative is that both sides will remain dependent upon the decisions of leaders who will be able to exploit their fear and confusion, always with destructive consequences. Americans need only look at George W. Bush's Iraq War to see the ease with which a leader can hide behind images of patriotism. By misleading an unquestioning public into supporting the invasion of another country, Bush caused immense harm to millions of people. If Americans had asked more questions and demanded more answers, rather than projecting their fear and confusion upon an enemy whose image had been cultivated by neo-conservatives for over a decade, the lies of the Bush administration would have been exposed and the invasion could have been averted.

Belief systems that are founded upon cultural and religious identities are often problematic. People have fought and died for symbols and dubious ideas since the beginning of time. And that is the question: Must we sacrifice our lives and the lives of our children for assumptions and beliefs that inhibit us from understanding the reality of the other? The reader must answer that question for himself.

I do believe that Judaism and most Jews value integrity, ethical behavior and justice. Accordingly, I have described how the commonly accepted historiography of the Jewish people's struggle for a homeland

---

apparatus needed a body that would co-ordinate its agencies, coordinate the messages and become a platform for co-operation between all the agencies that deal with communication relations and public diplomacy ["Special spin body gets media on message, says Israel," Rachel Shabi, *The Guardian*, January 2, 2009]."

has had the effect of denigrating the Palestinian people's struggle for *their* homeland. I have tried to show how our unconscious fear and confusion prevent us from looking and acting with compassion and, therefore, from noticing the destructive consequences of our behavior. The Jewish State was founded with great urgency upon ethical and moral considerations. To withhold these same considerations from the Palestinian people devalues the rationale for Israel's birth. The Jewish people, more than any other group, are capable of understanding the despair that seeps into the social, psychological and political fabric of the dispossessed.

* * * *

The Israel-Palestine conflict is as much a part of the history of the Jewish people as the Hebrew prophets, the Babylonian captivity, the Diaspora, and, above all, the Holocaust. For those who recognize the importance of preserving a record of the genocide of six million Jews, distorting and denying Israel's treatment of the Palestinian people merges them into the same mind stream as Mahmoud Ahmadinejad and other Holocaust deniers and provides the Iranian leader with a pulpit from which to claim the Holocaust never happened. Likewise, if we automatically bring up the Holocaust to defend the actions of the Jewish state, we will be guilty of exploiting its horrors in order to promote selfish political manipulation.

For his appalling rhetoric, Ahmadinejad's name is spoken with disgust by Jews and Israelis. They wonder how he can be so ignorant. The Holocaust is one of the most documented events in human history. How unreasonable, then, that the mention of another well-documented event, the ongoing Palestinian tragedy, elicits repeated denials and similar disgust from the very people who scorn Ahmadinejad. Like him, deniers of the Palestinian tragedy refuse to examine the available documentation. How are they any less ignorant?

Must the cries of the Jewish people drown out the cries of the Palestinian people? Must the memory of one tragedy suppress the memory of another? Or do the survivors of one of the greatest evils in history have a responsibility to all of mankind to insure that *never again* will another people have their humanity taken from them? Abraham Burg:

> All is compared to the Shoah, dwarfed by the Shoah, and therefore all is allowed – be it fences, sieges . . . curfews, food and water deprivation, or unexplained killings. All is permitted because we have been through the Shoah and you will not tell us how to behave.[10]

Each year, when Israel celebrates its birth, the Palestinians mourn their Nakba (Catastrophe). Imagine the pain Palestinians feel when they peer from behind the separation wall at their historic homeland and see strangers celebrating victory over their people, whose only crime was to have lived in the wrong place at the wrong time. Because the Palestinians inhabited a land another people coveted they became the enemies of Zionism. In the view of the Israeli nation the Palestinians created the discord between the two peoples because they were unwilling to acquiesce, to erase the reality of three thousand years of existence and accept the Zionist narrative of Israel's genesis. But no Israeli citizen would ever be willing to acquiesce and accept denials of the Holocaust. Israel's second Prime Minister, Moshe Sharett, admitted: "There is no Arab who is not harmed by the Jews' entry into the country."[11] Ben-Gurion was also cognizant of this injustice, as he made clear in his comment to Zionist leader Nahum Goldmann:

> Why should the Arabs make peace? If I was an Arab leader I would never make terms with Israel. That is natural: We have taken their country. Sure God promised it to us, but what does that matter to them? Our God is not theirs. We come from Israel, but two thousand years ago, and what is that to them? There has been anti-Semitism, the Nazis, Hitler, Auschwitz, but was that their fault? They only see one thing: We have come here and stolen their country. Why should they accept that?[12]

Perhaps the Arabs were more forgiving than Ben-Gurion. Benny Morris's research reveals the following: "Israeli and Western documentation indicates that windows of opportunity for peacemaking between Israel and several of its neighbors certainly existed during late 1948 – July 1952."[13] One missed opportunity occurred when Ben-Gurion spurned U.N. mediator Ralph Bunche's plea that he meet with Syrian president, Hosni Al- Za'im.[14] Za'im had proposed a comprehensive peace with Israel that included full economic cooperation and an offer to take in 300,000 Palestinian refugees.[15] Ze'ev Maoz explains the repercussions of Ben-Gurion's rejection:

> Had Israel been willing to adopt a more forthcoming position early on, the Za'im initiative could have paved the way for a model of refugee resettlement that Israel could use as a precedent for other agreements with Arab states with large numbers of Palestinian refugees. The whole refugee question would have taken on an entirely different form. As it turns out, the refugee issue continues to haunt Israeli peace policy to the very day.[16]

Ben-Gurion would not let go of his dream of a Greater Israel. He and Zionists like him were so single-minded in pursuit of their goals that they trampled on the Palestinian people's right to self-determination. By its very nature Zionism had to dispossess the Palestinians of much of their land in order to realize its goal of a Jewish state. Vladimir (Ze'ev) Jabotinsky said: "A voluntary reconciliation with the Arabs is out of the question either now or in the future . . . . Zionism is a colonization adventure and therefore it stands or falls on the question of armed force."[17]

In the first quarter of the twentieth century, Jabotinsky theorized that an unbreakable *Iron Wall* was necessary to protect the Zionist venture, and that armed force was the only means that would compel the Arabs to accept the existence of a Jewish state. Ben-Ami points out that in 1937 – after the Peel Commission* recommended partitioning the land into Palestinian and Jewish states – Ben-Gurion said that the Jewish state would have "'an outstanding army' that would ensure that 'we won't be constrained from settling in the rest of the country, whether out of accord

---

* The Peel Commission (1936-1937), also known as the Palestine Royal Commission, was established during the Arab revolt (1936-1939) to inquire into the causes of conflict between Jews and Arabs. It concluded that the British Mandate should be abolished and Palestine divided into Jewish and Arab states.

and mutual understanding with the Arab neighbours or otherwise.'"[18] Also in 1937, Ben-Gurion said that if endorsing partition would have meant "'relinquishing our historic rights over the whole land of Israel, then I would reject the state.'"[19] Nearing the end of his life, wiser and more contemplative, the retired Ben-Gurion told Tom Segev: "If I have to choose between a small Israel, without territories, but with peace, and a greater Israel without peace, I prefer a small Israel."[20]

Naturally, most Palestinians have never been willing to cooperate with policies designed to dispossess them of their land. Yet, when some act violently the motivation behind their behavior is seldom considered. Instead, they are looked upon as inhabiting a pathological society that teaches hatred of Jews. Why do Palestinian acts of violence warrant being labeled as terrorism while Israeli acts do not? General Shlomo Gazit, former chief of Israeli military intelligence, admitted: "Nobody can reject or condemn the revolt of a people that has been suffering under military occupation for forty-five years against occupation force."[21]

In a November 2003 interview for *Yedioth Ahronoth*, Carmi Gilon, Ami Ayalon, Avraham Shalom and Yaakov Peri, all former heads of Shin Bet, warned that Israel was "heading downhill towards near-catastrophe" unless it makes peace with the Palestinians. They argued that taking unilateral steps, such as withdrawing from Gaza and the West Bank, would improve Israel's economy, "minimize terror and . . . raise Israel's status in the eyes of the world." Shalom, Shin Bet head from 1980 to 1986, said that Israel's policies were "contrary to the desire for peace" and "We must once and for all admit there is another side, that it has feelings, that it is suffering and that we are behaving disgracefully... this entire behavior is the result of the occupation."[22]

In 2002, during an important political broadcast, Ayalon was asked: "Don't you think we can win the war against the Palestinians?" His reply: "Don't you understand that 'winning' this war would be the worst thing that could happen to Israel?"[23]

In 1938 Ben-Gurion said:

> But in the political field we are the attackers and the Arabs are those defending themselves. . . . We live in the Diaspora and want only to . . . gain possession of . . . the land from them.[24]

Eighteen years later, after an Egyptian ambush killed Kibbutz Nahal Oz's security officer, Ro'i Rothberg, Moshe Dayan, in a moment of introspection, beseeched his listeners:

> Let us not today cast blame on the murderers. What can we say against their terrible hatred of us? For eight years now they have sat in the refugee camps of Gaza, and have watched how, before their very eyes, we have turned their lands and villages, where they and their forefathers previously dwelled, into our home. It is not among the Arabs of Gaza, but in our own midst that we must seek Ro'i's blood. How did we shut our eyes and refuse to look squarely at our fate and see, in all its brutality, the fate of our generation? Can we forget that this group of youngsters, sitting in Nahal-'Oz, carries the heavy gates of Gaza on their shoulders? [25]

The words of Ben-Gurion, Dayan and the former heads of Shin Bet provide a broader context in which to understand militant Palestinian organizations. No matter how distasteful their methods, the fact remains that they are resisting a foreign power, just as the Irgun and Stern Gang resisted the British Mandate. Yet, members of these Palestinian groups are looked upon as terrorists, while members of the Jewish groups are looked upon as freedom fighters. All of these organizations deliberately murdered innocent civilians.

* * * *

In 1924 the U.S. Congress passed the Johnson-Lodge Immigration Act. Its purpose was to curtail Jewish immigration to America. [26] Not until the passage of the Immigration and Nationality Act of 1965 would U.S. policy change. Even Hitler's ascent to power in the 1930s had little influence on U.S. immigration policy. Nor, in the first few years of the 1940s, when news of the genocide grew more widespread, did the U.S. act urgently to help the Jews. The U.S. State Department justified its silence by explaining that winning the war as soon as possible was the most pressing objective. Only when Secretary of the Treasury Henry Morgenthau prevailed upon President Roosevelt did the American government establish the War Refugee Board in January 1944. [27] The Board's mandate was to find safe havens for Jews and to bring relief supplies to concentration camps. Although the board saved about 200,000

Jews from the death factories, it was "never able to accomplish what it was charged with doing because of the lack of cooperation extended by the United States government and even President Roosevelt. WRB director Pehle described their work as too little, too late."[28]

Dennis Ross recounts a conversation Roosevelt had with the King of Saudi Arabia regarding the immigration to Palestine of Jewish survivors of the death camps:

> While the Arabs at the time did not deny the great crime committed against the Jewish people, they did not see why they should pay for it. When President Roosevelt saw Ibn Saud, the King of Saudi Arabia, in 1945 and tried to persuade him that the extraordinary suffering of the Jews should make the Arabs open and hospitable to the Jewish interests in Palestine, the King was unmoved, emphasizing that the Germans, not the Arabs, should pay: "Make the enemy and the oppressor pay . . . Amends should be made by the criminal, not by the innocent bystander. What injury have Arabs done to the Jews of Europe? It is the Christian Germans who stole their homes and lives."[29]*

Although Roosevelt was slow to come to the aid of Europe's downtrodden Jews, during the latter stages of the war he proposed that allied countries open their doors to 500,000 European Jewish refugees. The United States and Britain were willing to take in 150,000 each and the rest appeared ready to take in the other 200,000. The president sent close friend and adviser Morris Ernst to garner support from influential American Jewish organizations. The response was fierce opposition to Roosevelt's program and the accusation that Ernst was a traitor to his people. "Amazed and insulted" by this reaction, Ernst describes the organizations' opposition as arising out of "a deep, genuine, often

---

* Also in 1945 the Arab League issued the Alexandria Protocol, which stated: "[The Arab League was] second to none in regretting the woes which have been inflicted on the Jews of Europe by European dictatorial states. But the question of these Jews should not be confused with Zionism, for there can be no greater injustice and aggression than solving the problem of the Jews of Europe by another injustice, that is, by inflicting injustice on the Palestinian Arabs [Hurewitz, Struggle for Palestine, 192; cited by Morris, *1948*, p. 26]."

fanatical emotional vested interest in putting over the Palestinian movement [Zionism]."[30]*

Under pressure from these organizations, Roosevelt's idea was abandoned. The United States and Europe continued to limit Jewish immigration, resolving instead to support Jewish exodus to Palestine. By ignoring legitimate Arab concerns, the western powers transferred European responsibility for the post-War Jewish refugee problem onto the populace of the Middle East. Amos Oz criticizes the Europeans whose decisions affected two cultures:

> One of the things that makes this conflict particularly hard is the fact that the Israeli-Palestinian, the Israeli-Arab conflict, is essentially a conflict between two victims. Two victims of the same oppressor. Europe – which colonized the Arab world, exploited it, humiliated it, trampled upon its culture, controlled it and used it as an imperialistic playground – is the same Europe that discriminated against the Jews, persecuted them, harassed them, and finally, mass-murdered them in an unprecedented crime of genocide.[31]

The Palestinian people were forced to pay a heavy price for the persecution and extermination of the Jews because of the failure of Britain, the United States and the rest of the free world to come to terms with their own anti-Semitism. How would Americans react if foreign powers imposed the mass immigration of a group of non-indigenous people onto American soil and decided the new arrivals were entitled to displace local populations and settle significant areas of U.S. territory for their own homeland?

In *The Disinherited*, Fawaz Turki describes how Palestinians interpreted the mass immigration of Jews to their homeland:

> The Western world, which had long tormented and abused the Jewish people, hastened to bless an event that saw an end to their victims' suffering. A debt was to be paid. Who was to pay

---

* Ernst, a Jewish attorney, was known for his defense of James Joyce and Havelock Ellis against obscenity charges for their respective books, *Ulysses* and *Psychology of Sex*.

it and where it was to be paid were not seen as of the essence, so long as it was not paid by Europeans in Europe.[32]

At the 1961 trial of Nazi war criminal Adolf Eichmann, the prosecution's final witness was Israeli lawyer, Aharon Hoter-Yishai. Following Germany's surrender at the end of the Second World War, Hoter-Yishai was in charge of coordinating the search for Jewish survivors throughout Europe. He described a Polish town where, out of six thousand Jewish residents, only fifteen survived the death factories; and after the war, as they made their way home from the displaced persons camps, four were murdered. Hannah Arendt paraphrased Hoter-Yishai's testimony:

> And yet Mr. Hoter-Yishai told the simple truth: those who had survived the ghettos and camps, who had come out alive from the nightmare of absolute helplessness and abandonment – as though the world was a jungle and they its prey – had only one wish, to go where they would never see a non-Jew again.[33]

For those who had outlived the trauma of pogroms and daily oppression or who had survived the Holocaust, a Jewish State had a powerful appeal. If the Jewish experience in eastern and central Europe before the rise of Hitler argued for a Jewish State, the Holocaust demanded it. But no matter how excruciating, the history of Jewish suffering cannot justify the dispossession and subjugation of the Palestinian people.

* * * *

For Palestinians, the Balfour Declaration of November 2, 1917 had already signaled the start of their dispossession. England had decided to "view with favour the establishment in Palestine of a national home for the Jewish people. . ."* Balfour's thinking on behalf of His Majesty's government (George V) was not meant to express an egalitarian sensibility. In 1919, Balfour wrote:

> For in Palestine we do not propose even to go through the form of consulting the wishes of the present inhabitants of the

---

* See Appendix VII for full text of the Balfour Declaration.

country. . . .Zionism, be it right or wrong, good or bad, is rooted in age-long traditions, in present needs, in future hopes, of far profounder import than the desires and prejudices of the 700,000 Arabs who now inhabit that ancient land. . . . Whatever deference should be paid to those who live there, the Powers [League of Nations] in their selection of a mandatory do not propose, as I understand the matter, to consult them.[34]

In 1923, Lord Cavendish, Great Britain's Secretary of State for the colonies, circulated a cabinet paper – first prepared in 1917 – that described the Balfour Declaration as a "'war measure,' whose purpose was to enlist sympathy for the Allied side from powerful Jewish interests around the world."[35] One early interest was the Ottoman Empire, whose Young Turkey Party had taken power just a few years before the start of the Great War. The British Foreign Office's flawed intelligence, which had determined that the new Ottoman rulers were Jews, was one of the reasons Britain decided to support the establishment of a Jewish homeland in Palestine. They hoped to convince the Empire to join the Allied Powers. In reality, the Young Turks were nationalists who discriminated against Armenians, Greeks, Arabs and Jews.[36]

The Balfour Declaration was the culmination of months of consideration on the part of the British Foreign Office, which had conducted meetings with Zionist leader Chaim Weizmann. Noticeably absent from these meetings was a Palestinian counterpart to Weizmann. The critical issue for Britain was how to win over German Jewry to the Allied cause and how to persuade both Russia – with her six million Jews – and America to enter the war against Germany.

While England may have been successful in concealing her ulterior motives, she failed to contain Arab frustration at Jewish immigration. Neither England nor the Yishuv cared enough about the native population to take into account the Arab view that the Balfour Declaration's safeguard clause was being overlooked: "[I]t being clearly understood that nothing shall be done which may prejudice the civil and religious rights of existing non-Jewish communities in Palestine. . . ." They ignored how Zionist policies that only benefited Jews confirmed Arab fears of dispossession; and they underestimated the effect these policies had in creating the breeding ground for Arab anger and despair.

In 1921 Winston Churchill bluntly observed: "The cause of unrest in Palestine, and the only cause, arises from the Zionist movement, and from our promises and pledges in regard to it."[37] Churchill had been even more explicit two years earlier when he pointed out that "the Jews, whom we are pledged to introduce into Palestine . . . take it for granted that the local population will be cleared out to suit their convenience."[38] On May 19, 1936, David Ben-Gurion said:

> [Arabs] see . . . exactly the opposite of what we see. . . . They see the best lands passing into our hands. . . . There is a fundamental conflict. We and they want the same thing: We both want Palestine. . . . By our very presence and progress here, [we] have nurtured the [Arab] movement.[39]

The Shaw Commission of 1930, in its report on the 1929 riots, and the Peel Commission of 1937 both came to the same conclusion as Churchill: that Jews and Arabs had lived in relative accord until a Jewish movement that originated in Europe implanted itself in Palestine, intent on turning the land into a Jewish state.

An Ultra-Orthodox Israeli sabra (native), speaking in broken English, explained the problem in simple terms:

> I am from Al Quds [Jerusalem]. I'm a witness. I know the Arabs; the Arabs are very good, no problem until the Zionist movement start. My grandmother tell me before the Zionist movement start they baby sitting each other's kids. They borrow both from each other like brothers. The idea of Zionism – you take away the land from the Palestinians, from the Arabs – started all the fighting. Not Arabs the problem; not Jews the problem, not Judaism, not Muslims, only Zionism.[40]

Shlomo Ben-Ami:

> As the irresistible drive of the Zionist settlers to possess the land gained in strength, as their population increased in size and their political institutions became consolidated, the Palestinian Arabs were driven to respond more and more as a group, and articulate their national identity to counter the threatening advance of Zionism. In a way, Zionism and Palestinian nationalism

developed as twin movements, each feeding and nurturing the other.[41]

Ben-Gurion again:

> Were I an Arab . . . I would rise up against immigration liable sometime in the future to hand the country . . . over to Jewish rule. What Arab cannot do his math and understand that immigration at the rate of 60,000 a year means a Jewish state *in all* Palestine.[42]

The Palestinians did rise up to defend their country from Jewish rule. Ben-Gurion, of course, understood their actions perfectly well, but he responded by attributing anti-Semitic motives to their struggle. Norman Finkelstein:

> The Zionist movement inferred behind Palestinian resistance to Jewish settlement a generic (and genetic) anti-Semitism – Jewish settlers "being murdered", as Ben-Gurion put it, "simply because they were Jews" – in order to conceal from the outside world and itself the rational and legitimate grievances of the indigenous population.[43]

Karen Armstrong, a former Catholic nun and one of the world's leading religious scholars:

> Anti-Semitism is a Christian vice. Hatred of the Jews became marked in the Muslim world only after the creation of the state of Israel in 1948 and the subsequent loss of Arab Palestine. It is significant that Muslims were compelled to import anti-Jewish myths from Europe, and translate into Arabic such virulently anti-Semitic texts as *The Protocols of the Elders of Zion*, because they had no such traditions of their own. Because of this new hostility towards the Jewish people, some Muslims now quote the passages in the Quran that refer to Muhammad's struggle with the three rebellious Jewish tribes to justify their prejudice. By taking these verses out of context, they have distorted both the message of the Quran and the attitude of the Prophet, who felt no such hatred of Judaism.[44]

During the Nazi era the belief in an inborn Arab hatred of Jews was embodied in the person of Nazi supporter Muhammad Haj Amin al-

Husseini, former Grand Mufti of Jerusalem, whose radio broadcasts throughout the Middle East were designed to rally support for the Nazis against the "British-Zionist-Bolshevik forces."[*][45]

Under Ottoman law, which the British had largely incorporated into their administration, a Muslim electoral college was responsible for nominating three candidates to the position of Mufti. Although the young al-Husseini – in his mid-twenties – was not among the nominees, the British government rejected tradition and unilaterally named him to the post.[46]

Al-Husseini symbolized the apparent Arab thirst for the extermination of the Jewish people which, in turn, stimulated Jewish fear and hatred of Arabs. Thus, as the feud between Jews and Arabs grew more rancorous, the latter were depicted as harboring deadly ambitions, lacking only the resources for their realization. But the image of al-Husseini, grafted onto the common Arab, left out part of the equation. What was missing was the fact that the Mufti's efforts failed to promote a pro-Nazi movement among the Arabs of Palestine, though some groups did appear elsewhere in the Middle East.

If it is true that Arabs have an inborn hatred of Jews, how were Sephardic Jews able to find refuge in North Africa, Turkey and other Muslim lands during the Spanish Inquisition? What about the tens of thousands of Palestinians who fought for the British during World War II and hundreds of thousands of African Muslims who participated in the liberation of France from the Nazi occupation and Vichy government?[+] Another forgotten piece of history is described by American Muslim Imam Zaid Shakir, scholar in residence at the Zaytuna Institute of Berkeley, California:

> Perhaps the greatest testimony to the Muslims who actively
> opposed fascism is the work of the Paris Mosque in protecting

---

* The Mufti was the chief jurist of Muslim religious law. The label "Bolshevik" was often used to refer to Jews, based on the belief that the leaders of the Bolshevik revolution were of Jewish origin.

+ "As many as half of the free French forces that landed in southern France in 1944 were Africans, the overwhelming majority of them Muslims." Zaid Shakir, "Obsessed with Defamation and Slander," *Tikkun Magazine*.

Jewish children from the Nazis, who were sending French Jews – men, women, and children – to perish in the death camps of Eastern Europe. The mosque itself was built by the French government in appreciation of the 500,000 Muslims who had fought for France during World War I, with 100,000 losing their lives in the trenches. It is estimated that the mosque helped to save over 1,700 Jewish children, by providing them with shelter, transit, and Muslim names.[47]

The Zionist/Jewish image of Jew-hating Arabs was further bolstered in the 1950s with the rise of Egyptian strongman, Gamal Abd al-Nasser. At the time, Nasser was the most powerful and charismatic leader in the Arab world. The anti-colonial and pan-Arabic nationalism he espoused instilled fear in the hearts of Jews worldwide, contributing to the belief that Arabs were unwavering in their desire to rid the Middle East of a Jewish state. The rhetoric of Nasser, and of much of the Arab world, was flagrantly confrontational. In 1963, for example, *Cairo Radio* announced: "Israel is the cancer, the malignant wound, in the body of Arabism, for which there is no cure but eradication."[48] Nevertheless, privately, Nasser tried to initiate peace talks with Israel. He was assisted by members of the British and Maltese governments as well as Quaker organization emissaries, but was rebuffed each time. In 1962, *London Times* editor Dennis Hamilton met with Nasser, who told him: "If I could meet with Ben-Gurion for two-three hours we would be able to settle the Israeli-Arab conflict."[49]

After the 1967 war,

Marshall Tito of Yugoslavia formulated a peace plan . . . that called basically for a full Israeli withdrawal from the conquered territories in exchange for full demilitarization and other security guarantees in the evacuated areas, as well as an "end to the call for an Arab state of Palestine." Egypt and Jordan agreed, but Israel did not, deeming it "one-sided."[50]

In April 1969, Jordan's King Hussein proposed a six-point peace settlement: "with the 'personal authority' of Nasser . . . 'our sole demand upon Israel is the withdrawal of its armed forces from all territories occupied in the June 1967 war, and the implementation of all other provisions of the Security Council Resolution'."[51]* One day later, Israel rejected Hussein's plan.

Throughout this period Ben-Gurion repeatedly referred to Nasser as the "Hitler of the Middle East," a phrase that reverberated throughout Jewish communities all over the world. As a child the images that reference conjured in my mind contributed to my distrust of Arabs and my fear for Israel and the Jewish people's survival.

As long as Nasser held power in Egypt, Ben-Gurion preferred war to peace. The Jewish leader envisioned the overthrow of Nasser and his replacement by a regime agreeable to peace with Israel on its terms. Ben-Ami explains that Ben-Gurion also envisioned partitioning "Jordan between Iraq and Israel," the annexation of southern Lebanon "and the creation of a [Christian] Maronite state in the north . . . ."[52] His goal was to make the Middle East conform to the existence of Israel. He even spoke of a "Third Kingdom of Israel."[53] Whether Ben-Gurion's expansion plans could have been realized is moot. The Soviet Union and the United States were unwilling to play any part in his dreams. They even considered expelling Israel from the United Nations.

In 1967 Israel's occupation of Arab territory encouraged a nationalistic fervor that blinded it to the consequences of its success. Moshe Dayan:

> There should be no Jew who says 'that's enough', no-one who says 'we are nearing the end of the road.' . . . It is the same with the land. . . . Your duty is not to stop; it is to keep your sword unsheathed, to have faith, to keep the flag flying. You must not call a halt – heaven forbid – and say 'that's all; up to here. . .' For that is not all.[54]

---

* Finkelstein, *Image and Reality*, p. 156: "Regarding Hussein's proposal, U Thant (320-1) reports that 'Israel for the first time was offered an explicit public pledge of free navigation through the Suez Canal' (emphasis in original). For a 'five-point' Nasser initiative – 'declaration of non-belligerence', 'respect for the territorial integrity of all countries of the Middle East, including Israel, in recognized and secure borders', etc.– immediately condemned by Eban as a 'plan to liquidate Israel', cf. Newsweek, 10 February 1969 and ARR, 1–14 February 1969."

Nasser died in 1970 and was succeeded by Anwar Sadat who, in 1971, offered peace if Israel returned the Egyptian territories it had occupied since 1967. Sadat's overture was rejected by Prime Minister Golda Meir.[55] This set the stage for the 1973 Yom Kippur War, in which Egypt and its Arab allies enjoyed a string of early successes. Although Israel emerged from the war intact, the casualties incurred forced its strategists to reconsider peace negotiations. Sensing new possibilities, Sadat took the initiative and made overtures to Israel that culminated in the Camp David Accords and the 1979 Egyptian-Israeli Peace Treaty. Had Israel accepted Sadat's virtually identical proposal in 1971, thousands of lives would have been spared. Still, Israel did not learn from that mistake. Lust for land and its failure to honor the terms of the Camp David Accords that call for full autonomy for the Palestinians have resulted in the conditions we see today. From an Israeli perspective, Palestinian corruption and lack of unity have been obstacles to peace in recent years. However, both problems are consequences of a forty-year occupation that has torn a society apart. And to argue that Hamas is not now and has never been a partner for peace is to ignore the fact that Hamas was Israel's answer to Fatah.

Three former Israeli Prime Ministers exemplify Israel's refusal to accept responsibility for the dispossession and expulsion of the Palestinian people. In 1971, Golda Meir said, "This country exists as the fulfillment of a promise made by God Himself. It would be ridiculous to ask it to account for its legitimacy."[56]

Menachem Begin constantly invoked the Nazi genocide during his political career to justify violent or acquisitive behavior. His reflexive use of the Holocaust limited his ability to consider the consequences of Israel's actions. Israel's invasion of Lebanon in 1982 ignited criticism throughout the international community. Begin, who was prime minister at the time, argued that by virtue of their silence during Hitler's reign of terror, Israel's critics had forfeited the moral authority to judge Israel. He told the Knesset: "No one, anywhere in the world, can preach morality to our people." After the bloody massacres at Sabra and Shatila, Begin reacted to criticism from the *London Times*: "A newspaper that supported the treachery of the Munich agreement [to dismember Czechoslovakia in the 1930s] should be very careful in preaching morality to a small nation fighting for its life."[57] Amos Oz responded to Begin's defense of Israeli policy: "But Mr. Begin, Adolf Hitler died thirty-seven years ago. Unfortunately or not, it is a fact: Hitler is not in hiding in Nabatea, in Sidon, or in Beirut. He is dead and gone."[58]

In 2001, Ariel Sharon, frozen in time like Begin, asserted: "Israel may have the right to put others on trial, but certainly no one has the right to put the Jewish people and the State of Israel on trial."[59]

Golda Meir's reliance on the Almighty, Begin and Sharon's appeals to morality and the aggressive behavior championed by Moshe Dayan, sought to excuse some of the most dreadful acts imaginable, including their own. The truth is that Israel has to be in a perpetual state of conflict against a "pathologically hostile" culture if it is to actualize the Zionist goal of the acquisition of more Palestinian land. And Jews who compare Arabs and Palestinians to Nazis will always support strict military domination as an alternative to genocide.

* * * *

Anna Baltzer describes an incident that epitomizes the effects of decades of occupation and oppression. One day Anna went with her friend Jamie to the Palestinian village of Yanoun. Situated in the Jordan Valley, Yanoun has been a target of right-wing Jews from the nearby settlement of Itamar, who want the land for themselves:

> Jamie took us for a tour through the village. Children at every house ran outside to greet us and their parents smiled from doorways. Jamie knew everyone by name and politely played the game of refusing tea until finally there's no point and you just have to give in. In one house, there was a little curly-haired redhead named Alima. "Alima's one of my favorite kids in Yanoun," Jamie told us. "When she first saw me, she thought I was a settler coming to take her family away and started screaming hysterically. It took the family 15 minutes to calm her down and explain who I was. I've finally earned her trust."[60]

Israel has replaced its people's legacy of ethics and justice with the misbegotten belief that by brutalizing the alleged enemy its people will be spared the same treatment. Do the Jewish people really deserve a state of their own if non-Jews, by their very presence, are to be treated so inhumanely? Yitzhak Rabin spent his entire life in Palestine/Israel. He fought in the 1948 war; he led his country's armed forces as chief-of-staff. He served as its Minister of Defense. He served twice as prime minister. And he finally realized that "ruling over another people has corrupted us."

* * * *

The Israel-Palestine conflict is not primarily about two religions, each with an historical antipathy to the other, nor is it about one culture with a propensity for violence and an aversion to compromise. The religious fanaticism and demonization from both sides are the result of two peoples, with attachments to different narratives, competing for one land. Rarely, if ever, have any of us questioned the accuracy of the stories we have chosen to identify with. If we had, we would have discovered that the "enemy" is only human, that his behavior has never occurred in a vacuum but has always been part of a drama in which we have also played roles, and that even the most violent among us is a mirror image of who we might have been under different circumstances. We would have understood that blaming the other as the cause of conflict is itself a cause of conflict.

These insights are essential. They lead us to question why Palestinians who are tormented by their second-class citizenship, Muslim extremists who are enraged at the desecration of Islamic Holy Land, and Jews who are angry with Israel's policies feel the way they do. They further lead to the dual realization that peace is, first and foremost, an individual responsibility and that only by transmuting fear and confusion into compassion and clarity can our differences be healed. Eventually these insights will manifest in the collective mind of mankind and in the world.

* * * *

T'shuvah is one of Judaism's fundamental principles. It means repentance and denotes a journey through personal darkness to the light of understanding; its actualization depends upon transformation. What, then, is the essence of transformation if it is not about releasing our conditioning, and returning to our natural state of compassion and non-separateness?

Some mystical sects of Judaism say that "The purpose of the Jewish people is to bring blessing to the world . . . .,"[61] and G-d accompanies "each and every one of us to transform darkness and evil into light and blessing,"[62] and "The reason G-d created the world is so that we should improve it and make the entire creation into a 'Holy Temple. . . .'"[63] In the spirit of these postulations, how does one account for the heartbreak of the Palestinian nation that coincides with the birth of the Jewish State and continues under its occupation? Rabbi Tuvia Bolton explains:

> Maimonides points out that there are various types of prophesy but what they all have in common is they inspire man to transform bad to good and follow the will of the Creator; the Torah. . . . But one of the biggest problems of all is that people don't want to change. That is why they rejected the prophets; they don't believe it's possible to be rid of hatred, depression, destructive desires and habits. In other words they become addicted to darkness and exile. But it's never too late.[64]

Professor Marc H. Ellis:

> Jewish outreach in the twenty-first century may be equivalent to non-Jews reaching out to Jews in the Nazi era. This raises a further fundamental question as to whether Jewish empowerment at the expense of another people represents a healing for the Jewish people or whether Jews can only be healed of the trauma of the Holocaust when Palestinians are healed of their own trauma of displacement and humiliation.[65]

My answer to Ellis is that as long as we see the world in terms of us against them, we will have no choice but to identify ourselves as victims or aggressors, in the constant stress of battle, disconnected from our hearts, living in fear. There can be no present, only the agonizing past, as if calamity and misfortune are realities in every moment. In that traumatized vision we must be prepared to unleash our own holocaust upon others so that it can *never again* be unleashed upon us. The Jewish people, and all people, can only be healed when the Palestinian people, and all people, are healed.

Breakthrough

Conclusion

Early in the process of writing this book, I emailed the first few chapters of my rudimentary manuscript to a close friend whose unique way of seeing things and skill at transferring his thoughts onto paper often opened my mind to new and enriching ideas.

His opinion was important to me, both for what I wrote and how I wrote it. A few days later, he telephoned to tell me that although my writing style needed improvement, my insights were enlightening and had the potential to guide people to a deeper understanding of how we create conflict in our lives and in our society. He also said that he had been so affected by my story that he'd had a dream that captured the spirit of my transformation. He felt inspired to write it down immediately upon waking. Since the dream's crystal clarity was unmistakable to both of us, I asked him if I could share it with my readers. He kindly agreed. It is entitled *The Truth*. I have reprinted it exactly as he wrote it.

The Truth

One night I had a dream. I was debating in a university with a professor about the pros and cons of U.S. foreign policy in the Middle East.

The dream was somewhat confusing (as dreams often can be). We seemed to be jumping around amongst various subjects.

But then we focused on Israel and the Palestinian issue. A sudden righteous certainty possessed me. I found myself in a long monologue against the professor. My arguments coalesced into a fiery rush of verbiage.

I was looking right at the professor, landing body shot after body shot. The fire of my mind let loose and possessed me. It had a sort of magnificent life of its own, as if I was alive in a force greater than what I knew in daily life.

Everything I'd always longed to give into was happening. I was the knife of the ego, razor sharp, freed from any convention that would prevent me from cutting and slashing, from drawing blood, from terrorizing my enemy.

The professor was silent. He had no other choice than to be silent. He was shocked, and then I could see he was afraid. His fear became his communication, and I heard it. A part of me from somewhere else, from eons of time into eternity, programmed in my cells, *felt* him. And I could not continue.

I stopped and knew some shame. As he felt safer I apologized. I told him that I was a fool. I had always tended to be a fool. I asked him to forgive me. He looked at me. He seemed vulnerable and tender. My heart was crushed by his beauty. How beautiful he was! I began to praise him. I told him directly that he was beautiful. He smiled. He said, "It is all right." He invited me to walk with him and see his university.

We walked through the university. It seemed like the university I had attended. Some of the buildings were ones I had studied in. The professor let me ponder them. Then he took me by the arm and invited me to walk along the beach. The beach was one I used to surf by my university. The waves were huge and beautiful, great windswept walls of water and light. I watched them with fascination.

We came to a group of young children playing on the beach. They appeared as if out of nowhere. The professor looked at them and then at me. He didn't speak. I looked at the children. They were very young. As I looked, I knew love. It was effortless attraction, pure feeling in my heart. I wanted to spend eternity watching and loving these children. I never wanted to be out of this love.

I awoke.

That morning I reflected on the dream. I had a thought: "The only thing we can see with certainty about another country is that there must be many, many beautiful children there."

Epilogue: Reflections on Awakening

*Before anything is emanated, there was only **The Infinite**. **The Infinite** was all that existed. Similarly, after it brought into being that which exists, there is nothing but **The Infinite**. You cannot find anything that exists apart from it. . . . If there were **The Infinite** would be limited, subject to duality, God forbid! Rather, God is everything that exists . . . present in everything and everything comes into being from it. . . . There is nothing but it.* Zohar: The Book of Splendor, 1:57b[1]

My realization happened spontaneously, like an unforeseen gift or an inheritance that one does not expect. It expressed itself as identification or connection with all beings. This sense of non-separateness had always been present – as I am sure it is with everyone – but it was hidden beneath layers of attachment to beliefs that supported and shaped a limited identity. When fear ceased to enliven those beliefs, non-separateness revealed itself. My new sensitivity came from the heart, beyond the duality of the mind, and it manifested without any conscious effort on my part. The relief it brought was not indicative of a talent that set me apart from anyone else. I was certain that my mind could never have created this dawning of clarity and freedom. The gifts I received, in the form of insights, did not result from the engagement of conventional thought in order to solve a problem, seek a resolution, or gain reprieve from suffering. Although my mind registered the insights, the insights were the fruits of a transformation that took place when the mind let go of a belief system that had held me in its grip for most of a lifetime.

A few weeks after this event I began to share my new condition with friends. Some asked how I could have been so abruptly converted from blind tolerance of almost any Israeli conduct to unmistakable recognition of the agony suffered by the Palestinians, and advocacy for their right to equality. My friends were looking for an historical narrative. Their request felt a bit awkward because the breakthrough itself was an unknowable event that "happened" in the eternal present. Frankly, I wasn't sure how it had come to pass.

Non-ordinary occurrences like mine do not easily lend themselves to common language because they are not experiences in the usual sense of the word. The identity we ordinarily refer to as "I" or "me" can only exist within the framework of time; and time, with its past, present and future, is inseparable from experience. Since my transformation took place outside of time, in the *Now*, there was no separate self, or me, having an experience. An equally valid way to describe the occurrence is to turn the previous sentence around and say that because there was no separate self-sense having an experience the transformation took place outside of time. The lack of a separate self and the transcendence of time are interdependent and coincident. This unique physics is why I did not recognize the dissolution of emotions that happened while reading *Beyond Chutzpah*. There was no separate self able to record their disappearance and there was no period of time during which their disappearance could have been recorded. Words such as awakening or breakthrough imply the passage of time. Taken literally they are misleading, but as pointers they offer glimpses into the inexpressible.

A good analogy to awakening is the instant before the Big Bang. The world-to-be was a self-existing, infinitesimal speck that, mysterious unto itself, contained, or was the potential for, time and space but was itself not within time and space. Then its creative potential was released, giving birth to the universe. In my awakening it was as if I had reversed the historic order and returned to the zero point of non-differentiation, before the one becomes many, prior to the creation of separateness (and in my case, exclusive identification as a Jew or American).

My understanding is that the non-separate state is in truth the *only* state. It is beyond all relative phenomena, and yet contains all relative phenomena as itself without separation. All other states are impermanent and arise out of and decay back into this always-existing source of existence. From this perspective, my conditioned beliefs had been an illusion that never really existed or had any substance in the first place. Like all things, they too decayed and were absorbed back into their original state. Although my narrative implies that a transformation occurred from non-awakening to awakening, in fact, when the awakening "occurred," there was the intuition that the awakened state is always already the case, that it is primary, that there is no other state; nor could there be another state because there is only this: the unchanging and eternal Present.*

Finding a way to describe my actual transformation has been and remains a challenge. One discussion that required less effort was an explication of the factors that pushed me in a certain direction, to a place from where I could fall more easily into the timeless moment. Here I was able to satisfy my friends' request for a linear explanation of the events that culminated in transformation.

To begin with, I pointed to Bill and Westley's repudiation of my portrayal of Israel's rivalry with its neighbors. Even though I knew where they normally stood on this issue, I was sure that both of my friends would finally side with me over the egregiousness of Hezbollah's operations, especially coming just weeks after Hamas's capture of Israeli soldier Gilad Shalit from the Southern Gaza/Israel border. If the aggression of one terrorist group couldn't persuade them that Israel was an innocent victim of hatred, I figured the aggression of two groups would. But my emotional response to the start of the Second Lebanon War had led me to misjudge Bill and Westley, and their lack of empathy for my point of view stoked the fires of frustration and hopelessness.

When Sam unexpectedly called, I was near the peak of this anguish. By letting me speak without judging or arguing with me, he helped me let go of some of my pain. Then, in a relaxed manner, he offered me a chance to learn more about the roots of this latest belligerence. From that time on I resolved to carry out my own exploration and establish, once and for all, whether or not my assumptions were rooted in fact.

My decision led me to Norman Finkelstein's book. As I read *Beyond Chutzpah*, the empathy I acquired for the Palestinian people broadened my vision to include all people, without a preference for one group versus another. That serendipitous expansion showed me that my commitment to a limited identity and its beliefs and judgments had left me incapable of real compassion and clarity. The outcome of that understanding was a breakthrough in consciousness.

---

* I am again indebted to Adi Da for the words "always already the case," which apply to my understanding.

My characteristic need for justice was also fertile soil for transformation. To profit from a superior stance based on false evidence would have felt unprincipled to me. Similarly, I was unwilling to avoid real evidence that might undermine my position, simply to maintain my dogmatic convictions. In that light, and given the potency of Finkelstein's discourse, I had no alternative to undergoing a crisis that brought my personal integrity into alignment with the persuasiveness of the material I was reading.

In truth, I will never really know how this revelation came about. The most honest statement I can make is that if there was a specific cause, my mind was, and is, unable to conceive what that cause may have been. However, neither knowing the cause of change nor undergoing a change as dramatic as mine is a necessary precondition for developing clarity about the disagreements between individuals or groups of people. All that is required is the willingness to assess one's beliefs with honesty and to follow wherever the facts lead.

Appendices

Appendix I – Maps

Projection of the West Bank Final Status Map presented
by Israel, Camp David, July 2000

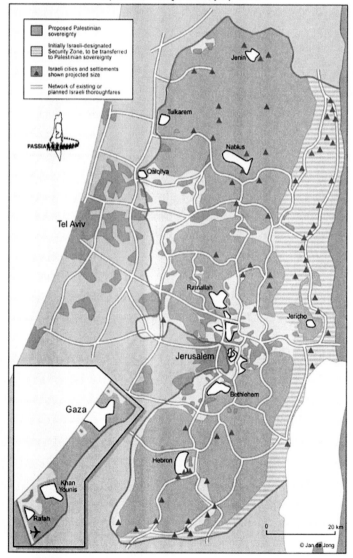

**Palestinian Academic Society for the Study of International Affairs
(PASSIA)**

Breakthrough

Palestinian loss of land, 1946 - 2007

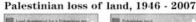

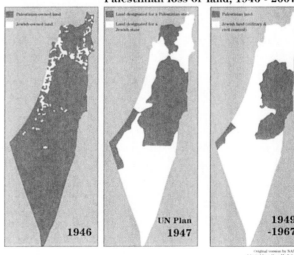

Map source and text adapted from:
www.annainthemiddleeast.com/photos/maps_media
I am indebted to Anna Baltzer for providing this material.

MAP 1:
By 1946, Jewish immigrants had purchased about 6-8% of the land. These were Jews migrating mostly from Europe either because they were Zionists working towards the creation of a Jewish state or because they had nowhere else to go.

These European Jews were distinct from the indigenous Jewish population – some of whose ancestors had lived in relative harmony with Muslims and Christians for thousands of years until widespread Zionist immigration began.

MAP 2:
In 1947, in the wake of the Nazi Holocaust, the United Nations proposed to give the Jewish people 54% of historic Palestine for the creation of a Jewish state, leaving Palestinian Christians and Muslims with less than half of their homeland. The Palestinians formally rejected the U. N. proposal.

Realizing that a Jewish state was not possible with a non-Jewish majority, Zionist leaders organized the mass expulsion of the greater part of the non-Jewish population. In their own words, they "cleansed" the land of these non-Jews. This event became known to Israelis as "The War of Independence" and to Palestinians as "Al-Nakba," meaning in Arabic, "The Catastrophe."

MAP 3:

Zionist forces advanced even further, increasing their control beyond the 54% proposed by the UN to 78% of historic Palestine. In the process they depopulated and destroyed more than 500 villages, committed more than 50 massacres, and dispossessed more than 750,000 Christians and Muslims. In May 1948, after several months of these expulsions, Zionist forces declared the formation of the State of Israel. With this pronouncement, the neighboring Arab countries entered the area. It is notable that Arab forces only entered areas designated for an Arab state – which Zionist forces had claimed as their own – and not those areas proposed for a Jewish state.

This narrative is very different from the one many Jews and Americans have grown up with – that Jewish refugees innocently arrived, minding their own business, wishing only to live in peace with their neighbors… and then Arab countries invaded because they hated Jews. In this common narrative there is no mention that the expulsion of Palestinian Christians and Muslims began before a single Arab soldier set foot in the area.

The expulsions continued until early 1949 by which time a Jewish majority had taken root in the 78% of the area now known as present-day Israel. Today's Jewish majority is not an organic one. Rather, it is an artificial majority, intentionally maintained by preventing the return of Christians and Muslims who still have rights to the land.

(It is within this context that one can understand what it means to have a Jewish state in historic Palestine: The existence of a Jewish state demographically requires discrimination against non-Jews in the area. This is something that I – and many other Jews around the world – cannot accept; that in order to create safe space for one people, we must deny safe space to another. This is unethical and it is an illusion – ultimately the Zionist project puts everyone in more danger.)

Breakthrough

MAP 4:

In 1967, Israel occupied all remaining Palestinian lands: the West Bank, Gaza Strip, and East Jerusalem, annexing the latter. Over the past 40 plus years, through a complex system of settlements, outposts, checkpoints, roadblocks, the Wall, and military bases, Israel has continued its expropriation of Palestinian owned land. The colonial expansion didn't end in 1949 nor did it begin in 1967; it has continued throughout Israel's existence. Occupation is only the most recent step in this ongoing process.

Appendices

Appendix II – Population in Palestine-Israel, 1882-2004

	JEWISH	NON-JEWISH
1882	24,000	276,000
1918	60,000	600,000
1931	174,610	861,211
1936	384,078	982,614
1946	543,000	1,267,037
1948	716,700	156,000
1950	1,203,000	167,100
1960	1,911,300	239,100
1970	2,582,000	440,100
1980	3,282,700	639,000
1990	3,946,700	875,000
2000	4,955,400	1,413,900
2004	5,237,600	1,631,900

Source: Jewish Virtual Library, "Jewish and Non-Jewish Population of Palestine-Israel: 1517 – 2004.

Appendix III – Balfour Declaration

November 2nd, 1917

Dear Lord Rothschild,

I have much pleasure in conveying to you, on behalf of His Majesty's Government, the following declaration of sympathy with Jewish Zionist aspirations which has been submitted to, and approved by, the Cabinet:

"His Majesty's Government view with favour the establishment in Palestine of a national home for the Jewish people, and will use their best endeavours to facilitate the achievement of this object, it being clearly understood that nothing shall be done which may prejudice the civil and religious rights of existing non-Jewish communities in Palestine, or the rights and political status enjoyed by Jews in any other country".

I should be grateful if you would bring this declaration to the knowledge of the Zionist Federation.

Yours sincerely

Arthur James Balfour

Appendix IV – Abraham Foxman's Review of *Palestine Peace Not Apartheid*

Abraham Foxman "Judging a Book by Its Cover and Its Content," A Review of *"Palestine Peace Not Apartheid"* by Jimmy Carter.

One should never judge a book by its cover, but in the case of former President Jimmy Carter's latest work, "Palestine Peace Not Apartheid", we should make an exception. All one really needs to know about this biased account is found in the title.

It is truly shocking, at a time of Islamic extremism running rampant, of suicide bombs polluting cities in Europe, Asia and the Middle East, of Iran publicly stating its desire to wipe Israel off the map and building nuclear weapons to achieve that end, of the missile and rocket attacks by Hezbollah and Hamas on Israel, that Jimmy Carter can to a large degree only see Israel as the party responsible for conflict between Israel and the Palestinians.

In some ways, Carter's book reminds me of the outlandish paper on "The Israel Lobby and U.S. Foreign Policy" by professors John Mearsheimer and Stephen Walt, though he doesn't go to their extremes. Like them, his examination of almost every issue concerning the conflict results in blaming Israel for most or all of what has gone wrong.

Listen to his conclusions: "Israel's continued control and colonization of Palestinian land have been the primary obstacles to a comprehensive peace agreement in the Holy Land." And, "The bottom line is this: Peace will come to Israel and the Middle East only when the Israeli government is willing to comply with international law, with the road map for peace…".

In order to reach such a simplistic and distorted view of the region, Carter has to ignore or downplay the continuing examples of Palestinian rejection of Israel and terrorism, which have been part of the equation from the beginning and which are strong as ever today. He has to minimize or condemn all the instances of Israel's peace offers and withdrawals, most particularly former Israeli Prime Minister Ehud Barak's initiative at Camp David in 2000, Prime Minister Ariel Sharon's disengagement from Gaza in 2005 and current Prime Minister Ehud Olmert's campaign pledge to withdraw from the West Bank. And he has to frame every example of Palestinian distress as simply the product of Israeli repression instead of Palestinian extremism, e.g., the economic condition of the Palestinians, which has much to do with the continued terrorism against Israel.

Much as in the paper of Mearsheimer and Walt, one doesn't have to be a pro-Israel advocate to recognize that the issues in the long conflict are a lot more complicated than Carter would portray. It's particularly revealing, that at a time when even many Arab leaders are recognizing the destructive and dangerous policies of the Palestinians, Carter can hardly bring himself to speak of such matters.

It is not the goals that Carter seeks that are so troubling -- he calls for a two-state solution, with Palestinians and Israelis living securely in two states, which, of course, is the policy of Israel -- but his obsession with blaming Israel for these goals not being achieved.

The problem with this approach is two-fold. He unjustly encourages Israel-bashers around the world. The legitimizing factor of being able to quote a former President of the United States and winner of the Nobel Peace Prize cannot be overestimated.

Secondly, this gives comfort to the extremists on the Palestinian side who are reinforced in their extremism by this kind of "analysis." In the end, it is the Palestinians themselves who are hurt by such a biased approach because they become even further entrenched in their illusions about weakening Israel and the need not to change.

As disturbing as Carter's simplistic approach is, however, even more disturbing is his picking up on the Mearsheimer -Walt theme of Jewish control of American policy, though in much more abbreviated form and not being the focus of his work. Referring to U.S. policy and the "condoning" of Israel's actions, Carter says: "There are constant and vehement political and media debates in Israel concerning its policies in the West Bank but because of powerful political, economic, and religious forces in the U.S., Israeli government decisions are rarely questioned or condemned, voices from Jerusalem dominate our media, and most American citizens are unaware of circumstances in the occupied territories." In other words, the old canard and conspiracy theory of Jewish control of the media, Congress, and the U.S. government is rearing its ugly head in the person of a former President.

It is sad that Mr. Carter would attempt to use his influence in this way. It is dangerous because he will be used by elements that want to undermine support for Israel in this country.

Ultimately, we have faith in the good sense, fairness and understanding of the American people. They know that life in the Middle East is much more complicated and will require seeing all sides of the issue, something President Carter doesn't seem to be interested in doing.

Breakthrough

Notes

Chapter 1: In the Beginning

1. Meir Schneider, *Movement for Self-Healing* (New World Library, 2004), p. 3.
2. Ibid, pp. 236-7.
3. Ibid, p. 237.
4. Michael Karpin and Ina Friedmann, *Murder in the Name of God, the Plot to Kill Yitzhak Rabin* (New York: Granta 1999), cited by www.novelguide.com/a/discover/exgi_0001_0001_0/exgi_0001_0001_0 _00077.html.

Chapter 2: Resistance

1. Rabbi Ken Spiro, "Crash Course in Jewish History Part 49," www.aish.com/jl/h/48952111.html.

Chapter 3: Awakening

1. Norman Finkelstein, *Beyond Chutzpah: On the Misuse of Anti-Semitism and the Abuse of History* (Berkeley: University of California Press, 2005), p. 27.
2. Ibid, p. 30.
3. Ibid, p. 194; Finkelstein cites B'Tselem, "Land Grab: Israel's Settlement Policy in the West Bank (Jerusalem May, 2002)."
4. Ibid, p. 197; also see note 14, quoted from Amnesty International, "Surviving Under Siege: The Impact of Movement Restrictions on the Right to Work" (London, September 2003).
5. Ibid, p. 222.
6. Ibid; cited from B'Tselem, Yael Stein, "Position Paper: Israel's Assassination Policy: Extra-judicial Executions."
7. Merriam-Webster's online dictionary: m-w.com/dictionary/projection; 6b.

Chapter 4: Alan Dershowitz and Norman Finkelstein

1. Finkelstein, *Beyond Chutzpah*, p. 91; emphasis in original.
2. Human Rights Watch, *Investigation into Unlawful Use of Force in the West Bank, Gaza Strip, and Northern Israel, October 4 through October 11*, 20 October 2000, Volume 12, Number 3(E), www.unhcr.org/refworld/docid/3ae6a86e4.html [accessed 5 March

2010], cited by Finkelstein, *Beyond Chutzpah*, p. 101.

3. Amnesty International, *Israel And The Occupied Territories: The Excessive Use of Lethal Force*, pp. 6, 8, October 2000, http://www.amnesty.org/en/library/asset/MDE15/041/2000/en/e3b756c a-dd23-11dd-8595-5f956bd70248/mde150412000en.pdf, cited by Finkelstein, *Beyond Chutzpah*, p. 101.

4. B'Tselem, *Trigger Happy: Unjustified Shooting and Violation of the Open-Fire Regulations during the al-Aqsa Intifada*, p. 7, March 2002, cited by Finkelstein, p. 101, *Beyond Chutzpah*, btselem.org/Download/200203_Trigger_Happy_Eng.pdf.

5. Finkelstein, p. 109, *Beyond Chutzpah*, emphasis in original. *The Case for Israel* quote is from page 120 of that book.

6. Human Rights Watch, *In a Dark Hour: the Use of Civilians during IDF Arrest Operations*, p. 2, Vol. 14, No. 2 (E), April 2002, cited by Finkelstein, *Beyond Chutzpah*, p. 110.

7. For "deliberate targeting" see Amnesty International, *Broken lives – a year of intifada*, 2001, p. 20, http://www.amnesty.org/en/library/asset/MDE15/083/2001/en/081c258 3-d8e7-11dd-ad8c-f3d4445c118e/mde150832001en.pdf.

   For "reckless shooting, shelling . . . ." and lack of judicial investigations see Killing the Future: Children in the Line of Fire, 2002, amnesty.org/en/library/asset/MDE15/147/2002/en/8c752a76-d7a4-11dd-b024-21932cd2170d/mde151472002en.pdf, Amnesty International.

   For torture of minors see B'Tselem, Torture of Palestinian Minors in the Gush Etzion Police Station, July 2001, p. 2 of full report. All of the above cited by Finkelstein, *Beyond Chutzpah*, pp. 112-13.

8. Alan Dershowitz, *The Case For Israel* (Hoboken, NJ: John Wiley and Sons, Inc., 2003), p. 42. Cited by Finkelstein, *Beyond Chutzpah*, pp. 280-1.

9. Finkelstein, *Beyond Chutzpah*, p. 280. Quote is from Benny Morris, *Righteous Victims: A History of the Zionist-Arab Conflict, 1881-1999* (New York, 1999), p. 138.

10. Finkelstein, *Beyond Chutzpah*, p. 209. See n. 7 citing the New York Times, Greg Myre, "Trial of Palestinian Leader Focuses Attention on Israeli Courts," May 5, 2003; bold print in original.

11. Email correspondence from Patrick Callahan to Alan Dershowitz, June 15, 2006; www.alandershowitz.com/publications/docs/depaulletter.htm.

12. Letter from Alan Dershowitz to Patrick Callahan, September 18, 2006; www.alandershowitz.com/publications/docs/depaulletter.htm.

13. Patricia Cohen, "Outspoken Political Scientist Denied Tenure at DePaul, New York Times, June 11, 2007.

14. "Suppressing Critics of Israel: The Campaign against Norman Finkelstein," by Bitta Mostofi, May 10, 2007, electronicintifada.net/v2/article6881.shtml.

15. Frank Menetrez, "Dershowitz v. Finkelstein: Who's Right and Who's Wrong?" April 30, 2007, counterpunch.org/menetrez04302007.html.

16. Ibid.

17. Finkelstein, *Beyond Chutzpah*, p. 161, see also Amnesty International, Death by Shaking: The Case of Abd al-Samad Harizat (October 1995) (autopsy reports) and "Israel & the Occupied Territories: Shaking as a Form of Torture – Death in Custody of 'Abd al-Samad Harizat," Physicians for Human Rights, October 1995.

18. Menetrez, cited from *The Case for Israel*, pp. 137-138.

19. Finkelstein, *Beyond Chutzpah*, pp. 160-161; see Note 47, Public Committee Against Torture v. Israel (HCJ 5100/94), 27 and B'Tselem, Interrogation, pp. 32-36.

20. Menetrez, "Dershowitz v. Finkelstein."

21. Ibid.

22. Finkelstein, *Beyond Chutzpah*, p. 230.

23. Ibid, Emphasis in the original.

24. Menetrez.

25. "Norman Finkelstein's Obscenities," Front Page Magazine, August 22, 2006, www://97.74.65.51/readArticle.aspx?ARTID=2952.

Chapter 5: The Righteous

1. Excerpted from *Der Judenstaat (The Jewish State)* by Theodore Herzl. See Jewish Virtual Library.org.

2. Yakov M. Rabkin, *A Threat from Within: A Century of Jewish Opposition to Zionism* (Canada: Zed Books, 2006) p. 20.

3. Shlomo Ben-Ami, *Scars of War, Wounds of Peace: The Israeli-Arab Tragedy* (Oxford University Press, 2006), p. xii.

4. Yitzhak Shamir, *Maariv*, February 21, 1997.

5. Rabkin, p. 19.

6. Ibid, p. 17.

7. Gideon Levy, "Time to poll Israelis on continuing occupation," *Haaretz*,

September 13, 2009.

8. Jerusalem Talmud, Sanhedrin 4:1 (22a).

9. Judaica Press: Complete Tanach;
    www.chabad.org/library/article_cdo/aid/9974/jewish/Chapter-10.htm.

10. Ibid, www.chabad.org/library/article_cdo/aid/8213/jewish/Chapter-18.htm.

11. G. Neuburger, "The Difference between Judaism and Zionism," jewsnotzionists.org/differencejudzion.html.

Chapter 6: Abraham Foxman and Jimmy Carter

1. http://dictionary.reference.com/browse/apartheid.

2. Humanitarian Award Winners: Lifetime Achievement Award Winners: 1998; Wikipedia.

3. ADL, "A Guide For Activists." Wikipedia, "Anti-Defamation League."

4. Quoted in the documentary film *Jimmy Carter*, shown on American Experience, PBS. Brinkley's biography of Carter is *The Unfinished Presidency: Jimmy Carter's Journey Beyond the White House* (New (New York: Viking, 1998).

5. Oslo, October 11, 2002.

6. Abraham Foxman, "Judging a Book by Its Cover and Its Content," www.adl.org/israel/carter_book_review.asp.

7. Jimmy Carter, *Palestine Peace Not Apartheid* (New York: Simon & Schuster, 2006), pp. 14-15.

8. Werner T. Farr, LTC, U.S. Army, "The Third Temple's Holy of Holies: Israel's Nuclear Weapons."

9. Carter, p. 35.

10. Ben-Ami, pp. 166-7.

11. Carter, p. 89.

12. Joshua Ronen, "Poll: 58% of Israelis back Oslo process," Tel Aviv University, June 7, 2001, April 28, 2008; Wikipedia, "Camp David Accords."

13. Daniel Levy, "So Pro-Israel That it Hurts," Haaretz, March 23, 2006; Campus-Watch.org/article/id/2485.

14. Ibid.

15. Zbigniew Brzezinski, "A Dangerous Exemption." This article is available in "The War over Israel's Influence," July/August 2006, mearsheimer.uchicago.edu/pdfs/A0042.pdf.

16. Noam Chomsky, "The Israel Lobby?"

www.zmag.org/znet/viewArticle/4134.

17. Carter, pp. 208-9.

18. Ibid, p. 108-9.

19. Ibid, p. 147.

20. Ibid, p. 114.

21. Ibid, pp. 118-19.

22. Ibid, pp. 125-6.

23. Hannah Arendt, *Eichmann in Jerusalem: A Report on the Banality of Evil* (New York: Viking Press, 1963), p. 276; emphasis in original.

24. "Onslaught: Israel's Attack On Gaza & The Rule of Law, December 27, 2008 – January 18, 2009," Report of the National Lawyers Guild Delegation To Gaza, February 2009.

25. Carter, p. 216.

26. Carter, p. 151.

27. Ibid.

28. Ibid.

29. Ibid, pp. 151-2.

30. Ibid, p. 150.

31. Ibid, p. 152.

32. Ibid.

33. Clayton Swisher, *The Truth about Camp David: The Untold Story about the Collapse of the Middle East Peace Process* (New York: Nations Books, 2004), p. 283.

34. Aaron David Miller, *The Much Too Promised Land* (New York: Bantam Dell, 2008), p. 297.

35. Swisher, p. 352.

36. Ibid, p.353.

37. Carter, pp. 175-6.

38. Alvaro de Soto, *End of Mission Report*, May 2007, paragraph 21.

39. Morris, *Righteous Victims*, p. 268.

40. Akiva Eldar, Haaretz, November 24, 2003.

41. Maariv, November 2, 1973.

42. Zeev Maoz, *Defending the Holy Land: A Critical Analysis of Israel's Security and Foreign Policy* (University of Michigan Press: 2006), p. 388.

43. Mary Elizabeth King, *A Quiet Revolution: The First Palestinian Intifada and Nonviolent Resistance* (New York: Nations Books, 2007), pp. 219 and 257-58. For a fuller discussion of Palestinian strategies during the

First Intifada see King, pp. 203-239.

44. Al-Haq/Law in the Service of Man, Punishing a Nation: Human Rights Violations during the Palestinian Uprising, December 1987–December 1988 (Boston: South End Press, 1990), 4. Cited by King, p. 9.

45. King (p. 9), citing Lieutenant Colonel Yehuda Weintraub, IDF spokesperson and head of information, Tel Aviv, records pursuant to a telephone request of March 18, 1997, trans. Reuven Gal. See n. 41, p. 362.

46. Stanley Cohen, "Criminology and the Uprising," *Tikkun Magazine*, September–October 1988, 60. Cited by King, n. 36, p. 361.

47. Gene Sharp, "Intifidah and Nonviolent Struggle," 7; cited by King, p. 258.

48. King, p. 324. Author's note: in her book, King names Muhammad Jadallah as one of the leaders of Palestinian nonviolence. I believe the correct surname is Jaradat. When I visited the West Bank I met with advocates of nonviolence, none of whom were familiar with Muhammad Jadallah. They were familiar with Muhammad Jaradat of Badil Resource Center for Palestinian Residency and Refugee Rights. I spoke with Mr. Jaradat who confirmed that he was indeed a leader of nonviolence during the First Intifada and had been imprisoned.

49. Sari Nusseibeh, "In a Different Time Zone," 29. Cited by King, p. 324.

50. King, p. 324.

51. Stephen Zunes, AlterNet, "America's Hidden Role in Hamas's Rise to Power," www.alternet.org/world/116855.

52. King, p. 172; see n. 36, p. 402: "Rubinstein, then correspondent for Davar, 'National Conference on Nonviolent Sanctions,'" Albert Einstein Institution, Cambridge, Massachusetts, as cited in Robert B. Ashmore, "Nonviolence as an Intifada Strategy," American-Arab Affairs 32 (1990): 98.

53. Morris, *Righteous Victims*, p. 657.

54. Robert A. Pape, *Dying to Win: the Strategic Logic of Suicide Terrorism* (New York: 2005), p. 4.

55. Ibid.

56. Israeli foreign ministry spokesperson, Yigal Caspi; cited by King, p. 269; see note 98, p. 433 and note 138, p. 391.

57. Swisher, p. 155.

58. John Daniszewski, "Remarks on Terror Become Fighting Words in Israel," Los Angeles Times, March 11, 1998;

http://articles.latimes.com/1998/mar/11/news/mn-27709.

59. Pape, pp. 11-12.
60. New York Times, April 22, 2007, "But First Deal With Israeli Apartheid in Palestine!" Author's Emphasis.
www.cnifoundation.org/images/stories/nytfullpage/nyt2007.04.22/nyt2007.04.22.pdf.
61. Julie Bosman, "Carter Book Stirs Furor With its View of Israelis' 'Apartheid'" New York Times December 14, 2006.
62. Chris Kahn, "Carter Prays with Rabbis Angered by Book," The Associated Press, December 13, 2006. www.washingtonpost.com/wp-dyn/content/article/2006/12/13/AR2006121300822.html.

Chapter 7: Interview with Ali

1. Carter, p. 34.

Chapter 8: Purity of Arms

1. Avi Shlaim, "How Israel brought Gaza to the brink of humanitarian catastrophe," *The Guardian*, January 7, 2009.
2. Israel Defense Forces website; http://dover.idf.il/IDF.
3. Reuven Gal, *A Portrait of the Israeli Soldier* (Greenwood Press, 1986), p. 239.
4. Morris, *Righteous Victims*, pp. 196-7.
5. Benny Morris, *1948: The First Arab-Israeli War* (Yale University Press, 2008), pp. 404-5.
6. Morris, *1948*, p. 405.
7. Ibid.
8. Ibid, p. 219; also see Note 193, p. 463.
9. Ilan Pappe, *The Ethnic Cleansing of Palestine* (One World: Oxford, 2006), p. 57.
10. Ibid, p. 69.
11. Ibid.
12. Ben-Gurion's Diary, January 1, 1948; cited by Pappe, p. 69.
13. Morris, *1948*, p. 103.
14. Pappe, pp. 77-78.
15. Pappe, p. 78.
16. Ibid.
17. Ben-Ami, p. 43.

18. Ibid.
19. Hannah Arendt, *The Jewish Writings,* edited by Jerome Kohn and Ron H. Feldman (New York: Schocken, 2007), p. 418.
20. Pappe, p. 91.
21. HIS Commander Yavne [Yitzhak Levy] to HIS-AD [Haganah Intelligence Service-Arab Department], 12 April 1948; Yizhar Be'er, "The Hidden Villages," Kol Ha'ir, Jerusalem, 25 November 1988. Cited by Benny Morris, *1948*, p. 127.
22. Morris, *Righteous Victims*, p. 208.
23. Morris, *1948*, p. 127.
24. I. F. Stone, *New York Review of Books*, August 3, 1967.
25. Menachem Begin, *The Revolt: Story of the Irgun* (London: W.H. Allen, 1951), p. 164; cited by Hirst, p. 253.
26. New York Jewish Newsletter, October, 1960.
27. Sylvain Cypel, *Walled: Israeli Society at an Impasse* (Other Press: New York, 2005), p. 69: (Ankori quote in Gresh and Vidal 2003, p. 148).
28. Morris, *Righteous Victims*, p. 208. On page 442, n. 53 of *1948*, Morris cites: "Yavne to HIS-AD, 12 April 1948, IDFA [Israeli Defense Forces Archive] 5254/49//372."
29. Norman Finkelstein, *Image and Reality of the Israel-Palestine Conflict* (Verso, Second Edition, 2003), p. 224, n. 16.
30. Yediot Aharonot, April 4, 1972, cited by Hirst, p. 251.
31. Morris, *1948*, p. 126.
32. Ibid.
33. Morris, *Righteous Victims*, p. 208.
34. Reported by Gai Erlich on May 6, 1992; article appearing in Ha'ir, a weekly magazine published by *Haaretz*. Quote cited by Cypel, p. 42.
35. Unnamed Palestinian woman interviewed in *Occupation 101*, a documentary film by Sufyan Omeish and Abdallah Omeish. A Triple Eye Films Production, www.occupation101.com/about.html.
36. David Hirst, *The Gun and the Olive Branch: The Roots of Violence in the Middle East* (New York: Thunder's Mouth Press-Nation Books, 2003), pp. 249-50.
37. Report of the Criminal Investigation Division, Palestine Government, No. 179/110/17/GS, 13, 15, 16 April 1948. Lapierre and Collins, p. 276. Cited by Hirst, pp. 250-51.
38. Pappe, p. 110.
39. Ibid, pp. 111-113.

40. Hans Lebrecht, *The Palestinians: History and Present*, p. 176-7; cited by Pappe, p. 112.
41. Pappe, pp. 230-1.
42. Ibid, p. 231.
43. Ibid, p. 197.
44. Ibid, p. 196.
45. *The Paratroopers' Book* (Hebrew), Tel Aviv, 1969, as cited in *The Other Israel* (New York: Doubleday, 1972), p. 72. Cited by Hirst, p. 309.
46. Baruch Kimmerling, *Politicide: Ariel Sharon's War against the Palestinians* (London: Verso Books, 2003), pp. 48-9.
47. Morris, *Righteous Victims*, p. 273.
48. Ibid, p. 275.
49. Ibid, p. 274.
50. Kimmerling, *Politicide*, p. 49.
51. E.H. Hutchison, *Violent Truce: A Military Observer Looks at the Arab-Israeli Conflict 1951-1955* (Devin-Adair, 1955), pp. 152-8. Cited by Hirst, p. 308.
52. Kimmerling, *Politicide*, p. 49.
53. "Orders, Operation Shoshana," Maj. Shmuel Meller in the name of Col. Meir Amit, General Staff Branch/Operations, to OC Central Command, OC Unit 101, etc., Oct. 13, 1953; and "Orders, Operation Shoshana," Maj. Alex Sharon, in the name of Central Command's operations officer, Lt. Col. David Elazar, to OC unit 101, etc., October 13, 1953, both in IDFA [Israeli Defense Forces Archive] 644/56//207. Cited by Morris, *Righteous Victims*, p. 278.
54. Kennett Love, *Suez: The Twice-Fought War*, p. 54; cited by Hirst, p. 308.
55. Hirst, p. 308.
56. Kimmerling, *Politicide*, p. 50.
57. Ibid.
58. Hirst. Also see note 20, p. 330.
59. Tom Segev, *The Seventh Million: The Israelis and the Holocaust*, (New York: 2000), p. 299. Also see Baruch Kimmerling and Joel Migdal, *The Palestinian People: A History* (Cambridge MA: Harvard University Press, 2003), 195-96.
60. Segev, *The Seventh Million*, p. 299.
61. Ibid, p. 300.

62. Ibid.

63. Aharon Zisling at cabinet meeting, 27 June 1948, Hakibbutz Hameuhad Archive (Zisling), section 9, container 9, file 3. Segev, *The Seventh Million*, pp. 301-2.

64. Segev, *The Seventh Million*, pp. 301-2.

65. Kimmerling and Migdal, pp. 195-96.

66. "Tom Segev on Atrocity at Kfar Kasem," November 2, 2006, Meretz Weblog; http://meretzusa.blogspot.com/2006/11/tom-segev-on-atrocity-at-kafr-kasem.html#c116262151510601118.

67. SCO [Supreme Court Opinions (Jerusalem, Ministry of Justice)], 1960, XLIV: 410. Cited by Segev, *The Seventh Million*, p. 301.

68. "Tom Segev on Atrocity at Kfar Kasem."

69. Tom Segev, *1967: Israel, The War, and the Year that Transformed the Middle East* (New York, 2005), pp. 443-4.

70. Ibid, p. 443.

71. Ibid, pp. 444-6. "Extremely graphic" statement made by Alon Gan, a PhD candidate at Tel Aviv University who wrote his dissertation on *Soldiers Talk*.

72. Noam Chomsky, *Fateful Triangle: The United States, Israel and the Palestinians* (South End Press Classics, 1999), pp. 130-1.

73. Ibid, p. 131.

74. Ibid.

75. Ibid, p. 132.

76. Aharon Bachar, "Do not say: We did not know, we did not hear," *Yediot Ahronot*, Dec. 3, 1982. Cited by Chomsky, p. 131.

77. "The Gangrene of the Occupation," Al Hamishmar, February 19, 1982. Cited by Chomsky, *Fateful Triangle* , p. 142 and Anna Baltzer, *Witness in Palestine: A Jewish American Woman in the Occupied Territories* (Boulder: Paradigm Publishers, 2007), p. 379. Al Hamishmar was an Israeli daily newspaper published from 1943 to 1995.

78. Yoram Peri, Davar, Dec. 10, 1982. Cited by Chomsky, p. 132.

79. Chris Hedges, "Israel's Barrier to Peace," Truthdig, July 25, 2006.

80. Amnesty International, "Israel and the Occupied Territories: Conflict, occupation and patriarchy. Women carry the burden," Section 4, March 31, 2005, http://unispal.un.org/unispal.nsf/0/abe29ca944af099385256fd50055f789?OpenDocument.

81. Cypel, pp. 70-1.

82. Human Rights Watch, "Why They Died," Part I, Executive Summary, September 5, 2007. Amnesty International ["Lebanon: Deliberate Destruction or 'Collateral Damage'? Israeli Attacks on Civilian Infrastructure"] estimates that a third of Lebanese killed were children.

83. Amnesty International, "Lebanon: Deliberate Destruction."

84. Human Rights Watch, "Why They Died," Part VI, "Hezbollah Conduct During the War."

85. Ibid, Part VII, "Israeli Conduct During the War Civilian Deaths."

86. Ibid.

87. Ibid.

88. Sultan, *Tragedy in South Lebanon: The Israeli-Hezbollah War of 2006*, (Scarletta Press, 2008), p. 60.

89. American Task Force for Lebanon, "A Million Unexploded Cluster Bomblets: The Deadly Legacy of Israel's Assault on Lebanon," by George T. Cody, PhD.

90. Ibid.

91. Ibid.

92. Isabel Kershner, "Israel Won't Prosecute Over Use of Cluster Bombs in Lebanon," *News York Times*, December 25, 2007.

93. Michael Sfard, "The commander's criminal intent," *Haaretz*, Oct 12, 2008.

94. Yaron London, "The Dahiya Strategy: Israel finally realizes that Arabs should be accountable for their leaders' acts," October 6, 2008, YNetNews.com.

95. Amir Mizroch and Brenda Gazzar, "Israel sets new rules on Lebanon targets," November 7, 2008, The *Jerusalem Post*, Israel.jpost.com.

96. Hirst, p. 119.

97. Livia Rokach, *Israel's Sacred Terrorism: A Study Based on Moshe Sharett's 'Personal Diary' and Other Documents* (Association of Arab-American University Graduates, Belmont, Massachusetts, 1980), p. 38; cited by Hirst, p. 118.

Chapter 9: Gaza

1. Cypel, p. 400.

2. Dr Samir Quota, director of research for the Gaza Community Mental Health Programme, quoted in "The Journal of Palestine Studies," Summer 1996, p.84. Cited by "The Origin of the Palestine-Israel Conflict," Third Edition, Published by Jews for Justice in the Middle

East.

3. Disengagement Plan of Prime Minister Ariel Sharon – Revised, May 28, 2004, "3. Security situation following the relocation," www.knesset.gov.il/process/docs/DisengageSharon_eng_revised.htm.

4. Ari Shavit, "The Big Freeze," *Haaretz*, October 8, 2004.

5. Ibid.

6. Alvaro de Soto, *End of Mission Report*, paragraph 16; also see note 126.

7. Avi Shlaim, Democracy Now: the War and Peace Report with Amy Goodman, January 14, 2009.

8. Tanya Reinhart, *The Road Map To Nowhere: Israel/Palestine Since 2003* (London, New York: Verso, 2006), p. 31.

9. Amotz Asa-El, Herb Keino and Gil Hoffman, "My Algeria is Here," Interview with Ariel Sharon, *Jerusalem Post*, September 9, 2004. Cited by Reinhart, 47.

10. The Disengagement Plan of Prime Minister Ariel Sharon, "Overview, Clause F," April 16, 2004, *Haaretz*, www.multaqa.org/pdfs/sharon%20disengagment%20plan.pdf.

11. "28 Feb, 2006: Suspicion: Israel has classified areas near Gaza perimeter fence as 'killing zones,'" B'Tselem.

12. Chris McGreal, "Palestinians Hit by Sonic Boom Airwaves," *Guardian Unlimited*, November 3, 2005, nogw.com/download/2005_pal_sonic_boom_air_raids.pdf.

13. Eyad El-Sarraj, "Stunning Gaza!" Electronic Intifada, September 28, 2005. Dr. Sarraj is commissioner-general of the Palestinian Independent Commission for Citizens Rights. Cited by Reinhart, pp. 140-1.

14. McGreal, "Palestinians Hit by Sonic Boom Airwaves."

15. Ibid.

16. "Hamas Sweeps to Election Victory," BBC News, January 26, 2006, http://news.bbc.co.uk/2/hi/middle_east/4650788.stm.

17. Professor Ephraim Yaar and Professor Tamar Hermann, Peace Index' January, 2006; *Haaretz*, February 8, 2006; cited by Reinhart, p. 145.

18. Amos Harel, "IDF: Hamas Will Abide by Ceasefire Even After PA Election," *Haaretz*, January 21, 2006; cited by Reinhart, p. 145.

19. Ibid, p. 150.

20. Shlaim, "How Israel brought Gaza to the brink of humanitarian catastrophe."

21. Noam Chomsky, "'Exterminate all the Brutes:'" Gaza 2009," January 19, 2009, www.chomsky.info/articles/20090119.htm.

22. Ibid.

23. B'Tselem, "Act of Vengeance: Israel's Bombing of the Gaza Power Plant and its Effects," Status Report September 2006.

24. Gideon Levy, "Gaza's Darkness," September 3, 2006, *Haaretz*.

25. Ibid.

26. "Sonic booms in the sky over Gaza," B'Tselem.

27. David Rose, "The Gaza Bombshell," *Vanity Fair Magazine*, April 2008. Rose's article is based in large part on "confidential documents, corroborated by outraged former and current U.S. officials. . . ."

28. Ethan Bronner, "Gaza Truce May be Revived by Necessity," *New York Times*, December 19, 2008.

29. Ibid.

30. Shlaim, "How Israel brought Gaza to the brink of humanitarian catastrophe."

31. IICC, "The Six Months of the Lull Arrangement," p. 2, www.terrorism-info.org.il/malam_multimedia/English/eng_n/pdf/hamas_e017.pdf

32. Ibid, p. 3.

33. Ibid, p. 2.

34. Ibid, p. 3.

35. Ibid, p. 9.

36. Chris McGreal, "Why Israel Went to War in Gaza," *The Observer*, January 4, 2009.

37. Ibid.

38. Ibid.

39. Daniel Levy, "Gaza and the Obama Effect – Ending the War," The Huffington Post, January 15, 2009.

40. "Israel Rejected Hamas Ceasefire Offer in December," *Huffington Post*, January 9, 2009.

41. Johann Hari, "The Nightmare of Netanyahu Returns," February 6, 2009, *The Independent*, www.commondreams.org/view/2009/02/06-8.

42. Reuters, "Israel Kills Scores in Gaza Airstrikes," December 27, 2008.

43. Human Rights in Palestine and Other Occupied Arab Territories: Report of the United Nations Fact Finding Mission on the Gaza Conflict (henceforth cited as *Goldstone Report*), p. 11.

44. Christiana Voniati, "Chomsky on Gaza," February 16, 2009; www.countercurrents.org.

45. Amnesty International, "Israel/Gaza: Operation 'Cast Lead': 22 days of Death and Destruction," 2009.

46. Press Release: "9 Sept. 2009: B'Tselem publishes complete fatality figures from Operation Cast Lead."

47. U.N. General Assembly, Human Rights Council, HUMAN RIGHTS SITUATION IN PALESTINE AND OTHER OCCUPIED ARAB TERRITORIES: Written statement submitted by International Organization for the Elimination of all Forms of Racial Discrimination (EAFORD, a non-governmental organization in special consultative status, "The Children Killed in an Invasion the World Did Nothing About," February 23, 2009, A/HRC/10/NGO/2, Emphasis in original.

48. Ibid.

49. Ibid.

50. "Onslaught: Israel's Attack on Gaza & the Rule of Law, December 27, 2008 – January 18, 2009," Report of the National Lawyers Guild Delegation to Gaza, February 2009.

51. "Israel/Gaza: Operation 'Cast Lead': 22 days of Death and Destruction," July 2, 2009, Amnesty International, p. 1.

52. Ibid, p. 48.

53. Breaking the Silence, "Soldiers Testimonies from Operation Cast Lead, Gaza, 2009," p. 8. Breaking the Silence cross references the testimonies of soldiers with other soldiers in order to verify that the reports it publishes are accurate.

54. Israel Ministry of Health, "Exposure to White Phosphorus," January 15, 2009, cited by Human Rights Watch, *Israel: White Phosphorus Use Evidence of War Crimes*, "Rain of Fire," Part 3, March 25, 2009.

55. Ibid.

56. Human Rights Watch, *Israel: White Phosphorus Use Evidence of War Crimes*, hrw.org/en/news/2009/03/25/israel-white-phosphorus-use-evidence-war-crimes.

57. "White Flag Deaths: Killings of Palestinian Civilians during Operation Cast Lead," August 2009, p. 2, Zunia.org.

58. Alison Flood, "Hay Festival: Tutu calls for urgent solution to Israeli-Palestine conflict," May 28, 2009, guardian.co.uk.

59. James Hider in Jerusalem, "Israeli soldiers admit to deliberate killing of Gaza civilians," March 20, 2009, *The Times Online*, timesonline.co.uk/tol/news/world/middle_east/article5939611.ece.

60. Ethan Bronner, "Soldiers Accounts of Gaza Killings Raise Furor in Israel," *New York Times*, March 19, 2009.

61. Uri Avnery's Column, "Bananas," April 7, 2009, http://zope.gush-shalom.org/home/en/channels/avnery/1246739493.

62. Ibid.

63. Breaking the Silence, Soldiers Testimonies from Operation Cast Lead, Gaza, 2009, p. 44.

64. Photo of tee shirt at news.sky.com/skynews/Home/World-News/Israeli-Army-T-Shirts-Mock-Killing-Palestinian-Women-And-Children-During-Gaza-Offensive/Article/200903315245946.

65. *Report of the Independent Fact Finding Committee on Gaza: No Safe Place*, April 30, 2009, p. 85.

66. "Onslaught: Israel's Attack On Gaza & The Rule of Law, December 27, 2008 – January 18, 2009," Report of the National Lawyers Guild Delegation To Gaza, February 2009.

67. Dina Kraft, "Gazan Doctor and Peace Advocate Loses 3 Daughters to Israeli Fire and Asks Why," *New York Times*, January 17, 2009.

68. Bronner, "Soldiers Accounts of Gaza Killings Raise Furor in Israel."

69. Ethan Bronner, "Parsing Gains of Gaza War," *New York Times*, January 18, 2009.

70. Zeev Schiff quote cited by Chomsky, "Exterminate all the Brutes." Antony Lowenstein cites the same quote in "The Eternal Victim," January 26, 2009, adbusters.org/blogs/adbusters_blog/eternal_victim.

71. Al-Hamishmar, May 10, 1978, cited by Hirst, 568.

72. Maoz, p. 484.

73. For a comprehensive description of Goldstone's credentials see "Tikkun's Interview with Judge Richard Goldstone," *Tikkun Magazine*, tikkun.org/article.php/20091002111513371. ORT, the Society for Trades and Agricultural Labour, was founded in Russia in 1880 "to provide employable skills for Russia's impoverished Jewish people;" www.ort.org/info/default.htm.

74. "Goldstone's daughter: My father's participation softened UN Gaza report," by *Haaretz Service*, September 16, 2009.

75. *Goldstone Report*, p. 523.

76. Ibid, p. 7.

77. Ibid, p. 199.

78. Ibid, p. 198.

79. Ibid, p. 11. This finding is in large part based on "the Government of Israel July 2009 report on the military operations."

80. Ibid, p. 12.

81. Ibid, p. 525.
82. Ibid, p. 524.
83. Ibid, p. 525.
84. Ibid, pp. 315-6.
85. Ibid, p. 324.
86. Ibid, p. 537.
87. Ibid, p. 525.
88. United Nations Press Release, September 15, 2009, "UN Fact Finding Mission finds strong evidence of war crimes and crimes against humanity committed during the Gaza conflict; calls for end to impunity."
89. *Goldstone Report*, p. 526.
90. Amira Hass, "The One Thing Worse than Denying the Gaza Report," *Haaretz*, September 27, 2009.
91. Gideon Levy, "Disgrace in the Hague," *Haaretz*, September 17, 2009.
92. "IDF Announcement: Findings from Cast Lead Investigations: Conclusion of Investigations into Central Claims and Issues in Operation Cast Lead" April 22, 2009, *Israel Defense Force Spokesperson* website.
93. Ibid.
94. Amnesty International, "Israel/Gaza: Operation 'Cast Lead': 22 Days of Death and Destruction," p. 93.
95. *Goldstone Report*, p. 508.
96. Shalhevet Zohar and Jpost.com Staff, "Peres: Goldstone Report Mocks History," *Jerusalem Post*, September 16, 2009.
97. Ehud Barak, "At the U.N., Terrorism Pays," September 25, 2009, *Wall Street Journal*.
98. *Goldstone Report*. See pp. 558-74 for text of letters between Goldstone and Leshno-Yaar.
99. Uri Avnery's Column, "UM-Shmum, UM-Boom," Gush Shalom, September 19, 2009.
100. *Goldstone Report*, p. 562.
101. Ibid, p.573.
102. Ibid, p. 450.
103. Ibid, p. 459.
104. Ibid, p. 527.
105. Ibid, p. 379
106. Ibid, p. 374.
107. Ibid, p. 375.
108. Ibid.

109. Nathan Guttman, "A Quick Burial for Goldstone's Report on Gaza," Jewish Daily Forward, September 23, 2009.

110. Uri Avnery's Column, "Scoundrel with Permission," November 14, 2009, http://zope.gush-shalom.org/home/en/channels/avnery/1258253296.

111. "Tikkun's Interview with Richard Goldstone."

112. Ethan Bronner, "Israelis United on War as Censure Rises Abroad," *New York Times*, January 12, 2009, www.nytimes.com/2009/01/13/world/middleeast/13israel.html?th&emc =th.

113. Alvaro de Soto, *End of Mission Report*, Footnote 6, p. 31.

114. Sherifa Zuhur, "Hamas and Israel: Conflicting Strategies of Group-Based Politics," December 2008, 15, fas.org/man/eprint/zuhur.pdf. Emphasis in original.

115. Letter signed by Dr. Ahmed Yousef, Deputy of the Foreign Affairs Ministry, Former Senior Political Advisor to Prime Minister Ismael Hanniya.

116. Hari, "The Nightmare of Netanyahu Returns."

117. Amira Hass, "Haniyeh: Hamas willing to accept Palestinian state with 1967 borders,'" *Haaretz*, November 9, 2008, www.haaretz.com/hasen/spages/1035414.html.

118. Storer H. Rowley, "Jimmy Carter on the Middle East," *Chicago Tribune*, February 1, 2009.

119. Roger Cohen, "The Fierce Urgency of Peace," *New York Times*, March 26, 2009.

120. mecaforpeace.org/downloads/Water_Proposal_Sep09(2).pdf, "Water for the Children," Middle East Children's Alliance, September 2009. Emphasis in original.

121. Ben-Ami, pp. 328-9.

122. Olmert quotes reported by Ethan Bronner: "Olmert Says Israel Should Pull Out of West Bank," *The New York Times*, September 29, 2008.

123. U.N. General Assembly, Human Rights Council, HUMAN RIGHTS SITUATION IN PALESTINE AND OTHER OCCUPIED ARAB TERRITORIES: "The Children Killed in an Invasion the World Did Nothing About."

Chapter 10: Interview with Fatima

1. "The Gaza Strip – One Big Prison," B'Tselem.

2. "Analysis /Israel wrecked Arafat, crowned Hamas, and gave birth to Al-Qaida in Gaza," by Nehemia Shtrasler, August 18, 2009, *Haaretz*.

Chapter 11: Hebron

1. Yaakov Raz, Introduction to Motti Golani's *Milkhamot Lo Kor'ot MeAtzman – Al Zikharon, Koakh OuBekhirah* (Wars Never Come by Themselves: On Memory, Force, and Choice), 2002, cited by Cypel, p. 101.

2. Report of the Commission on the Palestine Disturbances of August 1929, Cmd. 3530 (1930), pp. 124-131; Cited by United Nations Information System on the Question of Palestine (UNISPAL), http://unispal.un.org/unispal.nsf/0/AEAC80E740C782E4852561150071 FDB0, "The Origins and Evolution of the Palestine Problem: 1917-1988," Section VI: "Mandated Palestine – Palestinian Resistance/The revolt of 1929."

3. Ibid, p. 150.

4. OCHA – The United Nations Office for the Coordination of Humanitarian Affairs, *The Humanitarian Impact on Palestinians of Israeli Settlements and Other Infrastructure in the West Bank*, p. 96; July 2007.

5. Rabbi Ed Snitkoff, "Settling All the Land: The Birth and Growth of Gush Emunim," My JewishLearning.com. myjewishlearning.com/ideas_belief/LandIsrael/modern_landisrael/Relig iousZionism/GushEmunim.htm.

6. Ian Lustick, *For the Land and the Lord: Jewish Fundamentalism in Israel* (New York: Council on Foreign Relations Press, 1988), p. 84.

7. Ibid, p. 77.

8. Ibid, p. 78. Lustick is quoting Hanan Porat, one of the founders of Gush Emunim.

9. Cypel, p. 202.

10. Cited by Ben-Ami, p. 150.

11. "Settlements in Focus – Hebron," 2005, Peace Now.

12. OCHA: *Humanitarian Impact*, p. 96.

13. Ibid.

14. Ibid, p. 100, caption under photograph.

15. Cypel, p. 301.

16. Ibid.

17. "Ghost Town: Israel's Separation Policy and Forced Eviction of

Palestinians From the Center of Hebron," B'Tselem, May 2007; Joint Report with the Association for Civil Rights in Israel, Summary.

18. Ibid.

19. Ibid.

20. www.shovrimshtika.org/UserFiles/File//hevron-englishforweb.pdf, p. 4.

21. B'Tselem, "Standing Idly By: Non-enforcement of the Law on Settlers, Hebron, 26-28 July 2002." www.btselem.org/English/Press_Releases/20020808.asp.

22. Kimmerling, *Politicide*, n. 13, pp. 157-8.

23. Carter, p. 120.

24. www.shovrimshtika.org/about_e.asp.

25. Breaking the Silence, Soldiers Testimonies from Hebron, 2005-2007, Testimony 20. Printed in Jerusalem; April 2008.

26. B'Tselem: "Soldiers' Abuse of Palestinians in Hebron, 3 December 2002," www.btselem.org/English/Press_Releases/20021230.asp,

27. Cypel, pp. 378-9.

28. www.shovrimshtika.org/UserFiles/File//hevron-englishforweb.pdf, p. 5.

29. Ami Kronfeld "The Shoe is on the Other Foot," http://seruv.org.il/MoreArticles/English/AmichaiKronfeldEng_1.htm

30. "Our reign of terror, by the Israeli army." Donald McIntire. April 19, 2008; *The Independent World*, http://independent.co.uk/news/world/middle-east/our-reign-of-terror-by-the-Israeli-army-811769.html.

31. www.shovrimshtika.org/article_e.asp?id=14&page=1.

32. Cecil Roth, *The Jewish Contribution to Civilization* (Hebrew Publishing Co., 1978), 343f; cited in the Walking Stick Newsletter, emailed July 2, 2008.

33. Gershon Winkler, Walking Stick Newsletter.

34. Baltzer, p. 46.

35. Ibid, p. 86.

36. Cypel, p. 105.

37. Ibid, p. 381.

38. Ibid, from *Haaretz* interview, translated in Courier International, December 11-17, 2003, p. 684.

39. Breaking the Silence, Soldiers Testimonies From Hebron 2005-2007, Testimony 19, pp. 30-31.

40. "I didn't suggest we kill Palestinians," by Ruthie Blum, *The Jerusalem Post*, October 10, 2007.

41. Kimmerling and Migdal, p. 178.

42. "Olmert Condemns Settler Pogrom," BBC News.

43. www.counterpunch.org/mermelstein12252008.html.

44. King, p. 165.

45. www.yeshgvul.org/about_e.asp.

46. www.yeshgvul.org/index_e.asp.

47. King, p. 252.

48. Press Conference, November 27, 1967; cited by Cypel, pp. 472-3.

49. Ben-Ami, p. 152, cites Yemimah Rosenthal (ed.), *Yitzhak Rabin, Prime Minister of Israel, A Selection of Documents from His Life*, Jerusalem, 2005.

50. Anthony Lewis, "Abroad at Home; The Logic of Peace," *New York Times*, May 20, 1994; cited by King, N. 77, p. 428.

51. Reinhart, p. 173.

52. Noam Chomsky, "Middle East Diplomacy: Continuities and Changes," *Z Magazine*, December, 1991. Dayan was speaking to Shimon Peres at a Rafi meeting in September, 1967.

Chapter 12: Seizures, Settlements and the Security Fence

1. Mechon Mamre (The Mamre Institute), mechon-mamre.org/p/pt/pt0319.htm.

2. Israeli Ministry of Defense, "Israel's Security Fence," www.securityfence.mod.gov.il/Pages/ENG/purpose.htm; Author's emphasis.

3. The Anti-Terrorist Fence vs. Terrorism; Israel Ministry of Foreign Affairs, Israel Diplomatic Network, securityfence.mfa.gov.il/mfm/web/main/missionhome.asp?MissionID=45187&.

4. OCHA, *Humanitarian Impact*, p. 48; July 2007.

5. Israeli Ministry of Defense, www.securityfence.mod.gov.il/Pages/ENG/questions.htm#q20.

6. Amnesty International, "Israel and the Occupied territories: The place of the fence/wall in international law."

7. OCHA, *Humanitarian Impact*, p. 48.

8. Ibid, p. 110.

9. Ibid, p. 46, caption below photograph.

10. Ibid, p. 48.

11. Ibid, pp. 82, 84.

12. "Red Cross Report Says Israel Disregards Humanitarian Law," Steven Erlanger, *New York Times*, May 15, 2007.

13. Chris McGreal, "Israelis use barrier and 55-year-old law to quietly seize Palestinians' land," January 31, 2005, *The Guardian*, guardian.co.uk/world/2005/jan/31/israel.

14. "American citizen critically injured after being shot in head by Israeli forces in Ni'lin," March 13, 2009, International Solidarity Movement, http://palsolidarity.org/2009/03/5324.

15. "Israel and the Occupied Territories: Conflict, occupation and patriarchy. Women carry the burden," Amnesty International.

16. ICJ, "Ruling on Israeli Security Wall," Judge El-Araby Concurring Opinion, July 9, 2004.

17. Israeli Ministry of Defense, www.securityfence.mod.gov.il/Pages/ENG/Humanitarian.htm; author's emphasis.

18. Ministry of Defense, "Israel's Security Fence," www.securityfence.mod.gov.il/Pages/ENG/questions.htm#q20.

19. http://electronicintifada.net/v2/article2187.shtml.

20. Zuhur, "Hamas and Israel: Conflicting Strategies of Group-Based Politics," December 2008, Strategic Studies Institute, U.S. Army War College.

21. Akiva Eldar, "Tutu to Haaretz: Arabs paying the price of the Holocaust," August 28, 2009, *Haaretz*.

22. OCHA, *Humanitarian Impact*, p. 128.

23. B'Tselem, "Under the Guise of Security: Routing the Separation Barrier to Enable the Expansion of Israeli Settlements in the West Bank," December 2005.

24. OCHA, *Humanitarian Impact*, p. 124; author's emphasis.

25. Meron Rapoport, "The Spirit of the Commander Prevails," *Haaretz*, May 27, 2007, www.haaretz.com/hasen/spages/861228.html.

26. OCHA, *Humanitarian Impact*, p. 56, endnote 33.

27. Ibid.

28. Cabinet Decision 883, Section B.2; Cabinet Decision 2077, Section B.4; cited by B'Tselem, "Under the Guise of Security," p. 8. Emphasis in original.

29. "UN Laments Choking of Bethlehem," BBC News, May 2, 2009.

30. "Living in the Shadow of the Wall (Bethlehem District)," by Ida Audeh,

Electronic Intifada, November 16, 2003,
electronicintifada.net/v2/article2191.shtml.

31. "UN Laments Choking of Bethlehem," May 7, 2009, BBC News,
news.bbc.co.uk/2/hi/middle_east/8037467.stm

32. OCHA, *Humanitarian Impact*, p. 8.

33. "Land Grab,"
btselem.org/English/Publications/Summaries/200205_Land_Grab.asp

34. "Israel and the Occupied Territories: Conflict, Occupation and
Patriarchy. Women Carry the Burden," Amnesty International.

35. Jonathan Cook, "Turkey's Fallout with Israel Deals Blow to Settlers,"
counterpunch.org/cook03252009.html.

36. "Israel Evicts Palestinians From Their Homes," by Isabel Kershner,
New York Times, August 3, 2009.

37. Ibid.

38. On letterhead of the Ministry of Interior; Director of Population,
Immigration and Border Authority, the State of Israel, "Freedom of
Information Law," November 5, 2009,
hamoked.org.il/items/110588.pdf.

39. HaMoked: Center for the Defence of the Individual, December 1, 2009,
http://www.hamoked.org.il/news_main_en.asp?id=870.

40. BBC News, "Israel condemned over evictions," August 2, 2009,
news.bbc.co.uk/2/hi/8180743.stm.

41. Amy Teibel, "Israel to build 700 new apartments in east Jerusalem,"
Associated Press, December 28, 2009.

42. OCHA, "The Planning Crisis in East Jerusalem: Understanding the
Phenomenon of 'Illegal' Construction," Special Focus, April 2009.

43. Richard Miron, Chief Public Information Officer, Office of the United
Nations Special Coordinator, March 2009. Cited by OCHA, "The
Planning Crisis in East Jerusalem."

44. "Red Cross Report Says Israel Disregards Humanitarian Law," *New
York Times*, May 15, 2007.

45. OCHA: *Humanitarian Impact*, pp. 34-5; July 2007.

46. OCHA, "The Planning Crisis in East Jerusalem."

47. Chris McGreal, "Israelis use barrier and 55-year-old law to quietly seize
Palestinians' land," *Guardian*, January 31, 2005.
www.fromoccupiedpalestine.org/node/1485.

48. Kimmerling and Migdal, p. 173.

49. Absentees' Property Law, March 14, 1950, paragraph 1(b)(1)(i-iii); unispal.un.org/unispal.nsf/9a798adbf322aff38525617b006d88d7/e0b71 9e95e3b494885256f9a005ab90a?OpenDocument.

50. Absentees' Property Law, paragraph 6, sections (a) & (b).

51. Ibid, paragraphs 16 &17.

52. Hirst, p. 359.

53. Danny Seidemann, "The Separation Barrier and the Abuse of Security," December 8, 2004; *Foundation for Middle East Peace*, http://legacy.fmep.org/analysis/articles/separation_barrier.html.

54. Reinhart, p. 161.

55. OCHA, *Humanitarian Impact*, p. 114.

56. Carter, p. 121.

57. Rapoport, "The Spirit of the Commander Prevails."

58. Agence France Presse, cited by Cypel, p. 300.

59. James Akins, "Why Do They Hate Us?" *In These Times Magazine*, December 24, 2001, thirdworldtraveler.com.

Chapter 13: The Self-Hating Jew

1. Cypel, pp. 117-18.

2. "Alan Dershowitz Blasts President Jimmy Carter on Shalom TV," Youtube.com.

3. Marc H. Ellis, *Israel and Palestine: Out of the Ashes* (London: Pluto Press, 2002), p. 27.

4. Ibid, p. 28.

5. Ibid, p. 27.

6. Irina Klepfisz, *Dreams of an Insomniac: Jewish Feminist Essays, Reflections and Diatribes* (Portland, Oregon: Eighth Mountain, 1990), cited by Ellis, p. 28.

7. Sara Roy, "How Can Children of the Holocaust Do Such Things? A Jewish Plea," April 7/8, 2007. www.counterpunch.org/roy04072007.html.

8. masada2000.org/list-TUVWXYZ.html.

9. www.jewishcurrents.org/2007-may-wecker.htm.

10. Voniati, "Chomsky on Gaza." Chomsky explains that Eban used "Zionism" to refer to "the policies of the state of Israel."

Chapter 14: Interview with Leah

1. Laura Gelfond Feldinger, "Settling Their Differences," *Jerusalem Post*, October 15, 2009.

Chapter 15: Redemption

1. Herzl, p. 80.
2. Hans Kohn, "Ahad Ha'am: Nationalist with a Difference" in Gary Smith (ed.): *Zionism: The Dream and the Reality* (New York, Harper and Row, 1974), pp. 31-32, cited by UNISPAL, "The Origins and Evolution of the Palestine Problem: 1917-1988,"Part II, "The Balfour Declaration."
3. Ibid.
4. Cypel, note 11, p. 496.
5. The "dead Arab" quote, which was reported by Abraham Burg, and the reference to brutalizing prisoners, can be found in Chomsky, *Fateful Triangle*, p. 129. Stone-throwing incident and drugged roaches quotes are footnoted by Chomsky on p. 130.
6. Dennis Ross, *The Missing Peace: The Inside Story of the Fight for Middle East Peace* (New York: Farrar, Strauss and Giroux, 2004), p. 115.
7. Israel Ministry of Foreign Affairs: "The Declaration of the Establishment of the State of Israel."
8. Ross, p. 773.
9. Many scholars have acknowledged Khalidi and Childer's studies. See, for example, Hirst, pp. 136-7, and "In Memoriam: Erskine Childers, 1929-1996" by Ian Williams, *Washington Report on Middle Eastern Affairs*.
10. Avraham Burg, *The Holocaust is Over, We Must Rise from its Ashes* (Palgrave MacMillan, 2008); cited by John Mearsheimer, "Invoking the Holocaust to Defend the Occupation," December 10, 2008, www.silviacattori.net/article 640.html.
11. Anita Shapira, *Land and Power: the Zionist Resort to Force, 1881-1948* (Stanford University Press, 2000), pp. 310-11, cited by Morris, *Righteous Victims*, p. 136.
12. Nahum Goldmann, *Jewish Paradox* (Littlehampton Book Services, 1st Edition, 1978), 99. Cited by Morris, *1948*, p. 393.
13. Morris, *Righteous Victims*, p. 268.

14. Naeim Giladi, *Ben-Gurions's Scandals: How the Haganah & the Mossad Eliminated Jews* (Glilit Publishing Co., Inc., 1992) p. 16.

15. Maoz, pp. 391-5; Ben-Ami, p. 64.

16. Maoz, p. 395; also see pp. 391-394.

17. Vladimir Jabotinsky, *The Iron Wall*, 1923; www.scribd.com/doc/6200102/zionist-quotes.

18. Ben-Ami, p. 25.

19. Ibid.

20. From an interview at Ben-Gurion home conducted by Tom Segev, Yosef Avner, and Avraham Kushner, "Nitsots's Conversation with David Ben-Gurion," Nitsots, 28 April 1968, p. 2; cited by Segev, *The Seventh Million*, p. 468.

21. *Yediot Aharonot*, August 12 1993, cited by Tariq Ali in New Left Review, March-April 2006, "Mid-Point in the Middle East?"

22. *Haaretz* Service and Agencies: "Ex-Shin Bet heads warn of 'catastrophe' without peace deal," November 14, 2003.

23. Cypel, note 4, p. 497.

24. Protocol of Meeting of JAE [Jewish Agency Executive], 7 July 1938, BGA [David Ben-Gurion Archive], cited by Morris, *1948*, p. 393.

25. Morris, *Righteous Victims*, pp. 287-8.

26. Bernard Avishai, *The Tragedy of Zionism: Revolution and Democracy in the Land of Israel* (New York: Farrar, Straus, Giroux 1985), p. 116.

27. Shoah Resource Center, War Refugee Board, www.yadvashem.org/odot_pdf/Microsoft Word - 6488.pdf.

28. Ibid.

29. Ross, pp. 34-35.

30. Morris Ernst, *So Far, So Good*, (New York: Harper, 1948); www.cactus48.com/holocaust.html.

31. Amos Oz, *How to Cure A Fanatic* (Princeton University Press, 2002), p. 15.

32. Cited by Kimmerling and Migdal, pp. 136-137.

33. Arendt, *Eichmann in Jerusalem*, p. 226.

34. Arthur James Balfour, "11 August 1919 Memorandum Respecting Syria, Palestine, and Mesopotamia," 132187/2117/44A, Documents on British Foreign Policy 1919-1939, ed. E. L. Woodward and Rohan Butler, vol. 4, 1919 (London: H. M. Stationery Office, 1952), 345; cited by King, pp. 29-30.

35. Doreen Ingrams, *Palestine Papers, 1917-1922: Seeds of Conflict*

(London: John Murray, 1972), 173; cited by King, note 23, p. 365.

36. David Fromkin, *A Peace to End All Peace* (New York: Henry Holt and Co., 1989), pp. 42-43.

37. William Baker, *Theft of a Nation*, cited at campintl.org/cabook3.html.

38. Fromkin, p. 494.

39. Shabtai Teveth, *Ben-Gurion and the Palestinian Arabs: From Peace to War* (Oxford University Press, 1985), 165-6. Quoted by Morris, *Righteous Victims*, p. 136.

40. *Occupation 101*.

41. Ben-Ami, pp. 5-6.

42. Teveth, 1985, 166-68. Cited by Morris, *Righteous Victims*, p. 122; author's emphasis.

43. David Ben-Gurion, *My Talks with Arab* Leaders (New York: Third Press, 1973), p. 3, cited by Finkelstein, *Image and Reality of the Israel-Palestine Conflict*, p. xiii.

44. Karen Armstrong, *Islam: A Short History* (New York: Modern Library Paperback Edition, 2002), pp. 21-22.

45. Kimmerling and Migdal, p. 142.

46. Fromkin, p. 517-18. See also Jewish Virtual Library, jewishvirtuallibrary.org/jsource/biography/mufti.html.

47. Kimmerling and Migdal, p. 142.

48. Ben-Ami, p. 86.

49. Giladi, p. 71; also see pp. 65-74 for further discussion of Nasser's attempts to negotiate with Israel.

50. Finkelstein, *Image and Reality*, p. 154.

51. Ibid, p. 156; also see note 13, p. 263: "For Hussein plan, cf. ARR, 1–15 April 1969, and Dishon, MER, 1969–70, 15.

52. Ben-Ami, p. 82.

53. Ibid, p. 83.

54. *Ha'olam Hazeh*, July 8, 1968, cited by David Hirst, p. 348.

55. Morris, *Righteous Victims*, p. 668.

56. Le Monde, November 15, 1971; cited at www.netanyahu.org/golquotonjer.html.

57. Segev, *The Seventh Million*, p. 399.

58. Ibid, p. 400.

59. BBC News Online, March 25, 2001; http://news.bbc.co.uk/2/hi/middle_east/1241371.stm.

60. Baltzer, p. 45.

Notes

61. Parshas Vayeishev United Lubavitcher Yeshiva, December 14, 2006, www.ulyop.net/dvar/archive.php?id=000095.

62. www.ohrtmimim.org/Torah_Default.asp?id=1390; Rabbi Tuvia Bolton, Ohr Tmimim, commentary on Parshat Bo (5767).

63. Bolton, Ohr Tmimim, commentary on Parshat Re'eh (5768), www.ohrtmimim.org/Torah_Default.asp?id=2300.

64. Bolton, Ohr Tmimim, commentary on Parshat Shoftim (5767), www.ohrtmimim.org/Torah_default.asp?id=1599.

65. Ellis, p. 11.

Epilogue: Reflections on Awakening

1. Isaiah Tishby, M*ishnat ha-Zohar*, 2.159, cited by David Ariel, *Kabbalah*: *The Mystic Quest in Judaism* (Rowman & Littlefield Publishers, 2006), p. 62-3. Emphasis in original. The Zohar is the major Kabalistic text.

Breakthrough

Bibliography

Hannah Arendt

Eichmann in Jerusalem: A Report on the Banality of Evil (New York: Viking Press, 1963).

The Jewish Writings, edited by Jerome Kohn and Ron H. Feldman (New York: Schocken, 2007).

Karen Armstrong

Islam: A Short History (New York: Modern Library Paperback Edition, 2002).

Bernard Avishai

The Tragedy of Zionism: Revolution and Democracy in the Land of Israel (New York: Farrar, Straus, Giroux 1985).

Anna Baltzer

Witness in Palestine: A Jewish American Woman in the Occupied Territories (Boulder: Paradigm Publishers, 2007).

Menachem Begin

The Revolt: Story of the Irgun (London: W.H. Allen, 1951).

Shlomo Ben-Ami

Scars of War, Wounds of Peace: The Israeli-Arab Tragedy (Oxford University Press, 2006).

David Ben-Gurion

My Talks with Arab Leaders (New York: Third Press, 1973).

Avraham Burg

The Holocaust is Over, We Must Rise from its Ashes (Palgrave MacMillan, 2008).

Jimmy Carter

Palestine Peace Not Apartheid (New York: Simon & Schuster, 2006).

Noam Chomsky

Fateful Triangle: The United States, Israel and the Palestinians (South End Press Classics, 1999).

Sylvain Cypel

Walled: Israeli Society at an Impasse (Other Press: New York, 2005).

Alan Dershowitz

The Case for Israel (Hoboken, NJ: John Wiley and Sons, Inc., 2003).

Marc H. Ellis

Israel and Palestine: Out of the Ashes (London: Pluto Press, 2002).

Norman Finkelstein

Beyond Chutzpah: On the Misuse of Anti-Semitism and the Abuse of History (Berkeley: University of California Press, 2005).

Image and Reality of the Israel-Palestine Conflict, (Verso, Second Edition, 2003).

Simha Flapan

The Birth of Israel: Myths and Realities (New York: Pantheon, 1987).

David Fromkin

A Peace to End All Peace (New York: Henry Holt and Co., 1989).

Reuven Gal

A Portrait of the Israeli Soldier (Greenwood Press, 1986).

James L. Gelvin

The Israel-Palestine Conflict: One Hundred Years of War (Cambridge University Press, 2005).

Naeim Giladi

Ben-Gurions's Scandals: How the Haganah & the Mossad Eliminated Jews (Glilit Publishing Co., Inc., 1992).

Rabbi Joseph Ginsburg; Professor Herman Branover, Rabbi Menachem M. Schneerson

Mind Over Matter: The Lubavitcher Rebbe on Science, Technology and Medicine (Shamir, 2004).

Nahum Goldmann
Jewish Paradox (Littlehampton Book Services, 1st Edition, 1978).

Theodore Herzl
The Jewish State (Paperback), (Lulu.com, 2009).

David Hirst
The Gun and the Olive Branch: The Roots of Violence in the Middle East (New York: Thunder's Mouth Press-Nation Books, 2003).

E.H. Hutchison
Violent Truce: A Military Observer Looks at the Arab-Israeli Conflict 1951-1955 (Devin-Adair, 1955).

Doreen Ingrams
Palestine Papers, 1917-1922: Seeds of Conflict (London: John Murray, 1972).

Baruch Kimmerling
Politicide: Ariel Sharon's War against the Palestinians, (London: Verso Books, 2003).

Baruch Kimmerling and Joel S. Migdal
The Palestinian People: A History, (Cambridge MA: Harvard University Press, 2003).

Mary Elizabeth King
A Quiet Revolution: The First Palestinian Intifada and Nonviolent Resistance (New York: Nations Books, 2007).

Irena Klepfisz
Dreams of an Insomniac: Jewish Feminist Essays, Reflections and Diatribes (Portland, Oregon: Eighth Mountain, 1990).

Joel Kovel
Overcoming Zionism: Creating a Single Democratic State in Israel/Palestine (Pluto Press: London), 2007.

Dominique Lapierre and Larry Collins
O Jerusalem (Simon and Schuster: New York), 1972.

Ian Lustick

> *For the Land and the Lord: Jewish Fundamentalism in Israel* (New York: Council on Foreign Relations Press, 1988).

Zeev Maoz

> *Defending the Holy Land: A Critical Analysis of Israel's Security and Foreign Policy* (University of Michigan Press: 2006).

Aaron David Miller

> *The Much Too Promised Land* (New York: Bantam Dell, 2008).

Miguel Angel Moratinos

> *The Moratinos Report on the Israeli-Palestinian Talks at Taba* (January 27, 2001).

Benny Morris

> *The Birth of the Palestinian Refugee Problem* (Cambridge University Press, 1987).

> *1948: The First Arab-Israeli War* (Yale University Press, 2008).

> *Righteous Victims: A History of the Zionist-Arab Conflict, 1881-1999* (New York, 1999).

Amos Oz

> *How to Cure A Fanatic* (Princeton University Press, 2002).

Robert A. Pape

> *Dying to Win: the Strategic Logic of Suicide Terrorism* (New York: 2005).

Ilan Pappe

> *The Ethnic Cleansing of Palestine* (One World: Oxford, 2006).

Yakov M. Rabkin

> *A Threat from Within: A Century of Jewish Opposition to Zionism* (Canada: Zed Books, 2006).

Tanya Reinhart

> *The Road Map to Nowhere: Israel/Palestine Since 2003* (London, New York: Verso, 2006).

Livia Rokach

*Israel's Sacred Terrorism: A Study Based on Moshe Sharett's 'Personal Diary' and Other Documents (*Association of Arab-American University Graduates, Belmont, Massachusetts, 1980).

Dennis Ross

The Missing Peace: The Inside Story of the Fight for Middle East Peace (New York: Farrar, Strauss and Giroux, 2004).

Cecil Roth

The Jewish Contribution to Civilization (Hebrew Publishing Co., 1978).

Meir Schneider

Movement for Self-Healing (New World Library, 2004).

Tom Segev

1967: Israel, the War and the Year that Transformed the Middle East (New York, 2005).

The Seventh Million: The Israelis and the Holocaust (New York: 2000).

Anita Shapira

Land and Power: the Zionist Resort to Force, 1881-1948 (Stanford University Press, 2000).

Cathy Sultan

Tragedy in South Lebanon: The Israeli-Hezbollah War of 2006 (Scarletta Press, 2008).

Clayton Swisher

The Truth about Camp David: The Untold Story about the Collapse of the Middle East Peace Process (New York: Nations Books, 2004).

Shabtai Teveth

Ben-Gurion and the Palestinian Arabs: From Peace to War (Oxford University Press, 1985).

Breakthrough

Acknowledgments

I doubt that I would have finished this project without the encouragement of a number of friends who believed in the importance of my message. There are four people in particular whom I wish to thank: Marcia Lee for her advice during the early stages of the book and for starting me off on the right foot; Anna Baltzer for several very insightful suggestions; and Upahar for his review of the entire manuscript and the many suggestions he made that undoubtedly improved the book's quality. Most of all I would like to thank my old friend Chris Boys, who served as my editor. There is no question that if this book has awakened a greater self-awareness in the reader and a more humane perspective on the Israel-Palestine conflict he owes a debt of gratitude to Chris. Chris's insights and ability to tap into my own understanding were crucial factors in the final shape of this book. His unique ability is what allowed him to have his dream, "The Truth," which I believe perfectly summarizes my awakening.

I also wish to humbly thank all people everywhere who have had the courage to question their beliefs and indoctrination and fight for the rights and equality of others less fortunate than they are. This includes many of the sources I have quoted in this book, some of whom have had to fear for their lives or careers because of the threat they represent to those who are not yet ready to awaken to the light of understanding and compassion.

Breakthrough

Index

About the Author

Richard Forer was born in Trenton New Jersey in 1948. His father was an attorney and his uncle, Joseph Forer, a noted civil rights litigator and lead attorney with the National Lawyers Guild. His younger brother is an attorney and former President of one of the largest Reform synagogues on the East coast and his identical twin brother is a prominent member of an Ultra-Orthodox sect of Judaism. Forer is a practitioner of the Meir Schneider Self-Healing Method, a unique system of healing developed by an Israeli.